American Ethnicity

The Dynamics and Consequences of Discrimination

FOURTH EDITION

Adalberto Aguirre, Jr.
University of California, Riverside

Jonathan H. Turner
University of California, Riverside

Boston   Burr Ridge, IL   Dubuque, IA   Madison, WI   New York
San Francisco   St. Louis   Bangkok   Bogotá   Caracas   Kuala Lumpur
Lisbon   London   Madrid   Mexico City   Milan   Montreal   New Delhi
Santiago   Seoul   Singapore   Sydney   Taipei   Toronto

Higher Education

AMERICAN ETHNICITY: THE DYNAMICS AND CONSEQUENCES OF DISCRIMINATION

Published by McGraw-Hill, a business unit of The McGraw-Hill Companies, Inc., 1221 Avenue of the Americas, New York, NY, 10020. Copyright © 2004, 2001, 1998, 1995 by The McGraw-Hill Companies, Inc. All rights reserved. No part of this publication may be reproduced or distributed in any form or by any means, or stored in a database or retrieval system, without the prior written consent of The McGraw-Hill Companies, Inc., including, but not limited to, in any network or other electronic storage or transmission, or broadcast for distance learning. Some ancillaries, including electronic and print components, may not be available to customers outside the United States.

This book is printed on acid-free paper.

1 2 3 4 5 6 7 8 9 0 FGR/FGR 0 9 8 7 6 5 4 3

ISBN 0-07-282426-3

Publisher: *Phillip A. Butcher*
Sponsoring editor: *Sherith H. Pankratz*
Developmental editor: *Katherine Blake*
Senior marketing manager: *Daniel M. Loch*
Producer, Media technology: *Jessica Bodie*
Senior project manager: *Rebecca Nordbrock*
Production supervisor: *Carol A. Bielski*
Coordinator of freelance design: *Mary E. Kazak*
Supplement associate: *Kathleen Boylan*
Manager, Photo research: *Brian J. Pecko*
Associate art editor: *Cristin Yancey*
Cover art and design: *Eric Kass/Lodge Design*
Typeface: *10/12 Palatino*
Compositor: *Lachina Publishing Services*
Printer: *Quebecor World Fairfield Inc.*

Library of Congress Cataloging-in-Publication Data

Aguirre, Adalberto.
    American ethnicity : the dynamics and consequences of discrimination / Adalberto Aguirre, Jr., Jonathan H. Turner.—4th ed.
        p.   cm.
    Includes bibliographical references and index.
    ISBN 0-07-282426-3 (pbk. : acid-free paper)
        1. United States—Race relations. 2. United States—Ethnic relations 3. Discrimination—United States. 4. Ethnicity—United States. I. Turner, Jonathan H. II. Title.
E184.A1A38   2004
305.8'00973—dc21   2003051271

www.mhhe.com

About the Authors

ADALBERTO AGUIRRE, JR., is Professor of Sociology, University of California at Riverside. He is the author of over seven books and many articles in professional journals. Among his books related to this effort are *Race, Racism and the Death Penalty in the United States; Perspectives on Race and Ethnicity in American Criminal Justice; Chicanos in Higher Education: Issues and Dilemmas for the 21st Century; Chicanos and Intelligence Testing;* and *Women and Minority Faculty in the Academic Workplace.*

JONATHAN H. TURNER is Distinguished Professor of Sociology, University of California at Riverside. He is the author of twenty-six books and many articles in professional journals. Among his books related to this effort are *Oppression: A Sociohistory of Black-White Relations, American Society: Problems of Structure, Social Problems in America,* and *Inequality: Privilege & Poverty in America.*

To Our Wives,
Carmen Alicia Aguirre
Alexandra Maryanski

Contents in Brief

Contents

Preface

Our first glimpses of the twenty-first century have shown that American society continues to be shaped by the social forces associated with growing numbers of racial and ethnic populations. Whereas in its early formation American society was shaped by waves of European immigrants who forged ethnic identities within a hegemonious ethnic ideology, the last four decades of the twentieth century were witness to an increasing number of immigrants arriving from Asia, Mexico, and Central America who made diversity more noticeable in the social fabric of American society. Increasing diversity not only has become more noticeable, but it also has become more volatile in the social relations of everyday life.

For example, California's nativist response to immigrants—the implementation of Propositions 187 and 227—is reflective of the battle zone that dominates the everyday lives of minority persons as they seek presence and voice in American society. The tragic events of September 11th, 2001, were also a signal that discrimination and prejudice continue to be used as weapons against racial, ethnic, and religious minorities perceived as threats to American society.

As we take our first steps into the twenty-first century, these changing ethnic demographics will continue to dominate public discourse in the United States, as a dominant Anglo population perceives threats to its social opportunities. We argue in this book that tensions between ethnic populations and a dominant Anglo population represent the core of *ethnic stratification* in American society.

Conceptual Framework

Our goal in this book is to understand how social dynamics, such as prejudice and discrimination, have affected the participation of ethnic minorities in American society. To this end, we employ a conceptual framework incorporating key ideas from theories about ethnic stratification in an effort to organize historical and census data pertaining to ethnic populations in the United States. The great virtue of using a unified conceptual framework to organize the data is that it facilitates comparison between the ethnic populations in the United States on the same social dimensions.

Our analysis of each ethnic group in America begins with a few simple questions:

1. What share of resources does the ethnic group receive?
2. What are the major resource outcomes for ethnic groups in the United States in terms of income, education, health care, housing, and other valued resources?

We then explore how past and present discrimination can account for inequality in the distribution of resources among various ethnic groups.

In examining the dynamics of discrimination, we call attention to important factors, such as the sense of threat experienced by those who discriminate, the varying degrees of identifiability of people as targets of discrimination, the negative stereotypes that are created to legitimize discrimination, and—most importantly—the institutionalization of discrimination in economic, political, legal, educational, and housing patterns. These forces, as they have fueled and shaped discrimination, have created a system of ethnic stratification that reinforces the very discriminatory social forces that created this system of stratification in the first place. A major challenge for American society in the new century is to attack the discriminatory social forces that produce ethnic stratification. This challenge, however, is an especially difficult one given the rapid growth of ethnic populations in American society and the increasing and inevitable threat perceived by a dominant Anglo population as it confronts their rapid growth.

New to the Fourth Edition

In each chapter, statistics and data tables have been updated with 2000 census data. One of the major changes in the 2000 U.S. census was the introduction of multiple race categories from which a person could choose. For example, a person could choose to identify with only one race—such as Asian—or with a combination of two or more—such as Asian and White or Asian and White and African American. For our purposes, we use the race-only categories in the data tables. We anticipate a much more comprehensive analysis of how "race alone" and "race in combination" categories interface with social, economic, and educational characteristics of racial and ethnic populations in the United States as the data become available from the U.S. Census Bureau.

Other Additions/Changes

- We have added discussion of the increasing significance of "race" and ethnicity; the changing ethnic composition of America; abusive practices such as environmental racism and racial profiling; the relationship between poverty rate and discrimination against ethnic populations; residential segregation among various ethnic populations; the problems faced by Native American youth; hate crimes against Arabs and Muslims after September 11, 2001; the depiction of Italian Americans in the HBO series *The Sopranos;* the struggle for social justice in the twenty-first century; and a summary of the major court decisions relating to affirmative action in higher education.

- We now include a list of key terms (with page references) at the end of each chapter. A glossary will be available on the companion website.
- To streamline the text and concentrate on American ethnicity, consistent with the title, we have dropped the chapter on ethnic tensions worldwide.
- Ten of the 31 boxes are new.

Supplements

An *Instructor's Manual* is available to instructors on the password-protected Instructor's section of the companion Website. It is organized to correspond to the nine chapters in the text. Each chapter offers a chapter overview, a chapter outline, a list of key terms and concepts, discussion questions, suggested readings, and suggested Web links.

A *Computerized Test Bank* offers multiple-choice, true–false, fill-in-the-blank, and essay questions for each chapter.

Website

The companion website, with sections "For the Student" and "For the Instructor," provides information about the book, including an overview, a summary of key features and what's new in the fourth edition; information about the authors; chapter quizzes with feedback; a glossary; Web exercises; and an annotated list of Web links. Non–text-specific content on this site includes a list of professional resources (e.g., professional journals); links to Websites offering Census 2000 information; and a comprehensive guide (annotated and listed by category) of films and videos in the areas of race, ethnicity, class, and gender.

Visit the website by going to:
www.mhhe.com/aguirre4
or
www.mhhe.com/raceclassgender

Acknowledgments

We have amassed a large number of debts in writing this book. First, we wish to thank the reviewers of the fourth edition, who provided many helpful comments and suggestions that helped make this a better book. They include Clifford Broman, Michigan State University; Heather Beth Johnson, Lehigh University; Ivy Kennelly, George Washington University; Ralph Pyle, Michigan State University; and Sarah Soule, University of Arizona.

We would also like to acknowledge once again those who reviewed the previous editions of this book and whose contributions helped us lay the groundwork for the fourth edition: E. M. Beck, University of Georgia; Larry Carps, Northwestern Michigan College; Richard M. Cramer, University of North Carolina at Chapel Hill; Timothy Evans, Community College of Allegheny County; Jan Fiola, Moorhead State University; Charles Green, CUNY–Hunter College; Meg Wilkes Karraker, University of St. Thomas; Peter Kivisto, Augustana College; Peter Melvoin, Bellevue Community College; Luis Alfredo Posas, Minnesota State University–Mankato; Ernest Quimby, Howard University; Peter I. Rose, Smith College; Ellen Rosengarten, Sinclair Community College; Peter Singelmann, University of Missouri–Kansas City; Becky Thompson, Simmons College; George Wilson, University of Miami; and S. Rowan Wolf, Portland Community College.

The following individuals were invaluable in assisting us with the research for population statistics: Manuel de la Puenta and Edna Paisano at the U.S. Bureau of the Census; Ruth McKay at the U.S. Department of Labor Statistics; Tony Hernandez at the Hispanic Resarch Center, Arizona State University; and Georges Vernez at the Rand Corporation. Our thanks go to David Baker of Riverside Community College for serving as a sounding board for many of the issues raised in this book and for his revision of the Instructor's Manual and Computerized Test Bank that accompany the fourth edition. Our special thanks go to Clara Dean for helping us bring coherency to the manuscript. Finally, we give our heartfelt thanks to our families for giving us the space and time to complete this book.

Our purpose in writing this book continues to be one of providing students and teachers in the social sciences with a "working text"—an information tool that provides both the student and teacher with the resources needed to build around it. For example, many of you have commented on your ability to use supplementary materials, such as journal articles, to enhance the utility of this text in your classes. We are encouraged by your comments, because they tell us that the conceptual and comparative organization of the text serves as a valuable tool in the teaching and learning process. For those of you who have shared your thoughts and suggestions about *American Ethnicity* with us, we encourage you to continue doing so. We have been especially encouraged by those faculty who have shared with us student comments about the book or student reviews of the book. We hope others will also be encouraged to share their thoughts and suggestions with us. Please feel free to contact either one of us at:

aguirre@citrus.ucr.edu   jonathan.turner@ucr.edu

Adalberto Aguirre, Jr.
Jonathan H. Turner

CHAPTER 1

Ethnicity and Ethnic Relations

*E*thnic strife exists everywhere in the world today. People hate each other with a passion that is sometimes difficult to understand, and in many places, the protagonists seem to be locked in a cycle of mutually escalating violence. People are often proud of their ethnic heritage, and equally often they are suspicious of the heritage of others, seeing another ethnic population as a potential threat to their well-being. Thus, we must reluctantly conclude that ethnicity is a force that mobilizes people's emotions ranging from a sense of ethnic pride, on the one side, to fear and hatred of other ethnics, on the other. In very few places are tolerance and mutual understanding of ethnic differences accepted as normal, or even as desirable. True, ideologies often preach ethnic tolerance and celebration of diversity, but in actual practice, most of the world reveals ethnic tensions, open conflict, and in a few cases, efforts to exterminate others who are seen as different. Tensions are often so profound that societies are de-evolving, breaking apart along ethnic lines. The Soviet Union has collapsed around old ethnic lines; Yugoslavia has disintegrated into episodes of ethnic cleansing; Czechoslovakia is now two nations; French-speaking Canadians want to break away from the union; and India and Pakistan stand ready to use their newfound nuclear weapons as they dispute over the borders that were created to partition ethnic subpopulations. For those populations who cannot be split into new nations, the tensions persist, often erupting into violence and almost always producing systematic efforts at discriminations. And when ethnics migrate to new lands, they almost always encounter discrimination and, at times, violence. Thus, the world is filled with ethnic tension and outright conflict. Noisy and threatening protests, long-term oppression, terrorist bombings, mass killings, and war can be found everywhere on the globe. Ethnicity is one of the most volatile forces of the twenty-first century.

Why does ethnic tension and racial hatred persist in patterns of human organization? Why did the early white settlers in North America, for example, kill so many Native Americans? Why did slavery exist? Why are neo-Nazi hate groups emerging in Germany? Why are churches attended by African Americans arson targets? Why do Catholics and Protestants in Northern Ireland wall themselves off from each other? Why do ethnic jokes about Polacks, Wops, Japs, Jews, and others still persist in America at the beginning of the twenty-first century? Why do European-origin Americans so fear Latinos? And so the questions go.

Our goal in this book is to answer these and the many related questions that can be asked about ethnicity. Our emphasis is on American ethnic tensions, and compared to the violence and killings in many parts of the world, the dynamics of ethnicity in America can appear rather muted. This is not to say, however, that tensions among American ethnics are not severe. On the contrary, the existing divisions among ethnics in the United States are at a critical phase; America will either become a viable multiethnic society, or it will degenerate into patterns of hatred and violence so evident in our nation's past and so clear in much of the world today. The task before us, then, is to understand American ethnic antagonisms; and with this understanding, perhaps we can better appreciate what needs to be done in order to reduce the conflicts among ethnic groups in America.

In this chapter, we will get started in this task by clarifying basic concepts. To understand a phenomenon like ethnicity, we need to define key terms that will be used to understand how this phenomenon operates. So let us begin with a conceptual mapping of our subject; and in the next chapter, we can turn to theorizing about the dynamic properties of American ethnic relations.

RACE AND ETHNICITY

The term "race" connotes biological differences among peoples—skin color, facial features, stature, and the like—that are transmitted from generation to generation. As such, these biological differences are seen as permanent characteristics of people. The notion of race does not make much sense as a biological concept, however, because the physical characteristics that make people distinctive are trivial. A few alleles on genes are what account for these differences, and, most importantly, these alleles are on genes that are not determinative of basic biological functions. These biological differences are, in essence, superficial. Moreover, they do not mark clear boundaries: Where does "black" end and "white" begin? Is the child of an Asian mother and a European father more Asian or more European?

Even though biological differences are superficial and difficult to use as markers of boundaries between peoples, they are important sociologically. For if people believe that others are biologically distinctive, they tend to respond to them as being different. And when people associate superficial biological differences with variations in psychological, intellectual, and behavioral makeup, they may feel justified in treating members of a distinctive group in discriminatory ways. For example, if some individuals in a society consider dark skin an important distinction, and this distinction becomes associated in their minds with differences in the behavior of "black people," then this superficial biological difference will influence how those with black skin are treated in that society.

How, then, should we conceptualize the notion of "race" if it does not make much biological sense? Our answer is to subordinate and incorporate the idea of race into a broad definition of *ethnicity*. When a subpopulation of individuals reveals, or is perceived to reveal, shared historical experiences as well as unique organizational, behavioral, and cultural characteristics, it exhibits its ethnicity. For instance, when country of origin, religion, family practices, interpersonal style, language, beliefs, values, and other characteristics are used to demark a population of individuals from others, then ethnicity is operating. The more visible the characteristics marking ethnicity, the more likely it is that those in an ethnic category will be treated differently.

Here is where race or presumptions of biological differences become a part of ethnicity. Physical features like skin color and facial features can be used as highly visible markers of organizational, behavioral, and cultural differences among individuals. When someone is labeled "black," more than skin color is involved; whole clusters of assumptions about historical experiences, behavior, organization, and culture are associated with this label. The same is true for labels such as "white," "Asian," "Mexican," "Jew," and "Indian."

In fact, as we will come to see, labels are often self-fulfilling in creating and sustaining ethnicity. If people are given a label because of their skin color and then discriminated against as if they were different, they will react to such treatment by behaving and organizing in ways that are indeed distinctive. Once behavioral and organizational differences exist and are elaborated culturally into norms, beliefs, and other systems of symbols, they become an additional marker of differences, both justifying the earlier label and the distinctive treatment of these others as somehow "different." So, if biological distinctiveness can become a part of the label for denoting populations, then biology becomes an aspect of the social dynamics producing and sustaining ethnicity. Indeed, racial labels are like turbochargers in ethnic relations: They escalate the heat and power of emotions and tensions.

The notion of race and ethnicity are thus social constructions. They are conceptions, often inaccurate, that people have of what makes certain people different and unique. Over the last twenty years in America, especially in the last decade, ethnicity appears to have taken on greater significance. Why should this be so? One reason is perhaps obvious: American society is one of the most ethnically diverse in the world, and so, it is natural for people to notice this simple fact of life. But more is involved. An additional force raising perceptions of ethnicity has been social movements that draw attention to discrimination against a particular group, especially as laws and other policies like "affirmative action" have been designed to compensate for past patterns of discrimination against a particular ethnic population. Another reason is the rapidly changing proportions of various ethnic groups in America, with some increasing as a proportion of the total population while others are declining. Such shifts in the ethnic composition often make people aware of ethnic differences, particularly if they feel threatened by demographic changes. Still another reason is the widespread attention paid to ethnicity in schools and the media.

When ethnicity gains publicity, and particularly if it becomes a hot-button political issue, it becomes more salient in people's minds. And finally, the U.S. Census Bureau, which collects data on the characteristics of the American population, emphasizes ethnicity; indeed, many of the questions on the census forms are devoted to a person's ethnic background. The Census Bureau increasingly uses the concept of race, especially in its efforts to discover "mixed race" segments of the population (see Box 1.1).

It is difficult, therefore, to not be aware of ethnicity in American society. As attention is called to ethnicity, it takes on more reality and shapes how Americans think about themselves and others around them. While some of this reflection can be positive, much of what individuals think about is negative, perceiving others as somehow different and threatening. In the end, when ethnic differences are on people's minds, tensions among ethnic groups inevitably increase.

ETHNIC GROUPS

What is a group? Sociologists generally define a group as a gathering of individuals in face-to-face interaction. According to this definition, an ethnic "group" would be a number of interacting individuals distinguished by their ethnicity. Not every one of these individuals interacts face to face, but they may interact in various social settings. Obviously, when we use the term "ethnic group," we have something much bigger, broader, more inclusive in mind. *Subpopulations* of individuals in a society can be distinguished by their history as well as their distinctive behavior, organization, culture, and, perhaps, superficial biological features. An *ethnic group* is a subpopulation of individuals who are labeled and categorized by the general population and, often, by the members of a group itself as being of a particular type of ethnicity. They reveal a unique history as well as distinctive behavioral, organizational, and cultural characteristics, and, as a result, they often are treated differently by others. In addition to the term "ethnic group," in this text we use the terms *ethnic subpopulation* and *ethnic population*, which more accurately describe the groups that we are discussing.

MINORITY GROUPS

What is a *minority group*? Louis Wirth (1945:347) long ago offered the basic definition, the general thrust of which is still used today: "A group of people who, because of their physical or cultural characteristics, are singled out from others in the society in which they live for differential and unequal treatment and who therefore regard themselves as objects of collective discrimination." There are many problems with this definition, however. First, it is not a group but members of a larger subpopulation who are singled out for unequal treatment. Second, the label "minority" is not always accurate; sometimes it is a majority, as was the case historically in South Africa, that is discriminated against. Thus, we should begin to revise this traditional definition of "minority group" by

---

Box 1.1
The Increasing Significance of "Race"

Despite the fact that "race" has no real meaning in a biological sense, the U.S. Census Bureau has increased its use of the term to denote ethnicity. In so doing, the Bureau is implicitly suggesting that people are biologically different, although this is far from its intent. In the 2000 census, for example, the Bureau asked questions about "mixed" ancestry and race, placing everybody in a "race" and constructing summary data in terms of "race" rather than "ethnicity." Persons responding to the question on *race* in the 2000 census could choose from the following five categories: White, Black or African American, American Indian and Alaska Native, Asian, and Native Hawaiian and Other Pacific Islander. A sixth racial category, "some other race," was provided for those persons unable to identify with one of the five racial categories. In an effort to document the number of multiracial persons in the U.S. population, persons could also respond to the *race* question by selecting either one of the following categories: race alone or race in combination. Persons in the "race alone" category reported only one race category, while persons in the "race in combination" category reported two or more race categories.

One result from the treatment of "race" in the 2000 census is that the Census Bureau now tabulates the population by "race," downplaying the notion of ethnicity which, we feel, is the more appropriate label. Curiously, "Hispanics" are often separated from other whites, and one frequently finds tables with labels denoting the distribution of "races" for the non-Hispanic population. In this way, Latinos who are seen as part of the "white race" are separated in calculations on "Hispanics," resulting in the cumbersome categories of "non-Hispanic White" and "White Hispanics." This partitioning of whites into two categories only highlights the insignificance of race as a marker of difference and the importance of ethnicity.

The intent of the Bureau was, no doubt, benign; it simply needed a label for people of mixed ethnic backgrounds. But, in using the term "race," the Bureau suggests that the offspring of people from different ethnic groups are of a "mixed race" which makes no sense biologically. They are, in reality, of mixed ethnic ancestry rather than race. In the end, this kind of tabulation makes "race" ever-more salient in people's minds, and as ethnic differences become perceived as "racial differences," the lines dividing ethnic subpopulations can harden.

---

acknowledging what it really means: an ethnic subpopulation in a society subject to discrimination by members of *more powerful ethnic subpopulations*. Usually the victimized subpopulation is a numerical minority, and the more powerful discriminators are in the majority. Since this is not always true, however, the important issue is this: Which ethnic subpopulation has the power to discriminate? The more powerful subpopulation is the dominant or superordinate ethnic group, and the less powerful ethnic subpopulation is the subordinate group. This latter terminology, which revolves around dominance and subordination, more accurately frames the issues that were once classified as "minority group relations."

prejudice: an attitude
discrimination: an action

ETHNIC DISCRIMINATION

Phrases like "unequal treatment" and "distinctive treatment" have been used rather loosely thus far. These and related terms can be consolidated by one key term: "discrimination." In general, *discrimination* is the process by which an individual, group, or subpopulation of individuals acts in ways that deny another individual, group, or subpopulation access to valued resources. So, in the context of ethnic relations, *ethnic discrimination* is the process by which the members of a more powerful and dominant ethnic subpopulation deny the members of another, less powerful and subordinate ethnic subpopulation full access to valued resources—jobs, income, education, health, prestige, power, or anything that the members of a society value.

Today, the term *reverse discrimination* is often used to emphasize that programs designed to overcome the effects of past discrimination against members of a subordinate subpopulation often deny some members of the dominant subpopulation equal access to valued resources. What makes these programs so controversial is that those denied access to resources—say, particular classes of jobs—are usually not the ones who engaged in discrimination in the past. Thus, they feel cheated and angry—emotions that the victims of discrimination almost always feel. The phrase "reverse discrimination" is pejorative in that it emphasizes the net loss of resources for those who may no longer discriminate but whose forefathers did; and so, they ask: Is this fair? On the other side, those who must live with the legacy of past discrimination ask: How are the effects of past discrimination to be overcome? There is no easy answer to either of these questions, but one thing is clear: The term "discrimination" often becomes the centerpiece of ideological and political debate over ethnic tensions (Kinder and Sanders, 1990; Thomas, 1990; Feagins, 1990; Ross, 1990).

The process of discrimination is the most important force sustaining ethnicity in a society. Discrimination denies some people access to what is valued, making it a highly volatile process. Because discrimination varies in nature, degree, and form, we need to identify some of its dimensions.

Types of Discrimination

The ways in which discrimination is perpetrated against an ethnic population vary considerably. The most intense form is *genocide*, when members of an ethnic subpopulation are killed or, potentially, an entire ethnic group is exterminated. The Nazi death camps with their gas chambers constituted an effort at genocide; the exposure of Native Americans to diseases and then the carnage of the Indian wars resulted in the virtual genocide of the original population in America. More recently, the *ethnic cleansing* policies of the Serbians in the former Yugoslavia are another example of genocidal behavior.

Expulsion is a somewhat less intense form of discrimination because those who are exiled from a society retain access to at least one highly valued resource: life. Expulsion is a common form of discrimination. For example,

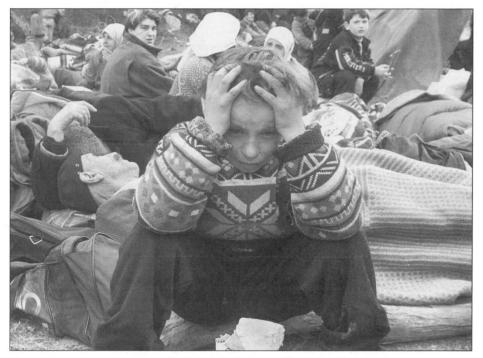

Those fleeing from ethnic conflict often find themselves refugees in a strange country, as is the case with this ethnic Albanian boy who fled his home in Kosovo into Macedonia to escape war in the former Yugoslavia.

during the time of slavery in the United States, several American presidents, including Abraham Lincoln, considered the creation of a black state in Africa to which "free" black people would be sent. Expulsion is usually forced, but it is often the case that one group makes life so miserable for another that the latter leaves "voluntarily." Thus, the concept of expulsion has ambiguity: If we confine its use only to cases in which people are thrown out of a country by direct coercion, the importance of indirect expulsion, people's lives made sufficiently miserable that they pack up and leave, is underemphasized.

Segregation is a process of spatially isolating an ethnic subpopulation in areas where they cannot have the same access to valued resources as do those who are not isolated. For instance, as we will see in Chapter 4, most African Americans were confined to the decaying cores of large cities during the post–World War II era by governmental and private housing policies; and as a result, they were denied access to the jobs, schools, and housing enjoyed by white Americans who moved to suburbia. The black townships and various rules of residence in South Africa mark another segregation pattern that historically denied access to resources. The Indian reservations that dot the American landscape are yet another form of segregation.

Box 1.2
Residential Segregation

Over the years, a series of statistical procedures have been developed to calculate the degree of residential segregation among various ethnic populations. The details of these calculations need not concern us here, but in essence, the higher the number for the "index of dissimilarity" the less likely are members of various ethnic groups to live in the same neighborhoods. A number of zero would mean no segregation while a score approaching 100 would signal complete segregation. The index is calculated for all metropolitan areas and for cities that have more than 25,000 residents, with each area or city given an index score for any two ethnic groups. The average index scores between non-Hispanic whites and other ethnic groups are as follows for cities and metropolitan areas:

	Cities	Metropolitan Areas
White–Black	45	59
White–Asian	32	45
White–Hispanic	35	43
White–American Indian	39	59

Segregation is thus higher in metropolitan areas than cities, a finding that should not be surprising since non-Hispanic whites were the first to move out of the cities to suburbia. It should be emphasized that these are only averages; the range of scores varies enormously. For example, the score for blacks and whites reveals a high of 87 in Chicago and a low of 18 in Newark, California. The number 87 means that 87 percent of whites in Chicago would have to move to a new neighborhood for whites to be evenly distributed throughout the city. Even when cities reveal a high proportion of African Americans, the index can still be high. For instance, New York is 25 percent African American but still has a score of 85; Philadelphia is 43 percent black with a score of 81; Boston is 24 percent black and has a score of 76. The highest score for non-Hispanic whites and Hispanics is 77, with the lowest score being 12; in New York, which is 27 percent Hispanic, the index score is still 70; in Los Angeles with 47 percent Hispanic, the score is 67. For whites and Asians, the highest score is 69 and lowest is 15; New York and Los Angeles, which are both 10 percent Asian, have, respectively, scores of 54 and 49.

Thus segregation is still very evident in American society, and African Americans are the most segregated. When people are segregated, they are typically denied access to valued resources, such as adequate housing, good schools, health care, and better-paying jobs.

Source: Frey and Myers (2002).

Exclusion is a pattern of discrimination that denies members of an ethnic group certain positions, independent of the effects of segregation. Slaves were denied basic citizenship rights. Up to just a few decades ago, African Americans were excluded from most craft unions; even in industrial unions, they were allowed to rise only to certain grade levels and not beyond. For many decades, African Americans and Latinos in the Southwest were excluded from the political arena through poll taxes, literacy tests, gerrymandering of districts, and other exclusionary tactics. Exclusion in the job sphere is especially harmful because it denies members of an ethnic group the money they could use to buy other valued resources—health care, housing, education, and political power. Exclusion from the political arena denies an ethnic group the power to move out of its subordinate position.

Selective inclusion is the process of allowing members of ethnic subpopulations into certain positions, while at the same time excluding them from other positions. For instance, Jews in Europe historically were excluded from most economic, social, and political positions but were included in the world of finance. In the United States, early Asian immigrants were allowed access to some positions—the Chinese were laborers on the railroads and later ran small service businesses. According to Takaki (1993), the Japanese were denied access to the industrial labor market in California during the 1920s; as a result, many moved into the agricultural labor market, in which they used their entrepreneurial skills to become successful farmers and land owners. Today, many Asian immigrants are given easy access to ownership of small retail businesses but are excluded, to some degree, from white- and blue-collar positions in large companies. In the past and still today, Mexican American laborers were included in the low-wage farm labor workforce and, later, in other low-paying jobs in light industry, but they were excluded from better-paying economic positions as well as positions in the political and educational arena. Thus *exclusion* and *selective inclusion* tend to operate simultaneously, in a pincerlike movement that denies access to some positions and opens access only to those areas that are often (though not always) financially unrewarding or lacking in power and prestige.

Abusive practices are patterns of action against the victims of discrimination by members of other ethnic groups and particularly by those charged with enforcement of the law. These practices may be intentional, but often they are not. However, for their victims it makes little difference because they must suffer. For example, in the United States it is typically in neighborhoods inhabited by poor and relatively powerless ethnic groups that environmental problems are, literally, dumped. Disposal sites are generally near the poor, causing some to label this process *environmental racism* (Bullard, 2000; Farhat, 2002). Or, to take another example, what is now labeled *racial profiling* occurs every single day in American cities, with officers using ethnic markers to assess the likelihood of potential crime. The result is that members of particular ethnic populations are likely to be singled out for special surveillance and potential harassment by police officers (Johnson, 2000; Russell, 2001). These kinds of practices typically make the difficult lives of the ethnic poor even more difficult, and in so doing, they ensure that it will be hard for members of these ethnic groups to gain a greater share of resources.

The intensity of discrimination varies according to its type: from genocide and expulsion to physical segregation to exclusion, selective inclusion, and abuse. None is pleasant, if you are on the receiving end. These patterns of discrimination have been implemented in various ways, but the underlying mechanisms of discrimination are much the same, as we explore below.

The Institutionalization of Discrimination

Acts by individuals to deny others access to valued resources are the most salient form of discrimination. When a white refuses to sell a house to an Asian, when a police officer physically abuses a member of a minority group, or when a supervisor refuses to promote an ethnic worker and these actions are taken simply because a person is a member of an ethnic group, discrimination is at work. These examples are isolated acts of discrimination if (1) they are not sanctioned by cultural values, beliefs, and norms; (2) they are not performed as a matter of policy within an organized structure such as a corporation, police department, board of realtors, school, or factory; and (3) they are not frequent and pervasive in the informal contact among people within an organization. In contrast, *institutionalized discrimination* exists when these individual acts are sanctioned by cultural values, beliefs, laws, and norms; when they are part of the way a social structure normally operates; and when they are a pervasive and persistent feature of the contact among people.

The distinction between isolated acts of discrimination and institutionalized discrimination is easier to make in a definition than in practice. For example, when discrimination is institutionalized in one sphere—say, housing practices— it becomes easier to commit acts of discrimination in other arenas, such as schooling, politics, or jobs. If enough people practice such isolated acts of informal discrimination, these acts become institutionalized. In the United States, civil rights laws and cultural beliefs do not condone discrimination as they once did; indeed, they demand that all individuals be given equal access to schools, jobs, housing, and other important resources. They even mandate punishments for those who discriminate, and they have led to the creation of watchdog and enforcement agencies. Yet, individual acts of informal discrimination are so widespread in many communities that discrimination is informally institutionalized even in the face of formal prohibitions.

Thus, the process of institutionalized discrimination is subtle and complex. It can operate at formal and informal levels, and these two levels can even be in contradiction. Isolated acts of discrimination can increase in frequency when they constitute a normatively sanctioned and, hence, institutionalized form of discrimination.

The subtlety and complexity of institutionalized discrimination is demonstrated in the lingering effect of past patterns of discrimination that are now

Prejudicial attitudes toward black people created a context in which Africans were auctioned off to the highest bidder.

formally banned and no longer practiced. The legacy and cumulative effects of past discrimination can be so great that they prevent ethnic subpopulations from gaining equal access to resources. Many blacks (and Native Americans, Latinos, and others) are systematically denied by their present circumstances the same access to valued resources as whites have. Even if we could assume that no employer, real estate agent, teacher, or police officer currently acts in a discriminatory way, many African Americans and other ethnic groups would not have the same degree of access to resources as white Americans have because of their present location in segregated slums with a long history of exclusion from most spheres of mainstream life in America. Many African Americans today live in urban slums away from decent schools, housing, and jobs because of past patterns of discrimination. In this environment, they do not acquire the education, job skills, or motivation that would enable them to leave the slums and take advantage of new opportunities that were not available even thirty years ago. Thus, sometimes the legacy of the past operates as a barrier in the present and constitutes a pervasive pattern of discrimination. We must acknowledge that institutionalized discrimination has a lag effect beyond the period in the past when individuals and organizations practiced discrimination routinely.

Another facet of institutionalized discrimination is that it is often unintentional. This is certainly the case with the holdover effects of past discrimination, but more is involved. To take the most obvious example in the United States today—schools—it is now clear that the school curriculum, testing procedures, and classroom activities place some ethnic students at a disadvantage in comparison with other students. This type of discrimination is not intentional, at least in most instances; and it could be argued (albeit problematically) that schools facilitate the acquisition of the critical skills necessary for success and for overcoming the effects of past discrimination. Yet, if the schools are organized in ways that are, for example, alien to students, that are unresponsive to the problems of poor children or immigrant children, and that are insensitive to the distinctive culture of a minority population, then the schools can become a source of discrimination. Students will have difficulty adjusting and will become discouraged—dropping out and finding themselves with few prospects for jobs and income. The school may not have intended this to occur—indeed, just the opposite—but the very nature of its structure and operation has worked to discourage students and, in so doing, has subtly and inadvertently discriminated against students whose access to resources is dramatically lowered when they drop out (Hilliard, 1988; Medina, 1988; Trueba, 1986; McCarthy, 1990). In a society that uses educational credentials as a quick and easy way to sort people out in a labor market, the consequences for members of ethnic subpopulations who find the school experience unrewarding extend to all spheres of their life—job, home, income, and health.

Thus, the institutionalization of discrimination is an important force in ethnic relations. The pattern of institutionalization affects the type of segregation, exclusion, selective inclusion, and abuse that a subordinate ethnic subpopulation experiences, if it is not killed off or sent away. As the pattern of institutionalized discrimination changes, so do patterns of segregation, exclusion, selective inclusion, and abuse.

ETHNIC STRATIFICATION

Discrimination, as it operates to segregate, exclude, and selectively include members of a subordinate ethnic subpopulation within a society, produces a system of ethnic stratification. Because discrimination determines how many and which types of valued resources the members of an ethnic subpopulation are likely to have, it establishes the location of an ethnic subpopulation within the stratification system of a society. Moreover, discrimination also determines the patterns of mobility, if any, across social class lines.

For our purposes, *ethnic stratification* refers to several interrelated processes:

1. The amount, level, and type of resources—such as jobs, education, health, money, power, and prestige—an ethnic subpopulation typically receives.
2. The degree to which these resource shares locate most members of an ethnic subpopulation in various social hierarchies.
3. The extent to which these resource shares contribute to those distinctive behaviors, organizations, and cultural systems that provide justification to the dominant group for making the ethnic subpopulation targets of discrimination.

We can take almost any ethnic group—Latinos, for example (see Chapter 6)—and determine their average income, their level of political representation, and their average years of education. In performing this exercise, we soon find that, on the whole, many Latinos in America have relatively low incomes, are underrepresented in the halls of political power, and attain less education than Anglo-Americans. The statistics can be determined by simple counts of average income, years of education, and number of political offices held. The numbers show the share of resources that Latinos possess in American society. One often finds, in addition, differences in the shares of resources *within* an ethnic subpopulation. There are affluent Latinos as well as very poor ones; their average level of affluence, power, and prestige tends to vary in terms of which subpopulation—Mexican American, Cuban, Puerto Rican, South or Central American—is being addressed. Yet, when ethnic stratification is in evidence, a majority of a subpopulation does reveal a particular level and configuration of resource shares. On various social hierarchies—power, income and wealth, prestige, and education—a profile of resource shares locates a majority of the ethnic group at a particular place in the broader system of stratification. There are always deviations, of course, but when ethnic stratification is in force, these deviations apply to a minority of cases. Some Latinos, such as Mexican Americans, are located near the bottom of the power, income and wealth, prestige, and education hierarchies, thereby placing them in the lower and working classes. There are middle- and upper-class Mexican Americans, to be sure, but they are a tiny minority of this subpopulation as a whole. This profile of resource shares and the resulting location on various social hierarchies contribute to the distinctiveness of Mexican Americans and, as a consequence, justify new and continuing prejudices and discrimination against them, thereby perpetuating the ethnic dimensions of social stratification.

In general, discrimination causes members of an ethnic subpopulation to be (1) overrepresented in lower and working classes or (2) overrepresented in a narrow range of middle-class positions, usually in small businesses of various kinds. As discrimination lessens, mobility to other classes and positions within classes occurs, but a holdover effect persists that limits such mobility for many.

Institutionalized discrimination, as it segregates, excludes, and selectively includes, determines the kinds and shares of resources received by members of an ethnic subpopulation; these shares locate them on society's hierarchies. By virtue of its pattern of resource shares and location on various social hierarchies, an ethnic subpopulation's distinctiveness is created and sustained. Thus, the principal consequence of ethnic discrimination is to give the broader stratification system in a society an ethnic dimension, one that is often more tension-producing and volatile than the normal antagonisms between members of different social classes.

One rough measure of the effects of ethnic discrimination is the rate of poverty among various ethnic groups. The higher the poverty rate, the more an ethnic population has been subject to discrimination. Members of this population have been denied equal access to quality education and, thereby, jobs and income. However, poverty alone cannot tell us the complete story because some ethnics, like many Asians in America, are more affluent, although discrimination has often forced them to occupy a limited range of professions. But, for a quick view of where ethnics stand in the overall stratification system, the rates of poverty can give us an early picture as to which groups have been victimized the most. In Figure 1.1, the rates of poverty for various ethnic groups are reported for whites (both Hispanics and non-Hispanics), Hispanics alone, non-Hispanics alone, Asian/Pacific Islanders, and African Americans. Similar time-series data are not available for Native Americans, but their poverty rate over the last three years has been about 25 percent. As is evident in the figure, blacks have the highest rate, followed by Latinos or Hispanics; and coupled with Native Americans, these three ethnic groups are well above the overall poverty rate of 11.7 percent of the population, which translates into almost 33 million people. Non-Hispanic whites and Asian/Pacific Islanders are below the overall rate, although within the Asian/Pacific Islanders category there is wide variation, with some Asian minorities well above and others below the overall poverty rate and with many Pacific Islander groups well above this overall rate. Thus, rates of poverty represent the cumulative effects of discrimination over time; and they give us a starting point in assessing which groups have been subjected to the most intense discrimination.

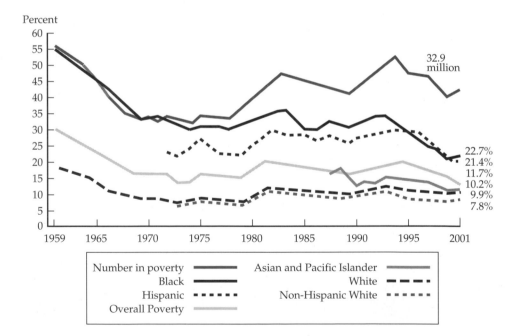

FIGURE 1.1 Poverty Rates by Race and Hispanic Origin: 1959 to 2001

Source: U.S. Bureau of the Census, Current Population Survey, 1960–2002 Annual Demographic Supplements.

ETHNIC PREJUDICE

The terms "prejudice" and "discrimination" are often uttered together, for it is presumed that prejudiced people discriminate, and vice versa. *Prejudice* is a set of beliefs and stereotypes about a category of people; hence, *ethnic prejudices* are beliefs and stereotypes about designated subpopulations who share certain identifying characteristics—biological, behavioral, organizational, or cultural—or at least are perceived to share these identifying characteristics. Those prejudices that lead to, and are used to justify, discrimination are negative, emphasizing the undesirable features of a subpopulation.

Does prejudice invariably lead to discrimination? In a classic study in the early 1930s, Richard La Piere (1934) observed in his travels with a Chinese couple that, despite a climate of hostility toward Asians in the United States at that time, the couple was served and treated courteously at hotels, motels, and restaurants. He was puzzled by this observation because all the attitude surveys at that time revealed extreme prejudice by white Americans toward the Chinese. La Piere sent a questionnaire to the owners of the establishments where he and his Asian companions had experienced courteous service, asking if they would "accept members of the Chinese race as guests in your establishment." More than 90 percent said no, thus demonstrating that prejudice and discrimination do not always go together.

Robert Merton (1949) defined four categories of people in his analysis of the relationship between prejudice and discrimination:

1. *All-weather liberals* who are not prejudiced and do not discriminate.
2. *Reluctant liberals* who are unprejudiced but will discriminate when it is in their interest to do so.
3. *Timid bigots* who are prejudiced but afraid to show it.
4. *Active bigots* who are prejudiced and quite willing to discriminate.

In La Piere's study of motel owners, then, he encountered timid bigots who, in face-to-face contact with an ethnic group, did not implement their prejudices.

Even though prejudice does not always translate into discrimination, it is an important force in ethnic relations, for several reasons. First, prejudicial beliefs and stereotypes highlight, usually unfairly and inaccurately, certain characteristics of an ethnic subpopulation. By spotlighting these characteristics, they make ethnic group members more identifiable, alerting others to their existence, separating them from the majority, and potentially making them easier targets for discrimination. Second, prejudices present negative images of an ethnic group, legitimizing discrimination against such "undesirable" persons. Third, prejudices arouse fears about, and anger toward, an ethnic group, placing members of the ethnic group in constant tension with those who are prejudiced and, often, making them vulnerable to unprovoked acts of discrimination. Fourth, prejudice creates a general climate of intolerance for differences not only in a selected ethnic group but in other categories of individuals as well (such as the disabled or the elderly).

Prejudice may generate potential or actual discrimination, but the reverse is also true: Acts of discrimination can generate prejudice or, as is often the case, reinforce existing prejudices. Most people feel they must justify their acts of discrimination; in a society like the United States, where cultural values emphasize equality and freedom, discrimination, which violates these values, has to be rationalized and made to seem appropriate. Prejudice is one mechanism for doing this because it makes the denial of freedom and equality seem acceptable "in this one case" since "after all, these people are so . . . (fill in the prejudice)." Those who are victims of discrimination react in different ways: sometimes passively and other times aggressively. The results of people's reaction against prejudice and discrimination vary—prejudicial stereotypes are sometimes reinforced, other times changed or eliminated.

Thus, prejudicial beliefs based on negative and stereotypical portrayals of an ethnic subpopulation stimulate and sustain ethnic tensions. Such beliefs do not always translate into direct discriminatory action, but they target, highlight the negative, arouse fears and anger, and create a culture of intolerance that can erupt into discriminatory acts or legitimate those that have been practiced in the past. Prejudice provides the rationale for discrimination, either before or after the fact, and is thus central to understanding discrimination and patterns of ethnic stratification.

ADAPTATIONS TO PREJUDICE AND DISCRIMINATION

When confronted with discrimination, members of a subordinate subpopulation respond. Usually, they seek to make the best of a difficult situation. Depending upon the nature and magnitude of discrimination, as well as upon other social conditions, several responses are possible: (1) passive acceptance, (2) marginal participation, (3) assimilation, (4) withdrawal and self-segregation, (5) rebellion and revolt, and (6) organized protest. Different segments of a minority population may resort to several of these adaptations at the same time, or a population may pass through different patterns of adaptation.

Passive Acceptance

If the power of an ethnic group is small and the magnitude of the discrimination great, members of the group may have no choice but to accept the discrimination. During the slavery era in the United States it was virtually impossible for African slaves to do anything but accept subjugation. Yet, even under severely oppressive conditions, populations acquire interpersonal techniques for dealing with their oppressors while maintaining their sense of identity and dignity. The stereotypical slave, as portrayed in Harriet Beecher Stowe's *Uncle Tom's Cabin*, offers a vivid example of such techniques. Uncle Tom's bowing and scraping and repeated use of the phrase "Yes sir, yes sir" allowed him to gain favor with white people and to enjoy some degree of privilege. *Passive acceptance,* then, is often not passive but, rather, active manipulation of a situation. Some slaves were able to develop their own culture and to enjoy some of the basic pleasures of life through the appearance of passive acceptance. Of course, such a pattern of adjustment tends to perpetuate itself; the subordinate population does not initiate change, and the majority is not pressured to cease its discriminatory practices.

Marginal Participation

At times, subordinate ethnic subpopulations can find a niche where they can use their creative resources and prosper. In essence, these subpopulations are allowed *marginal participation.* For example, Jews have often been able to find business opportunities and to prosper in societies that actively discriminated against them. At the turn of the century and up to the present, many Chinese Americans were able to prosper in small businesses providing services to the white American majority. Such marginal niches are created when the majority is not inclined to enter a specialized field. Marginal participation tends to be most successful when the minority population is small and does not enter areas dominated by the majority. It is probably for this reason that African Americans and Chicanos have been unable to find specialized niches; their numbers are simply too great.

Assimilation

Assimilation is the process by which the members of an ethnic group become part of the broader culture and society, losing their distinctive character. Minorities that are less identifiable biologically and culturally are more readily assimilated. Ethnic populations that can be easily identified, however, have greater difficulty assimilating. It is for this reason that white ethnic groups in America, such as the Protestant Irish and Germans, have become largely assimilated, although enclaves are thriving in some large eastern cities. Other Caucasian migrants, such as Poles, Italians, and Catholic Irish, have also tended to assimilate, although the East and Midwest have cohesive ethnic cultures of these populations. African Americans, on the other hand, have had a more difficult time assimilating because of their visibility and the resulting ease with which the majority can locate them as targets of discrimination.

Withdrawal and Self-Segregation

Another adaptation to discrimination is withdrawal and the creation of a self-sustaining "society" within the broader society. Such *self-segregation* enables a population to create and support their own communities, businesses, schools, leadership, churches, and other social forms. For example, the early black Muslim movement in America advocated a separate African American community,

Nonviolent protest proved to be an effective tool in securing for African Americans their civil rights. Here, Martin Luther King, Jr., leads a civil rights march on Washington, D.C., August 1963.

self-supporting and isolated from "white" institutions. Urban communities as well as rural communes were established and still prosper, although there has been a clear trend away from complete withdrawal and isolation among many black Muslims. Self-segregation is a difficult adaptation to maintain. Opportunities are necessarily limited compared to those in the broader society. As a result, some seek these outside opportunities. Moreover, economic, political, and social isolation is often difficult to sustain in urban, media-dominated societies, in which alternatives and options constantly present themselves.

Rebellion and Revolt

Subordinate ethnic subpopulations do not always accept, assimilate, withdraw, or marginally participate. Frequently they rebel. Such *rebellion* can take a number of forms, one being general hostility and aggressive behavior toward the majority. Few white Americans would feel comfortable walking through a black ghetto or a Chicano barrio, because they fear that there is some likelihood of intimidation and assault. Another form of rebellion is rioting, such as the widespread urban riots in the United States in the 1960s and the turmoil

---

Box 1.3

Reported Ancestry of Americans

The U.S. Bureau of the Census polls people on their ancestry. They can select up to two ancestries, but they are not required to report any. Nonetheless, the results of this poll are interesting and roughly correspond to the official count of the 2000 census.

Non-Hispanic White	**75.1%**	Asian	**3.6%**
German	15.2	Chinese	0.9
Irish	10.8	Filipino	0.7
English	8.7	Asian Indian	0.6
American	7.2	Korean	0.4
Italian	5.5	Vietnamese	0.4
Polish	3.2	Other	0.3
French	2.9	Pacific Islander	**0.14%**
Scottish	1.8	Hawaiian	0.05
Dutch	1.6	Guamanian	0.02
Norwegian	1.6	Samoan	0.03
Scots-Irish	1.5	Other	0.04
Swedish	1.4	Latino	**12.6%**
Other	3.6	Mexican	7.3
Black	**12.3%**	Puerto Rican	1.2
Native American	**0.8%**	Cuban	0.4
		Other	3.6

Source: U.S. Bureau of the Census 2000, Social Science Data Analysis Network (SSDAN), 2002.

---

associated with the Rodney King beating in Los Angeles in the early 1990s. All forms of rebellion involve minorities' "striking back" and venting their frustrations, and at times, these revolts become extremely violent, mobilizing people for mass killings.

Organized Protest

Rebellious outbursts are often part of a larger social movement, and, hence may become *organized protests,* when subordinate ethnic groups become organized to make broad-based and concerted efforts to change patterns of discrimination. The civil rights movement represents one such effort. Beginning with sit-ins and freedom rides in the 1960s, progressing to large-scale demonstrations (sometimes boiling over into riots), and culminating in creation of successful national organizations that effectively changed many legal and social patterns, the civil rights movement of African Americans successfully challenged pervasive discriminatory practices. The movement has been far from totally successful, however, since substantial integration of African Americans into the American mainstream has not occurred. But when an ethnic population is large and organized, it can generate political power and initiate some degree of social change. When minorities become majorities in cities and regions, as was the case in the late twentieth century in the United States, they can wield additional power and can force changes in old patterns of discrimination.

SUMMARY

Ethnic antagonism is one of the oldest and most pervasive dimensions of human social organization. To study this phenomenon, it is necessary to define terms and key concepts. The term "race" is of little importance biologically, but it is relevant sociologically. For if people perceive and believe others to be biologically distinctive and different, superficial biological traits become an important consideration in the formation of ethnicity. For our purposes, "ethnicity" refers to the history as well as the behavioral, organizational, and cultural features of people that make them distinctive and distinguishable from others. People can be distinguished on the basis of superficial biological traits, but these traits are associated with presumed behavioral, organizational, and cultural features—that is, with ethnicity.

The term "ethnic group" is commonly used, but we prefer the term "ethnic subpopulation." The latter term emphasizes the fact that people who are distinguished on the basis of an interrelated cluster of characteristics—biological, cultural, behavioral, and organizational—constitute a population more than a closed group. They are not all necessarily engaged in face-to-face contact, as the notion of "group" implies. To be sure, people's involvement in local groups and other structures sustains their distinctive patterns of organization, but these do not embrace the population as a whole. Ethnic subpopulations exist, instead, within a larger, more inclusive population. This point is not merely semantic; it is fundamental to an understanding of the dynamics of ethnicity.

The term "minority group" is also limited. Not all ethnic subpopulations subject to discrimination are minorities. They can constitute the majority in a community or in a nation as a whole. The underlying issue is *power*. Which groups have the power to limit the activities of other groups? More accurate terms are "*super*ordinate ethnic subpopulations" and "*sub*ordinate ethnic subpopulations."

Discrimination is the process of denying others access to valued resources. Ethnic discrimination occurs when members of a superordinate ethnic subpopulation are able to limit or deny members of a subordinate ethnic population access to valued resources—jobs, income, education, power, health care, and anything that is valued and prized in a society. Ethnic discrimination surfaces in several different forms: genocide, or the systematic killing of members in a subordinate ethnic population; expulsion, or the exiling of all or selected members of an ethnic population; segregation, or the spatial confinement or isolation of members of an ethnic group so that they have difficulty gaining access to resources; exclusion, or the denial of rights to positions in a society that provide access to valued resources; and selective inclusion, or the confinement of members of an ethnic subpopulation to a narrow range of positions in the society. In addition to these forms of discrimination are a wide range of abusive practices against targeted ethnics. These types of discrimination gain effectiveness as discrimination becomes institutionalized. We define "institutionalized discrimination" as individual acts of discrimination that are (1) pervasive; (2) culturally supported in norms, beliefs, and values; and (3) lodged in social structures as matters of policy and practice. The more institutionalized the discrimination is, the more a subordinate ethnic subpopulation is segregated, excluded, and selectively included, while being vulnerable to genocide and expulsion. Discrimination is thus the central process underlying ethnic problems in society.

Institutionalized discrimination produces ethnic stratification. When members of a subordinate ethnic subpopulation receive only certain types and levels of valued resources, it becomes possible to establish their location on the social hierarchies of society. On the basis of this location, the distinctiveness of an ethnic group is retained, thereby making it a target of further prejudice and discrimination.

"Prejudice" refers to negative and stigmatizing beliefs, concepts, and stereotypes about people; "ethnic prejudice" is based on negative beliefs, conceptions, and stereotypes about members of a subpopulation distinguishable in terms of their history and biological, behavioral, cultural, and organizational features. Prejudice and discrimination are not perfectly correlated, but discrimination cannot be easily institutionalized without widespread prejudice among dominant ethnic subpopulations.

Prejudice and discrimination force their targets to respond and adapt. Assimilation, or the elimination of ethnically distinct characteristics and adoption of those of the superordinate ethnic population, is one method of adaptation. At the other extreme are rebellion and revolt against superordinate ethnic groups, the goal being redistribution of power and, hence, the patterns of discrimination. Another response to discrimination is organized protest, often arising out of or even prompting acts of rebellion, in which ethnic groups and their allies organize to change patterns of discrimination. Yet another response is withdrawal and self-segregation of the subordinate ethnic group in order to isolate itself from the discriminatory acts of others. Members of an ethnic group may choose to accept their position passively, or they may participate marginally, finding narrow niches in which they can secure resources.

This chapter has presented many useful terms and distinctions that will deepen our understanding of and provide a perspective on ethnic relations in America. These terms and distinctions do not explain ethnic relations; they merely describe them. We also need to know *why* people focus on perceived ethnic differences, *why* they discriminate, *why* they hold prejudices, and *why* superordinate populations force subordinate groups to adapt in certain ways. Explaining these "why" issues is the job of theory. Within the framework of definitions and distinctions developed in this chapter, we can now move on to explore the theories that have been used to explain ethnicity, prejudice, discrimination, and other aspects of ethnic relations.

POINTS OF DEBATE

In any society where distinct ethnic subpopulations exist, the issue of ethnicity is a subject of debate and controversy. No society revealing ethnic differences has ever been able to organize itself in ways that avoid the tension and conflict accompanying ethnic identity. The United States is not an exception; indeed, American society is one of the few in history that has sought to integrate so many large and diverse ethnic subpopulations into its cultural core. The problems of ethnicity in the United States have stimulated and continue to create many points of debate. When reading the coming chapters, keep in mind the following controversial issues.

1. The "first American dilemma": How can a society that values equality and freedom engage in systematic discrimination against minority subpopulations? This question is rhetorical because the evidence is irrefutable that discrimination has occurred, and continues to occur, on a massive and long-term scale. Can the accumulated effects of such discrimination be undone?

2. The "second American dilemma": Can the values of freedom and equality be used to justify efforts to compensate the descendants of past discrimination? An affirmative answer to this question has many implications, all of which are debatable: (a) Are Americans willing to spend billions of tax dollars to create jobs, housing, and educational programs to overcome the effects of past discrimination? (b) Is private enterprise willing or able to participate on a massive scale in creating jobs for members of particular ethnic groups who have been the victims of this legacy of discrimination? (c) Are white Americans willing to give up some of their access to valued resources so that disadvantaged minority groups can increase their access, or is such action simply going to encourage accusations of "reverse discrimination"?

3. If Americans are unwilling to meet the challenges posed by the second American dilemma, what is the alternative? Conflict and violence among ethnic groups are escalating; poverty among ethnic groups is on the rise; out-of-wedlock childbearing is reaching epidemic proportions (now 63 percent) among African Americans; substance abuse and other social problems among minority groups are growing; the number of crimes committed by minority group members is increasing; and innumerable problems are arising from the accumulated effects of past discrimination. This reality confronts Americans in their daily lives. What is to be done? Nothing? Build more prisons? Hire more police? Actively try to address the problems at enormous cost? What are the viable options? Such questions are ultimately part of any discussion of ethnicity in America.

KEY TERMS

active bigots, 15

all-weather liberals, 15

assimilation, 17

discrimination, 6

environmental racism, 9

ethnic cleansing, 6

ethnic discrimination, 6

ethnic group, 4

ethnic population, 4

ethnic prejudice, 15

ethnic stratification, 12

ethnic subpopulation, 4

ethnicity, 3

exclusion, 9

expulsion, 6

genocide, 6

institutionalized discrimination, 10

marginal participation, 17

minority group, 4

organized protests, 19

passive acceptance, 17

prejudice, 15

race, 5

racial profiling, 9

rebellion, 18

reluctant liberals, 15

reverse discrimination, 6

segregation, 7

selective inclusion, 9

self-segregation, 17

subpopulation, 4

timid bigots, 15

CHAPTER 2

Explaining Ethnic Relations

A *theory* tries to explain *why* specific events occur. In the context of ethnic relations, then, theories seek to explain why ethnic distinctions are made in the first place, why they are sustained over time, why some ethnic groups discriminate against others with varying degrees of severity, why prejudice exists, why some ethnic groups remain identifiable, and why others melt into the dominant culture.

Many different theories exist concerning ethnic relations. Our goal in this chapter is to pull these theories together so that we have a coherent framework within which to examine specific ethnic groups in America—African Americans, Latinos, Native Americans, Asian Americans, and European-origin white ethnics. The first step is to review the range of diversity in existing theories; later we can incorporate the strengths of each theory into a more general one that can guide us throughout our review of ethnic relations in America.

THEORIES OF ETHNIC RELATIONS

Assimilation Theories

Part of the early American creed was a belief that successive waves of ethnic immigrants could be incorporated into the mainstream of social life. Robert Park, one of the earliest American theorists on ethnic relations, saw such assimilation as "a process of interpenetration and fusion in which persons and groups acquire the memories, sentiments, and attitudes of other groups, and, by sharing their experience and history, are incorporated with them into a common cultural life" (Park and Burgess, 1924:735).

Park proposed stages of assimilation, beginning with contact among diverse ethnic groups. Out of such contact comes a *competitive phase*, in which ethnic populations compete over resources, such as jobs, living space, and political representation. The next stage is an unstable *accommodation*, in which immigrants and their descendants are forced to change and adapt to their new environment. During this phase, there is some degree of stabilization of relations between immigrants and those in the host society, even if this accommodation forces migrants into lower social strata. Moreover, once ethnic stratification exists, the

24

pace of assimilation is dramatically reduced, although Park believed that, ultimately, even a lower-class, subordinate ethnic subpopulation could be *assimilated*. It might take hundreds of years, but eventually assimilation would occur. Thus, the last phase in Park's theory is assimilation in which the migrant ethnic merges with other ethnic groups (Park, 1950).

More recent assimilation theories have been more explicit about (1) the nature of the host society and culture to which migrant ethnic groups must adapt and (2) the various types, levels, and degrees of assimilation that can develop. For instance, as Milton Gordon (1964) emphasizes, it is to "the middle class cultural patterns of . . . white, Anglo-Saxon" culture that immigrants to the United States have had to adapt. Various ethnic subpopulations may evidence, however, different degrees of progress in adapting to the dominant Anglo-Saxon culture. *Cultural assimilation* occurs when the values, beliefs, dogmas, ideologies, language, and other systems of symbols of the dominant culture are adopted. Most ethnic groups become, to varying degrees, culturally assimilated. In contrast to cultural assimilation, *structural assimilation* occurs when migrant ethnic groups become members of the primary groups within dominant ethnic subpopulations—their families, close friends, cliques within clubs, and groups within organizations. Gordon emphasizes that structural assimilation is more difficult to achieve than cultural assimilation because it involves penetration into the close interactions and associations of dominant ethnic groups. Even when members of ethnic groups penetrate more secondary and formal organizational structures—schools, workplaces, and political arenas—they may still lack more primary and personal ties with members of dominant ethnic groups.

Other types of assimilation are based on the degree of cultural and structural assimilation an ethnic group is able to achieve: *marital assimilation*, or the emergence of high rates of intermarriage between the migrant and dominant ethnic groups; *identification assimilation*, in which individuals no longer see themselves as distinctive and, like members of dominant groups, stake their personal identities to participation and success in the mainstream institutions of a society; *attitude-receptional assimilation*, or the lack of prejudicial attitudes and stereotyping on the part of both dominant and migrant ethnic groups; *behavioral-receptional assimilation*, or the absence of intentional discrimination by dominant ethnic groups against subordinate ethnic groups; and *civic assimilation*, or the reduction of conflict between ethnic groups over basic values and access to the political arena.

According to Gordon, assimilation occurs over generations in the United States. By the third generation, a considerable amount of assimilation has occurred, especially among white ethnic groups. They have become culturally assimilated; they have made inroads into the primary groups or, at the very least, into the organizations of the Anglo-Saxon core; they have begun to intermarry with members of other ethnic groups; they identify with the institutional system; they are victims and perpetrators of fewer prejudices, stereotypes, and acts of discrimination; and they are engaged in less conflict over values and political rights. But what about nonwhite ethnic groups? For them, the assimilation process, Gordon (1981) admits, is slower, but he is optimistic that even the most identifiable subordinate ethnic groups in America—African Americans and Native Americans—are on the path to further assimilation.

Assimilation theories probably paint an overly benign view of ethnic relations, viewing assimilation as inexorable. Yet, they provide us with a way to measure how far an ethnic group has moved into the dominant culture along various dimensions—cultural, structural, marital, identification, attitude, behavioral, political. Indeed, the amount and pace of assimilation along these dimensions provide clues about how much and what type of discrimination has been working against an ethnic subpopulation. For example, if we find that, after hundreds of years of coexistence with the dominant Anglo-Saxon society, African Americans and Native Americans are structurally unassimilated and only partially assimilated in terms of culture, reveal low rates of intermarriage with other ethnic groups, identify only partially with the society and its institutions, suffer many prejudicial stereotypes, experience acts of discrimination, and remain partially disenfranchised from the political arena, then it is likely that massive informal and institutional discrimination exists and has existed. Assimilation theories do not explain how these discriminatory forces operate, but they provide a sense of what their consequences are.

Pluralism Theories

Partially in reaction to the "melting pot" assumption underlying most assimilation theories are those theories that stress the process of maintaining patterns of ethnicity. Indeed, the maintenance of distinctive cultural, organizational, and behavioral characteristics is often a way of coping with discrimination. A distinct ethnic identity provides sources of support and guidance in a sometimes hostile world. When ethnic identity is nurtured, a pluralistic and permanent mosaic of ethnic subpopulations becomes evident.

Most scholars who subscribe to this more pluralistic view do not deny that some assimilation into the dominant segments of a society occurs. Rather, they argue, ethnicity remains a powerful force, even among white ethnic groups who are often presumed to be fully assimilated. Nathan Glazer and Daniel Moynihan (1970) were among the first to emphasize that even as many of their customs are replaced with those of the dominant Anglo-Saxon society, white ethnic groups continue to reveal residential, behavioral, organizational, and cultural patterns that mark their distinctive ethnic identity, one that subtly separates them from the middle-class, Anglo-Saxon Protestant core.

The term *ethnogenesis* is often employed to describe this process of creating a distinctive ethnicity as a means of adapting to discrimination, even as some degree of assimilation occurs. Andrew Greeley (1971, 1974) has been one of the most forceful advocates of this position, arguing that there is considerable ethnic diversity in America that simply cannot be explained by assimilation models. Ethnic groups not only retain elements of their past but they also construct and create new ways of adjusting to discrimination. As generations pass, and ethnic groups come to share many characteristics with the dominant white,

Anglo-Saxon Protestant segments of society, they selectively retain elements of their ethnic heritage and they create new elements. For example, third- and even fourth-generation Irish Americans, Poles, and Italians continue to display their ethnic identities; moreover, they often strive to create new symbols to mark with pride their ethnic heritage.

Pluralistic theories offer an important corrective to assimilation theories, but they do not explain adequately the broader social forces that cause and sustain discrimination. If ethnic pluralism is, to some degree, a consequence of discrimination, these theories have little to say about those forces producing such discrimination. They are, instead, concerned with ethnogenesis, per se, rather than the external structures in the society that set ethnogenesis in motion.

Biological Theories

The spectacular rise of sociobiology in recent decades has produced another kind of theory of ethnogenesis. This theory is different from pluralist theories in its emphasis on the biological underpinnings of ethnicity. What are these biological underpinnings? The basic position of early sociobiology was that the units of natural selection are the genes, rather than the individual. The individual is, from a sociobiological point of view, only a temporary house or vessel for genes that seek to survive in the gene pool. Thus, genes are seen as "selfish" and as driven to maximize their fitness, or their capacity to remain in the gene pool. Sociobiological theories of ethnicity, then, start with these assumptions and see them as a driving force operating to produce and sustain ethnicity (Turner and Maryanski, 1993). How do these evolutionary and biological forces operate? Pierre van den Berghe (1981) has provided the most forceful argument from a sociobiological perspective; let us examine his answer to this question.

According to van den Berghe and most sociobiologists, social structures are merely "survival machines" that exist to maintain the fitness of genes. Sociobiologists have introduced two concepts to explain why "selfish genes" create social structures or "survival machines." One concept is *kin selection* or *inclusive fitness*, which holds that family structures are a strategy allowing males and females to maximize their fitness by keeping as much of their genetic material as possible in the gene pool. Moreover, when family members help each other, they are ensuring that a portion of their genes remains in the pool (since brothers, sisters, parents, and offspring all share 50 percent of the same genes; grandparents, half siblings, uncles, aunts, nieces, and nephews share 25 percent of their genes; and first cousins, half nephews, and great grandchildren share 12 percent of their genes). Thus, familism is simply a strategy that allows genes to stay in the pool. The other concept is *reciprocal altruism*, which was developed to explain why nonfamily members help each other survive; for if maximization of fitness is the goal of genes, an explanation is needed for the fact that people help others with whom they do not share any genes. Reciprocal altruism seeks to provide this explanation: People offer assistance to nonkin because they know that at some future time their acts of altruism will be reciprocated by those they help. Such reciprocation promotes fitness and, thereby, enables individuals to keep their genes in the pool.

Van den Berghe uses these two concepts—kin selection and reciprocal altruism—to explain ethnicity. He extends the idea of kin selection to a larger subpopulation. Historically, larger kin groups (composed of lineages) constituted a breeding population of close and distant kin who sustained trust and solidarity with one another and mistrusted other breeding populations. Van den Berghe coins the term *ethny* for "ethnic group." An ethny is an extension of these more primordial breeding populations, a cluster of kinship circles created by endogamy (in which mate selection is confined to specific groups) and territoriality (physical proximity of its members and relative isolation from non-members). An ethny represents a reproductive strategy for maximizing fitness beyond the narrower confines of kinship, because by forming an ethny—even a very large one of millions of people—individuals create bonds with those who can help preserve their fitness, whether by actually sharing genes or, more typically, by reciprocal acts of altruism with fellow ethnys. An ethny is, therefore, a manifestation of more basic "urges" to help "those like oneself." Although ethnys become genetically diluted as their numbers increase and become subject to social and cultural definitions, the very tendency to form and sustain ethnys is the result of natural selection, which produced biological tendencies for people who share genetic material to help each other.

Thus, sociobiology provides an evolutionary explanation—a highly controversial one, we might add—for why members of an ethnic group band together and maintain distinctiveness. While this perspective has not gained a wide following among sociologists, sociobiology has taken center stage in the field of biology; as a result, we need to be aware of theories emanating from this quarter.

Human Ecology Theories

Also drawing inspiration from biology are ecological theories stressing the forces of competition, selection, and "speciation" of distinctive ethnic groupings. Robert Park's assimilation theory was couched in a larger ecological framework for analyzing urban areas (Park, 1916; Park and Burgess, 1924). This framework emphasized that living patterns in urban areas are produced by competition for scarce resources—land, housing, and jobs. Human groups exist in a kind of Darwinian struggle for survival, each trying to find a viable social niche. Thus, as populations migrate to urban areas, they accelerate the level of competition for resources with those already present and, Park believed, set in motion the processes of accommodation and assimilation.

More recent ecological theories stress that competition for resources often escalates the level of conflict between ethnic subpopulations, forcing subordinate ethnic groups into segregated housing niches and a narrow range of economic positions. Once members of an ethnic group find such niches, their boundaries and distinctiveness are preserved, thereby making them easier targets of discrimination. Susan Olzak (1986, 1992) is one of several scholars working in the human ecology tradition. Her theory holds that violence between ethnic subpopulations, especially attacks by members of the dominant group on subordinate groupings, occurs when members of subordinate ethnic subpopulations move into the occupational and housing niches of superordinate groups. Acts of violence against these mobile subordinates increase as members of the dominant subpopulation feel threatened. For example, Olzak (1992) has documented Anglo-Saxon Protestant attacks on nineteenth- and twentieth-century European immigrants in two scenarios: (1) when the number of immigrants expanded and (2) when economic recessions occurred. She concludes that under these conditions European immigrants were seen as a threat to the housing and occupational niches occupied by Anglo-Saxon Protestants (Roediger, 1991). These two conditions could provide reasons for the dramatic intensification of white violence against African Americans as they began to leave the rural South in the early decades of this century and to emigrate to northern cities as a low-wage labor force in tight labor markets, although it should be emphasized that African Americans and white Americans had come into conflict as early as the 1830s (Roediger, 1991). As greater numbers of African-origin people migrated north, European immigrants who had recently secured a foothold in American society felt threatened and, as a result, attacked blacks and developed intense prejudices, some of which persist to this day.

These ecological theories emphasize the relative size of ethnic subpopulations, their patterns of migration, their movement into various social niches, and their competition with other ethnic groups in markets for housing and jobs. Out of such competition come conflicts, often violent, that maintain prejudices and boundaries between antagonistic ethnic subpopulations. Thus, competition does not always lead to easy assimilation, as Park (1950) hoped, but to partitions and pluralism, punctuated by tension and conflict.

Power and Stratification Theories

Stratification theories emphasize how the process of discrimination produces overrepresentation of members of ethnic subpopulations in various social classes. All of these theories place considerable emphasis on the mobilization of power in order to control where ethnic groups are placed in the class system. Yet, each stresses a somewhat different aspect of how power is used to create systems of ethnic stratification.

Caste Theories   In the early 1940s, W. Lloyd Warner and colleagues described black–white relations as constituting a *caste system* in which African Americans were confined to lower socioeconomic positions, denied access to power, prevented from intermarriage, and segregated in their own living space (Warner, 1941; Warner and Srole, 1945). African Americans thus constituted a distinctive caste that white Americans maintained for their own privileges.

Oliver C. Cox (1948) added a Marxist twist to this argument, emphasizing that the capitalist class of owners and managers of industry has been crucial to the castelike subordination of African Americans. The importation of slaves was a business enterprise in which European capitalists bought and sold cheap labor—slaves—to capitalistic plantations in the South. Once capitalists set this pattern of using Africans as a source of cheap labor and higher profits, it needed to be legitimated by highly prejudiced beliefs and stereotypes based on the biological characteristics of the "black race." Thus, exploitive practices are tied to the actions and interests of economic elites who mobilize power and ideologies in order to have a ready, desperate, and low-cost labor pool available for exploitation. From these early caste theories, the emphasis on power and stratification has taken a number of directions. Let us examine some representative theories.

Colonialism Theories   Colonialism theories draw inspiration from the analysis of the dynamics of European colonialism in the past. *External colonialism* is the process by which one nation controls the political and economic activities of another, less developed and less powerful society. Robert Blauner (1969:396) has identified four components of what he terms the *colonization complex:* (1) forced entry into a territory and its population, (2) alteration or destruction of the indigenous culture and patterns of social organization, (3) domination of the indigenous population by representatives of the invading society, and (4) justification of such activities with highly prejudicial, racist beliefs and stereotypes.

      This basic theory has also been used to study *internal colonialism* (Blauner, 1969, 1972), in which the dynamics of the colonization complex are seen to operate *within* a society. From the internal colonization perspective, much of the history of ethnic relations in America has involved the establishment of successive internal colonies of people who are not white and who are dominated by descendants of the original Anglo-Saxon Protestant colonists. For example, African Americans constitute a colony within white America because institutionalized discrimination maintains white control over the economic, educational, and political opportunities of many African Americans. This situation, it is argued, is little different from that in South Africa, where until recently a white minority, made up of the descendants of British, Dutch, and German colonists, exerted institutional control over the black population.

      The motivations behind internal colonialism in the United States were twofold: (1) the need for cheap labor to increase profits and (2) the desire to take and control land, first from the Native Americans and later from the Mexicans. As Robert Blauner (1969) notes, the desire for inexpensive labor led to the creation of slavery; the desire to control the agricultural base and land of Mexicans in the Southwest was the reason white Americans pushed Mexicans into a low-wage labor pool. Similarly, the attempted genocide of Native Americans was a way for Europeans to take their land, forcing those who survived to live on reservations—a very visible type of internal colony.

      In order to create internal colonies, government must actively participate. It must provide the coercive force needed to control those who are "colonized," while legitimating patterns of domination with laws. Thus, by virtue of their control of the state, the descendants of early European white immigrants have been able to create and sustain internal colonies for long periods of time.

Split-Labor Market Theories   Split-labor market theories are much like ecological theories in their emphasis on competition between ethnic groups for resources, but they bring the mobilization and use of power to the forefront. Indeed, split-labor market theories make up for what is often considered a deficiency in ecological theories: the lack of sufficient attention to power and how the dominant class in society uses power to foster ethnic antagonism for its own benefit. *Split-labor market theories* emphasize that markets for labor become partitioned, with members of certain ethnic groups confined to some jobs in the labor market and not allowed to work in other, typically higher-paying jobs. The pressure to split the labor market comes from those in the more powerful ethnic populations who fear that they might lose their advantage if the labor market were to be opened up to other groups who would be willing to work for less and who would increase the supply of labor relative to the market's demand, thereby driving wages down as more workers competed for jobs.

Edna Bonacich (1972) has developed the most important split-labor market theory. This theory has been applied to black–white relations in America (Bonacich, 1976) and to ethnic populations in other societies. The basic argument is that capitalists, or those who own and manage large businesses, have an interest in high profits. One way to raise or maintain profits is to keep labor costs low; so capitalists try to import cheap labor in order to undercut higher-wage labor. Thus, for example, low-wage African American workers were imported from the South by northern industrialists as "strike breakers" in the 1920s and 1930s in order to undermine the efforts of white workers to unionize and to develop a power base for securing higher wages and better working conditions (Bonacich, 1976). And just as ecological theory would have predicted, acts of violence against African Americans increased dramatically in the 1920s.

Threatened workers sometimes react not only violently to efforts at undermining their wages but also politically and economically. At times they enlist government to exclude an ethnic group, but this is almost always impossible when powerful capitalists have an interest in supporting and sponsoring an influx of low-wage workers. A fallback strategy is for threatened workers to create formal and informal ways of "splitting the labor market" such that a subordinate minority is excluded from the more privileged positions in this market. As a result, members of the subordinate ethnic group often find themselves forced to compete with each other for a narrow range of less privileged and less secure positions. For example, as we will see in later chapters, for more than a century after the Civil War African Americans were excluded from most skilled craft unions and included in only some positions in industrial unions, creating a split in the labor market between its white and black sectors.

Thus, competition involves more than two antagonistic ethnic groups; it also involves third parties who wield power and who wish to maximize profits by stimulating competition between ethnic groups in labor markets. Such actions fuel both competition and threat, leading to discrimination ranging from acts of violence to institutionalization of a split-labor market.

Split-Class Theories   Class theories emphasize economic exploitation of the lower classes by those in the higher classes. Added to this dynamic, however, is the recognition that each class includes segments or sectors that are isolated and hence subject to discriminatory practices. Theories of this sort, such as one developed by Mario Barrera (1979), generally begin with a Marxian view of the class system composed of (1) capitalists who control the investment of capital and who thereby regulate production and the purchase of labor; (2) managers who do the administrative work for capitalists and who, thereby, have control of workers; (3) petit bourgeoisie who own small businesses and buy labor; and (4) members of the working class who constitute the majority of workers and who sell their labor for salaries and wages. Aside from the conflicts of interest among these classes, Barrera argues, there are splits *within* each class along ethnic lines. Members of some ethnic subpopulations are subordinate within a class and are often relegated to the less desirable, lower-paying, and less secure jobs within this class. Moreover, these members can become a reserve labor force within a class, especially the large working class, in which they constitute a pool of excess labor that can be hired when needed for low wages and thrown back into the pool when not needed.

For example, within the working classes, subordinate ethnic minorities were until recently almost always excluded from the most desirable jobs— unionized craft positions (carpenters, plumbers, electricians, sheet metal workers, welders, machine workers, and the like)—and dramatically overrepresented in low-skill, low-pay, and low-job-security positions (day laborers, seasonal workers, and domestics). This is still the case, though somewhat less so, for African, Latino, and Native Americans. In Europe, Jews were historically confined to a few positions (trade, finance); even today in the United States, Jews are overrepresented in certain middle-class occupations and businesses (retail sales in certain spheres such as clothing, as well as accounting, finance, college teaching, and medicine), but they tend to be underrepresented in other spheres. Many Asian groups—Koreans, Vietnamese, and Chinese, for example—are confined to small retail and service businesses and underrepresented in other middle-class occupations and professions. Thus, there are splits in social classes, just as there are in labor markets. Indeed, splits in labor markets may extend beyond lower-paying jobs and operate in other, more affluent and privileged spheres.

Middleman Minority Theories   One process that creates splits in the middle class is described by *middleman minority theories*. Not all ethnic groups occupy lower castes and classes, nor are all confined to internal colonies. In fact, some are overrepresented in the petit bourgeoisie, or small businesses that often rely on family labor and ethnic networks (for credit, customers, and other needed aspects of doing business). They are *middlemen* along several potential dimensions: (1) They have middle, or moderate, levels of resources; (2) they serve as distribution links between producers of goods and those who buy them; and (3) in Marxist terms (Bonacich, 1973), they are the "go-betweens" (as small retail store owners) between members of elite classes and subordinate classes.

The various explanations for the formation of middleman minorities are basically the same (Blalock, 1967; Bonacich, 1973; Turner and Bonacich, 1980): Certain minorities bring to a host society entrepreneurial skills and perhaps some capital. Ironically, these very attributes pose a threat to dominant groups, and so these minorities are excluded from many middle-class positions and allowed to operate only those businesses that serve their own ethnic group, other oppressed ethnics, and, occasionally, more elite ethnic groups. Once these "middlemen" become lodged in these middle niches, movement to economic niches controlled by dominant groups is threatening and, hence, likely to engender discrimination, which keeps its ethnic victims confined. The clients of middleman minorities, especially those in the lower social classes, also tend to exhibit hostility toward the petit bourgeoisie, who are viewed as mercenary and exploitive. For example, tensions have emerged between African American residents and Korean business owners in ghetto areas. As demonstrated by the attacks on these businesses during the rioting in Los Angeles in the early 1990s, this hostility can translate into violence. At other times, boycotts against a middleman minority—as in the case of certain Korean stores in New York—are initiated as a way to vent hostility against perceptions of maltreatment. Such hostilities from potential competitors and clients force the members of a middleman minority to withdraw into an ethnic enclave and to be perceived as "clannish," thereby perpetuating hostility toward them.

We have now presented in very general terms the range of theories on ethnic relations. There are many variations of the theories discussed above, but the basic types of theoretical approaches have been summarized. As is evident, each theory stresses some processes, while ignoring others. Some appear to apply to a single ethnic group in America, whereas others seem more general and generic. How, then, can this theoretical diversity be pulled together in an analysis of ethnicity in America? Our answer to this question is to create an even more general theory that can incorporate the strong points of existing theories, while simplifying the explanation of ethnic relations. Good theory should not be complicated; rather, it should be simple and parsimonious.

A UNIFIED THEORY OF ETHNIC RELATIONS

Let us begin by emphasizing the central force in ethnic relations: *discrimination* against a subordinate subpopulation. The greater the level of discrimination and the more it is institutionalized across many social arenas, the more likely is a subpopulation to develop and retain a distinctive ethnic identity. Thus, if forms of discrimination, such as violence, exclusion, selective inclusion, abusive practices, and segregation, are practiced against a subpopulation, its members will become a clearly identifiable ethnic group. Conversely, the less the discrimination practiced against an identifiable subpopulation, the less distinctive will be its ethnicity and the more likely it is that it will assimilate.

Of course, at times elements of ethnicity are retained without the threat of discrimination. Many white ethnic groups—Irish Catholics, Poles, Italians, and others in America—have tried to maintain elements of their ethnicity, such as holidays, festivals, religion, and community organizations. These ethnic elements are not immediately apparent, however; they do not define and distinguish these subpopulations in a highly visible way. Moreover, all these ethnic groups were at one time victims of discrimination; and so the effort to retain ethnicity is a holdover effect of past discrimination, in which members of the subpopulation selectively retain certain symbols and rituals of the past. Other ethnic groups, such as the Basques in America, have retained a considerable number of their ethnic traditions without ever having experienced high levels of overt discrimination. This maintenance of ethnicity has been accomplished by retaining Basque communities, patterns of intragroup marriage, important rituals and festivals, and language. Even here, though, assimilation is slowly occurring because there is relatively little outside discrimination to force Basques to retreat into their ethnic traditions. Thus, ethnicity can be retained, to an extent and for a while, without discrimination; ultimately, however, the intensity of discrimination determines whether a subpopulation remains distinctively ethnic in culture, behavior, and organization or becomes assimilated into the societal mainstream.

Another force involved in creating and maintaining ethnicity is the degree of *identifiability* of members of a subpopulation. To be targets of discrimination, members of a subpopulation need to be visible and readily identified. And so, the more distinctive members of a subpopulation are, the more likely they are to become targets of discrimination.

There are several bases for distinctiveness. One is biological, and so the more members of a subpopulation can be singled out in terms of biological features, such as skin color and eye shape, the more readily they can become targets of discrimination. It should come as no surprise, then, that the two ethnic groups most discriminated against in American society have been African Americans and Native Americans; after all, they can be identified biologically. Asians and Latinos have had a similar experience. Identifiability is also cultural—language, religious beliefs, normative practices, and other symbol systems. For example, if an American subpopulation uses a language other than English, has distinctive religious practices that deviate from Judeo-Christian traditions, and reveals norms that sanction behaviors and demeanors that are at odds with the American mainstream, that subpopulation becomes distinctive and identifiable. As a consequence, they are likely targets of discrimination. Behavioral and organizational characteristics also create identifiability. When members of an ethnic population have a noticeable interpersonal demeanor (such as speech styles, body language, or dress) and when they have unusual organizational structures (such as deviant kinship patterns, church practices, and business arrangements), they can become targets of discrimination.

Discrimination and identifiability are mutually reinforcing. If people can be identified and singled out for discrimination, then such acts of discrimination and their institutionalization force their victims to "remain with their own kind," among whom they interact, intermarry, and maintain their distinctive cultural, organizational, and behavioral patterns. Sometimes this maintenance of ethnic patterns is a defensive reaction, and other times it is merely the only option for segregated and excluded peoples. Most typically, however, it is a mixture of the two. Once a subpopulation is forced to maintain its identity as a result of discrimination, ironically it becomes an easier target for further discrimination. This is particularly likely to be the case if rates of marriage within the ethnic group maintain biological distinctiveness, but other bases of distinctiveness—cultural, behavioral, and organizational—are also important. As biological, cultural, behavioral, and organizational features of a subpopulation become intertwined and intercorrelated, then the members of a subpopulation become ever more visible targets of discrimination. This cycle of identifiability, discrimination, maintenance of identifiability, and further discrimination is often difficult to break—as has certainly been the case for African Americans, Native Americans, most Latinos, and some Asians (Aguirre and Baker, 1993). In contrast, for ethnic groups who are not biologically distinguishable because of skin color or facial features, it has been easier to break the cycle and to filter into the mainstream, as has been the case for members of most white European ethnic groups.

Identifiability and discrimination affect the levels and types of valued resources available to an ethnic subpopulation, such as income, power, and prestige. Resources such as human capital (skills and education) and financial capital (savings) that ethnics bring with them when they come to America are also important. But ultimately discrimination determines which resources members of a population can have and how those resources can be used. Discrimination shapes how and where immigrants who bring human and financial resources with them may use their imported resources, and as a consequence, it will affect the kinds and levels of resources they can accumulate. Discrimination keeps existing ethnic groups in the lower socioeconomic stratum and those immigrants who do not bring human or financial capital with them from acquiring resources. Whether channeling the further acquisition of resources among those with some capital or denying resources to those without capital, discrimination works to maintain identifiability indirectly because the levels and types of resources that members of a population possess influence their behavioral, cultural, and organizational characteristics. When a population has little money, low levels of education (and hence prestige in a credentialed society like the United States), and few channels of acquiring power, it develops distinctive characteristics which, in turn, make its members easier targets for further discrimination. For example, African Americans, Native Americans, and most Latinos have become even more visible as targets of discrimination because of their low *shares of valued resources.* Or when a population uses its financial resources to make more money but is excluded from positions of power and prestige, it also becomes distinctive, often arousing hostility over its wealth. As a result, it also can become a target of discrimination. For instance, most Asian middleman minorities have experienced this phenomenon, as have Jews over centuries of persecution in Europe and discrimination in the United States.

Figure 2.1 is a diagram of the relationships among *discrimination, identifiability,* and *resource levels.* If a population can be easily identified, it is likely to be a target of discrimination; if there is discrimination, this population develops a typical share of resources, which in turn increases its identifiability. We have added to this cycle another feature: *degree of ethnic stratification.* If a pattern of resource shares becomes discernible, then it usually creates distinctive pockets of ethnicity within the strata of society. For example, if African Americans are consistently overrepresented in the lower social strata, this situation increases their identifiability as somehow "not measuring up" to societal standards, and, as a result, it provides a further basis for discrimination which, in turn, perpetuates their meager shares of resources and their location in the stratification system.

As discrimination denies people access to resources, it limits their capacity to fight back or to move away from their situation. If a subpopulation does not have access to channels of power, how can it fight discrimination? If it does not

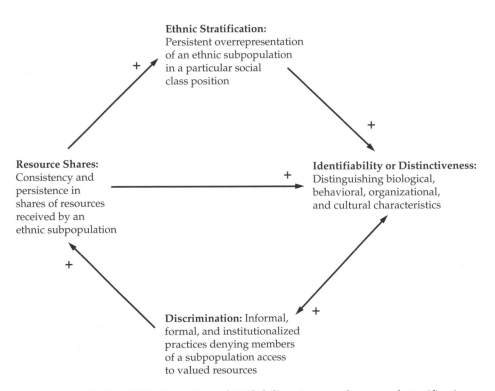

FIGURE 2.1 Cycles of discrimination, identifiability, resource shares, and stratification.
+ = increases or has a positive effect on.

have access to a good education, which leads to job opportunities and prestige, how does it become upwardly mobile? If it does not have money, how does it improve? Thus, resource shares also determine how people respond to discrimination; if their options are limited, they are more likely to accept their plight and, as a consequence, remain identifiable targets of further discrimination.

Figure 2.1 illustrates the reinforcing dynamics in the cycle of discrimination, identifiability, resource shares, and stratification—as denoted by the positive signs on the arrows. Each one increases the values of the other in the direction specified by the arrows. If these were the only processes involved in the cycles, they would be difficult to break. But other forces are involved, some of which work to intensify these cycles, a few to mitigate their effects.

Why do people discriminate? Is identifiability the only reason? Ethnic identifiability alone is not enough to generate the high levels of discrimination that perpetuate the cycles portrayed in Figure 2.1. At least one additional force is needed: *a sense of threat*. If a subordinate ethnic group is perceived as threatening the political power, the economic well-being, the cultural symbols (language, customs, values, and beliefs), the social structures (community organization, social clubs, rituals, and holidays), and/or the basic institutions (economy, politics, family, church, school, and medicine) of a dominant ethnic group, this perception will translate into hostility, fueling the fires of discrimination. For example, slavery may have persisted long after it was economically viable because there was great fear about the social, economic, and political consequences of a large mass of freed slaves. This fear mobilized considerable hostility toward black people in the decades before and after the Civil War, resulting in violent acts (hangings, shootings) and efforts to reinstitutionalize in law and practice the oppression of African Americans (Turner and Singleton, 1978; Singleton and Turner, 1975; Turner, Singleton, and Musick, 1984). A more recent example is how the large influx of Latinos, especially Mexicans, into the United States has aroused fears about its effects on the economy, the existing balance of power, and schools. This fear has resulted in hostility and discriminatory practices. Recent Asian immigrants—Koreans and Vietnamese, for instance—are sometimes seen as a threat to small-business owners because many of them possess both human and financial capital and are willing to work long hours with pooled family labor. They are, in essence, more successful than some white ethnic groups in many entrepreneurial niches, thereby arousing hostility. Moreover, their success in these niches limits opportunities for other ethnic groups—African Americans and Latinos, for example—who may wish to start small businesses as a way to rise from their particular place in the system of ethnic stratification. The result is hostility and discrimination against these middleman minorities. Thus, the greater the sense of threat experienced by superordinate ethnic groups (and, at times, subordinate ones as well) over the influx or existence of another ethnic subpopulation, the greater is their hostility toward this subordinate population and the more likely they are to engage in discriminatory acts and to institutionalize these acts.

Which forces create a sense of threat? Is distinctiveness enough? Our sense is that two additional features of an ethnic subpopulation operate to generate hostility. One is the *size* of an ethnic population. A large number of immigrants or a large subordinate ethnic group poses a threat because they might (1) work for less money than the dominant ethnic groups (out of desperation for job opportunities), (2) upset the balance of political power if they become enfranchised, and (3) change existing cultural and organizational patterns if they influence the mainstream. Thus, African Americans and Latinos pose a threat to the dominant Anglo-Saxon population because of their large numbers; and as a result, they are discriminated against in order to preserve what white ethnic groups see as "the American way of life." When an ethnic group is large, intense discrimination, fueled by a sense of threat, will usually force them to the bottom of the stratification system because there are too many people to be channeled into a narrow range of middleman minority niches and because they cannot be allowed to "dilute" the dominant culture and its institutions. Of course, when ethnic groups are denied access to resources and pushed into a lower socioeconomic group, they maintain their ethnicity, which increases the identifiability that poses a threat—often more imagined than real. But more is involved: Large numbers of oppressed ethnic subpopulations sometimes become hostile, which causes the dominant ethnic groups to experience an escalated sense of threat. Intense discrimination against a large ethnic population only exacerbates the level of threat that prompted the discrimination; hence the cycle of threat, discrimination, hostile reaction to discrimination, escalated threat, and renewed discrimination is perpetuated.

Another force that creates a sense of threat is the *entrepreneurial resources*—occupational skills, education, money, and organizational abilities—that an ethnic population possesses. Usually, however, ethnic groups with entrepreneurial resources are small; hence, through discrimination, it is possible to channel them into a narrow range of middleman minority niches or a limited number of professions. The ability of these ethnic groups to outperform segments of the dominant population in economic enterprises is threatening and arouses hostility, which results in efforts to confine them to niches and positions that reduce head-to-head competition with the members of the dominant population and, perhaps, places them in competition with other subordinate minorities. Under these conditions, the resentment of the victims of discrimination is reduced because they can enjoy economic success in at least some activities, thus weakening the cycle. Because many Asian immigrants in America possess entrepreneurial resources, they have been shunted into middleman minority niches or selected professions. Yet, over time, it is difficult to maintain this kind of confinement because these ethnic groups, and their successive generations of offspring, possess skills, capital, and education that make them valuable in the mainstream; and if they can acquire at least the veneer of the cultural mainstream, they can often penetrate mainstream institutions. Because their numbers are relatively small, coupled with increased rates of intermarriage with members of the dominant ethnic subpopulation, their penetration is less threatening and arouses less hostility than would be the case with larger ethnic populations.

Thus, the level of threat posed by superordinate ethnic groups is increased not only by their distinctiveness but also by their size and entrepreneurial resources. Large numbers of ethnic groups threaten to "overrun" the mainstream, and the possession of entrepreneurial resources among ethnic groups threatens entrenched small businesses and professions.

How is this sense of threat and hostility sustained over time? The answer resides in another central aspect of ethnic relations: *negative beliefs and stereotypes.* Here is where prejudice becomes a significant force in ethnic relations. When dominant ethnic groups feel threatened, they develop prejudices and portray those who threaten them in a negative light. If the sense of threat is severe, these negative portrayals are codified into a series of beliefs and stereotypes about the perceived undesirable characteristics and qualities of a subordinate ethnic population. Ironically, such portrayals tend to heighten the potential "menace" of the ethnic group, thereby escalating the sense of threat, which, in turn, leads to more negative portrayals. For example, the initial justification for not freeing slaves in America was that they were "childlike" and hence incapable of "managing for themselves" (Turner and Singleton, 1978). But as the abolitionist movement gained momentum, and as the sense of threat experienced by some white Americans increased correspondingly, these portrayals became ever more vicious, shifting to a view of black males as sexually aggressive and as lusting after white women whom they were prepared to rape if ever set free. Such portrayals escalated the sense of threat in the minds of white southerners, resulting in ever more aggressive discrimination against African Americans. According to Jordan (1968:151) the perception that "Negro men lusted after white women" intensified white prejudice.

Codified beliefs and stereotypes not only escalate the sense of threat, which then ratchets up the level of discrimination, but also legitimate discrimination: If an ethnic group is seen to have "undesirable" qualities, it is only appropriate that its members be segregated and excluded from the mainstream. And as discrimination sets in motion the cycles outlined in Figure 2.1, it appears to justify itself because the victims of discrimination tend to maintain those biological, behavioral, cultural, and organizational features that are portrayed in a negative light by stereotypes. As a consequence, the failure of ethnic groups to "change" (ignoring the obvious fact that discrimination prevents change) escalates the sense of threat and organizes the negative beliefs and stereotypes into a codified dogma. For example, Jews in Europe were denied access to many positions and forced into a narrow range of retail, finance, and professional niches; as they operated successfully in these niches and did not change their ethnic characteristics, the stereotypes about them—clannish, anti-Christian, financially ruthless, and so on—became ever more codified, thereby justifying more hostility, discrimination, and prejudice.

Figure 2.2 summarizes dynamics escalating discrimination. People discriminate when they feel threatened by the presence of an ethnic group. This sense of threat increases when the threatening ethnic group is large and/or when it has entrepreneurial or educational resources. When threatened, those who would discriminate justify their actions by formulating negative beliefs

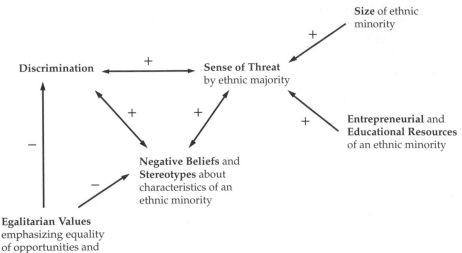

FIGURE 2.2 Forces increasing and decreasing ethnic discrimination.
+ = increases or has a positive effect on.
− = decreases or has a negative effect on.

and stereotypes about the undesirable qualities of their victims. Ironically, as they formulate these stereotypes, the negative portrayal makes discriminators perceive their victims as more threatening, thus making them even more disposed to discriminate. Moreover, discriminating against an ethnic group makes it more threatening, because discriminators implicitly know that their victims will be hostile. This hostility, whether or not fully acknowledged by discriminators, will always make an ethnic group more menacing, thereby justifying abusive practices and other types of discrimination to "keep them in line" which, of course, arouses more resentments that make the ethnic minority even more threatening. As the positive arrows in Figure 2.2 underscore, these processes are self-reinforcing and, indeed, can become self-escalating. Threat escalates discrimination, and discrimination increases the sense of threat. As negative stereotypes are developed to justify discrimination, these negative portrayals make people more threatening and, thereby, justify negative beliefs and further discrimination.

We are now in a position to put the cycles portrayed in Figures 2.1 and 2.2 together so that we can see how discrimination, as fueled by threat and negative stereotypes, leads to ethnic stratification. In Figure 2.3, we have blended the first two figures. Threat increases with growing size and entrepreneurial/educational resources of an ethnic minority, setting into motion the formation of negative beliefs that, along with the fear that threat generates, pushes people to discriminate against an ethnic minority. As discrimination occurs, mem-

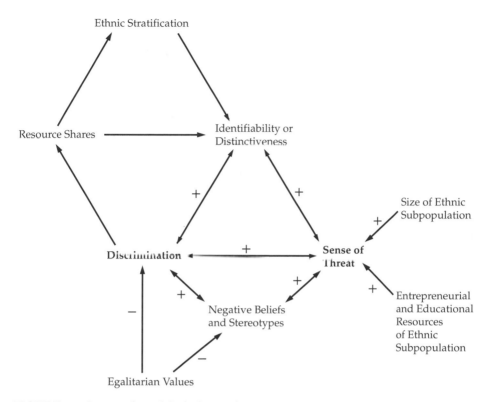

FIGURE 2.3 A general model of ethnic relations.
+ = increases or has a positive effect on.
− = decreases or has a negative effect on.

bers of ethnic groups are denied resources and are generally segregated, forcing them to live and marry with "their own kind." As a result of their shares of resources that confine them to a given stratum in the stratification system as well as their high rates of interaction and intermarriage, both biological and cultural patterns are sustained, thereby making an ethnic group more identifiable and, hence, an easier target of discrimination.

As can be seen with all of the positively signed arrows, these dynamics, once unleashed, are self-reinforcing. Each one sets the other into motion; and it is for this reason that it is often difficult to break these vicious cycles revolving around discrimination. In American society, however, there has been one force working against discrimination and negative stereotyping: powerful egalitarian values. The arrow coming up from the bottom of Figures 2.2 and 2.3 emphasizes this important force that can act to reduce discrimination and stereotyping. Americans believe that people should be treated equally and be given equal opportunities, and these core values have always stood in opposition to ethnic

Box 2.1
What Do Americans Mean by Egalitarian?

Affirmative action policies have, over the last two decades, generated so much controversy that it is reasonable to ask: Why the controversy? The answer ultimately resides in two approaches for realizing egalitarian values. The first, clearly stated in the Declaration of Independence, stresses equality for individuals rather than social categories; and as this value has become translated into social policies, the goal has been to equalize *opportunities for individuals.* The second approach, initiated under Richard Nixon's presidency in the 1970s, emphasizes equality for groups; and as this policy has been implemented under more recent affirmative action programs, the focus has been on *equality of results.*

As Seymour Martin Lipset (1991:209) has argued, these policies represent a clash of two basic American values: egalitarianism versus individualism. *Individualism* stresses that people get ahead through their own efforts and hard work; and when combined with *egalitarianism,* the result is a commitment to providing compensatory help to those individuals whose circumstances keep them from realizing their full potential for hard work and success. But, when equality is stressed over individualism, the commitment is to assuring that certain categories of people—minorities and women, for example—achieve proportionate representation and results when compared to those who have been more advantaged. In this latter commitment, emphasis is on giving preferences to certain categories of individuals in order to compensate for past discrimination.

Public opinion polls in the United States have been consistent and overwhelming in their endorsement of individualistic egalitarianism. The American public is opposed to group-preference approaches; and even among minorities, who could be helped by these approaches, a clear majority is opposed to them as well. Yet, Americans are strongly in support of programs that will help individuals, *as individuals* rather than as a social category, overcome the disadvantages that come with present and past discrimination. It should not be surprising, then, that affirmative action—when seen as group preferences—should be so hotly debated, and that Americans have come to disagree with virtually all policies

discrimination. Obviously, Americans have often been willing to live with this contradiction between their values and their acts of discrimination, but the existence of these values has served historically as a rallying point for civil rights movements designed to eliminate discrimination.

The model in Figure 2.3 will guide our organization of each chapter on an ethnic group. We will begin by asking about the resource shares of an ethnic group. Are they overrepresented in poverty? What kinds of jobs do they have? How much education do they receive? How long do they live? Answers to these questions tell us about the respective shares of resources of an ethnic population and are a good indicator of present or past discrimination. Present resource shares tell us about the past. Has a subpopulation been denied access based upon a group-preference interpretation of egalitarianism. Whether this feeling on the part of the American public is good, bad, right, or wrong in some ultimate moral sense is less relevant than the fact that Americans view group preferences as unfair. In contrast, they do not feel that compensatory efforts— special programs in education and job training, for example—are unfair; indeed, Americans see these kinds of efforts as necessary to overcome present, as well as the legacy of the past, discrimination.

Another basic American value is *humanitarianism*—that is, those who have suffered through no fault of their own should be helped. In the minds of most Americans this value is mixed with individualism and egalitarianism to produce a clear desire for programs to help individuals realize more opportunities, regardless of their social category. Those who are poor and who have been victims of discrimination need compensatory help *as individuals* to realize their potential. This is as far as Americans appear to be willing to go in their humanitarianism; relatively small percentages of Americans believe that categories of individuals should be given preferential treatment. Indeed, programs that are perceived to give preferential treatment to social categories—whether this perception is accurate or not is another matter—are seen as undesirable. Hence, efforts on the part of policy makers to overcome the effects of present and past discrimination will need to be careful in constructing these programs; if they are not, programs will encounter negative evaluation by the conditional humanitarianism of most Americans: Equality of opportunity is okay; equality of outcome through group preferences is not okay.

Yet, it can be asked: Without group preferences, can the cumulative effects of discrimination over hundreds of years really be overcome? Can any compensatory educational program, for example, overcome the effects of being raised in a graffiti- and bullet-marked public housing project infested by gangs and drug dealers? Or, can women ever overcome discrimination by anything but group preferences in assuring their access to job categories dominated by men? In reality, the answer to these questions is probably no, but Americans think otherwise, or think group preferences won't work either; and, it is reasonable to assume, programs to realize egalitarian values in the face of past and present discrimination will always be limited by what the public perceives as fair and unfair.

to valued resources and forced to live at the bottom or in a narrow range of middle slots in the stratification system of American society?

Next, we can review the history of *discrimination* against this ethnic group, paying particular attention to its institutionalization in the economic, governmental, and educational structures. We should also understand how and why an ethnic group remains *distinctive* or *identifiable* and, as such, an easy target for discrimination. We must then delve into questions about the *sense of threat* engendered by an identifiable ethnic population and how this sense of threat is related to its size and entrepreneurial resources. Then, we can turn to the *negative beliefs* and *stereotypes* to see how they have legitimized discrimination, while escalating the sense of threat. Finally, we need to examine the impact of *egalitarian values* imposing challenges to prejudicial beliefs and stereotypes about an ethnic group and to patterns of institutionalized discrimination that have denied this group access to resources. In this context, we can assess political and social movements that have arisen in recent years or that are likely to emerge in the future.

How can these self-reinforcing processes be broken? Rebellion and revolt, political mobilization, formation of a social movement, and other acts may force dominant ethnic groups to make concessions. Also, as noted earlier, the existence of egalitarian values, as portrayed in the lower portion of Figures 2.2 and 2.3, may stimulate change. The negative arrows pointing to prejudicial and negative beliefs as well as to discrimination indicate that such values stand in contradiction to prejudice and discrimination. Of course, in societies without such values, the cycles portrayed in Figure 2.3 are allowed to operate, up to the point of revolt and conflict. But in the United States, where values of equality and freedom are pervasive, they legitimate opposition movements to discriminatory practices—for example, the abolitionist movement that denounced slavery and the civil rights movement that culminated in a series of federal laws in the 1960s formally outlawing discrimination. Without the existence of such egalitarian values in the dominant culture, oppressed ethnic groups must accept discrimination, migrate to a more favorable environment, or incur the risks of rebellion. Historically, acceptance and migration have been the most common responses of subordinate ethnic groups; protest by a subordinate minority is usually crushed, unless the population is large and the dominant groups weak, or unless the ethnic group has allies within or outside the society. Only recently in world history have egalitarian values become a powerful force; patterns of discrimination and ethnic stratification have been a prominent feature of human societies for millennia. Since egalitarian values are hardly universal in the world today, ethnic stratification and tensions will remain part of human society in the future. This is assuredly the case when one considers that the United States, which subscribes to powerful egalitarian values, has yet to break the cycles portrayed in Figure 2.3.

The definitions in Chapter 1, coupled with the theoretical explanation offered in this chapter, provide us with a means for examining ethnic relations in America. More specifically, the model depicted in Figure 2.3 can be viewed as a springboard for discussion about each ethnic subpopulation to be examined in the chapters to follow.

When noticeable differences of an ethnic subpopulation are perceived to pose a threat, they lead to discrimination. Large ethnic populations or smaller ones with entrepreneurial skills are most likely to generate a sense of threat among dominant ethnics. This sense of threat leads people to construct negative beliefs and stereotypes about ethnics; and these beliefs are used to legitimate discrimination.

Discrimination, itself, also encourages beliefs that can make such discrimination seem legitimate; and once codified, these beliefs encourage further discrimination. The effects of additional discrimination are to limit resource shares of ethnic groups, maintain their identity and vulnerability to discrimination, and to force them into habitual locations in the stratification system; as these effects occur, a renewed cycle of threat, prejudice, and discrimination is unleashed against ethnic groups who "refuse to change" (again, ignoring the obvious reasons for why change is difficult).

The forces delineated in the theoretical model portrayed in Figure 2.3 will become the chapter headings and sections in subsequent discussions. They will provide a framework for systematically reviewing the past, present, and future of the most prominent ethnic subpopulations in America. And they will do more. Because these headings are derived from a theoretical model, they contribute to an explanation of *why* an ethnic subpopulation and members of the dominant Anglo-Saxon Protestant culture have formed a particular pattern of tension-provoking relations. By examining how the forces portrayed in Figure 2.3 have operated and interacted for a particular ethnic population, we will be able to explain what has occurred in the past, what is going on today, and what will be likely to happen in the future.

SUMMARY

Theories attempt to explain why a phenomenon exists and how it operates. Theories explaining ethnicity are diverse, each capturing an important dynamic but none incorporating all the key forces in ethnic relations. Assimilation theories emphasize the process by which members of an ethnic population become part of the mainstream of a society, but they do not adequately account for the persistence of ethnic differences and the conflicts these differences generate. Theories of ethnic pluralism arose in reaction to the "melting pot" basis of assimilation theories, arguing that the maintenance of ethnicity is often a way of coping with discrimination. More recent biological theories propose the possibility of humans' genetic tendencies to identify with and support members of their distinctive ethnic heritage. These biological theories are as controversial as earlier and often ethnocentric, if not racist, theories. Ecological theories emphasize that competition for scarce resources is a key force in creating and sustaining ethnic relations and that patterns of domination and subjugation among ethnic groups reflect this competition over valued resources such as jobs, incomes, and housing.

All stratification theories argue that ethnic groups are overrepresented in particular social strata because of the unequal distribution of power. Caste theories stress that many minority groups have been historically pushed to the bottom of the class system with rigid barriers preventing mobility out of this position. Colonialism theories emphasize that minority populations often become exploited "colonies" within a society—much like their international counterparts, the overseas colonies of one nation that subjugates the members of others and extracts their resources without a proportionate return. Split-labor market theories draw attention to the fact that patterns of discrimination are often created and sustained through the partitioning of labor markets so that dominant subpopulations can continue to enjoy their privilege while denying subordinate ethnic groups access to jobs and income. Split-class theories argue that divisions and partitions *within* social classes exist, with the least powerful typically confined to a lower class in order to maintain the privilege of the dominant sector within a class. Middleman minority theories use elements from split-labor market and split-class theories to explain how small pockets within ethnic subpopulations, mostly in a narrow range of business and entrepreneurial positions, emerge and succeed in the socioeconomic mainstream.

Finally, this chapter has sought to take the main tenets of each theory and synthesize them into a general model of ethnic discrimination in America. This model stresses several interrelated factors: ethnic identifiability, the threat that an ethnic population poses, the prejudicial stereotypes that are articulated, the resources possessed by an ethnic population, the size of an ethnic population, and the position of a subpopulation in the stratification system.

POINTS OF DEBATE

Each of the theories summarized in this chapter suggests points of debate, some of which are enumerated below.

1. Is assimilation the desired outcome of ethnic relations? Today, many argue that America must be a "pluralistic society," but this raises the question: How much pluralism is possible? Historically, no society has endured without a cultural core that absorbs elements of diverse ethnic populations while remaining intact. When "ethnic pluralism" translates into competing cultural cores, history has shown that societal disintegration follows. When "ethnic pluralism" refers to a limited range of traditions such as religious beliefs and rituals, distinctive ceremonies and holidays honoring a cultural heritage and important figures in this heritage, and even maintenance of a secondary language, the disintegrative potential of ethnicity is reduced. Can the cultural core, which is examined in Chapter 3, absorb important components of diverse ethnic populations? Must ethnic groups assimilate, and, if so, to what degree? What are the consequences for society if assimilation does not occur? To what degree are members of the dominant Anglo-Saxon cultural core willing to accommodate change?

2. Stratification theories emphasize that discrimination forces some ethnic groups into either lower-class positions or a narrow range of middleman positions. Inequality is one of the most volatile forces in human organization; when inequality takes on an ethnic dimension, it is doubly volatile. Because the socioeconomic position of many ethnic groups in America is the result of discrimination, it is reasonable to ask: How can the remaining patterns of discrimination be eliminated, or at least reduced? What can be done to compensate descendants of those who have experienced the most discrimination and those who live with the legacy of such discrimination? To the "second American dilemma," discussed in the points of debate section in Chapter 1, we now add a caveat: People who have been subjugated

for a long time become angry and strike back. Americans need to consider how they are to avoid the dangers of ethnic violence as a form of retaliation by those in lower socioeconomic positions.

3. Ethnic stratification is sustained by mutually reinforcing cycles (see Figures 2.1, 2.2, and 2.3); how can these cycles be broken? The identifiability cycle, especially when based upon physical features, can be broken by intermarriage. How willing are the members of both subordinate and dominant ethnic groups to accept this type of assimilation? When members of the dominant culture, as well as other subordinate ethnic groups, feel threatened, discrimination and prejudice emerge. How is this cycle to be broken, especially as competition for resources (as emphasized by ecological theories) intensifies? Are there enough jobs, houses, or educational credentials to go around? Are those who have these resources willing to see others acquire them if it costs them some of their own privilege? How much, if anything, are people willing to give up in the name of ethnic peace and egalitarianism? What are the consequences if privileged Americans are not willing to give up anything?

KEY TERMS

accommodation phase of
  assimilation, 24
assimilation theories, 24
attitude-receptional assimilation, 25
behavioral-receptional assimilation, 25
biological theories, 27
caste system, 29
caste theories, 29
civic assimilation, 25
colonialism theories, 30
colonization complex, 30
competitive phase of assimilation, 24
cultural assimilation, 25
egalitarian values, 44
egalitarianism, 42
ethnogenesis, 26
ethny, 28
external colonialism, 30
human ecology theories, 28

humanitarianism, 43
identifiability, 34
identification assimilation, 25
individualism, 42
internal colonialism, 30
kin selection (inclusive fitness), 27
marital assimilation, 25
middleman minority theories, 32
middlemen, 32
negative beliefs, 39
pluralism theories, 26
reciprocal altruism, 27
split-class theories, 32
split-labor market theories, 31
stereotypes, 39
stratification theories, 29
structural assimilation, 25
theory, 24

CHAPTER 3

The Anglo-Saxon Core and Ethnic Antagonism

Relations between ethnic groups almost always involve elements of domination and subordination: One ethnic subpopulation is able to impose its culture and institutional arrangements on another. In the United States, this process of cultural and institutional domination is complex because of the immigration of so many diverse ethnic groups, but one fact is clear: Anglo-Saxon culture and institutions often dictate and define what other ethnic populations must become (Gordon, 1964; Vargas, 1998). Each ethnic minority in America has been expected to adapt to this Anglo-Saxon core; and each has experienced discrimination by those who have sought to maintain the cultural symbols and institutional structure of this core. Thus, before exploring the lives of the most prominent ethnic minorities in the United States, let us explore the history of those dominant sociocultural traditions that have been imposed upon other ethnics.

EARLY COLONIZATION OF AMERICA

The Anglo-Saxons

The term *Anglo-Saxon* is a bit of a misnomer; it derives from northern Germanic tribes—the Saxons and Angles—that invaded England in the fifth and sixth centuries, displacing other tribes whose lives had already been disrupted by the invasions of the Celts from continental Europe and later the Romans. Other invaders followed, such as the Normans from France; and as a result, a considerable amount of mingling among continental and English cultures ensued. Thus, the English settlers who came to America were themselves a product of a long history of conquest and blending of ethnic subpopulations. And not only were Scots and Welsh (the remnants of the old Celts) part of the early "English" settlements, but in some areas significant numbers of Germans (as many as one-third in Pennsylvania) and Scandinavians were to follow, blending together with these "English Americans" to form the cultural core of America.

The white Anglo-Saxon core, clearly represented in this scene of the signing of the Declaration of Independence, was the dominant group that established the cultural and institutional agenda of the United States.

The term Anglo-Saxon (or one of its variants, *WASP—White Anglo-Saxon Protestant*) denotes a northern European cultural and institutional complex of ethnic traditions fused with, and dominated by, the English who were the first to settle North America in large numbers and to begin the process of colonization. We use the terms Anglo-Saxon and WASP, therefore, to denote an ethnic complex consisting of northern European ethnic stock with light, "white" skin; Protestant religious beliefs; Protestant-inspired values based on individualism, hard work, savings, and secular material success; and English cultural traditions (language, laws, and beliefs) and institutional structures (politics, economics, and education).

The Early Colonists

Although the early colonizers were predominantly English, there were significant numbers of Welsh and Scots. At first, the Welsh maintained their own communities, and even language traditions, but by the late 1600s, they were assimilated into the English core. Scots constituted a much larger population, coming from both the Highlands and Lowlands as well as from Ireland (where many Scots had earlier migrated). Like the Welsh, they were almost fully assimilated into English culture by the end of the seventeenth century. A few

Irish also lived in the early settlement communities, but the flood of Irish immigrants was to come much later.

Germans constituted the largest of the non–British Isle segment of early colonists, with almost all coming from the Protestant north. Later German immigrants were Catholics and Jews, but the early Germans were close to the English in terms of culture and institutional practices. Thus, it was not difficult for these Germans to change in ways compatible with English culture, although some distinctive German traditions remained in isolated communities. Other northern Europeans, such as Scandinavians, were not as prominent as Germans; their peak period of immigration was not to come until the late nineteenth century. Continental Europeans, such as the Dutch and French (who were settling in larger numbers in Canada), also immigrated, but again, they did not come to the early colonies en masse.

Thus, by the close of the eighteenth century in the aftermath of the Revolutionary War and in the early phases of the emergence of the United States as a nation, the American Historical Association (1932) estimates that 60.1 percent of the free, nonslave population was English, 14.0 percent Scotch and Scotch-Irish, 8.6 percent German, 3.6 percent Irish, 3.1 percent Dutch, 3.0 percent French or Swedish, and 7.6 percent other ethnic nationalities. The English dominated numerically for the first two centuries, especially if one includes other ethnic groups from the British Isles. This dominant group established the cultural and institutional agenda of the United States.

THE CULTURAL AND INSTITUTIONAL
LEGACY OF EARLY COLONIZATION

The Core Culture

Language Perhaps the single most important cultural legacy of the early settlers was the English language. Language was to become a litmus test for subsequent immigrants' right to be "American," for the early settlers demanded that English be spoken and that other immigrant populations adopt this language or suffer the consequences. Indeed, there was great agonizing over the "mongrelization" of the white, Anglo-Saxon culture by immigrants who spoke other languages. These concerns exist today, as is clearly evident in the "English-as-the-official-language" campaigns in Congress and some states.

Basic Values Many of the core values of America come from English Protestantism, as Max Weber [1905–1906 (1930)] emphasized in his famous analysis. As Weber stressed, the British brought with them to the Americas *ascetic Protestantism*, as personified in *Puritanism*, which emphasized salvation, hard work, abstinence from temptation, and religiosity. Weber's portrayal of asceticism—discipline, hard work, efficient use of time, rationality, accumulation and profit without moral temptation—can be seen in the core values of America. These values, in turn, have been used as a yardstick to see if ethnic immigrants "measure up." Those ethnic groups who have not been deemed hardworking, efficient, and disciplined have become targets of prejudicial beliefs and discriminatory practices.

Legal Tenets The basic tenets of American law owe much to British traditions, as modified by the colonists' adoption of ideas from eighteenth-century French philosophies. Law is to rule; people are to be equal before the law; laws are to be enacted by representatives of the people; and concentrations of power are to be limited or held in check by law. Despite the blending of French and British philosophical and legal traditions, much of the actual substance of early law in the colonies was English in origin. For example, the specific rights of property holders and obligations established by contracts were considered as important in the actual wording of substantive laws as the broader philosophical and constitutional concerns about equality, freedom, and justice. This disjunction between general constitutional principles, on the one hand, and state and local laws protecting property rights, on the other, enabled patterns of legally sanctioned discrimination to persist until the latter decades of the twentieth century.

The dominant systems of symbols in America—language, values, and laws—derive from the early English settlers. These core cultural components have, of course, been intermingled with those of other cultures and altered with changing circumstances, but more noticeable is the continuity of these symbols and their capacity to define how members of ethnic groups must speak, think, and behave.

The Core Institutional Structures

Economic Institutions The early American settlers came primarily for economic reasons. Colonial settlement was geared to the extraction of raw materials for English commerce and the creation of new markets for English goods. Other reasons for settlement—to escape religious persecution, to reduce the population, to arrest the Spanish and French advance in the hemisphere, and to search for a quicker passage to India—were secondary to the desire of the English Crown and commercial interests to develop America in ways that increased England's prosperity. The chartering of companies and granting of territory were the initial vehicles for transporting commercial capitalism to the colonies. Here, emphasis was placed on private property, contracts, and markets. The drive to take land, develop farms, kill or displace Native Americans, and import slaves was fueled by the effort to create markets that sent raw materials across the Atlantic and brought back finished goods from commercial and emerging industrial interests in England.

The Revolution freed this market-oriented economy from the chartered companies of the English Crown and created what eventually was to be a dynamic form of capitalism that relied upon disadvantaged and inexpensive ethnic labor. The enslavement of Africans was the first manifestation of this use of ethnic populations to extract profits; the mass killing of Native Americans was ultimately for the economic gains that came with their land and resources; the conquest of Mexican Americans in the Southwest marked a similar appropriation of land and subordination of an ethnic group for economic gain; finally, the large-scale importation of white ethnic groups from other parts of continental Europe and of Asians was used to sustain further expansion of industrial development. Thus, the legacy of early British commercial capitalism evolved into a system that depended upon subordinated ethnic labor—a situation that persists to the present day.

Political Institutions   As with legal tenets, the structure of government in the United States reflects the blending of seventeenth-century British political traditions (Hunnington, 1966) and eighteenth-century French social philosophy. The early colonists' concepts of decentered nationhood, representative government, decentralized power, and rule by law were greatly supplemented in the post-Revolutionary era by French thinking on equality, justice, individual rights, representative democracy, and checks and balances among legislative, judicial, and administrative branches of government. The result was a constitutional democracy that expounded high principles about justice, equality, and freedom but which also gave much political autonomy to local communities and the states.

   In actual practice, this decentralized system allowed for considerable disjunction between lofty constitutional principles—freedom, equality, and justice— and the actual operation of government. Both local and state laws perpetuating slavery, justifying land appropriation from Native Americans and Mexican Americans, and encouraging discrimination against ethnic groups employed as inexpensive laborers existed alongside egalitarian constitutional tenets. Moreover, these highly discriminatory laws and political practices were often sanctioned by all branches of the federal government in the name of territorial expansion, industrial and commercial development, private property rights, and, most importantly, *states' rights*. This same system existed within a democracy that attacked discrimination on the political and legal battlefields. The result was that ethnic groups and their allies from the dominant core gradually overcame the most blatant and formal patterns of discrimination by making appeals to constitutional principles, by taking power at the local level, and by forcing legislative changes in the laws at all levels of government.

Educational Institutions   Before the Revolution, schooling was private and available only to affluent, mostly Anglo-Saxon, citizens. Education was based largely on the tenets of English Protestantism, the core values that Protestantism spawned, the culture of western and northern Europe, and the views of commerce and politics held by the early English settlers. This early private system did not reach a large proportion of the population, but it became the model for the public schools, which later proliferated as an explicit and acknowledged means to "Americanize" newer and non-Protestant immigrants in the latter part of the eighteenth century and throughout the nineteenth and twentieth centuries. What typified these early schools and many public schools thereafter was an Anglo-Saxon Eurocentric curriculum. And even as a system of private

Catholic schools, along with other religious institutions, began to emerge, the substance of the secular curriculum in these schools contained the core values and beliefs of the early northern European settlers. Only recently has this curriculum begun to accommodate the realities of non-European immigration and of the legacy of slavery and Native American genocide. In many instances, however, this new material is viewed as a supplement to the core white, Anglo-Saxon, middle-class thrust of the school culture and curriculum. These new materials are designed as supplements to efforts at Americanizing those who were unsuccessfully assimilated, such as those Native Americans and African Americans who remain at the fringes of society, those who have resisted full assimilation, such as Mexicans and other Latino individuals, and those newer immigrants, such as various Asian groups, who must learn western and American ways.

Religious Institutions   The English brought with them Anglican and Congregational Protestantism, although these religions were not dominant by the Revolutionary era. The religious tone of the society was decidedly Protestant, however, with other religions, particularly Catholicism and Judaism, viewed most suspiciously. In fact, Will Herberg (1960) has argued that Catholicism, Judaism, and non-British Protestantism all accommodated themselves in terms of the language used in their services, the organization of their religious schools, and the format of their rituals. As increasing numbers of non-English Protestants and non-Protestants immigrated to America in the post-Revolutionary era, tolerance for religious pluralism became evident; yet this was a pluralism among unequal partners, for English religious traditions dictated how each religion was to be tolerated. To this day, hostility exists toward those religions that do not conform to the style and format of Protestantism.

ANGLO-SAXON HEGEMONY
AND THE DYNAMICS OF ETHNICITY

The Domination of the Anglo-Saxon Core

We can conclude, then, that the core cultural and institutional structures of the United States have been disproportionately influenced by the early English settlers. As founders of America, the English did not have to compete with rival cultural symbols and institutions from another equally developed population. For although Native Americans helped many of the early settlers survive the early winters, their institutional structures were unlikely to survive those of peoples from a much more technologically developed society. Unless the first settlers wanted to return to hunting and gathering or simple horticulture, Native American institutions could not out-compete those brought by an economically and militarily more developed population. Native Americans and their institutional structures were destroyed and displaced, as was their culture.

Once Anglo-Saxon culture and institutional structures were in place, Anglo-Saxons could set the terms of competition among ethnic groups—the nature of the playing field, the rules of the game, and the players who would be allowed in the game. In so doing, they could force other cultures and institutional systems to adapt to and adopt Anglo-Saxon ways. A conquering ethnic group, which has conquered and displaced the founding native stock, can usually establish itself before other ethnic migrants arrive and, as a consequence, will almost always be able to dominate.

Today, with two hundred years of immigration to complement the ancestors of African slaves, Latinos, and Native Americans, the descendants of Anglo-Saxons still hold a disproportionate number of elite positions (see Feagin, 1989:75–78, for a brief review). Not only are core cultural and basic institutional structures Anglo-Saxon but the elite members of this group are overrepresented by the descendants of those who came before the Revolution. Because these elite members have the power to influence beliefs and policy, Anglo-Saxons can disproportionately determine the cultural climate and institutional policies of American society today. We are not concluding that there is a concerted conspiracy to do so; rather, the elite Anglo-Saxons and their many assimilated allies from other ethnic groups, especially later European immigrants, simply view certain symbols and arrangements as more desirable, workable, and fair. Indeed, they are likely to believe that these symbols and arrangements offer the best chance for the disadvantaged to do better in American society.

The dominance of white ethnic groups, especially those in the Anglo-Saxon core as well as others who have adopted this core culture, is reflected in their economic well-being. White ethnic groups have lower rates of poverty and higher levels of wealth than Native Americans, African Americans, and Latinos (Farley, 1990:238; U.S. Bureau of the Census, 1991a, b, and c). Some Asians match or exceed non-Latino white Americans in income and wealth (see Chapter 7), but this fact does not detract from the basic point: White ethnic groups from the original core and later white immigrants who suffered enormously *until* they were absorbed into the core do well compared to those who were brought as slaves (African Americans), those who were killed by European diseases or instruments of violence (Native Americans), and those who were displaced by conquest in the Southwest (Mexican Americans). Latinos and Asians have also suffered, but not to the same degree as those whose human and material resources were taken away or used to build the society.

The Anglo-Saxon Core and the Dynamics of Discrimination

The imposition of the Anglo-Saxon core has not always been benign in the past, nor is it today. The dominance of the Anglo-Saxon core has led to patterns of ethnic antagonism along the lines discussed in Chapter 2. As each new ethnic group arrived, it posed a threat to this core: These ethnic groups tended to be non-Protestant, sometimes non-Christian; they were willing to work for less; they were sufficiently numerous to tip local balances of political power; they placed new burdens on schools and housing; and they brought different lan-

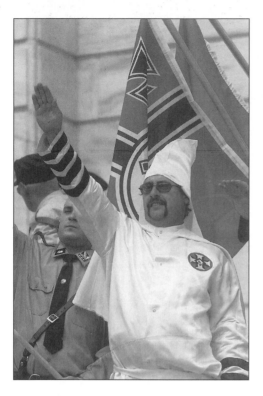

The Ku Klux Klan is not gone. Here Grand Dragon Mike McQueeny of Mercer, Wisconsin, gives the Nazi salute during a demonstration by several dozen neo-Nazi members on the steps of the Minnesota State Capital in August 2001.

guages, values, beliefs, and other symbol systems. This threat led to negative and prejudicial stereotyping of these newly arrived ethnic groups based on their inability to conform to the Anglo-Saxon core; these prejudicial beliefs legitimized discrimination in jobs, housing, education, and politics. Such discrimination was relatively easy to practice because recently arrived ethnic groups are identifiable in terms of culture (language, beliefs, traditions, values), behavior, imported institutions (religion, family), and, for many, physical appearance (skin color, facial features). Those who could adapt to Anglo-Saxon culture by changing their cultural or behavioral norms experienced less discrimination, especially if they were white. Groups who remained identifiable, but were small, and possessed entrepreneurial skills, tended to find middleman minority niches, even in the face of intense discrimination. Groups who were identifiable, large, and without skills or other resources tended to occupy lower socioeconomic positions.

As with each wave of immigration, the emancipation from slavery of African Americans and the mere survival of Native Americans and Mexicans set in motion these discriminatory dynamics. In the early years of settlement, in the seventeenth and eighteenth centuries, Africans were enslaved and Native Americans conquered; however, with the "freedom" and partial emergence of these populations, the Anglo-Saxon core had to adjust to the perceived threat against their predominance.

Box 3.1
The Changing Ethnic Composition of America

In addition to counting the current number of people in various ethnic groups, the Census Bureau also runs projections on the ethnic composition of America in the future. In the figures below, the actual proportion of the population represented by an ethnic group is reported for 2001, the most recent year available, and then the projections for 2025 and 2045 are made. What is immediately evident is that the non-Hispanic white core will decline from around 70 percent of the population today to around 55 percent in less than fifty years; African Americans will increase only a little, about 1 percent over the next forty years; and Native Americans will remain less than 1 percent of the total population. The decline of the white core is the result of an increase in the Asian/Pacific Islander population from 4 percent to over 8 percent and, more dramatically, in the Latino population from 12 percent to 23 percent. There is, then, a clear "Latinoization" of America under way, and particularly in certain regions of the country such as the Southwest, the eastern seaboard, and south Florida. As this transformation occurs, the culture of America will also change, but a change of this magnitude is always feared by those whose ways of life will be transformed to some unknown degree. Thus, the growth of the Asian and Hispanic populations will often be seen as threatening by not only whites but perhaps by African Americans as well.

Projections of Relative Size of Ethnic Populations
(Percentage of Total Population)*

	(Actual) 2001	2025	2045
Non-Hispanic white Americans	71.0%	62.0%	54.5%
Non-Hispanic African Americans	12.2	12.9	13.2
Non-Hispanic Native Americans	0.7	0.8	0.8
Non-Hispanic Asian/Pacific Islanders	4.0	6.2	8.4
Hispanic	12.1	18.2	23.1
	100.0	100.0	100.0

*Rounding of numbers causes figures to sum to 101%.

Source: U.S. Bureau of the Census (2002) Population Projections Program, Population Division.

Germans and Scandinavians began to migrate to America in the late eighteenth century and continued throughout the nineteenth century, as did many English. Their presence posed less threat to the Anglo-Saxon core than other ethnic populations, however, because of their Protestant and northern European heritage. But for the other ethnic groups, the dynamics of discrimination were always accelerated by the perception of new threats.

Abolitionist pressures to free slaves heightened the sense of threat in the South, and also in the North. As the country expanded westward, nations of

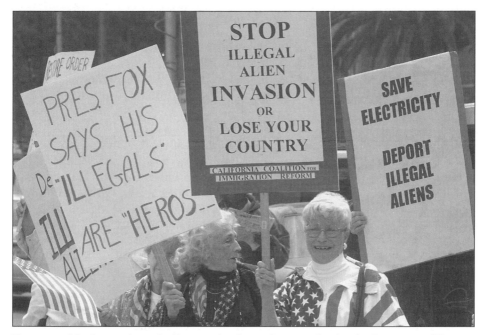

Demographic change is typically perceived as a threat to the Anglo-Saxon core. Here, in March 2001, members of the California Coalition for Immigration Reform protest in Century City against the looser border restrictions with Mexico advocated by Mexican President Vicente Fox.

Native Americans were successively conquered in the Indian Wars of the 1800s and shunted to various reservations. The Indians were viewed as a constant threat by the white settlers who had taken their land and destroyed their culture. Irish Catholics, the first of the non-Protestant Europeans, came between the 1830s and 1860s. Their large numbers unsettled the Anglo-Saxon core in America's key cities. The Chinese—the first Asian ethnic population—came in the 1850s to 1870s as railroad workers. Their non-Western ways posed a threat to the western extensions of the Anglo-Saxon core. The Mexicans of the Southwest were colonized and thrown off their land beginning in the 1850s. Those who remained in the United States were relegated to low-wage jobs—a condition that continued and was exacerbated in the Mexican migration into the Southwest throughout the twentieth century. In the 1880s through the first decades of the twentieth century, Italians, Jews from eastern Europe, and Poles entered in large numbers. The Japanese and Filipinos also arrived at this time, coming as agricultural workers, often via Hawaii, to the West Coast and bearing with them the "threat" of Asian and South Asian culture.

African Americans began to migrate to the Northeast and Midwest in the early decades of the twentieth century, competing with the white ethnic groups for employment. Puerto Ricans came to the Northeast in large numbers, starting in the 1940s and continuing to the present. Cubans began to come to south Florida in the 1960s and 1970s. Their presence evoked less fear because of their anticommunist views and professed desire to return to Cuba; but their large numbers and Latin culture pinched at Anglo sensibilities. And in the 1960s to the present, new Asian groups—Koreans, Vietnamese, Taiwanese, Chinese, Filipinos—have migrated to the United States. Each wave of immigration and migration has posed a threat to the integrity of the Anglo-Saxon core.

Although the culture and institution building of each wave of immigrants have broadened the culture and structure of American society beyond the original Anglo-Saxon core, this broadening has always involved the assimilation of immigrant cultures to the Anglo-Saxon core. Even with accommodation, however, the more visible dynamic has been ethnic antagonism—born of and sustained by threat, prejudice, and discrimination—between the new cultures and the older cultural core.

SUMMARY

Ethnic relations in America have been profoundly influenced by the cultural systems and institutional structures of the first colonizers. This is almost always the case when a more powerful population invades the territory of a less powerful population and, then, seeks to settle there. Throughout world history, this process has occurred again and again, but the New World added a different twist: The settlement and expansion of the conquering population required the accommodation of new waves of immigrants. Some immigrants were imported as slaves, but most came voluntarily from Europe and Asia. As Native Americans were virtually eliminated and isolated on reservations, and Mexicans were conquered and deposed, America became, literally, a land of opportunity for immigrants and migrants. The rapid industrialization of the East and Midwest, along with the expansion of agriculture and ranching in the West, created new opportunities, which stimulated a massive wave of immigration. Among the Europeans, those from north Europe were the first to come, followed by central and southern Europeans. Most of these Europeans initially settled in the East and emerging Midwest; later, they moved farther west. In addition to these white immigrants, Asian immigrants began to settle on the West Coast; some came before most northern and southern Europeans, but most came at about the same time as these Europeans.

These early immigrants, as well as those who arrived in the latter part of the twentieth century, have had to confront the Anglo-Saxon core, itself an amalgam of cultural and institutional systems of the British Isles, with significant infusions from German, Dutch, Scandinavian, and French cultural traditions. This core consisted of such cultural elements as the English language, English values and beliefs, and English legal tenets, along with mostly northern European institutional structures in economy, government, education, and religion. This core represented the environment to which other ethnic groups would have to adapt and which they would have to adopt, or live with the consequences if they did not. For white ethnic groups, assimilation was easier because of their European heritage and, most important, their skin color; for Asians, physical identifiability and their non-Western culture posed greater problems; for freed slaves, skin color in the face of extreme prejudice and discrimination made it very difficult to adapt to, much less adopt, all the elements of the core; for more recent immigrants—particularly Asians and Latinos—adjustment has not been easy because of the threats that these immigrants pose not only to many members of the Anglo-Saxon core but also to those earlier immigrants who have yet to fully adapt to this core.

Each wave of immigration, as well as each internal wave of migration of former slaves and of natives, and the mere existence of natives, has activated the dynamics of discrimination discussed in Chapter 2 and modeled in Figures 2.1, 2.2, and 2.3 on pages 36, 40, and 41. Each ethnic group has altered the Anglo-Saxon core, but only to a point; the persistence of ethnic tension indicates that not all ethnic groups can, are allowed to, or want to, assimilate.

POINTS OF DEBATE

Some of the most hotly contested issues in America today revolve around the conflict between subordinate ethnic groups and members of the dominant Anglo-Saxon core. Often as a reaction to discrimination, but also as a matter of preference, ethnic minority groups have sought to cultivate and maintain their distinctive cultural features and patterns of social organization, even if this means that they conflict with the Anglo-Saxon core. The resulting tension and conflict engenders many questions, some of which follow:

1. How flexible can the Anglo-Saxon core be in accommodating the key elements of other cultures and remain the core? Many argue that America must become pluralistic, but to what degree and at what expense? If a society has no clear cultural or institutional core, is such a society viable?
2. Has the existence of blatant and established discrimination in America forced ethnic groups to discard assimilation as an option? If so, has the United States passed the critical point after which accommodation is less likely than ethnic conflict? If this is so, what is to be done? What is the future of the United States if ethnic subpopulations polarize around distinctive cores?
3. Has the Anglo-Saxon core been inflexible, as is often charged by the victims of discrimination? There are clear signs that considerable change has occurred, as reflected in the massive contributions of all ethnic groups to the culture and structure of American society. Even those populations that have experienced severe discrimination have assimilated some elements of their culture. There are two important questions: Can the Anglo-Saxon

core absorb more? Are ethnic groups willing to give up more of their own cultural and institutional core in order to decrease the polarization between cores? If the answer is no to both questions, what is America's future?

KEY TERMS

Anglo-Saxon, 49
ascetic Protestantism, 50
Puritanism, 50

states' rights, 52
WASP, 49

CHAPTER 4

African Americans

Imported as slaves, treated as property to be bought and sold, denied citizenship rights, and considered less than human for much of American history, most African Americans have not been able to enjoy the benefits that come with living in the United States. The legacy of two hundred years of slavery, thirty years of post–Civil War oppression, and another century of systematic discrimination in housing, employment, education, and virtually every social sphere persists. Even as many of the old forms of discrimination have been dismantled since the mid-1960s, discrimination remains a central part of the African American experience (Jaynes and Williams, 1989; Farley and Allen, 1987; Schafer, 1993).

The effects of three hundred and fifty years of oppression are not suddenly undone, for the weight of the past stands as a barrier in the present (Pinkney, 1984). How does one overcome, for example, the effects of residing in inner-city slums and public housing projects, growing up in single-parent households, living in a social climate in which most young men have lost hope of finding employment and women are overburdened, attending crowded and often dangerous schools, and walking down crime-ridden streets (Caputo, 1993; Bullard, 1991)? These conditions did not suddenly emerge; rather, they are the product of past discrimination, and now they operate as a new kind of discriminatory barrier. White Americans often fail to recognize this fact. Indeed, African Americans are frequently condemned for not overcoming these barriers, as if centuries of massive oppression could be quickly eradicated by individual initiative and drive (Farley, 1987; Hughes and Madden, 1991; Blauner 1989). And so, even now, when institutionalized discrimination has been greatly reduced, the damage of the past remains, and few in the United States are seriously addressing this damage. Moreover, even as formal discrimination has decreased, subtle patterns of informal discrimination persist. As a result, today many African Americans are still denied equal access to the valued resources of society.

RESOURCE SHARES OF AFRICAN AMERICANS

The Impoverishment of African Americans

One very good indicator of how well, or badly, a subpopulation is doing in the United States is the rate of poverty. According to the U.S. Bureau of the Census, approximately 12 percent of the population is defined as "poor," meaning, in essence, people's incomes do not meet government-established standards for adequate food, housing, clothing, and other necessary resources. These standards have varied over the last fifty years, as have the income levels necessary to meet them, but they have remained constant in the last decade. African Americans are disproportionately poor, as Table 4.1 documents. As of 2000, close to 23 percent of African Americans were living in poverty; and this figure might be higher if the government's outmoded method for calculating poverty more accurately reflected the actual costs for many necessities of living (see Turner, 1992, for a review).

The Income of African Americans

In absolute terms, the income of African Americans has increased, even taking inflation into consideration; and relative to whites, blacks have made some gains, although they still lag behind whites.

Table 4.2 shows the ratio between black and white median family income from 1950 to 2000. With the exception of 1970, the ratio of black to white income remained relatively the same between 1950 and 1990. The 1980s saw a drop in the ratio to the levels of the 1950s and 1960s. The decrease between 1970 and 1990 was the result of (1) cutbacks in government job programs for the poor in general and African Americans living in the inner city in particular, (2) dramatic decreases in the number of relatively unskilled jobs in the economy, and, most importantly, (3) the rapid rise in female-headed single-parent families in the black population over the last two decades, at a time when white families increasingly became dual-income families (Jackson, 1993).

But despite these problems, median family income of blacks relative to that of whites increased between 1990 and 2000. The reason for this improvement is that nearly one in seven black families earns over $50,000, compared to

TABLE 4.1 Percentage of Black and White Americans Living in Poverty

Year	Black	White
2000	22.7%	7.4%
1990	30.7	10.0
1980	31.0	9.0
1970	33.5	9.9
1960	55.1	18.1

Source: U.S. Bureau of the Census, 1979a, 1983d, 1989a, 1991c, 1999, and 2002.

TABLE 4.2 Black Family Median Income as a Percentage
of White Median Income

Year	Ratio of Black to White Income %
2000	0.68
1990	0.59
1980	0.56
1970	0.64
1960	0.55
1950	0.54

Source: U.S. Bureau of the Census, 1979a, 1983d, 1989a, 1991c, 1999a, and 2002.

one in seventeen in 1967. Since the ratio of black to white income includes the incomes of this higher-income black middle class, poor blacks are much worse off relative to whites. Thus, the figures in Table 4.2 combine incomes of both African Americans who escaped poverty and those who did not; and since the figures extend to the 1950s, when there were very few middle-class blacks, these statistics show that more African Americans are poor now than in the past. Moreover, among these poor, a significant amount of income is derived from welfare and other government programs and, hence, does not signal participation in the job market, the occupational system, and the mainstream of American society. This lack of participation results in a pattern of marginalization among many in the African American community—a pattern that is difficult to change.

The Occupation Distribution of African Americans

There have been dramatic changes in the distribution of jobs among African Americans. In 1960, only 13 percent of blacks could be labeled "white-collar workers," whereas in 2000, 50 percent held white-collar jobs. This improvement, while significant, needs to be qualified by the kinds of white-collar jobs African Americans have been able to find. Many of these jobs are not high-paying because they are clerical and service jobs. Table 4.3 compares non-Hispanic

TABLE 4.3 Distribution of African Americans and Non-Hispanic Whites in Various Occupations, 2000

	Non-Hispanic Whites	African Americans
Managerial and professional	33.2%	21.7%
Technical, sales, administrative support	30.3	29.0
Service occupations	11.8	22.6
Precision production, craft, repair	10.9	7.8
Operators, fabricators, laborers	11.6	18.1
Farming, forestry, and fishing	2.3	0.8

Source: U.S. Bureau of the Census, 2002; Population Statistics, Social and Demographic.

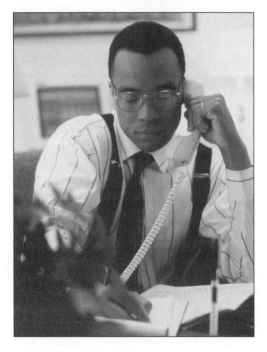

While the percentage of blacks in "white-collar" jobs has increased significantly (from 13 to 50 percent between 1960 and 2000), blacks remain underrepresented in higher-paying "managerial and professional" positions.

whites and blacks across the six major categories that the U.S. Bureau of the Census uses to classify occupations. In the higher-paying white-collar occupations like "managerial and professional," whites are much more likely to hold these better-paying jobs, while in the higher-paying blue collar categories, such as "precision production, craft, and repair," only 7.8 percent of blacks have these jobs. Indeed, the occupations most likely to be held by African Americans are in lower-paying blue-collar labor, service labor, and clerical white-collar work. Thus, although considerable progress has been made in opening up the occupational system to African Americans, they are still underrepresented in the high-end blue- and white-collar occupations, as was the case two decades ago (Bates, 1995; Darity and Myers, 2001; Farley and Allen, 1987; Swinton, 1989). The situation for African Americans becomes even more clouded when unemployment rates for non-Hispanic whites and blacks are compared (see Table 4.4). For many decades, African Americans were twice as likely to be unemployed.

Part of the explanation for the higher unemployment rate for African Americans is the greater percentage of black workers in service jobs, where employment is less secure, and in blue-collar jobs which, over the last forty years, have been decreasing. Some unemployment can be attributed to discrimination: More black workers are laid off than white workers.

Unemployment denies people access to resources such as money and dignity. The unemployed often turn to the welfare system, which further erodes their dignity and which, in light of Congress's effort to "reform" welfare in 1996, forces many onto the streets. Moreover, unemployment makes it difficult, if not

TABLE 4.4 Unemployment Rates for Black Workers Compared to White Workers

Year	Percentage of Black Unemployed	Percentage of White Unemployed	Ratio of Black to White Unemployment
2000	7.7%	3.4%	2.3%
1998	9.6	4.0	2.4
1994	11.5	5.3	2.2
1990	11.3	4.7	2.4
1980	13.2	6.3	2.1
1970	8.2	4.5	1.8
1960	10.2	4.9	2.1
1950	9.0	4.9	1.8

Source: U.S. Bureau of the Census, 1991c, 1993b, 1995, 1999a, and 2001.

impossible, to build a stable life around home, family, and hope for the future (Eggers and Massey, 1992; Caputo, 1993; Schneider and Phelan, 1990).

Educational Attainment of African Americans

Today, access to good jobs, income, and other resources depends upon a person's educational credentials. African American attendance in schools has, of course, been a hotly contested issue—from the early efforts at desegregation in the 1950s and 1960s to the controversy over forced busing in the 1970s and 1980s (Boozer et al., 1992). This situation alone signals the institutional inequities that have prevented blacks from attaining educational credentials equivalent to white Americans. Despite the desegregation controversy, which still rages on today, African Americans have made significant gains over the last decades in securing credentials that have increased their access to valued resources. As Table 4.5 shows, the gap between blacks and whites with high

TABLE 4.5 Educational Attainment Levels of Blacks and Whites*

Year	High School[†]		College[‡]	
	Blacks, %	Whites, %	Blacks, %	Whites, %
2000	79%	88%	17%	28%
1998	76	87	15	27
1994	73	82	13	23
1990	66	79	11	22
1980	51	69	8	17
1970	31	55	4	11
1960	20	43	3	8

*Persons 25 years old and over.
†Four years of high school.
‡Four years or more of college.
Source: U.S. Bureau of the Census, 1995, 1999a, and 2001.

school diplomas has been closing over the last forty years. Moreover, for most of this period, the percentage of African Americans who have completed four years of college increased, but so did the percentage of whites, thereby sustaining the wide gap between blacks and whites.

Housing of African Americans

Housing is a valued resource. Where one lives determines access to other resources—jobs, good schools, clean air, peace and quiet, lack of crime, and so on (Bullard, 1993; Whetstone, 1993). African Americans have endured a tremendous amount of discrimination in housing, and, as a consequence, they are disproportionately confined to the inner cities (Jaynes and Williams, 1989; Wildavsky, 1990; Farley, 1995). Furthermore, they are segregated more than any other large ethnic population in the United States. Table 4.6 shows the residential segregation index for blacks in representative metropolitan areas: A low number indicates mild levels of segregation, whereas a high score represents high levels (a score of 100 would signal complete segregation of blacks). Among the sixteen metropolitan areas with the largest black population, however, the index score rises considerably to about 80 (Jaynes and Williams, 1989:27). As the black population increases in a metropolitan area, the level of segregation increases dramatically. Yet, as the most recent analysis of segregation between blacks and whites indicates, the peak period of segregation may now have passed (Farley and Frey, 1994), although Table 4.6 reveals that considerable segregation persists. Table 4.7 underscores the fact that the degree of segregation is very high in the most segregated metropolitan areas. Even in the least segregated metropolitan areas, the index scores are still rather high. However, the recent reductions in white–black segregation can be accounted for by increases in the Latino population. Census data classify Latinos as white, and this ethnic group has nearly the same levels of poverty as blacks (McKinney and Schnare, 1989), and hence, these poor Latinos have become integrated with blacks in urban poverty.

TABLE 4.6 Trends in Residential Segregation of African Americans

Year	Degree of Segregation, %
2001	59%
1990	58
1980	53
1970	59
1960	56

Source: Harrison and Weinberg, 1992; McKinney and Schnare, 1989; U.S. Department of Housing and Urban Develpment, 1991; Frey and Myers, 2002.

TABLE 4.7 Segregation Indexes for Most and Least Segregated Metropolitan Areas, 2000

Most Segregated			Least Segregated		
Rank	Metropolitan Area	Index	Rank	Metropolitan Area	Index
1	Gary, IN PMSA*	88	1	Jacksonville, NC MSA	32
2	Detroit, MI PMSA	87	2	Yolo, CA PMSA	32
3	Milwaukee-Waukesha, WI PMSA	84	3	Lawrence, KS MSA	34
4	New York, NY PMSA	84	4	Santa Cruz-Watsonville, CA PSMA	34
5	Chicago, IL PMSA	84	5	Lawton, OK MSA	35
6	Newark, NJ PMSA	83	6	Boulder-Longmont, CO PSMA	37
7	Flint, MI PMSA	81	7	Redding, CA MSA	37
8	Buffalo-Niagara Falls, NY MSA	80	8	Boise City, ID MSA	37
9	Cleveland-Lorain-Elyria, OH PMSA	80	9	Fayetteville, NC MSA	38
10	Saginaw-Bay City-Midland, MI MSA**	79	10	Eugene-Springfield, OR MSA	38

*PSMA: Primary Metropolitan Statistical Area
**MSA: Metropolitan Statistical Area

Source: Frey and Meyers (2002).

Segregation of African Americans means that this minority is concentrated in inner cities and in city public housing. The result is that African Americans have (1) reduced access to jobs (because many companies have moved to the suburbs), (2) reduced capacity to go to good schools (because many inner-city schools are underfunded, overcrowded, and plagued with problems ranging from drugs and crime to high dropout rates), and (3) reduced ability to live and grow up outside the sphere of rampant crime, drug use, and gang activity (Calmore, 1993).

Life Span of African Americans

The ultimate resource is life. How long do you live? Figure 4.1 documents the life expectancy of whites and blacks in America over the last thirty years (National Vital Statistics Reports, 2002). While all Americans are living longer, the gap between whites and blacks remains rather high. An African American male will live, on average, to be 68.2 years old, while his white counterpart will live more than six years longer at 74.8 years. A black female will live about as long as a white male, at 74.9 years, but still five years less than her white counterpart, who can expect to live until she is 80 years old. Another way to examine inequalities in life expectancy is to compare infant mortality rates. White babies die at the rate of about 3.8 babies per 1,000 births, whereas black infants die at well over twice this rate, at 9.4 deaths per 1,000 births.

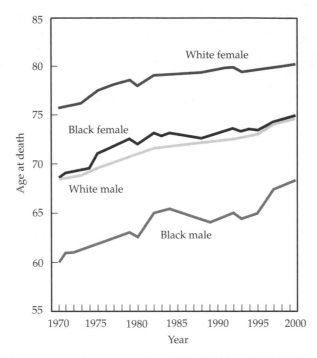

FIGURE 4.1 Life expectancy by race and sex: United States, 1970–2000.
Source: National Vital Statistics Reports, 2002.

These high infant mortality rates indicate that African Americans do not have full access to the medical care system in the United States. Some of the causes of death of African Americans are also revealing. African Americans are more than twice as likely than whites to die from diabetes, kidney disease, bacterial infections, and hypertension. More dramatically, they are almost six times more likely to die from homicide than are whites.

Thus, African Americans do not have the same level of access to money, jobs, education, housing, and health care as do white Americans and, as we will see, other ethnic groups (Wallace, 1990). Our goal is to understand how and why this inequity exists. In seeking an explanation, we will use our discussion in Chapter 2; and in fact, the reader may want to review Figures 2.1, 2.2, and 2.3 on pages 36, 40, and 41 before proceeding. As the model in Figure 2.3 predicts, the explanation for the plight of African Americans resides in easy identifiability as targets of discrimination, large numbers and lack of entrepreneurial skills, negative stereotyping and prejudice by members of the dominant society, and victimization through both institutionalized and informal discrimination.

THE DYNAMICS OF DISCRIMINATION
AGAINST AFRICAN AMERICANS

Identifiability of African Americans

Being black poses a problem in a white world: You stand out, and dramatically so. Black and white are perceived as opposite colors; a black person cannot easily "blend" into a predominantly white America. Skin color is, in the biological sense, a minor genetic trait; but in the sociological sense it is anything but minor. Identifiability makes people easy targets of discrimination. Most members of white ethnic groups look like the dominant population, and most Latinos are not physically identifiable as members of an ethnic group. Black people cannot shed their color, but commingling has occurred since the Africans were pressed into slavery, resulting in generations of individuals with various degrees of dark skin pigmentation. Interethnic marriages have increased somewhat in recent decades, further influencing the color balance of the American population. Yet, skin color, no matter what the permutation, continues to identify some as targets of discrimination.

Sociocultural traits also contribute to discrimination. Poverty and unemployment statistics for African Americans reflect their disproportionate representation in the lower classes; demeanor, speech, and dress further distinguish many members of the African American community. These characteristics are reinforced by black culture, which has evolved in reaction to slavery and the discrimination that blacks have endured since "emancipation."

Even when socioeconomic standing and/or culture are not obvious, skin color alone remains as a basis of discrimination. For example, Joe Feagin (1991) conducted in-depth interviews with black middle-class members and found that they experienced discrimination in public places, such as restaurants, stores, swimming pools, and parking areas. Thus, to be denied service, to be told to go, or to suffer epithets are still very common for blacks in America. The prejudice and discrimination that middle-class African Americans live with cannot be attributed to class or culture, but simply to skin color.

Negative Beliefs about African Americans

More than any other ethnic population in the United States, and perhaps in the world, African Americans have been the victims of negative beliefs and stereotypes. Negative beliefs have also reinforced the identifiability of blacks, making them unique in a negative way. Such stereotypes have then been used to legitimize discrimination in a society whose core values are based on liberty, freedom, and equality (Staples, 1975; Andrews, 1994).

In the early period of slavery, from 1650 to 1820, whites viewed Africans as "uncivilized heathens," "bestial," "sexually aggressive," and as suffering the "curse of God" who made them black (Jordan, 1968; Turner and Singleton, 1978). Although there is some debate as to whether all white southerners held such hard views (Roediger, 1991:24), these beliefs changed somewhat when

---

Box 4.1
The First "R"

Debra Van Ausdale and Joe R. Feagin recently conducted a study of children at a day care center. They observed how these young children interacted during the course of their play activities. What immediately became evident to the investigators is that children are very well aware of "race." Unlike much of the literature, which simply assumes that children pay little attention to markers of various ethnic groups, these investigators found that the opposite was the case. Very young children have rather sophisticated cognitive conceptions of "race"; moreover, they act on these conceptions. At times they reveal behaviors that can only be described as "racist." Thus, the broader cultural stereotypes of various ethnic groups are picked up rather early in children's lives; they learn from their parents, peers, media, and other sources a great deal of information about the first "R" long before they can read, write, and do arithmetic. For example, one three-year-old child picked up her cot and moved to the other side of the classroom during nap time. When the teacher asked why she did this, she replied that "I can't sleep next to a nigger." She then pointed to the four-year-old African American girl and uttered that "Niggers are stinky. I can't sleep next to one."

When young minority children are asked about their experiences with racism, they almost always report reactions like that of the little three-year-old girl. Imagine a legacy of such reactions, beginning at an early age, and perhaps we can get a sense of why minority children often feel uncomfortable around whites. What is interesting is that both professionals and the lay public simply fail to perceive that these kinds of reactions of the young to ethnic differences occur. There is, in a sense, a collective denial that young children, presumed to be so innocent, can also be racists.

Source: Van Ausdale and Feagin (2001).

---

abolitionists in the North challenged them. Slavery became a "positive good," protecting Africans from their "savage impulses" and responding to their "childlike dependency." Yet, even in the abolitionist North, stereotypes portrayed Africans as ignorant, lazy, and immoral (Fredrickson, 1971:51). During this period the *"black Sambo" stereotype* evolved (Boskin, 1986), which portrayed black people as childlike, helpless, shuffling, and fumbling (but with potentially aggressive tendencies).

After the Civil War, when the short-lived but significant gains of radical Reconstruction were undone, African Americans were portrayed as inferior because they had not been able to take advantage of the *equal opportunities* offered by Reconstruction. Even in enlightened circles, blacks were often portrayed as not having progressed as far as whites on the evolutionary scale; so, without segregation as well as supervision and control, African Americans would revert to their more primitive state. In the South, this state was perceived to be one of laziness, criminality, and lustfulness (especially for white women, a belief that conveniently overlooked some slaveholders' lust for black women); in the North, this state was viewed as one of childlike docility and kindness that needed to be channeled (by whites). Whether vicious or benign, treatment of African Americans was based on the belief that black people are biologically inferior and must be segregated (Fredrickson, 1971).

Between the world wars, from 1914 to 1941, evolutionary theory and results on intelligence tests were interpreted to confirm as "scientific fact" the inferiority of blacks, although social scientists began to attack this position and to argue that the differences between black people and white people (as well as all "races") were the result of environmental rather than biological differences. Yet, the prevailing belief continued to advocate segregation as necessary and desirable in order to prevent "black inferiority" from diminishing the white biological stock.

The post–World War II period saw a dramatic shift in beliefs about African Americans. A consensus slowly emerged in more progressive circles that segregation was harmful, that blacks were not innately inferior, that the appearance of inferiority reflected cultural deprivation stemming from undesirable environments, and that improvements in schooling, job opportunities, and neighborhoods were the key to making life better for African Americans. Such progressive beliefs began to shape broad public perceptions (though not universally), and perhaps more significantly, they began to affect federal governmental policies, at least to a degree. Yet, many still believed that integration was unnecessary and undesirable.

Today, beliefs about African Americans are mixed. Three decades ago, 65 percent of Americans believed that blacks were unmotivated, and only a decade ago almost 50 percent thought that blacks were lazy (see Turner and Payne, 2002, for a summary of the most recent poll results summarized below). These attitudes have softened somewhat, but not as much as one might think. Almost half of Americans still believe that African Americans lack motivation, and one-third see blacks as lazy. Moreover, public sentiment for government assistance for African Americans has turned much more harsh than it was at the peak of the Civil Rights movement in the 1960s. Only 40 percent of Americans think that government should aid blacks; and only 30 percent believe that government should ensure fair treatment in jobs. And, between 30 percent and 40 percent of Americans still think that blacks "should not go where they are not wanted" and that it is acceptable to "keep blacks out of the neighborhood." These kinds of attitudes make it extremely difficult for African Americans to feel comfortable in so many contexts critical to their well-being, because a significant proportion of the population holds negative beliefs about their motives and their rights to fair treatment.

Indeed, beliefs have hardened against help for African Americans over the last five years. Some people think that liberal policies have gone too far: *Affirmative action*, or measures designed to rectify past patterns of discrimination, is often seen to discriminate against white people; busing destroys neighborhood schools; and integration forces people to live near those whom they would rather avoid. Others believe that liberal policies have encouraged African Americans to depend on government for welfare, jobs, and education, thereby preventing many blacks from improving their lives. Many others, fearing the emergence of an urban underclass of angry, unemployed youth, have called for more government spending on programs to provide opportunities for African Americans. Some have urged the government and the private sector to provide real rather than illusory opportunities. Others feel that individuals and communities must develop their own resources to break the cycle of poverty and government dependency. This last outlook has gained some currency over the last few years and has been used to cut back federal aid programs for the poor in general and African Americans in particular. Some believe that "minorities are getting too much" at the expense of whites (Kluegel and Bobo, 1993). The passage of Proposition 209 (California Civil Rights Initiative) by the majority of California voters in the 1996 November election was fueled by the belief that "minorities had received more than their share" at the expense of white persons. And, in response to these sentiments, the welfare reform of 1996 ensures that the poor will get less, and for a shorter period of time.

What people say on a survey is often very different from what they really feel; and as a result, African Americans must constantly be aware that people will express in words or deeds their negative attitudes. White Americans cannot imagine what it is like to confront uncertainty in almost every situation about how one will be treated. This diffuse anxiety takes a heavy toll on African Americans who must constantly monitor others to see if negative attitudes toward them will become manifest, and few whites are willing to even consider the psychological costs to African Americans to say nothing of the sociological costs of experiencing subtle forms of discrimination in jobs, schools, public places, and neighborhoods.

Many studies document that when blacks and whites have opportunities to interact and associate, prejudicial attitudes decline. But this is at the interpersonal level; at a community level, a different picture emerges. Ironically, negative beliefs about African Americans tend to increase as their percentage of the local population increases. Marylee Taylor (1998), for example, found that whites' prejudices toward blacks increased as the percentage of blacks in a community rose. Even when blacks were highly segregated and, hence, not in contact with whites, prejudice increased. In contrast, prejudice did not increase significantly when the proportion of other minorities, such as Latinos, increased in a community. Thus, African Americans' presence escalates fears and prejudice in ways not typical of other minorities, and these prejudices represent an enormous burden to African Americans.

Institutionalized Discrimination against African Americans

Legal Discrimination   Dominant beliefs usually become codified into laws; in turn, these laws sanction certain types of behavior. So it was with beliefs about blacks in America, against whom it was once legal to discriminate. Moreover, undermining and, often, defying the law are informal discriminatory practices that are not codified but that are deemed appropriate in a climate in which the law makes discrimination acceptable.

Legal Discrimination under Slavery and in Slavery's Aftermath   It is difficult to determine whether the first Africans in America were slaves or indentured servants; the historical record is not clear on this point (Jordan, 1962). By the 1650s, however, there is evidence that some colonies had laws distinguishing between white and black servants, with black servants and their children consigned to servitude for life. By the early eighteenth century, the broad legal framework of slavery in the South had become clearly codified (Stampp, 1956; Starobin, 1970:7):

1. Blacks were to be slaves for life.
2. Slaves were *both* property and persons; owners held title to blacks as property and had some responsibilities to blacks as persons.
3. Children would inherit their mother's status as a slave.
4. Christian baptism did not automatically lead to freedom.
5. Marriages between blacks and whites were prohibited.
6. Blacks could not acquire or inherit property.
7. Blacks could not engage in litigation or enter into civil contracts; they could not testify against whites in court, nor could they sit on juries.

Such codes reaffirmed beliefs about the "bestiality" of slaves and legitimized slavery by making it acceptable for white Americans to buy slave labor. In the North, the laws were considerably more benign, but few questioned the biological inferiority of blacks or the norm of economic, educational, and political discrimination (Litwack, 1961:30–38; Fredrickson, 1971:1–43, 1981, 1988). With the admission of border and southern states to the Union in the early 1800s, a considerable amount of debate in Congress ensued over the legal rights of African-origin people. The coexistence of free blacks in the North and slaves in southern and border states made it difficult to define the constitutional rights of slaves in the growing Union. The issue was effectively avoided in 1821 when Missouri was admitted to the Union, for Congress enacted a loosely worded law that allowed the states to legislate as they pleased, with the proviso that no citizens "shall be excluded from the enjoyment of any of the privileges and immunities to which such citizen is entitled under the Constitution of the United States." Thereafter, until the Civil War, northern laws were increasingly relaxed, while southern legislatures passed ever more restrictive laws.

Abolitionist pleas for at least "humane treatment" of the "inferior race" were beginning to have a small impact on public opinion, and those states with few black residents began to accord them broader citizenship rights. However, these formal laws contradicted informal *Jim Crow practices* of the North, which, despite the lofty tenets of formal laws, excluded most African Americans from access to jobs, education, and housing (Woodward, 1966).

It appears likely that the abolitionist ideology was used retroactively to justify a massive northern invasion of the South for economic and political reasons.

Box 4.2
The Execution of Black Slaves

The following table provides some descriptive statistics for black slave executions in the United States between 1641 and 1865. Most black slave executions occurred in Deep South states. While black slaves were more likely to be executed for theft in Deep South states, they were just as likely to be executed for murder and rape regardless of geographical region. In general, black slaves were most often executed for murder, followed by participation in a slave revolt, rape, theft, arson, and poisoning. The most common form of execution was hanging, and most executed black slaves were males.

Selected Characteristics of Black Slave Executions in the United States, 1641–1865

	Deep South States*		Border States†		Northern States‡		Total	
	N	%	N	%	N	%	N	%
Criminal offense								
Murder	566	78%	105	15%	52	7%	723	100%
Rape	110	77	22	15	11	8	143	100
Theft	115	92	7	6	3	2	125	100
Slave revolt	207	84	8	3	31	13	246	100
Arson	45	67	7	10	15	23	67	100
Poisoning	51	88	2	3	5	9	58	100
Method of execution								
Hanging	1,351	85	158	10	87	5	1,596	100
Breaking on the wheel	31	47	3	5	32	48	66	100
Gibbeted	20	95	0	0	1	5	21	
Gender								
Male	1,179	83	136	10	106	7	1,421	100
Female	119	79	19	13	13	8	1,551	100

*Alabama, Arkansas, Florida, Georgia, Louisiana, Mississippi, North Carolina, South Carolina, Texas, and Virginia.
†Kentucky, Maryland, Tennessee, and West Virginia.
‡Illinois, Massachusetts, Missouri, New Jersey, New York, and Pennsylvania.

Source: Aguirre and Baker, 1999.

Nevertheless, the war abolished forever the institution of slavery, and, hence, the economic base of the South. In 1866, the abolition of slavery was formally ratified in the *Thirteenth Amendment*.

In reaction, southern states began to enact *black codes* restricting the rights of freed slaves. These codes were enforced through violence, which, for the remainder of the century, was to become the key to maintaining black subordination to whites. The details of these codes varied, but several restrictions were common to all of them. Blacks could not (1) vote, (2) serve on juries, (3) testify against whites, (4) carry arms, and (5) enter certain occupations (depending upon the state). The codes also stated that black vagrants could be consigned to forced labor. Thus, after the Civil War, the free South was unified in its attempts to impose new legal restrictions upon African Americans.

In reaction to these codes, the violence used to enforce them, and perceptions that President Andrew Johnson was being too conciliatory toward the South, radical Republicans in Congress began to assume control of Reconstruction. The radicals in Congress mounted a two-front legal attack on discrimination in the South by advocating (1) the division of the South into military districts and the enforcement of new constitutional conventions on each southern state and (2) the passage of the Fourteenth and Fifteenth Amendments, which were ratified by northern and reconstituted southern states in 1868 and 1870, respectively. The *Fourteenth Amendment* was an extension of an earlier civil rights act (vetoed by Johnson, and then overridden by Congress) that was designed to overrule the emerging *black codes*. The *Fifteenth Amendment* extended suffrage to African Americans. Reforms in the South were soon followed by the *Civil Rights Act of 1875*, which outlawed northern Jim Crow practices. In this way, Congress forced the South and, to a lesser extent, the North to accept black participation in mainstream American life.

Had radical Reconstruction continued over several generations, institutional discrimination in America would have been markedly reduced. However, by 1880, the radical Republicans had lost control of Congress and the presidency. Almost immediately, new exclusionary laws were passed at local and state levels. These laws were, in essence, a codification of informal practices of segregation and exclusion, reinforced by the ever-present threat of white violence (Williamson, 1984:229). In turn, the Supreme Court began to legitimize the reemergence of Jim Crow practices in the 1890s. First, the Court declared unconstitutional the Civil Rights Act of 1875, thus denying African Americans access to public conveyances and amusement facilities used by white Americans. Then, in 1896, the Court ruled in *Plessy v. Ferguson* that segregated facilities for blacks and whites were not in violation of the Thirteenth and Fourteenth Amendments to the Constitution, since, as the Court declared: "If one race be inferior to the other socially, the Constitution cannot put them on the same plane" (Pinkney, 1969:28).

Codifying exclusionary and segregationist practices in the highest laws of the land firmly established the culture and structure of discrimination in America, in both institutional and informal practice (Cella, 1982; Horowitz and Karit, 1969). It was with this national legal legacy that blacks entered the twentieth century (Steele, 1990). During this period, African Americans became increasingly urban. In the North, however, a myriad of discriminatory laws prevented black integration into white institutions and black participation in the world of white American affluence. Many did not consider such laws illegal or immoral; they were legitimized by the highest court in the land

Box 4.3
Over a Century after Plessy v. Ferguson

On June 7, 1892, Homer Plessy became part of an incident that would shape the entire twentieth century in America. Plessy was self-described as one-eighth "colored," and on this day he refused to move out of the "whites only" railroad car on the East Louisiana Railroad traveling between New Orleans and Covington. Plessy was seen to violate a two-year-old state law in Louisiana that required "separate but equal" facilities for blacks and whites. Plessy's refusal was staged to test the state law, but the Louisiana decision went against him.

The issue was important because throughout the South, except for South and North Carolina as well as Virginia, segregation laws had been rapidly emerging for intrastate travel on the railroads which, at this time, was the major means of long-distance travel. In the 1890s, it was not inevitable that black–white segregation would occur; it was, instead, entirely possible that these emerging state laws could be struck down and the process of integration—however slow and difficult—could have proceeded. The case went to the Supreme Court, and the history of black–white relations in America was forever changed in 1890. Justice Henry Billings Brown—a man who had grown up in the North—wrote for the majority opinion and argued that facilities need not be identical to be equal, and if blacks see their segregation as inferior, "it is not by reason of anything found in the act, but solely because the colored race chooses to put that construction on it." Thus, if blacks saw their segregation as a signal of inferiority, it was in their minds, not in the legal mandate. Writing a strong dissent was Justice John Marshall Harlan, a Kentuckian who had even been a Confederate officer, who predicted just what happened: The *Plessy v. Ferguson* decision would become the legal mantle for creating segregated facilities in all spheres, not just public transport.

It was not until the early 1950s that the *Plessy v. Ferguson* decision was overturned, but by then much of the damage had been done. White America had begun to move: up the occupational ladder, into the suburbs, into better schools, into colleges and universities, and into post–World War II prosperity. Blacks had been shut out during these critical decades between the *Plessy* decision and the *Brown v. Board of Education* decision in 1954, which declared segregated schools to be inherently unequal.

Source: Adapted from a syndicated column by Edwin M. Yoder, Jr., and from C. Vann Woodward's *The Strange Career of Jim Crow*, 1966.

and reflected the post–Civil War belief that blacks had been given a chance and had demonstrated their inferiority. These court decisions were subsequently reversed, but great damage had been done and informal discrimination in housing, jobs, education, and other spheres persists to this day. Such formal legal barriers and the informal climate of discrimination they created made up the legacy which African Americans sought to overturn in the civil rights movement in the twentieth century.

Legal Discrimination in the Twentieth Century   Through the first half of the twentieth century, state and local codes discriminated against blacks in many vital areas of life. In education, African Americans in the South attended segregated and inferior schools, a circumstance supported by state and local codes and enforced with threats of and actual violence from the white community. In housing, Federal Housing Authority (FHA) codes prevented integration of housing subsidized by the FHA, which confirmed and reaffirmed restrictive covenants in trust deeds (that certain ethnic groups could not own property in an area) and discriminatory lending practices of bankers. In the job market, most craft unions and many industrial unions established rules that either restricted or forbade black membership or created separate black auxiliary (and less powerful and effective) unions; in both cases, these practices prevented African Americans from moving beyond a narrow range of lower-paying jobs. In politics, especially in the South, state and local governments enacted voting laws that were differentially enforced for blacks and whites, a practice that kept African Americans disenfranchised. For example, in the 1890s and after, Alabama, Georgia, Louisiana, Mississippi, North Carolina, South Carolina, and Virginia all enforced literacy tests for blacks but not for whites (Bell, 1973). Since two-thirds of the black population in these states was illiterate at that time, the vast majority of African Americans were disenfranchised. Such literacy tests, often loaded with trick questions, were common well into the twentieth century. In contrast, illiterate whites could have the literacy requirement waived if they owned property or if they revealed a "good character" or could understand English. Across all sectors of society, then, African Americans confronted laws and rules that excluded them into the 1960s.

From this blatant legal discrimination—which reinforced and encouraged informal discrimination in housing, schools, jobs, and politics—the civil rights movement was born. For two decades, in the 1950s and 1960s, blacks and sympathetic whites organized to eliminate the legal basis of discrimination. They employed a broad array of tactics—lawsuits culminating in Supreme Court decisions, mass protests, boycotts, sit-ins, and lobbying in Congress. The first big legal victory was the 1954 Supreme Court decision in *Brown v. Board of Education of Topeka, Kansas,* which declared segregated schooling inherently inferior and, hence, discriminatory (Kluger, 1975). By the 1960s, public opinion outside the South had become sympathetic to the black struggle. The result was the enactment of a series of significant laws—the *Voting Rights Act of 1965* and the *Civil Rights Acts of 1964 and 1968.* Congress passed these laws to eliminate legal and informal discrimination in employment, unions, housing, voting booths, and schools.

These laws were not enacted until one hundred years after the Civil War. Although they have helped African Americans enormously in the latter half of this century, these relatively recent laws cannot reverse the damage done by a long history of legal discrimination. Indeed, it was during the one hundred years since the Civil War that the United States was transformed into an affluent,

industrial society; yet many African Americans were not allowed to be benefi-
ciaries of this national success.

Undoing the legacy of legal discrimination is a formidable challenge to American society in the new century. Unfortunately, the 1980s and early 1990s did not
evidence a strong commitment to meeting the challenge. In fact, there have even
been efforts recently to weaken some laws; for example, the Reagan and Bush
administrations sought to soften the Voting Rights Act by limiting funding for its
enforcement by the Justice Department, and by supporting a civil rights law that
virtually eliminated the Voting Rights Act. Moreover, attempts to reinterpret other
laws in the courts, especially with respect to the affirmative action policies stemming from the Civil Rights Act, and to enforce laws selectively, particularly with
respect to job and housing discrimination, have been made by Congress and the
presidents of the 1980s and 1990s. Most important is the virtual absence of political will to create laws to help African Americans overcome the cumulative effects
of legal exclusion from the American mainstream. This lack of political will exists
because the majority of Americans believe that today the inequities African Americans experience are the result of their lack of motivation and individual effort
(Kluegel and Smith, 1986; Kluegel and Bobo, 1993). When a voting majority does
not see the present problem, it is difficult to redress past discrimination. It is not
surprising, then, that many African Americans continue to meet obstacles in their
efforts to participate fully in the institutional structure—economy, education, politics, and housing—of the society.

Nowhere is the lack of knowledge about the cumulative effects of discrimination more evident than in the area of *affirmative action*. The civil rights laws of
the 1960s, as interpreted by Executive Order 11246, required organizations
doing business with, or receiving funds from, the government to increase
minority representation in those organizations (Jaynes and Williams, 1989:316).
In practice, these government mandates applied primarily to businesses receiving (directly or indirectly) government contracts, and to education, especially
higher education. As affirmative action policies were more rigorously enforced
in the 1970s and early 1980s, they became increasingly unpopular. Charges
(both legal and informal) of *reverse discrimination* could be heard from some
white employees and students. Moreover, one effect of affirmative action was
the creation of informal quotas favoring members of minority groups and, to a
lesser extent, women in male-dominated occupations and in the sphere of education; this public perception that quotas do indeed exist is then used to vali-
date the charge that some whites are the victims of discrimination. This charge
has led many people to believe that affirmative action no longer is about equality of opportunities but is about group preferences. Yet, without affirmative
action, or a similar policy, how are the effects of past discrimination to be overcome? Without some degree of preference afforded African Americans affected
by past discrimination, many will have difficulty achieving equality with white
Americans in school and in the workplace.

In recent decades, the courts have issued somewhat contradictory decisions (Marger, 1994:528; Jaynes and Williams, 1989), perhaps reflecting the

public's ambivalence over affirmative action. In some cases, such as *Weber v. Kaiser Aluminum* in 1979, the Supreme Court ruled that employers could use "race" as a criterion for hiring and could employ quotas. A year earlier, however, in *Bakke v. The Regents of the University of California,* the Supreme Court ruled in favor of Bakke, a white male who had been denied entrance into medical school because of quotas for minority students. During the Reagan and Bush administrations, the Supreme Court, which had been generally supportive of affirmative action, began to shift as new appointees to the Court began to influence decisions. Recent decisions not only have weakened the impact of affirmative action but have also made it more difficult for members of minority groups to prove in court that they have been victims of discrimination. As the Court's composition shifted again in the 1990s, it is difficult to predict the fate of affirmative action programs, but it is unlikely that any new laws will be enacted to bolster affirmative action programs in light of the general public's hostility to such programs (Takaki, 1987:223–32; Kluegel and Bobo, 1993). Indeed in 1996, the *Hopwood v. Texas* decision, the first major decision since *Bakke,* went against the University of Texas, which had sought to use "race" as a criterion for special admission policies; and in a highly controversial decision in 1996, the Board of Regents of the University of California eliminated race and ethnicity as criteria for special admission to the university, a decision that will be challenged in the courts but that, like the *Hopwood* ruling, will work against affirmative action as it was practiced in the 1970s and 1980s.

Despite gains in treatment by the legal system, the most volatile point of contact between African Americans and the legal system is the police. In a Gallup 1999 poll of blacks and whites on the question of whether or not the police profile blacks for questioning, 77 percent of African Americans believe that such targeting of blacks occurs, and four out of ten say that they have been stopped for no other reason than the color of their skin (Jet, 2000). This figure increases dramatically among young black men, 72 percent of whom indicate that they have been stopped, some many times. Despite these figures, it is rather surprising that a majority of African Americans have a positive opinion of their local police, but still over one-third do not. And a clear majority of African American men between the ages of eighteen and twenty-four have highly negative views about the police—not surprising since this is the targeted group. A somewhat surprising finding from the poll is that a majority of white Americans—some 56 percent—believe that police profiling of blacks is widespread. Thus, it is clear that negative stereotypes of young black males have worked against the black population who are much more likely to be stopped routinely and questioned by the police than are their white counterparts. Like all Americans, African Americans want to be treated fairly by the police, since this is the portion of the legal system that directly touches their lives. It is not clear that they get the same treatment, and indeed just the opposite appears to be the case. Most of the various mass "riots" and "revolts" of the last half of the twentieth century began with a "routine" police arrest; anger against not only the police but the larger white society often then led to violence that escalated

---

Box 4.4
When Whites Riot and Cover Up

Tulsa was a rapidly growing oil city in 1921. Oklahoma was producing over a third of the country's oil, with Tulsa producing about 90 percent of the state's total oil production. Oil production was driving Tulsa's economy and expanding job opportunities for black workers. However, there was an increasing sense of white nativism in Oklahoma that was being fueled by the Ku Klux Klan. Some portions of the white population began to resent the increasing social and occupational mobility of blacks in Tulsa.

On the morning of May 31, 1921, police arrested a black shoeshine man named Dick Rowland for allegedly assaulting a seventeen-year-old white female elevator operator. The arrest became the springboard for what became known as the *Tulsa Race War*. Despite the fact that the white female did not file charges against Rowland, rumors of his arrest caused 2,000 white persons to demonstrate outside the courthouse demanding that Rowland be lynched.

A confrontation between the white demonstrators and about 75 armed black war veterans who had approached the police offering to help defend the courthouse resulted in an outbreak of violence. According to witnesses, a shot was fired by someone. The white demonstrators assumed it was fired by one of the black war veterans. The black war veterans assumed it was fired by one of the white demonstrators. The clash between the two groups resulted in an invasion of as many as 10,000 whites creating havoc and destruction in a predominantly black neighborhood, Greenwood, home to Tulsa's black teachers, doctors, and laborers.

By the time the governor called in the National Guard on June 1 to bring things under control, about 700 African American families had fled the city looking for safety and about 4,000 African Americans were forced into internment camps

---

until the military was called in to restore order. At the opening of the twenty-first century, there is still anger at the police; and it may have the same disruptive potential that it has had in the past.

Economic Discrimination
Slavery and Its Aftermath   Prior to the Civil War, the economic organization of the South became heavily dependent upon a large slave population. While the historical record does not mark precisely when slavery was first institutionalized, it is clear that by 1670 most black people in America, adults and children, had been forced into lifelong servitude. Slavery became rapidly institutionalized because of the agricultural economy emerging in the South. In contrast to the North, which was beginning to industrialize and urbanize by the time of the American Revolution, the South remained heavily agricultural, relying on the export of cotton, tobacco, hemp, rice, wheat, and sugar. While different states tended to specialize in only some of these crops, they all had one feature in common: the reliance upon an inexpensive and relatively large

guarded by armed whites. The estimated death count was fewer than 10 whites and about 250 blacks. More than 30 blocks in Greenwood had been destroyed and more than 10,000 blacks were left homeless.

As tragic as the riot was for the black community in Tulsa, one of the saddest aspects of it became hidden in Tulsa's past. A lingering rumor about the Tulsa Race War was that many blacks, far more than estimates of white city officials, had been killed and buried in mass graves. The rumor led Don Ross, a state legislator, in 1996 to push through a bill forming the Tulsa Race Riot Commission. The Commission's mandate was to locate survivors of the riot in order to document its history, to determine if survivors were entitled to reparations, and to investigate the rumor about the mass graves.

The Commission's initial findings have confirmed the rumor of mass graves. Testifying before the Commission in September 1999, an 88-year-old man told the commissioners of seeing huge crates standing by unmarked pits in the paupers' section of the city's cemetery. Before he was told to move away from the crates, he admitted, he saw the bodies of four black men in one crate. State archaeologists have been charged with testing the ground in the city's cemetery with radar in order to see if such bodies lie underneath. According to the Commission's chairman, Bob Blackburn, recovering any remains will be the first step toward reconciliation between blacks and whites in Tulsa, and the breaking of a seventy-eight-year-old silence.

Source: This account of the Tulsa Race Riot was drawn from the following sources: Scott Ellsworth, *Death in a Promised Land: The Tulsa Race Riot of 1921* (Baton Rouge: Lousiana State University Press, 1982); R. Halliburton, "The Tulsa Race War of 1921," *Journal of Black Studies* 2 (1972): 333–57; "The Riot That Never Was," *The Economist*, April 24, 1999, p. 29; "Panel Seeks Clearer View of 1921 Tulsa Race Riot," *New York Times*, Feb. 21, 1999, p. 28; "Searching for Graves—and Justice—in Tulsa," *New York Times*, March 20, 1999, p. A14; "A City's Buried Shame," *Los Angeles Times*, Oct. 23, 1999, pp. A1, A16.

labor pool to cultivate large tracts of land. It is not clear whether slavery was the most efficient form of agricultural organization (see Fogel and Engerman, 1974; Genovese, 1965; Williamson, 1984:12–14), but the shortage of labor and the abundance of land in the southern colonies placed a high value on involuntary labor. As a result, slaves were used to initiate the plantation system, and once initiated, the system was operated to "keep in line" a large and potentially volatile population. The initial importation and enslavement of blacks in the seventeenth century was facilitated by the early settlers' cultural beliefs about the "bestial" nature and less-than-human status of Africans (Jordan, 1968). Such negative beliefs facilitated the accelerated pace of enslavement, a process that violated the official core values of American society.

The distribution of slaves in the South reflected the economic priorities and power relations within that part of the country (Stampp, 1956; Starobin, 1970:5). By 1860 there were about four million slaves in the South. Over 50 percent were owned by only 12 percent, who held the large tracts of fertile land that formed the basis of the southern economy. Slavery emerged and persisted largely because a small group of politically powerful landowners required cheap labor and made slavery acceptable in the agricultural sector of the economy, and then, to a very limited extent, in mining, iron production, textile manufacturing, and small industry (Lewis, 1979, 1989; Lander, 1969). Thus, by the dawn of the Civil War, most agriculture in the southern economy and a few industrial and craft sectors (Newton and Lewis, 1978) relied upon slave labor. The institutionalization of slavery in the southern economy, plus the fear of retaliatory violence by slaves, partially accounts for the resistance of this "peculiar institution" to change (Stampp, 1956).

The South countered abolitionist attacks on slavery by further codifying beliefs based on the "Sambo" stereotype (Turner and Singleton, 1978; Boskin, 1986). Although most abolitionists did not hold the Sambo stereotype, even the most radical abolitionist believed in the intellectual inferiority of blacks (Fredrickson, 1971). Differences in the northern and southern belief systems no doubt reflected the respective economic dependency of the northern and southern economies on slave labor. Because few blacks lived in the North, its economy remained unaffected by abolition or the colonization of the black population. In the South, however, the loss of slave labor threatened widespread disruption of the southern economy and lifestyle.

Only a war between the states could break the culturally legitimized institution of slavery in the South. During the brief period of radical Reconstruction afterward, large numbers of blacks gained access to many skilled trades and began to assume ownership of farms. But as noted earlier, Congress in 1877 changed its legislative mind toward ethnic relations. For thirty years thereafter African Americans were systematically excluded from skilled nonfarm occupations and thrust into tenant farming or low-wage labor for white landowners or into menial labor and domestic work in both rural and urban areas. Such a dramatic reversal of the economic policies of radical Reconstruction was legitimized by the limited conception of "equality" of the then-dominant laissez-faire ideology (economic and individual activity should go unregulated) and by the Social Darwinism ("survival of the fittest") of the late nineteenth century.

By the turn of the century, 90 percent of all African Americans remained in the South, with 75 percent living under oppressive conditions in rural areas. For a number of reasons, the quality of life for African Americans, especially those in rural areas, worsened dramatically during the early years of the twentieth century (Hamilton, 1964): (1) The high birthrates of rural families began to exceed their ability to secure sufficient income in the depressed economy of the South; (2) the nature of agriculture changed dramatically with mechanization and the consequent displacement of black labor; (3) the cotton industry, on which many blacks depended for survival, began to move to the Southwest and, then, was devastated by the boll weevil; and (4) many whites used violence—beatings, burnings, and lynchings—to maintain black subordination (Williamson, 1984:180–223; Rable, 1984; Tolnay and Beck, 1992; Aguirre and Baker, 1991). These and other "push factors" led blacks to migrate from the South into the urban areas of the North. By 1914, these "push factors" were combined with "pull factors" from northern cities: The onset of World War I

White violence against African Americans has historically been a means of control and domination. Here, in the twentieth century, two blacks were hanged without trial or due process for supposed crimes against whites.

had cut off European migration while rapidly expanding the very industrial production that had for decades drawn European migrants to American cities. Suddenly, there were economic opportunities for African Americans in northern cities, with the result that between 1914 and 1920, nearly one million blacks migrated to urban areas in the industrial North. This migration was to be the first of a series of large-scale shifts in the black population; by 1960 over three-fourths of that population resided in cities, with only one-half remaining in the South. Patterns of economic discrimination became urban as opposed to rural, and national in contrast to regional.

Many of the early migrants to northern cities initially found jobs during the peak of wartime production, but they also encountered white discrimination and violence (Bonacich, 1976). African Americans tended to live in segregated tenements that early European migrants had abandoned because of their dilapidated and unsafe condition; when blacks ventured into white neighborhoods and into certain occupations, acts or threats of violence frequently occurred. For example, twenty-five "race riots" broke out between June and October of 1919 (Turner, Singleton, and Musick, 1984). This violence was intensified as black laborers were used as strikebreakers in corporate America's effort to stifle the union movement. Whites attacked blacks, then black workers retaliated, bringing a counterattack by whites. The resulting violence forced police to quell such riots. The hostility toward blacks, based on the threat of job displacement, persists today in many urban areas of the Northeast and Midwest.

With the end of wartime production and the onset of the great depression of the 1930s, the economic situation of African Americans worsened once again. Unemployment and hunger increased, and even welfare allocations were differentially distributed among blacks and whites (Pinkney, 1969:33–34). The New Deal ushered in some changes, but the capacity of nascent civil rights groups to generate change was limited. Wage and job discrimination and exclusion from unions continued until well after World War II.

World War II, like World War I, caused a massive black migration to urban areas in both the North and South. As African Americans became concentrated in key wartime industries in urban areas, they began to exert political pressure, forcing President Roosevelt to ban discrimination in wartime industries and pressuring the Congress of Industrial Organizations (CIO) to allow some black workers into the unions' ranks (although most unions, especially craft unions, used informal means to keep black workers out, or in low-paying positions).

Patterns of Present-Day Discrimination   The effects of slavery and established patterns of discrimination remain today. Black workers are overrepresented in menial service jobs; they are underrepresented in professional and managerial occupations; they are twice as likely to be unemployed; they earn slightly less than two-thirds the wages of white workers; and they are twice as likely to be poor. This legacy of slavery costs all Americans a great deal in terms of (1) lost productivity among the large pool of potential black workers; (2) lost consumption of gainfully employed African Americans, which could, in turn, encourage production for all workers; (3) lost tax revenues from African Americans who lack a steady job; and (4) lost federal, state, and local revenues allocated to social welfare programs in order to maintain black households.

The legacy of economic discrimination has been compounded by other conditions over the last two decades:

1. The decrease in skilled and semiskilled blue-collar jobs in the economy at a time when most employment barriers have been eliminated.
2. The movement of employment opportunities to the suburbs, making employment difficult for inner-city blacks to secure because of past housing discrimination (see the section on this topic later in this chapter).
3. The decline in industrial union power and membership at a time when they have become fully open to blacks.

4. The increase in low-paying service jobs relative to the higher-paying and skilled blue-collar jobs that historically allowed many white immigrant ethnic groups to assimilate and become upwardly mobile.
5. The influx of new immigrants who compete with black workers and small-business owners for jobs.
6. The national fiscal crisis, which has reduced the amount of money available for social programs in general, and poverty programs in particular.
7. The resurgence of conservative beliefs that government cannot and should not try to solve the economic problems of African Americans (indeed, government is now seen as part of the problem in that it supports welfare dependency).

Thus, the economic plight of today's African Americans is difficult to address, even though many of the legal barriers to discrimination have been removed. Even though legal and institutional discrimination have receded, more subtle patterns of informal discrimination persist.

Many African Americans today continue to pay a penalty for their skin color when seeking jobs—assuming that they live in an area where they have access to jobs. For example, the Urban Institute in Washington, D.C., sent teams of black and white men as job seekers to over four hundred interviews for jobs advertised in the newspapers of Washington and Chicago. The workers were matched with identical qualifications. The results showed that 15 percent of the white applicants received job offers compared to 5 percent of the African Americans. During the job selection process, white men advanced to the next round of interviews 20 percent of the time, whereas black men did so only 7 percent of the time. White men reported rude or otherwise unfavorable treatment during the job-seeking process 27 percent of the time, while the corresponding figure for black men was 50 percent. These findings were confirmed in a landmark study by the Russell Sage Foundation (1999). Employers still hold many negative stereotypes about African Americans, and these prejudices influence their hiring decisions. In Detroit, for example, it took unskilled and unemployed whites 91 hours to generate a job offer, whereas it required 167 hours for a black to receive an offer. Beliefs that blacks are welfare dependent, that they are more likely to commit crimes, and that they are difficult to get along with all work to bias the hiring practices of employers against African Americans. These stereotypes are particularly pernicious because they place blacks at a disadvantage in job competition with recent immigrants who are not subject to these negative beliefs and who, as a result, are more likely to get jobs than blacks. Thus, despite Americans' beliefs that affirmative action guarantees African Americans favorable treatment, this study indicates that African Americans still experience discrimination.

Once employed, African Americans often are not promoted because of informal discriminatory practices, especially in white-collar corporate jobs. In another pioneering study on women and minorities in nine of the Fortune 500 corporations, the U.S. Department of Labor (1991) found a "glass ceiling" blocking these groups from access to "corporate pipelines" leading to mana-gerial and executive positions. African Americans, in particular, experience this subtle, almost invisible barrier in a variety of ways. First, blacks and other minority groups are more likely than whites to be placed in human resources and public relations positions, which, unlike sales and production jobs, are off the "fast track" to management. Second, blacks are more likely than whites to be excluded from networks, mentor programs, and policy-making committees; as a result, they do not acquire the contacts, information, and experience nec-essary for movement up the corporate ladder. Third, hiring at the executive level is typically conducted outside the human resources and personnel departments, without concern about affirmative action and without systematic efforts by corporate executives or their "head hunter" search firms to create a diverse pool of applicants. Instead, informal networks and discussions usually influence hiring at the higher levels of a corporation, the kind of contact from which African Americans are routinely excluded.

African Americans often encounter another pattern of informal, and per-haps at times inadvertent, discrimination when attempting to set up a busi-ness. For many white Americans, owning and running a business has been one path to affluence. For African Americans, however, this path is strewn with obstacles. African American–owned businesses tend to be economically marginal, labor-intensive proprietorships that must withstand heavy competi-tion from entrepreneurial immigrants vying for the same clientele. Also, it is more difficult for black Americans to secure credit than it is for white Ameri-cans since lending agencies use criteria that favor those with "white creden-tials" (such as higher education, current collateral, and high credit ratings) and those who intend to service white shopping-center clientele. However, while all small businesses are high-risk ventures, there is no evidence that black businesses in ghetto neighborhoods are any more risky than white ventures in white neighborhoods. For example, in the 1960s the Small Business Adminis-tration began extending loans in terms of criteria other than credit history and collateral. In 1964, 98 of 219 special loans went to African Americans; and only 8 of the 219 loans became delinquent and none were liquidated (Turner and Singleton, 1978). For a while the Minority Business Development Agency helped expand minority-owned businesses, but in the 1980s its resources and programs were cut back. Such cutbacks are a form of discrimination, espe-cially when it is recognized that African Americans do not receive Small Busi-ness Administration loans proportionate to their numbers in society. Almost thirty years later, the Federal Reserve Board of Boston issued a report showing that blacks were 60 percent more likely than whites to be rejected for bank loans (Smith, 1992). Thus, the public's perceptions of "preferences" for blacks are inaccurate.

Part of the informal process of discrimination are the criteria defining a good worker—criteria that are biased against African Americans in favor of white Americans. For instance, employers look at formal education creden-tials, which white Americans are more likely to have, for jobs that do not require them. Or, to take another example, only white speech styles and personal demeanor associated with middle-class subculture (which, in reality, are seldom related to actual job performance) are preferred in certain jobs (Jaynes and Williams, 1989:321). Invidious discrimination is thus built into the hiring practices of many of America's businesses—a discrimination that perpetuates the disadvantaged position of African Americans.

Political Discrimination   Without political power, it is difficult for those who experience discrimination to diminish it. Until recent decades, African Americans have been almost completely disenfranchised, with little or no political power. Even today, blacks' participation in the political arena is not proportionate to their numbers because of the long-established pattern of exclusion. Several historical facts explain the low level of political participation in the black community today:

1. Prior to the Civil War, blacks held the right to vote or hold office in only five states (all northern with very small black populations).
2. In the nineteenth century, blacks voted and held office in significant numbers only during the brief period of radical Reconstruction following the Civil War.
3. In the 1870s, when congressional commitment to Reconstruction had waned, when the presidential election of 1876 became deadlocked in the Electoral College and was thrown into Congress, Republicans abandoned the principles of Reconstruction in order to "buy" southern votes. The result was that blacks were systematically excluded from the polls, with virtually complete disenfranchisement in the South by 1895 (Kousser, 1974; Williamson, 1984:224–84).
4. Through a variety of tactics—from poll taxes through "literacy tests" to threats of violence—blacks living in the South remained politically excluded from the 1890s until well into the 1960s (Daniel, 1973). Urban blacks who lived in the North and South had somewhat more voting power, but a broad array of tactics kept many African Americans disenfranchised and diminished the power of those who participated in local and national elections.

Thus, the relative lack of black political power is largely a result of the long history of intended and deliberate political exclusion, especially in the South. The patterns of political discrimination have continued well into this century with strategies such as the poll tax, the "literacy test," and the "Constitution test," which were differentially enforced for African Americans and poor whites. When these measures were declared illegal, administrative obstruction—long lines, much paperwork, elaborate documentation of residence, and so forth—effectively prevented most African Americans from registering to vote. Underlying these obstructions was the frequently implemented threat of white violence visited on the homes of those blacks who sought to register to vote or who actually voted.

It was not until the mid-1960s that many of these exclusionary tactics were declared unconstitutional. With the Voting Rights Act of 1965, political partici- pation among blacks increased. However, the removal of these roadblocks and a growing political consciousness among African Americans caused discrimi- natory political strategies to shift from denying the vote to diluting the impact of black voting power by gerrymandering congressional districts in order to "break up" the ghetto as a voting bloc and spread its votes among two or more districts where whites outnumbered the now-divided African American vote.

In the decades following the civil rights movement and the Voting Rights Act of 1965, African Americans have made significant political gains, espe- cially at the state and local levels (Jaynes and Williams, 1989:208–9; Welch, 1990, Turner and Payne, 2002). Although black voter participation still lags behind that of whites, the elimination of most barriers to black electoral par- ticipation has led to significant changes. For example, approximately three hundred mayors are African American; many of the largest cities in the United States are governed by black mayors. Many city, county, and state leg- islators, municipal judges, constables, and sheriffs, and some standing and select committee chairs in Congress are black. Yet, even with this kind of political representation, African Americans still constitute considerably less than 2 percent of all elected offices and officials in the United States (Joint Center for Political Studies, 1977, 1996; Turner and Payne, 2002). Moreover, at the national level, where important policy decisions affecting blacks will be made, African Americans are not proportionately represented: less than 10 percent of Congress is black; there are no black senators; and aside from some high-profile cabinet members there are very few African Americans in top- level positions in the executive branch of government (Pohlmann, 1990; White, 1985; Turner and Payne, 2002).

Even in areas where African Americans have made real gains—political influence and control of large cities—they have come at a time when political and economic power has shifted to the suburbs and, because of the fiscal prob- lems of most large cities, to state and federal government. Black political con- trol of the large cities really means that black officials must deal with the finan- cial, educational, and social problems that were created by past discrimination and that caused many whites to move to the suburbs. "Control" over cities marked by poverty, gangs, deteriorating schools, high levels of crime, deficit budgets, slums, empty industrial buildings, and expensive social services is not likely to improve the political power base situation of African Americans. City politics does not greatly influence national politics, which is where most important political decisions affecting the welfare of African Americans are ultimately made.

African Americans are almost always elected in locations where they are the majority—with only a few exceptions. Significant numbers of white Amer- icans tend not to vote for black candidates, and so African Americans usually have power only where there is an overwhelming black constituency. Thus, while significant gains in political power are evident, African Americans remain underrepresented in the political system, a system that often fails to address their problems and needs.

Educational Discrimination
Educational Discrimination before and Immediately after the Civil War
By the dawn of the Civil War, all southern states had enacted compulsory ignorance laws for slaves. These laws, which some slaveholders chose to violate, prohibited whites from teaching slaves to read, write, and calculate. Moreover, clandestine schools for slaves operated everywhere in the South;

The U.S. Supreme Court ruled in 1954 (*Brown v. Board of Education*) that separate schools are unequal and thus unconstitutional, but local school boards were often slow to implement desegregation. In 1957 a federal court, in response to legal action by the NAACP, ordered Little Rock's Central High School to admit Elizabeth Eckford, shown here, and eight fellow black students.

and many freed slaves received education in segregated public facilities (Turner, Singleton, and Musick, 1984). In some states, such as North Carolina, literacy among blacks reached as high as 43 percent, but in the Deep South literacy was probably no more than 10 percent.

In the North, educational opportunities were much better for African Americans in the decades before the Civil War. Religious groups, some municipalities, and a number of philanthropists created educational opportunities for blacks. Yet, these opportunities were not universally available. At the higher-education level, the first black university—Lincoln University in Pennsylvania—opened its doors to a few students. In 1833, Oberlin College became the first *mainstream* college to admit African Americans in significant numbers.

After the Civil War, the establishment of free public schools in both the North and South was initiated (Cash, 1941:3–102). Yet, much of the education of African Americans occurred in private schools sponsored by religious societies and philanthropists. By the 1870s, state legislatures had mandated free public education for all citizens, and by 1880, one-third of all black children were registered in school (Weinberg, 1977:45–54). But during the 1880s, the tide turned against black education. Public funding at the local level slowed considerably, although African Americans were required to pay taxes for all schools, both white and black. In some southern states, government spending on African American schools became voluntary. Between 1870 and 1905, the sixteen southern states in which 90 percent of all southern African Americans lived spent one-fourth as much on black schools as they spent on white schools. Most of these black schools were vocational, providing literacy and teaching the rudiments of a trade.

By the dawn of the twentieth century, literacy among African Americans had increased to as much as 40 percent (Turner, Singleton, and Musick, 1984), but still, a system of dual education was firmly in place. This system of separate and decidedly unequal schools became more pronounced as blacks began to move to urban centers in the North and South.

Educational Discrimination in the Twentieth Century   In the urban areas of the North and South, school attendance and literacy increased, but in a segregated school system. In this system, the South spent two to three times as much on white students as on black students, assuring that the latter would receive an inferior education (Bullock, 1967). Moreover, despite gains in literacy within this unequal system, illiteracy among African Americans was six times that among whites, and as late as 1969, it was still four times that of whites. It was not until 1975 that black enrollment in schools reached parity with white enrollment (Turner, Singleton, and Musick, 1984:123). But the quality of education for African Americans was consistently inferior for the simple reason that schools were segregated. Between 1920 and 1940, the pattern of segregated schools spread throughout the United States. In the South, state legislators, local political figures, school boards, and courts all worked to create a separate educational system; in the North, housing discrimination and threats of white violence produced residential segregation, which led to separate school systems.

As this dual system was established, blacks and their white supporters began to raise questions (Kluger, 1975). In the late 1940s and early 1950s, the National Association for the Advancement of Colored People (NAACP) and The Urban League began to push not only for African American voting rights but also for equality in education. This effort culminated in the NAACP's successful appeal in 1954 before the Supreme Court stating that separate schools are unequal and, therefore, are in contradiction to the Fourteenth Amendment to the Constitution *(Brown v. Board of Education of Topeka)*. In rendering this landmark decision, however, the Supreme Court did not set a timetable for its implementation. Hence, local school boards dragged their feet, citing complexities and the need for additional time. Indeed, local officials routinely ignored court orders for desegregation. During the 1960s, however, black and white activism increased and led to the passage of the Civil Rights Act of 1964, which strengthened the federal government's hand in forcing the states to comply with desegregation orders; and hence, under the threat of withholding federal funds and military coercion, the states increased school integration, especially in the South.

A series of court decisions in the 1970s reinforced the push for school integration. In 1971 *(Swann v. Charlotte-MecKlenburg Board of Education)*, the Supreme Court ruled that busing was an appropriate tool for achieving integration; in 1973 *(Keyes v. Denver School District No. 1)*, the Court ruled that evidence of government actions to maintain segregation, such as site selection for schools or manipulation of attendance zones, was sufficient to require desegregation using busing and other means. Yet, in another series of decisions in the 1970s, the Court rejected the regionalization strategy, which would require suburban districts to be part of the desegregation effort in large cities. This latter set of decisions, coupled with white protests and violence over busing, has made the desegregation of the inner city a difficult process. And so, in the 1990s, half of all black students attended schools in which minority groups were overrepresented (Feagin, 1989:244).

In the period between 1920 and 1960, most black students in the South attended black colleges. In the 1950s, however, forced desegregation of state universities in the South began; today, there is little evidence of discrimination in admissions to public universities in either the South or North. At private colleges and universities, the picture is more complicated. A combination of sincere efforts to comply with affirmative action and fear of losing federal funds has led most private colleges and universities, especially those heavily involved in government-funded research, to recruit and assist members of minority groups, especially African Americans. For some institutions less dependent on federal monies, both explicit and covert discrimination in admittance procedures continues. Yet, current efforts by colleges and universities to recruit and assist African Americans have not succeeded in stemming the decrease in African American enrollment, particularly among males (Jaynes and Williams, 1989: 340–41).

African Americans have endured a long history of exclusion from the education system; even today they are overrepresented in poor, minority-filled
schools. While the data are inconclusive, some findings show that blacks who
attend integrated schools are more likely to graduate, attend college, and live
in integrated neighborhoods (Feagin, 1989:242). Thus, to the degree that
African Americans continue to cluster in the inner city, they are more likely to
attend segregated schools and less likely to attend college. In addition, housing segregation remains an important cause of discrimination in education.

As part of the general debate on school vouchers, proponents of using government money to finance private schools often point to the desire of minority
populations, particularly African Americans, to have options besides the public
schools. This sentiment is understandable because the public schools in ghetto
neighborhoods are notoriously bad, in just about every sense: state of repair of
the buildings, equipment and books, teacher qualifications, crowding of class-
rooms, drugs, and danger. Yet, if school vouchers were allowed, it is not so
clear that African Americans would be better off. If there were good private
schools in their neighborhoods, such a program might work. Otherwise, it
would be difficult for poor families to transport their children the distances to
private schools. Moreover, once public school monies go to private schools as
vouchers, the already underfinanced public schools would decline even further, giving those who cannot attend private schools an even worse public
school environment. True, in a voucher program, public schools could receive
vouchers but these would be insufficient to maintain old and decaying facilities, nor would they be sufficient to improve the quality of the curriculum and,
at the same time, maintain security. Thus, vouchers are unlikely to help the
very poor improve their level of access to quality education.

Housing Discrimination   One's place of residence determines access to other
valued resources—jobs, schools, public facilities, health care, and social services. When African Americans experience discrimination in housing, they
become isolated from the mainstream and are, in effect, excluded from other
social arenas, even if there is no intent to discriminate in these arenas. Housing
discrimination has confined many African Americans to inner cities at a time
when jobs have moved to the suburbs and transportation systems to the suburbs have decayed. Housing discrimination works against African Americans
not only in their efforts to find work but also in their capacity to gain access to
decent schools, public facilities, and services.

The first black migrants to northern cities were forced—not only by their
meager resources but also by threats of white violence and discriminatory land-
lord policies—into the decaying cores of the cities. While the wartime industries
of World War I provided many jobs, and while the geographical concentration
of cities allowed easy access from the ghetto to work, a *pattern* of African American residential isolation in urban areas had been initiated. This pattern was
often formalized in communities by restrictive covenants that forbade integrated neighborhoods. During the Great Depression of the 1930s, when economic opportunities vanished in the North and elsewhere, black migration to

the cities waned. During this period the federal government enacted highly discriminatory legislation that forged the current profile of urban America.

The most significant piece of legislation was the federal act creating the
Federal Housing Authority and the FHA mortgage loan guarantee program,
which subsidized home mortgages for whites. In the post–World War II
period, the FHA and the related Veterans Administration (VA) mortgage guarantee programs stimulated the rapid flight of white Americans from the cities
to the suburbs. African Americans were prevented from joining this flight
because of discriminatory administrative rules of law that stated that neighborhoods of "mixed races" could not be subsidized by the government. From
1950 to 1962, the year when President Kennedy finally issued an executive
order to the contrary, the practice of providing FHA and VA loan guarantees
primarily to white neighborhoods continued. Even after 1962, FHA policy was
"ineffectively integrationist."

Industry and commerce began to follow the white population to the suburbs; and eventually, as assembly-line production with its need for large tracts
of land came to dominate sectors of the economy, industry began to pull residents out of the cities. As industry and workers moved out of the city, commerce and service industries followed. Some African Americans were able to
commute to these jobs, but as mass transit services began to deteriorate in the
post–World War II period, commuting became difficult. At the same time, as
the tax base that financed city schools diminished, schools with heavy concentrations of black students languished for lack of financial resources. Furthermore, large suburban communities began to exert enormous political power in
metropolitan and statewide government. Thus, urban–suburban segregation,
largely created by FHA law, has profoundly limited African Americans' access
to jobs, quality schools, and political power.

To cope with the consequences of this segregation, other federal laws have
been enacted, but they have not eliminated slum conditions, and, more importantly, some have exacerbated patterns of segregation. One of the key legislative acts of the New Deal initiated public housing, which, by 1937, had
acquired the social purpose of eliminating substandard housing. Unfortunately, changes in the law in the late 1930s turned administration of the public
housing projects over to the cities, resulting in housing projects that were built
in existing slum areas, which, in turn, perpetuated black confinement to the
inner city. Urban renewal in the decades since the 1950s was another major
attempt to revitalize slum areas and to restore the decaying downtown commercial areas in order to attract middle-class suburbanites back to the city. The
result of the program was the destruction of slum housing, which forced the
poor into public housing projects where few wished to live. Model cities programs, introduced in the 1950s through the 1960s, have not done much better
because they do not attack the basic problem—urban–suburban segregation.

A crucial Supreme Court decision made even more difficult the breakdown
of urban–suburban inequities. In 1973 the Court ruled that suburban communities do have zoning control over patterns of land use in their communities. This
ruling allowed local suburban governments to alter the zoning of land tracts to

keep public housing and federally subsidized home-ownership programs for African Americans out of the suburbs.

Important civil rights legislation of the 1960s has been ineffective in counteracting discrimination because (1) it has often gone unenforced because the civil rights division of the Justice Department is understaffed, underfinanced, and, in the 1980s and today, was overtly unsympathetic and (2) it has placed the burden of litigation on the *individual* against whom discrimination has occurred—a personally and financially arduous process.

More importantly, this legislation does not address the fundamental need for a *mass* migration of African Americans to the suburbs (or a mass white migration to the cities). Of course, any such policy would encounter resistance in local communities, which, under the 1973 Supreme Court ruling, can "zone out" government-sponsored housing for African Americans. One of the ironies of housing laws is that from the mid-1930s until the mid-1960s, whites were given mortgage subsidies by the FHA and VA to move into the suburbs en masse, whereas current laws prevent a similar mass exodus of blacks. Moreover, current Supreme Court rulings prevent the implementation of massive federal programs to integrate the suburbs. Thus, suburban integration must happen slowly, on an individual-by-individual basis. These laws reinforce the discriminatory belief that the absence of African Americans from the suburbs is a result of their failure to avail themselves of "equal" educational and economic opportunities that would allow them to buy a house there.

Throughout the period of suburbanization of whites and confinement of blacks to the cities informal practices of *redlining* have persisted whereby residents of integrated neighborhoods or residents of less affluent neighborhoods with large numbers of African Americans have difficulty securing home mortgages. These practices are now so well documented that special enforcement of antiredlining laws now occurs; but because of the subtlety of the practice, it is often difficult to catch and prosecute the offenders. And even if one could assume that all redlining could be stopped, much of the damage has already been done: African Americans have been denied home ownership because banks would not lend them the money, while equivalently positioned whites have received mortgages and have been able to enjoy the benefits of home ownership (Minerbrook, 1993; Huskisson, 1988; and U.S. Commission on Civil Rights, 1996).

STRATIFICATION OF AFRICAN AMERICANS

Affluent and Poor African Americans: The Widening Gap

As a result of legal, economic, political, educational, and housing discrimination, significant numbers of black Americans have been pushed to the bottom rungs of the stratification system. Indeed, African American families were the only ethnic group to see poverty rates increase in the first years of the new century (U.S. Bureau of the Census, 2002). They tend to have few resources, as was documented at the outset of this chapter, and even fewer prospects for the future. Some African Americans have "made it" out of poverty and the lower socioeconomic stratum. Indeed, the percentage of black families that earn more than the national median family income—around $42,000 per year in 2001—has increased dramatically over the last decade. African Americans are thus divided by social class, and although many middle-class African Americans still encounter discrimination in public places, in jobs, in housing, and in education, they no longer live in poverty.

Many of those outside the middle class live in slums or, even worse, public housing projects in the inner city; they live in crime-ridden and dangerous neighborhoods; they send their children to inferior schools; they work—if they can find work—for low wages in jobs with little security, few benefits, and an uncertain future; they seek help from the welfare system, which erodes their self-respect and which, with new "reforms," will be even less helpful; and if they are women, they are often raising their children alone. Indeed, a majority of black children are now raised by single parents, most of whom are women living in poverty. Thus, the situation for poor blacks has been made worse by the disruption to the family structure.

The African American Underclass: Myth or Reality?

Many white Americans are concerned—indeed, even fearful—of perceived trends in the urban minority population, especially urban African Americans: more babies born out of wedlock; more unmarried women on welfare; more violent crime; more drug use and related crime; more school dropouts and illiteracy; and more unemployed males. Some believe that these social and

Poverty remains a problem for a significant number of African Americans. What some have labeled "the American underclass" is comprised in large part of poor blacks struggling with such social and economic woes as homelessness, joblessness, crime, welfare dependency, and fatherless families.

economic ills are concentrated in "the American underclass" which is presumed to be mostly black (Auletta, 1982). Currently, debate rages in the media, public, and academia over just what this underclass is, who belongs to it, how big it is, and how fast it is growing (Baca-Zinn, 1989; Fainstein, 1993). Definitions vary, but a reasonable one is the convergence of "a number of social ills including poverty, joblessness, crime, welfare dependency, fatherless families, and low levels of education or work-related skills" (Ricketts and Sawhill, 1988:316). Some sociologists are convinced that the black underclass represents a major problem in America (Wilson, 1987).

Documentation of this underclass among African Americans reveals, however, a somewhat different picture (Jencks, 1991:28–102): The proportion of black single mothers collecting welfare has declined since 1974; violent crime rates among blacks have declined; black dropout rates from schools declined in the 1980s; the gap in secondary school graduation rates has closed; and the percentage of 17-year-olds with basic reading skills steadily rose in the 1980s. However, some problems have grown worse: joblessness for males has risen, and the number of babies born out of wedlock has increased to over 65 percent among African Americans, resulting in an increase in single mothers. These data, then, do not support the existence of an African American underclass. The minority of African Americans who do meet the criteria of membership in an underclass receive much publicity, and the much larger African American population is further stigmatized by their activities.

Threats and Hostility toward African Americans

White hostility toward African Americans, and the resulting discrimination, have been fueled by a sense of threat. During slavery, many working-class whites, encouraged by slaveholders, feared the release of large numbers of blacks into the labor market and society in general (thereby destroying the "southern way of life"). When northern industries used African Americans as strikebreakers in the first decades of this century, white workers feared the loss of their jobs. Today, many white Americans fear "black violence" (fostered by the riots of the 1960s and 1990s, the increase in gang activities, the high crime rates, and the perception of a growing "underclass"). Moreover, specific fears about the "costs" of welfare as well as the "taking" of jobs through affirmative action have added to white fears.

These fears have translated into negative stereotypes of African Americans as prone to crime and violence, as morally and sexually promiscuous, as unwilling to work, and as draining the white taxpayers through welfare dependency. In turn, these stereotypes have been used to justify informal discrimination, the dismantling or underfunding of programs to help the urban poor, negligence in enforcing laws or policies prohibiting discriminatory practices against black workers, and, most important, hesitancy in mounting a serious effort at job creation for African Americans. The result is that African Americans' share of valued resources has not increased appreciably over the last two decades, even as formal discrimination has been greatly mitigated. This fact is used to further the negative belief that African Americans have "not taken advantage of their equal opportunities." For example, most media portrayals of black youth revolve around gangs and criminal activity in an attempt to symbolize their purported unwillingness to "take advantage of opportunity" in U.S. society (Lyman, 1990; Reed, 1993; Gomes and Williams, 1990).

RESPONDING TO DISCRIMINATION

Protest during Slavery

During slavery, African Americans were severely limited in what they could do to protest their situation. White violence and the plantation system, coupled with easy physical identification of black-skinned individuals, were extremely effective in maintaining oppressive social control. Music represented one form of protest; *Negro spirituals* depicted the troubles and dissatisfaction of African slaves. Sabotage, such as the burning of barns and destruction of farm tools, was another form of protest. Slaves also practiced quiet resistance, by faking illness and working slowly. Suicide and infanticide (to keep children from being enslaved) were other forms of protest. Running away was perhaps the most effective protest, although being caught meant severe punishment. The *Underground Railroad* to the North for freed slaves, created by northern abolitionists and humanitarians, made this form of protest somewhat successful. Open, and frequently violent, revolt was not uncommon throughout the slave era; Nat Turner's revolt in 1831 was the most famous because sixty whites were killed.

Protest after Slavery

The problem for freed slaves was to build institutions that could, in turn, become resources in their fight for greater equality. After the fall of radical Reconstruction, this became extremely difficult because of the imposition of Jim Crow laws and white violence. Yet, institutions were being built. The church became perhaps the most important and effective institution because it was difficult for whites to deny African Americans the right to worship; indeed, white Americans tended to see the church as pacifying the African American community. In reality, church leaders were the most effective protest organizers in the twentieth century.

Education represented another institution that was slowly built. Historically, gaining access to public schools had been difficult; yet black attendance, even in segregated schools, has increased dramatically from the end of the Civil War until today. In the 1990s, black high school graduation rates were on a par with those of whites, although new problems in dropout rates emerged in the late 1990s. A system of private *Negro colleges* emerged in the late 1800s as a means to circumvent the exclusion of African Americans from private and state colleges in the South. Over time, a public African American college network was created. Today, the challenge in higher education is to increase enrollment

---

Box 4.5
African American Women in the Civil Rights Movement

The most famous leaders of the civil rights movement are men, with Dr. Martin Luther King, Jr., being the most famous of all. But women were also leaders, playing key roles in initiating protests, mapping out strategies, and mobilizing necessary resources. Below are some of the most prominent and important black women in the civil rights movement:

Ella Baker: She was an officer of the National Association for the Advancement of Colored People, a founder of the Southern Christian Leadership Conference, and a supporter of the Student Nonviolent Coordinating Committee.

Daisy Bates: With the support of the NAACP, she played a major role in the integration of the Little Rock, Arkansas, public schools. Single-handedly she spearheaded a grassroots community campaign to enroll black children in all-white public schools.

Mary McLeod Bethune: She was president of the National Association of Colored Women from 1924 to 1928. She established the National Council of Negro Women in 1935, and President Franklin D. Roosevelt appointed Bethune as administrative assistant for Negro Affairs in 1936.

Mary Burks: As founder and first president of the Women's Political Council (WPC) of Montgomery, Alabama, she led the WPC in the Montgomery bus boycott of 1955–1956.

Septima Poinsette Clark: She established "citizenship schools," which combined the teaching of literacy with voting rights organization. The schools spread throughout the southeastern United States and were, in large part, responsible for voter registration of thousands of African American southerners.

Autherine Foster: She was the first black student at the University of Alabama (1956).

---

of black students in formerly exclusionary universities and, simultaneously, to sustain the black colleges, which were once the main source of higher education for African Americans in the South.

African Americans had begun to vote in large numbers during Reconstruction, but political organization was difficult in the post-Reconstruction South because of intense efforts to disenfranchise blacks (Williamson, 1984:224–58; McAdam, 1982:65–67, 1988). Indeed, only with the massive migration out of the South from 1910 to 1930 did African Americans gain political clout, albeit only in their new northern location; and even there, white violence and other tactics kept black voters from gaining political access. In 1940 in the South, no

Fannie Lou Hamer: She founded the Freedom Farm Cooperative in which 5,000 people were able to grow their own food and own 680 acres of land. In 1972 she helped found the National Women's Political Caucus.

Juanita Mitchell: In April 1942, she directed a citizens' march of two thousand people on Maryland's capitol in Annapolis that resulted in the appointment of the Governor's Interracial Commission, the appointment of black police officers, and an investigation into charges of police brutality in the black community.

Constance Motley: Serving as an associate counsel for the NAACP Legal Defense Fund over a period of twenty years, she prepared legal briefs for *Brown v. Board of Education* (1954).

Diane Nash: While a student at Fisk University, she was a key figure in the sit-in movement of the 1960s to remove segregation from restaurants, lunch counters, and theaters in Nashville, Tennessee.

Rosa Parks. Known for her December 1, 1955, refusal to surrender her seat to a white passenger in a crowded Montgomery, Alabama, bus, she was the spark for the Montgomery bus boycott.

Ida Wells: She was a newspaper columnist, writing for the *Conservator,* an African American newspaper in Chicago, and for the *Chicago Tribune.* Wells published a book in 1901, *Lynching and the Excuse for It,* in which she argued that lynching was used by whites to intimidate blacks from becoming involved in politics in order to maintain white power in the South. Wells was one of the founders of the NAACP in 1909.

Margaret Wilson: She became the first black woman to serve as chair of the board of directors for the NAACP.

Source: Bernice M. Barnett, "Invisible Southern Black Women Leaders in the Civil Rights Movement: The Triple Constraints of Gender, Race, and Class," *Gender & Society* 7(2): (1993) pp. 162–82; Jessie C. Smith (ed.), *Notable Black American Women* (Detroit, MI: Gale Research, 1992); Darlene C. Hine (ed.), *Black Women in America: An Historical Encyclopedia* (Brooklyn, NY: Carlson Publishing, 1993).

more than 10 percent of the eligible black voters were registered in any state; in most southern states the registration was under 5 percent, and for four states it was under 1 percent (McAdam, 1982:79). Yet, the existence of the NAACP and its frontal attack on Jim Crow during the 1930s led to a series of favorable Supreme Court decisions that reenfranchised African Americans in enough numbers to form an important voting block. During and after World War II, the black migration continued to the North and West, where the climate of political oppression was less severe. The stage was then set for the political mobilization of the 1960s (for a review of the NAACP and the career of Thurgood Marshall, see Rowan, 1993).

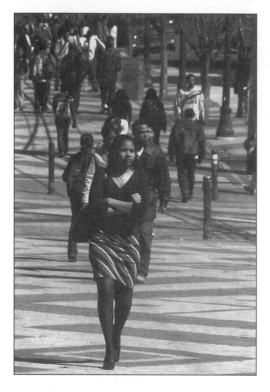

Nationally, colleges and universities are becoming increasingly more female. The imbalance is even more pronounced at historically black colleges such as Clark Atlanta University, where women comprise 71 percent of the student body.

Violence was a common occurrence in the post-Reconstruction era, right up through the interwar years. Until the 1940s, most violence by African Americans was in reaction to the violence initiated by whites, but from the 1940s on, and particularly in the 1960s, black rioting emerged as an effective form of protest, calling attention to problems and, at the same time, prodding fearful white Americans into limited responses to alleviate these problems.

The Last Fifty Years

Beginning in the 1940s and escalating during the 1950s and 1960s, black protest against continued subjugation took an array of forms: The NAACP continued to press its case in the courts, winning such important decisions as *Brown v. Board of Education of Topeka*; individual protests, such as Rosa Parks's refusal to go to the back of the bus, became the rallying cry for boycotts and other forms of collective protest; organized, nonviolent demonstrations, orchestrated by religious leaders such as Martin Luther King, Jr., and by civil rights organizations such as the Student Non-Violent Coordinating Committee, became an extremely effective tool in calling attention to and mobilizing broader sentiments against the continued segregation of public facilities (from lunch counters to schools); voter registration drives, especially after the Voting Rights Act of 1965, dramatically increased the voting power of African Americans; urban violence in the form of riots escalated in the 1960s, calling attention to and forcing a response from government; militant black political organizations and leaders, Malcolm X, the Black Panther party, the Black Muslims, some members, such as Stokely Carmichael, of the Student Nonviolent Coordinating Committee, began to advocate that acts of white violence and oppression should be met with equal force (for a history of the Black Panther party, see Hilliard and Cole, 1993).

These protests created a climate in the 1960s for the passage of a series of civil rights laws, which, in turn, facilitated more protest, more voter registration, more legal redress of grievances, more individual actions against acts of discrimination, more awareness among the general public about the plight of African Americans, and, for a time, more militancy in "black power" parties and organizations. For the first and only time since radical Reconstruction, the federal government, under Lyndon Johnson's Great Society initiative, seriously addressed the problems of the poor in general and African Americans in particular with a broad array of programs. During this period African Americans made significant gains in income and educational attainment, in assistance in housing and medical care, and in job training. Many of these gains have been undone over the last two decades; others have remained static. Today, even in the wake of the Los Angeles riots of 1992—the most costly in history—violent protest is less effective in the 1990s than in the 1960s. More effective is the growing voting power that has come with increased voter registration among African Americans.

The long history of protest has been, at best, only partially effective in combating discrimination. Protest has brought improvement in the economic, political, and social positions of African Americans, but the continued existence of poverty, segregation, and subtly institutionalized discrimination emphasizes that the descendants of the slaves must live under conditions that no other minority group in American history has had to endure. These conditions will, in the future, be the driving force behind further protests—from the violence of alienated gang members, to the retreat of separatist groups, to the legal assault on the more subtle forms of discrimination, and perhaps protests presently unforeseeable.

SUMMARY

African Americans were brought to the United States as slaves and were denied access to the most basic resources, even after slavery ended. Blacks have thus experienced higher rates of poverty, lower incomes, more segregation in housing, higher rates of unemployment, less access to higher education, and shorter life spans than virtually all other groups of Americans. Discrimination is relatively easy to practice against African Americans because their black skin makes them easy to identify. Historically, African Americans have had to endure some of the most vicious negative beliefs, which have been used to justify discrimination in jobs, housing, education, and all institutional spheres in American society. These beliefs and patterns of discrimination have been fueled by the white perception of a "black threat." Such forces have combined to institutionalize discrimination against black Americans.

In the legal arena, in pre–Civil War days, both free and enslaved blacks were denied all rights of citizenship. In the Jim Crow period after slavery and up to the 1960s, African Americans had to overcome a combination of laws, court decisions, and enforcement practices that sought to deny them access to the resources enjoyed by white Americans. In the economic sphere, black workers have been denied access to all categories of jobs, although in recent decades many African Americans have made dramatic progress in securing good jobs. As slaves, blacks were simply excluded from the political process. Their manumission followed by the rapid collapse of radical Reconstruction introduced the Jim Crow practices that kept blacks from registering to vote through the first half of the century. The civil rights movement begun in the late 1950s opened the door for large numbers of African Americans to participate in the American political process. In the educational arena, black slaves were deliberately kept illiterate; after slavery their exclusion from the educational system was maintained as long as possible, especially in the South. Separate schools for blacks and whites, as well as black colleges, represented the fall-back position during most of this century; and only over the last few decades has any significant school integration occurred, and such integration is still hampered by white resistance and the segregation of blacks from white neighborhoods.

In housing, African Americans are the most segregated minority in America, save for those Native Americans confined to reservations. Such segregation was created by white violence against blacks who ventured into white neighborhoods, by lending policies of banks, and by governmental housing programs.

This system of institutionalized discrimination has confined African Americans to the lowest strata of the class system in America, although in recent decades a significant proportion of the black population has been able to overcome discrimination and move into the middle classes. This movement has only highlighted the fate of those who have not been mobile.

POINTS OF DEBATE

African Americans are the only minority in America that was imported against their will as slaves. Slavery existed until 1865, ending with the Civil War. Except for the brief period of radical Reconstruction, new forms of vicious discrimination ensued. For most of the twentieth century, blacks were systematically denied access to jobs, housing, politics, and education, while being subjected to white violence and negative stereotypes. The legacy of these forces haunts America today, posing what we earlier termed the "second American dilemma": How is this legacy to be undone? In answering this question, some hotly debated issues emerge.

1. Does white America owe black America compensation for past acts of discrimination? If so, how much? Most Americans are now against forced busing to integrate schools. Many are antiwelfare, believing that welfare mothers have babies in order to increase their allotments; some are against higher taxes to support any social action programs. Some white Americans want to build more prisons to house those they fear. Many are more willing than in the past to live in integrated neighborhoods but worry (needlessly) about loss of property values. At the same time they complain about reverse discrimination when confronted with affirmative action programs that may limit their employment future. In light of these beliefs and attitudes, it will be difficult to address the legacy of the past, even if white America is sympathetic in the abstract. But are white Americans willing to live with the consequences of these attitudes? This poses another point of debate.

2. The legacy of discrimination against black Americans is manifest in two directions: One is the hard work and effort by many to overcome discrimination; the other is the entrapment of millions of African Americans in the pathologies of decaying urban areas. These pathologies revolve around drug use, violent crime, gang activity, high dropout rates from schools, very high rates of out-of-wedlock births, and an increasing number of single-parent households. Can America allow this to continue and not experience the consequences of these pathologies? Are Americans willing to allow them to fester, thereby putting an even harder and potentially more volatile edge on black–white relations in America?

3. Even in the wake of the most expensive riot in American history, in Los Angeles, Americans in the 1990s remained remarkably insensitive to the depth of the problems. Indeed, they continued to visualize the plight of African Americans in very individualistic terms, as a character flaw of blacks and not the structure of society. Can white Americans continue to blame only the victims of discrimination, and not also their own white ancestors, if not themselves? Anglo-Saxons tend to assume that they are a rational people who pragmatically assess costs and benefits. If blacks are not wise enough to realize the consequences of crime, drug use, out-of-wedlock babies, and unstable families, then they must accept the costs. But the costs will not be only on the victims; they will continue to spill over into the whole society in the form of the enormous costs of building more prisons, health care costs brought about by violence and drugs and despair, the loss of productive activity with so many alienated youth in gangs and the corresponding welfare burden, costs that will burden many mainstream aspects of American society. Thus, can white Americans afford to continue to hold such a narrow view of human behavior as expresses itself in their attitudes toward blacks without addressing the more deep-seated forces behind these social problems?

KEY TERMS / KEY LEGISLATION

Affirmative action, 78

Bakke v. The Regents of the University of California (1980), 79

black codes, 74

"black Sambo" stereotype, 70

Brown v. Board of Education of Topeka, Kansas (1954), 77

Civil Rights Act of 1875, 75

Civil Rights Acts of 1964 and 1968, 77

Fifteenth Amendment (1870), 75

Fourteenth Amendment (1868), 75

Hopwood v. Texas (1996), 79

Jim Crow practices, 73

Keyes v. Denver School District No. 1 (1973), 91

Negro colleges, 100

Plessy v. Ferguson (1896), 75

redlining, 94

reverse discrimination, 78

Swann v. Charlotte-MecKlenburg Board of Education (1971), 91

Thirteenth Amendment (1866), 74

Voting Rights Act of 1965, 77

Weber v. Kaiser Aluminum (1979), 79

CHAPTER 5

Native Americans

Leif Ericson and Christopher Columbus were comparative newcomers to the Americas. Long before their "discoveries," people began to cross the land bridge connecting Alaska with the Asian continent, perhaps as long ago as 40,000 years. They came in search of food, hunting wild game and gathering indigenous plant life, and they settled the entire face of North, Central, and South America. As they settled in distinctive niches, they evolved diverse cultures. Some, such as those among the Maya, Incas, and Aztecs, developed cultures and organizational structures as sophisticated as those in other parts of the world. In what was to become the United States, however, the several hundred societies and perhaps as many as three hundred language groups of the native people were comparatively simple, making them highly vulnerable to conquest by white Europeans. Some were hunters and gatherers, others focused on fishing, a few on herding, and some on horticulture. All constituted viable societies, but upon contact with Europeans, they were to be wholly or partially destroyed. The history of Native Americans[1] after European contact is thus one of conquest and domination.

ON THE VERGE OF EXTINCTION

We can only estimate how large the Native American population was prior to its contact with the Europeans. In 1860, Emmanuel Domenech (1860) estimated that the precontact population was between 16 and 17 million. One of the limitations of early estimates, however, is that they represent subjective impressions and extrapolations based on early contacts with villages and settlements (Snipp, 1989:6). The first generally accepted scientific estimate of the sixteenth-century Native American population was produced by James

---

[1]*A note on terminology:* Our use of the term "Native American" is intentional. First, we use it to emphasize the presence of the population prior to the arrival of European explorers. Implicit is the observation that Native Americans were not "discovered." Second, the term "Native American" encompasses a number of indigenous nations. Jaimes (1992:113) has noted, "American Indian Peoples whose territory lies within the borders of the United States hold compelling legal and moral rights to be treated as fully sovereign nations."

Mooney (1928), who estimated the North American aboriginal population to be about 1.2 million persons at the time of European contact. A more recent estimate puts the precontact population between 2 and 5 million (Snipp, 1989), although some still argue that the number was in fact much larger.

Figure 5.1 illustrates the decrease in the Native American population between 1600 and 1850, from around 2.5 million (a conservative estimate) to only around 200,000 (Spinden, 1928). This decline can be viewed only as genocide, or the virtual elimination of a population. Lack of immunity to European diseases, or what some have called "ecological warfare"; displacement from lands and consequent starvation; widespread killing in "war"; and cold-blooded murder account for this sudden drop (Merrell, 1984; Crosby, 1976). Thus, if we needed an indicator of discrimination against Native Americans, a tenfold drop in the size of the population is as good as any. But this figure does not tell the whole story, for even as the population has replenished itself over the last 150 years, it has done so amid the residue of those conditions that led to attempted genocide.

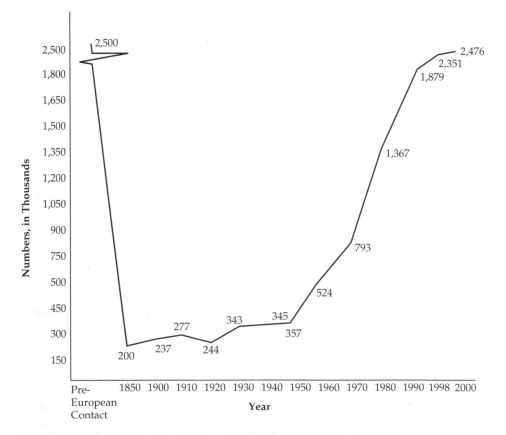

FIGURE 5.1 The Native American population from 1850 through 2000.

Over the last century, with the exception of the 1920s, the Native American population has grown for each census period. Part of the decrease in population during the 1920s has been attributed to an influenza epidemic. By 1930, however, the population was again growing, and by 1950, this growth began to accelerate, a trend that Snipp (1989) suggested constituted a Native American "baby boom" equivalent to the postwar boom among white Europeans. The result was that between 1950 and 2000, the Native American population grew by over 600 percent. This increase was caused by public policy toward Native Americans beginning to change in 1950, and attitudes shifting from fear and hate to sympathy and guilt. Improved health care resulted in lowered infant mortality rates and increased life expectancy for adults.

Another factor in this growth has been the increased willingness of Native Americans to be identified as such, resulting in the increased capability of government agencies, such as the U.S. Bureau of the Census, to identify them. The "self-pride" movements among disadvantaged ethnic groups in the 1960s, for example, increased the ethnic awareness of Native Americans; it became a matter of pride to identify oneself as an "Indian" because the term no longer carried such negative connotations and stereotypes. Indeed, some researchers have suggested that the increase in the Native American population between 1960 and 1980 is not solely the product of health programs (Passel, 1976; Passel and Berman, 1986; Clifton, 1989) but, rather, is a marker of increased ethnic pride as more and more people were willing to proclaim themselves as "American Indian" on U.S. census forms. However, increased ethnic pride may result in a high "overcount" of the American Indian population. According to Passel (1993), while 54 percent of the growth in the American Indian population between 1960 and 1990 could be attributed to demographic factors, 46 percent of the growth resulted from nondemographic factors. One of the most salient nondemographic factors is enhanced self-identification as an American Indian. Thus, there may be as many persons that perceive themselves as American Indians as there are "real" American Indians.

In an effort to sort out the actual numbers of Native Americans, the U.S. Bureau of the Census now asks questions about "mixed" ancestry (in their terms, "mixed races"). The count in Figure 5.1 is for those reporting *only* Native American, and in 2000, this number was 2.4 million individuals. If, however, people reported that they were Native American and members of another ethnic group, the number jumps to 4.1 million reporting some Native American ancestry. Table 5.1 summarizes the numbers of individuals reporting mixed ancestry with whites and blacks. Table 5.2 summarizes the respective counts for tribal groupings for both those reporting only Native American ancestry and for those reporting mixed ancestry. Figure 5.2 reports the count for the ten largest tribal groupings.

Native Americans represent less than 1 percent of the total population, slightly more if we count those of mixed ancestry. In only one state, Alaska, do Native Americans constitute more than 10 percent of the total population. Table 5.3 lists in rank order those states that had at least 1 percent of Native Americans in 2000. In Alaska, with the largest Native American population,

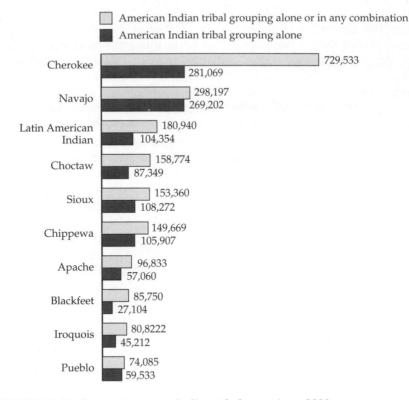

FIGURE 5.2 Ten largest American Indian tribal groupings: 2000.

Source: U.S. Bureau of the Census, 2002. Census 2000 Brief on the American Indian and Alaska Native Population.

TABLE 5.1 Reports on Native American Ancestry, Alone and in Combination with Other Ethnic Groups, 2000

Native Americans	
Alone	2,475,956
In combination with	
other ethnics	4,119,301
With whites	1,082,683
With blacks	182,494
With whites and blacks	112,207
With other combinations	265,961

Source: U.S. Bureau of the Census. Overview of Race and Hispanic Origin. Washington, D.C.: U.S. Census Bureau, 2001.

TABLE 5.2 Size of Tribal Groupings of Native Americans, 2000

Tribal Grouping	One Tribal Grouping Reported	American Indian and Alaska Native Tribal Grouping Alone or in Any Combination[1]
Total	2,423,531	4,119,310
Apache	57,060	96,833
Blackfeet	27,104	85,750
Cherokee	281,069	729,533
Cheyenne	11,191	18,204
Chickasaw	20,887	38,351
Chippewa	105,907	149,669
Choctaw	87,349	158,774
Colville	7,833	9,393
Comanche	10,120	19,376
Cree	2,488	7,734
Creek	40,223	71,310
Crow	9,117	13,394
Delaware	8,304	16,341
Houma	6,798	8,713
Iroquois	45,212	80,822
Kiowa	8,559	12,242
Latin American Indian	104,354	180,940
Lumbee	51,913	57,868
Menominee	7,883	9,840
Navajo	269,202	298,197
Osage	7,658	15,897
Ottawa	6,432	10,677
Paiute	9,705	13,532
Pima	8,519	11,493
Potawatomi	15,817	25,595
Pueblo	59,533	74,085
Puget Sound Salish	11,034	14,631
Seminole	12,431	27,431
Shoshone	7,739	12,026
Sioux	108,272	153,360
Tohono O'odham	17,466	20,087
Ute	7,309	10,385
Yakama	8,481	10,851
Yaqui	15,224	22,412
Yuman	7,295	8,976
Other specified American Indian tribes	240,521	357,658
American Indian tribe, not specified[2]	109,644	195,902
Alaska Athabascan	14,520	18,838
Aleut	11,941	16,978
Eskimo	45,919	54,761
Tlingit-Haida	14,825	22,365
Other specified Alaska Native tribes	2,552	3,973
Alaska Native tribe, not specified	6,161	8,702
American Indian or Alaska Native tribes, not specified	511,960	1,056,457

[1]The numbers by American Indian and Alaska Native tribal grouping do not add to the total population. This is because the American Indian and Alaska Native tribal groupings are tallies of the number of American Indian and Alaska Native *responses* rather than the number of American Indian and Alaska Native *respondents*. Respondents reporting several American Indian and Alaska Native tribes are counted several times. For example, a respondent reporting "Apache and Blackfeet" would be included in the Apache as well as Blackfeet numbers.
[2]Includes respondents who checked the "American Indian or Alaska Native" response category on the census questionnaire or wrote in a tribe not specified in the American Indian and Alaska Native Tribal Detailed Classification List for Census 2000.

Source: U.S. Bureau of the Census, 2002. Census 2000 Brief on the American Indian and Alaska Native Population.

TABLE 5.3 States Where Native Americans
Constitute At Least 1% of Population

State	Percent of State's Population
Alaska	15.6%
New Mexico	8.9
Oklahoma	8.0
South Dakota	7.3
Montana	6.0
Arizona	5.6
North Dakota	4.1
Wyoming	2.1
Washington	1.7
Utah	1.4
Oregon	1.4
Idaho	1.4
Minnesota	1.1

Source: U.S. Bureau of the Census, 2002. Census 2000 Brief on
the American Indian and Alaska Native Population.

the four largest tribal groupings are the Eskimo, Tlingit-Haida, Athabascan, and Aleut, as is reported in Figure 5.3. Only ten cities with 100,000 in population have over 1 percent of their population who are Native Americans, as is reported in Figure 5.4. Thus, although Native Americans constitute just a small percentage of the total population in the United States, they represent a significant subpopulation because they were here first. Since having contact with whites, they have been subject to especially brutal patterns of discrimination. Along with African Americans, who were imported as slaves, the aboriginals of the North American continent represent a special case because of the long history of discrimination that has denied them access to valued resources.

RESOURCE SHARES OF NATIVE AMERICANS

Compared with other ethnic populations in the United States, Native Americans have been severely constrained in their interaction with mainstream society. This isolation is the result of the numerous treaties between the U.S. government and the Native American tribes, which marginalized and subordinated them, thereby limiting their opportunities to secure valued resources (Deloria, 1976).

Income of Native Americans

Historically, Native Americans have had very low incomes, the lowest on average of any ethnic group. Over the last decade, however, the incomes of native Americans have risen somewhat and are now a bit higher than African

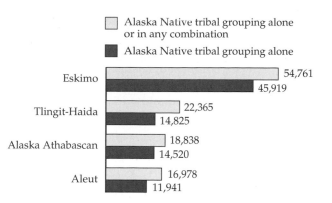

FIGURE 5.3 Largest Alaska Native tribal groupings: 2000.

Source: U.S. Bureau of the Census, 2002. Census 2000 Brief on the American Indian and Alaska Native Population.

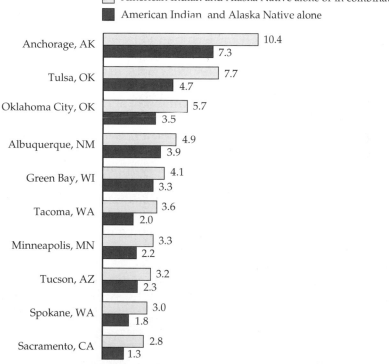

FIGURE 5.4 Ten places of 100,000 or more population with the highest percentage of Native Americans: 2000.

Source: U.S. Bureau of the Census, 2002. Census 2000 Brief on the American Indian and Alaska Native Population.

Americans but still lower than Latinos, non-Hispanic whites, and Asian/Pacific Islanders. Table 5.4 reports on the average median household income for the last three years for which data are available. These data may over-represent the income of Native Americans compared with other ethnic groups because households are often much larger, being composed of several generations. Even without this qualification, $32,000 is a very low income for an entire household; and when compared with non-Hispanic whites, Native American income is only 66 percent of white income.

Occupational Distribution of Native Americans

Native Americans are underrepresented in white-collar occupations and over-represented in service occupations. For example, in 1990 almost 42 percent of Native Americans were employed in white-collar occupations (managerial and professional; technical, sales, and administrative support) compared with 61 percent of white Americans. In contrast, 39 percent of Native Americans were employed in blue-collar occupations (service; operators, fabricators, and laborers) compared with 24 percent of white Americans (Table 5.5).

Occupational distributions for Native Americans are also based on their patterns of residence. In general, Native Americans living on the reservation are more likely to be employed in blue-collar occupations, whereas off-reservation Native Americans are more likely to be employed in white-collar occupations. Moreover, according to Snipp (1989:239), "About 32 percent of Indian men and 37 percent of Indian women living on or near a reservation are employed by federal and local government authorities, compared with 16 percent of men and 17 percent of women residing in nonreservation areas." Many of the government-created jobs for Native Americans living on reservations have been low-paying ones, particularly during the 1970s. Although federal programs have been instrumental in providing an array of public works jobs in trades and construction, like all such "make-work" it is subject to political more than economic forces and does not, therefore, lead to steady employment patterns. The large percentage of Native Americans in service occupations on reservations (contrasted with those living off the reservation) may not, according to Snipp (1989:241), "constitute a major source of employment for the

TABLE 5.4 Median Household Income of Native Americans, Three-Year Average, 1999–2001, Compared with Other Ethnic Groups

Native Americans	$32,116
African Americans	29,870
Latinos	33,439
Non-Hispanic whites	46,305
Asian/Pacific Islanders	55,026

Source: U.S. Bureau of the Census, 2002. *Money Income in the United States: 2001,* by C. DeNavas-Walt and R. W. Cleveland.

TABLE 5.5 Occupational Distribution among White Americans
and Native Americans, 1980 and 1990*

Occupation	White American Population, %		Native American Population, %	
	1980	1990	1980	1990
Managerial and professional	23.7%	28.3%	15.1%	14.4%
Technical, sales, and administrative support	33.4	32.9	23.9	27.4
Service	12.3	10.2	21.0	17.7
Farming, forestry, and fishing	2.6	2.4	5.0	3.8
Precision production, craft, and repair	11.9	12.0	12.9	15.0
Operators, fabricators, and laborers	16.2	14.2	22.3	21.7

*Only 1990 data are currently available.

Source: U.S. Bureau of the Census, 1985; 1990 census-detailed EEO occupations file.

American Indian labor force. . . . It is most likely that many traditional occupations for American Indians, such as traditional crafts (especially those purchased mainly by other Indians), provide a livelihood insufficient for survival and consequently may be practiced as an avocation and not as a principal source of income."

Educational Attainment of Native Americans

On average, the levels of education attained by Native Americans are below those attained by white Americans, although outcomes (e.g., completed years of schooling) at the high school and college levels have increased for the Native American population over the last few decades (see Table 5.6 on page 114). However, Native Americans still account for less than 1 percent of the undergraduate and graduate and professional degrees awarded in the United States (see Table 5.7 on page 115) (Chronicle of Higher Education, 2002).

The gains in education for Native Americans at the high school level may have been affected by the politics of education in the 1970s. During that time, both federal and state governments sought to improve high school graduation and college attendance rates of minority groups in general. Programs such as Upward Bound, for example, sought to increase the presence of minority high school graduates on college campuses; and while these education initiatives dramatically increased the high school graduation rates for Native Americans, a comparable increase in college completion did not materialize. Despite the fact that high school and college graduation rates more than doubled for Native Americans between 1970 and 1990, the gap in college completion between the whites and Native Americans closed very little.

TABLE 5.6 Educational Levels Attained by White Americans and Native Americans, 1970, 1980, and 1990*

	Less than Five Years of School			Four Years or More of High School			Four Years or More of College		
	1970	1980	1990	1970	1980	1990	1970	1980	1990
White Americans	4.5%	3.2%	2.4%	54.5%	69.6%	79.6%	11.3%	17.4%	22.2%
Native Americans	7.7	8.4	6.6	22.0	55.5	63.5	3.8	7.7	9.3

*Persons 25 years old and older. Only 1990 data available.

Source: U.S. Bureau of the Census, 1973a, 1985; 1990 Census of Population and Housing Summary, Tape File 3C.

TABLE 5.7 The Postsecondary Progress of Native Americans, 1981 through 2000

	1981		1990		2000	
Population	Undergraduate Degrees, %*	Graduate/ Professional Degrees, %†	Undergraduate Degrees, %	Graduate/ Professional Degrees, %	Undergraduate Degrees, %	Graduate/ Professional Degrees, %
White	87%	89%	85%	88%	74%	70%
Black	7	6	7	5	9	7
Latino	3	2	4	3	7	4
Asian	2	2	3	3	6	6
Native American	‡	‡	‡	‡	‡	‡

*Includes associate's and bachelor's degrees.

†Includes master's, doctor's, and first professional degrees.

‡ < 1 percent.

Source: U.S. Bureau of the Census, 1995; *The Chronicle of Higher Education Almanac,* August 27, 1999; *The Chronicle of Higher Education Almanac 2002–3,* August 30, 2002.

Life Span of Native Americans

Ignoring for the moment the genocidal practices of the past, Native Americans currently do not live on average as long as whites. Life expectancy, for example, for Native Americans in 1990 was 71 years compared to 74 years for whites (National Center for Health Statistics, 1991). Access to health care helps account for this difference, particularly the limited availability of prenatal care for Native Americans, which increases the chances of babies being born with low birth weight that, in turn, results in infant mortality.

In general, Native Americans have higher death rates during their life course than white Americans. In contrast to whites, Native Americans are twice as likely to be victims of accidents (motor vehicle accidents, drownings, and unintentional injuries such as household fire), more likely to be victims of homicide, twice as likely to commit suicide, and almost three times as likely to die from heart disease (U.S. Department of Health and Human Services, 1993). Thus, life is a resource that is less available to Native Americans than to whites and other ethnic groups.

Housing of Native Americans

Native Americans tend to have lower-quality housing than whites. They are less likely to live in owner-occupied housing, more likely to live in a mobile home, more likely to live in a smaller (that is, number of rooms) home, and more likely to have extra persons per room in each household (U.S. Bureau of the Census, 1973b, 1983a, 1993). Also, the quality of domestic life for many Native Americans is very different from that of most white Americans. For example, fewer Native American households have complete bathrooms, and fewer have access to public water, public sewers, complete kitchens, and telephones (Rumbelow, 2002). In 1990, 5 percent of the Native American population lived in housing units that lacked complete plumbing facilities, compared to 1 percent of the U.S. population as a whole. In addition, Native Americans tend to live in households that lack complete kitchen facilities (5 percent), depend on well water (17 percent), and are not connected to a public sewer system (67 percent). Comparable figures for the U.S. population are 1 percent, 14 percent, and 1 percent, respectively.

As we enter the twenty-first century, housing remains a serious social problem for Native Americans. While the development of public housing on Indian reservations in the 1960s was intended to alleviate overcrowding, more than 40 percent of Native Americans live in overcrowded or substandard housing (Biles, 2000). In testimony before the Senate Committee on Housing and Urban Affairs (2002), Franklin Raines, chairman and CEO of Fannie Mae, noted that low incomes and high poverty rates prevented Native Americans from qualifying for conventional mortgages. He noted in his testimony that in 1999 there were only 471 home mortgages on Indian lands even though an estimated 38,000 families had sufficient income to qualify for a mortgage. As a result, less than 33 percent of the Native American population owns homes compared with 67 percent of the U.S. population (General Accounting Office, 2002).

Aside from the quality of life in most Native American dwellings is the issue of where these dwellings are located. Some 25 percent of the native population lives on government-regulated reservations, separated and isolated from the general population, and another 15 percent live near the reservations. Thus, around 40 percent of the Native American population is dramatically segregated, not just by neighborhood but by territory. This situation, the legacy of past discrimination, forces a significant percentage of Native Americans to be dependent on economic opportunities on and around the reservation, which, typically, is isolated from mainstream society. Most Native Americans view this isolation in a positive light, as a way to recapture their quickly vanishing culture (Ambler, 1990). On the negative side, however, this segregation has increased dependency on the federal government, which in the past has not demonstrated great sympathy for maintaining Native American cultures.

Aside from isolation on reservations, Native Americans are segregated from non-Hispanic whites in metropolitan areas. Overall, Native Americans record a dissimilarity index of 43, which means that 43 percent of whites would

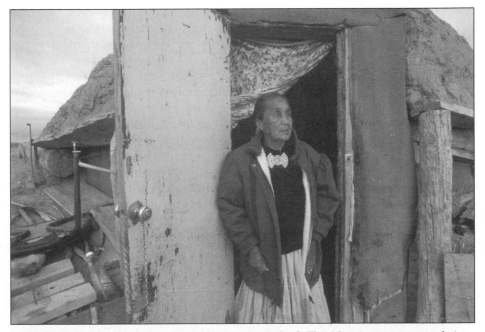

The housing of Native Americans is often substandard. This Navajo woman stands in front of her traditional Navajo hogan—a small octagonal dirt and wood home—on the Hopi Indian Reservation in Arizona. She has no plumbing or electricity.

have to move to new cities and neighborhoods within cities to achieve full integration. This is about the same dissimilarity index that Latinos and Asians reveal, but considerably less than African Americans. Table 5.8 summarizes the indexes of dissimilarity (segregation) for the highest and lowest ranked metropolitan areas.

Poverty of Native Americans

In the 1970s, the U.S. government officially acknowledged that Native Americans were the most impoverished group in the United States and that this population lived in conditions rivaling those found in the Third World (U.S. Department of Health, Education and Welfare, 1976). For example, at that time, 14 percent of Native Americans lived in crowded housing, 67 percent lived in houses without running water, 48 percent lived in houses without toilets, and 32 percent had no means of transportation. Thirty-three percent of Native American families were living below the poverty line compared to 8.6 percent of white families. Ten years later, 24 percent of Native American families were living below the poverty line compared to 7 percent of white families (Aguirre, 1990), but by 1990, conditions had worsened, with almost 36 percent of Native American families living below the poverty line.

More recently, the poverty rates of Native Americans have declined back to what they were in the 1980s, at around 24 percent. Table 5.9 reports the average rate of poverty for Native Americans over the last three years for which data are available (1999–2001) and compares these rates with those of other ethnic groups. As is evident, Native Americans are still the most impoverished ethnic group in America. They are over twice as likely than all other ethnics combined to be in poverty, and three times as likely as non-Hispanic whites to be in poverty.

TABLE 5.8 Metropolitan Areas with Highest and Lowest Dissimilarity Indexes for Non-Hispanic Whites and Native Americans

	Highest			Lowest	
Rank	Metropolitan Area	Index	Rank	Metropolitan Area	Index
1	Flagstaff, AZ-UT MSA	75	1	Panama City, FL MSA	20
2	New York, NY PMSA	75	2	Enid, OK MSA	22
3	Bergen-Passaic, NJ PMSA	72	3	Medford-Ashland, OR MSA	23
4	Yakima, WA MSA	72	4	Pedding, CA MSA	24
5	Nassau-Suffolk, NY PMSA	72	5	Eugene-Springfield, OR MSA	25
6	Newark, NJ PMSA	72	6	Pensacola, FL MSA	25
7	Tucson, AZ MSA	68	7	Yuba City, CA MSA	25
8	Pittsburgh, PA MSA	67	8	Atascadero-Paso Robles, CA MSA	27
9	Middlesex-Somerset-Hunterdon, NJ PMSA	64	9	Modesto, CA MSA	27
10	Chicago, IL PMSA	64	10	Oklahoma City, OK MSA	28

Source: Frey and Myers (2002).

TABLE 5.9 Poverty Rates for Native Americans, Three-Year Average, 1999–2001, Compared with Other Ethnic Groups

	Poor (%)
All groups	11.6%
Native Americans	24.5
African Americans	22.9
Latinos	21.9
Non-Hispanic whites	7.6
Asian/Pacific Islanders	10.3

Source: U.S. Bureau of the Census, 2002. *Poverty in the United States: 2001,* by B. D. Proctor and J. Dalaker.

THE DYNAMICS OF DISCRIMINATION AGAINST NATIVE AMERICANS

Identifiability of Native Americans

Movie stereotypes aside, it is not so easy to identify Native Americans physically, for such characteristics as high cheekbones, reddish complexion, black hair, almond-shaped eyes, and very little male facial hair are not universal among Native Americans, and any of these characteristics can be found among other populations (Snipp, 1989:26). In contrast to these popular notions of who "Indians" are, more explicit biological definitions seek to highlight the five genetic features unique to Native Americans: earwax texture, organic compounds in urine, blood types and Rh factor, fingerprint patterns, and the ability to taste the test chemical phenylthiocar bamide (Snipp, 1989). Although trivial in any genetic sense, some of these characteristics, especially those related to "blood quantum," were to become the bases for constructing a social definition of who is "Indian." The need to define an Indian based on blood quantum became important at the turn of the nineteenth century when the U.S. government took an active role in determining land rights for Indians and non-Indians in the western United States (Meyer, 1991; Harmon, 1990; Smits, 1991).

In the late nineteenth century, the U.S. government made a systematic attempt to identify Native Americans. Jaimes (1992) suggests that this effort stemmed more from an interest in limiting treaty obligations than in promoting collective identity among native peoples. The vehicle for doing so was a *blood quantum* measure, or the degree of "Indian blood" an individual possessed. *The Dawes Act of 1887*, also known as the General Allotment Act, empowered the government to "test" blood levels to identify someone as an "Indian" and thereby entitled to government treatment under treaty obligations. If this degree was below certain levels, then treaty obligations could be ignored.

To this day the *percentage of Indian blood* is an important bureaucratic marker for who is entitled to government assistance and who qualifies for special programs, such as affirmative action. For example, in 1986 the Department of Health

Box 5.1
What's in a Team Name?

The use of an ethnic label as a mascot is perhaps one of the most degrading things that can happen to a population. It is a sign of disrespect and low regard. If one doubts this conclusion, let us rename some prominent teams: The Washington Negroes, the Florida State Jews, the Cleveland Italians, or the Atlanta WASPs. Or, let's construct some new names that reflect the ethnicity of an area: The Los Angeles Dodgers can become Los Angeles Mexicans; the San Francisco 49ers can become the San Francisco Chinamen; the Anaheim Angels can become the Anaheim Viets; the Chicago Bears can become the Chicago Polacks; the New York Giants can become the New York Spics.

In the United States, no ethnic group other than Native Americans is used as a mascot. Yet, when efforts are made to change the name of a sports team on the basis of this inappropriate usage, there is often resistance. Some teams, such as the Stanford Cardinals (formerly the Indians), have changed their names, but most have not.

Atlanta Braves mascot, Homer the Brave.

and Human Services proposed that one-fourth blood quantum be a requirement for receiving medical services at Indian Health Service clinics (Snipp, 1989). In adopting this approach—which no other ethnic population must submit to—the government presumes that blood makes "Indians" a distinct race with certain behavioral propensities (Bieder, 1980). More materially, the earlier Dawes Act used "blood" to determine who was eligible for land or, more important, who was not entitled to land because of insufficient "Indian blood." As a consequence, between 1887 and 1934, the land base to which Native Americans were entitled was reduced from 138 million acres to 48 million acres (House Committee on Indian Affairs, 1934). For those Native Americans who did qualify to receive land, most found that the allocated land was arid or semiarid, almost useless for agriculture. In contrast, the most attractive and fertile native-occupied land was reserved for nonnative populations (Deloria and Lytle, 1983).

Negative Beliefs about Native Americans

Despite their visibility in U.S. popular culture, Native Americans did not earlier occupy a meaningful place in the sociohistorical fabric of U.S. society (Churchill, 1993). In the past, Native Americans often were either "noble savages" or "savage redmen" in movies and on television. Native Americans were stigmatized as pastoral relics in an industrial society: the cigar store Indian and the Indian face engraved on the nickel. Moreover, Native Americans often are portrayed as partially mute in popular culture. In American literature, "the Indian" tends to be a passive witness to others' actions. For example, Queequeg in *Moby Dick,* Tonto in *The Lone Ranger,* and Chief Broom in Ken Kesey's *One Flew Over the Cuckoo's Nest* do not speak. The same may be rightly said of most other Native American characters inhabiting the pages of Euroamerican fiction (Durham, 1992:428). And even the depiction of Native Americans as silent has resulted in a set of negative beliefs (Osborne, 1989; Jones, 1988; Churchill, 1992).

Savage Redmen   The portrayal of the Native American as a ruthless killer of white settlers in movies and television can be traced to the early stages of European contact (Stedman, 1982). As Europeans moved westward, they discovered that they would have to either remove the Native Americans from their lands or learn to share the land. Rather than attempt to live alongside the natives, European settlers decided to take the land. When the natives resisted, European settlers produced the ruthless savage stereotype (Brown, 1970; Shively, 1992). The death of European settlers was seen as a savage act imposed upon innocent people. Such stereotypes became common in the media of the time, which tended to sensationalize and caricature, and promoted a tidal wave of anti–Native American sentiment (O'Connor, 1980).

"Fat Cat" Capitalists   Land has always been a pivotal feature in conflicts between Native and white Americans. One of the more recent negative beliefs is that Native Americans have become "fat cats" from the minerals and

---

Box 5.2
"Whites" As Team Mascots

In Box 5.1 we asked the question, "What's in a team name?" The focus is on the use of Native Americans as mascots for team sports. While most white persons may not see a problem with sports teams using Indians as mascots, how would white people respond if they were used as a sport team mascot?

An intramural basketball team organized by Native American students at the University of Northern Colorado adopted "Fightin' Whites" as their team mascot. The team is made-up of Anglo, Native American, and Hispanic players. The team T-shirt symbolizes the "Fightin' White" as a 1950s-style white man with dimples and shiny, tidy hair. The T-shirt bears the slogan "Every thang's gonna be all white!" According to the students, they adopted "Fightin' Whites" as their mascot because they wanted to raise awareness about culturally insensitive mascots in a community (Eaton, Colorado) debate regarding a local high school's use of an Indian mascot. The high school's mascot is a caricature of a hook-nosed Indian brave wearing a loincloth, a feather sticking out of his braid, and arms crossed over a bare chest.

Ray White, a Mohawk on the college basketball team, said about the team mascot, "It's not meant to be vicious; it is meant to be humorous. It puts people in our shoes, and then we can say, 'Now you know how it is, and now you can make a judgment.'"

White persons in Eaton have expressed their disappointment with the basketball team's "Fightin' Whites" mascot, especially because it has caused Native Americans to become more vocal about their opposition to the high school's mascot. A white resident in the community reflects its sentiments: "It's gone on for years. Why are they just now bringing it up? If they are offended, sorry, but, I mean, why? How is this offending you? They say, 'The big nose, the potbelly,' but those are little things. There are other issues in the world to be worried about."

---

resources on their land—a belief that is empirically wrong in light of their poverty rates (Anderson, 1992). At issue is the potential wealth in Indian lands—oil, natural gas, uranium, or other resources. Churchill and LaDuke (1992:241) note that "approximately one-third of all western U.S. low-sulphur coal, 20 percent of known U.S. reserves of oil and natural gas, and over one-half of all U.S. uranium deposits lie under the reservations."

The stereotype of Native Americans as "fat cats" is negative in that it implies that Native Americans are undeserving of these resources. Similar to the early stereotype of Native Americans as "unwanted land occupants," the negative portrayal of Native Americans as "fat cats" reinforces their perceived threat to white society and its control of resources. This stereotype has facilitated the federal government's transfer of mineral-rich Native American lands to U.S. control (LaDuke, 1981) and has limited the amount of opposition by

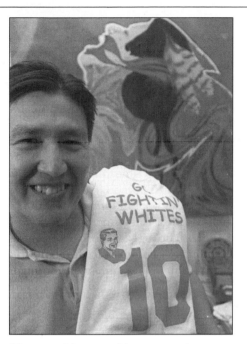

How would most whites respond to seeing a Native American sports team adopt "Fightin' White" as their team mascot?

What do you think? Should Native Americans adopt mascots based on white cultural stereotypes as a strategy for convincing sports teams to remove mascots based on Native American cultural stereotypes?

Source: Julie Cart, "Irked by Mascot, Team Retaliates," *Los Angeles Times* (March 15, 2002), p. A12.

white society in the appropriation of these mineral-rich lands. For example, the bulk of the ore-bearing portion of the copper belt found on the Papago reservation during the 1920s was removed from the Papago domain by the U.S. Congress.

The expansion of casinos on Indian reservations has created a new version of the "fat cat" capitalist stereotype. The "casino fat cat capitalist" depicts Indians as millionaires with luxury homes and automobiles, and an unlimited source of money from Indian casinos. According to Barlett and Steele (2002), the "new" fat cats in Indian casinos are non-Indians who serve as investors and consultants and who pocket as much as 40 percent of the total revenue generated by Indian casinos. However, the reality for Native Americans is that while a few tribes have made their members wealthy, the vast majority of Native Americans do not benefit from Indian casinos (Safire, 2002). For example,

---

Box 5.3

The Cost of Indian Identifiability: The Passage
of the Indian–White Miscegenation Laws

The Disney studios made a lot of money bringing the story of Pocahontas to the movie public. The image of Pocahontas was romanticized in popular thinking to show the "noble" character of Indian and white relations. The reality, however, is that the marriage between Pocahontas and John Rolfe in Virginia in 1614 was hardly representative of the times, let alone a catalyst for other Indian–white marriages.

The English colonists were surely not very interested in promoting marriages between whites and Indians, but instead were more interested in promoting their "racial purity" by controlling such interracial marriages. For one thing, the English colonists were unwilling to accept Indians, even Christianized ones, as equals. According to Karen Woods (1999:51), the passage of Indian–white *miscegenation laws* was a means for white men to assert "power over people of color and over white women."

According to Woods, the English colonists' fears of blood mixture between Indians and whites resulted in the passage of these laws that prohibited marriage between Indians and whites, and that outlined harsh punishments for white women giving birth to "interracial bastards." Indian–white miscegenation laws were passed in Virginia (1691), North Carolina (1715), Massachusetts (1786), Rhode Island (1798), and Maine (1821). Most of the other colonies and surrounding territories avoided the existence of Indian–white miscegenation laws by enacting laws prohibiting the "entry" or "settlement" of Indians.

Source: Karen Woods, "Law Making: A 'Wicked and Mischievous Connection': The Origins of Indian–White Miscegenation Law," *Legal Studies Forum* 23:37–70 (1999).

---

twenty-three tribes with casinos earning more than $100 million a year accounted for 56 percent of the $8.2 billion in total Indian gaming revenues in 1998—yet, the tribes' members comprise about 5 percent of the total Native American population (Pace, 2001). One can observe in Table 5.10 that Indian gaming benefits the smaller tribes, while the larger tribes, such as the Navajo and Zuni, do not receive any gaming revenue—revenue that could significantly improve the quality of life for the Navajo and Zuni by improving housing conditions and reducing poverty.

Early negative stereotypes emerged out of conflict with Native Americans, and these stereotypes became an active force in legitimating virtual genocide, in encouraging land grabs, and in establishing patterns of institutionalized discrimination. More recent stereotypes, such as the image that economic problems have been redressed through casino revenues, could lead to a decrease in the government's efforts to redress the long-standing poverty of Native Americans.

TABLE 5.10 Annual Casino Revenue for Select Indian Tribes

Tribe	Population	Casino Revenue per Member*	Federal Aid per Member
Navajo	260,010	$ 0	$ 912
Hopi	11,267	0	2,006
Mississippi Choctaw	8,823	25,048	5,717
Seminole	2,817	87,682	8,540
Mashantucket Pequot	677	1,624,815	2,304
Miccosukee	400	250,000	20,560
Santa Ynez	159	1,257,862	8,360

*Based on annual casino revenue divided by the number of tribal members. Of course, if the actual "profits" that go to the tribes were divided by the number of tribal members, the per-member amounts would be dramatically lower.

Source: Barlett et al. (2002).

Institutionalized Discrimination against Native Americans

Legal Discrimination The early European explorers and settlers described the Native American as innocent, ingenuous, friendly, and naked. In a sense, the Native American was seen as childish—one of the early stereotypes about them (Jarvenpa, 1985). As more European settlers arrived, English concepts of property—land transfer, titles, deeds—were inserted into the relations between the settlers and the natives (Delgado and Stefancic, 1992). It is not surprising to find, then, that much of discrimination against Native Americans was tied very closely to the legalistic legitimation of land grabs by European settlers. The bulk of this discrimination is found in legal documents, especially treaties, that defined the nature of Native Americans' presence and residence on their own land.

The taking of Native American land by whites was philosophically legitimized by the principle of *Manifest Destiny,* in which "European Americans believed that through divine ordination and the natural superiority of the white race, they had a right (and indeed an obligation) to seize and occupy all of North America. . . . During the nineteenth and twentieth centuries, the philosophy of Manifest Destiny was accompanied by several pieces of legislation that accomplished under . . . law that which would not have been legally justifiable through military force" (Morris, 1992:67). Some of the central pieces of legislation that defined the U.S. government's relationship with Native Americans include the following (Churchill and Morris, 1992).

- *The Indian Removal Act (1830).* Andrew Jackson used this act to force the mass relocation of the Creek, Cherokee, Choctaw, Seminole, and other Indian nations during the 1830s. The intent was to open up the territory east of the Mississippi for settlement by white Americans and their African slaves.
- *The Major Crimes Act (1885).* This act allowed the United States to extend its jurisdiction into Native American territories. Since the sovereignty of Native American territories was defined by treaty, this act nullified the

---

Box 5.4
Who Were the Real "Savages"?

Historical analyses dispute the stereotype of the wagon train of white settlers being attacked by hordes of "screaming Indians" (Hurtado and Iverson, 1994). Between 1840 and 1860, when the Plains migrations occurred, some 250,000 white settlers crossed the Great Plains on their way farther west. During this period 362 white Americans and 426 Native Americans died in all the recorded battles. Cooperation was much more common between migrants and natives. For example, regarding Indian and white relations on the California frontier, Hurtado (1982:245) has noted that "instead of resisting the whites, restricting settlement, and impeding development, California's Indians worked obediently in the whites' fields and homes in return for food and shelter."

The real savagery came from federal troops and federal agents who sought to pacify the Native Americans, killing them arbitrarily and making their lands available to the white settlers. While the Native Americans certainly defended themselves, most of the massacres were committed against Native Americans. In the early 1800s, Governor William Henry Harrison of Indiana expressed concern that "a great many of the Inhabitants of the Fronteers [*sic*] consider the murdering of the Indians in the highest degree meritorius" (quoted in Edmunds, 1983:262). As Figure 5.1 demonstrates, the vast majority of Native Americans were killed by 1850.

treaty's purpose, which had permitted Native Americans to exercise their own jurisdiction within their own territories.

- *The General Allotment Act (1887).* Also known as the "Dawes Act," this act was designed to break up the collective ownership of Indian lands by requiring Indians to identify themselves by means of a "blood quantum" code. Under the act, "full-blood Indians" received the deeds to land parcels over which the U.S. government exercised control for twenty-five years, and "mixed-blood Indians" received "patents in fee simple"—basically land rental agreements—and were forced to accept U.S. citizenship. As a result of the act's implementation, the United States acquired over 100 million acres of Native American land between 1887 and 1934.
- *The Indian Citizenship Act (1924).* This act confers U.S. citizenship on all Native Americans born within the territorial limits of the United States. The act's purpose was to curtail the demand for indigenous identity among Native Americans. To protest, the Hopi and Onondaga refuse to acknowledge the act by issuing their own tribal passports.
- *The Indian Claims Commission Act (1946).* There is some speculation that this act originated, in part, as a response to the role the United States played at the Nuremberg trials. The act was designed to provide legal recourse to those Native Americans who felt that their land was unjustly taken away from them. The act established the Claims Commission, which was

responsible for hearing cases brought forward by Native Americans. The commission, however, was not empowered to return land to any Native American; rather, it was required to assign a monetary value to the land in question—"at the time it was taken." As a result, awards given out by the commission tended to be very small. In general, the act gave the United States the tool with which to legitimize its claim to Native American lands.

- *The Relocation Act (1956).* This act created job training centers in urban areas for Native Americans. The purpose of the act was to force Native Americans off the reservation by offering job training opportunities only in urban areas. Native Americans participating in the job training programs were required to sign formal agreements that they would not return to their reservations.
- *The Alaska Native Claims Settlement Act (1971).* The act removed the sovereign status of the Indian nations in Alaska by incorporating them into the United States. Approximately 44 million acres of Native American lands were turned into U.S. assets. The importance of this act is that the incorporation of Native American lands included the oil beneath and the timber on top.

Treaties were the first step in the colonization of Native Americans. Most of the legal concepts—such as land deeds and land tenure—were foreign to natives, but they accepted treaties as a "good-faith" attempt at coexistence with the whites. Native Americans perceived treaties as a recognition of their sovereignty as Indian nations and assumed that they were on an equal legal footing with the United States. The second step in the colonization of native Americans was congressional legislation, such as the acts reviewed above, which became a tool for displacing Native Americans from their lands (McDonnel, 1991; Parker, 1989). Congress's efforts to alter the original treaties with Native American nations were motivated by the white settlers' demands for yet more land. Without their land, Native Americans lost their sovereign status and became a fully colonized population.

All these manipulations of the law increasingly undermined the promises of the 1787 Northwest Ordinance:

> The utmost faith shall always be observed towards the Indians; their land and property shall never be taken from them without their consent; and in their property . . . they shall never be invaded or disturbed . . . ; but laws founded in justice and humanity shall from time to time be made, for preventing wrongs being done to them, and for preserving peace and friendship with them.

Such laws, as it turns out, were used as a tool for doing great wrong.

Political Discrimination   Native Americans were squeezed politically both ways: The treaties defined each native nation as a "foreign" government, albeit heavily regulated by the U.S. Congress. Hence, the members of these "Indian nations" could vote and exercise their political rights only within their "tribe" and "tribal council." Not until 1924 with passage of the Indian Citizenship Act could they vote outside their reservation. Even after 1924, when

---

Box 5.5
What's in a Gravesite?

Obviously, dead bodies are in a gravesite. Only Native Americans, as a conquered people, have had to endure the desecration of their gravesites and the religious-cultural significance of these sites. Let us propose an alternative scenario: A crew of Native American archaeologists arrives at a cemetery in which members of an ethnic group are buried. They lay a grid over the site, and with careful picking, dusting, sorting, and recording, they then empty the gravesite of its bones. These are then carted back to a reservation, where they are stored in large drawers, labeled and numbered, and used for research by Native American scholars who want to know about a particular ethnic group. Perhaps some of the bones are reassembled and put on display; maybe some are dressed up in native costumes and put on display in a reservation museum.

Few non–Native Americans would tolerate such treatment of their ancestors. And yet, many Americans cannot understand why Native Americans are upset at the desecration of their ancestral burial grounds.

In an attempt to prevent further removal of artifacts from Indian burial grounds, the U.S. Congress approved the Native American Graves Protection and Repatriation Act of 1990 (Coughlin, 1994; Tsosie, 1999). Two important provisions in the act are (1) museums are required to notify tribal groups of remains for which the tribes may have a claim or cultural link and (2) goods excavated on federal or tribal land belong to the Indian tribal group that claims the goods.

Native Americans could vote, discriminatory practices—literacy tests, poll taxes, informal discrimination, gerrymandering of districts—were used to discourage their voting. Thus, Native Americans were excluded from full political participation and of course from assuming local, state, and national political offices. At the same time, regulation by the *Bureau of Indian Affairs (BIA)*, whose key administrators have traditionally been whites, limited Native Americans in their ability to determine their fate on the reservations where they could vote. John Collier, for example, Commissioner of Indian Affairs from 1933 to 1945, accused the Bureau of Indian Affairs of despotism rooted in rules and regulations that sought to dispossess Indians from their lands and increase the Indians' impoverishment (Kelly, 1975; Kunitz, 1971).

In recent years, Native Americans have gained more political power. They have increased their numbers at the voting booths and, consequently, in political office—particularly at local levels. Also, the BIA has become less restrictive and more sensitive to the needs and interests of its clients. Yet, the legacy of past discrimination remains today, and its consequences for the Native Americans need to be discussed.

The Political Consequences of Being Conquered "Nations"   As we have noted, treaties were utilized to subdue and then dislocate Native Americans from their land—thereby opening up the land to white settlers. By dislocating them from their lands, the federal government removed the basis—land—on which Native Americans could demand political sovereignty (Deloria, 1969; Brown, 1970); with a reduced territorial land base over which they could exercise political power, Native Americans lost power vis-à-vis white Americans. According to Deloria (1992) the concepts embedded in the treaty agreements between Native Americans and the federal government were rooted in the idea of the European ministate. European states would utilize diplomatic relationships, such as treaties, to coexist with other populations within a territory. However, such relationships enabled the stronger, more powerful participant to dominate the weaker, less powerful participant. As a result, the door was open to take land from or to colonize the land of the weaker participant, and as colonization proceeded, less care and concern in negotiations with Native Americans was necessary.

Native Americans entered treaty agreements with the belief that they would be accorded equal political status with the United States and did not perceive treaty agreements as the basis by which an expanding nation, the United States, would usurp their lands. According to Deloria (1992:269), it was Native Americans' misperception of treaty agreements that resulted in their being regarded as "suspect" in the political infrastructure of U.S. society:

> Formal diplomatic relations were established with the various indigenous peoples and international political status was accorded them. The difficulty, however, was one of perception. European mini-states had family relationships with the rulers of larger nations, they were contiguous to the powerful countries of Europe, and they represented long-standing historical traditions going back to the time of original settlement when the barbaric tribes had divided the Roman Empire. Indians could not claim this history and since they were of a different "race," and had different religions, languages, and cultures altogether, their political rights, even when phrased in European terms, were always considered to be intellectually suspect.

Treaties were a blatant expression of political discrimination by the United States against Native Americans. To enhance the political colonization of Native Americans established by treaty, the federal government utilized legislation such as the Major Crimes Act (1885), General Allotment Act (1887), Indian Citizenship Act (1924), and Indian Reorganization Act (1934) to extend its jurisdiction over Native American lands (Williams, 1990). This legislation gave the federal government absolute control over land tenure and the political governance of "Indian nations." Indeed, the federal government increased the role of nonnatives in tribal decision making, and according to Robbins (1992:90), this colonial administration of natives often operates under the guise and illusion of self-determination by tribal councils:

> The current reality is that American Indian governance within the United States has been converted into something very different from that which traditionally prevailed, or anything remotely resembling the exercise of national self-determination. Through the unilateral assertion of U.S. "plenary power"

over Indian affairs, a doctrine forcefully articulated in the 1885 *United States v. Kagama* case, the status of indigenous national governments has been subordinated to that of the federal government. . . . Under legislation such as Public Law 280, which emerged during the 1950s, the status of Indian nations has been in many cases again unilaterally lowered by the United States, this time to a level below that of the states, placing the indigenous governments affected by the change in approximately the same postures as counties. . . . In sum, it is accurate to observe, as has been noted elsewhere, that American Indian nations within the geography presently claimed by the United States exist in a condition of "internal colonization."

Political Control by the BIA   The BIA was originally housed in the War Department (the precursor to the current Department of Defense), a clear signal that the bureau was designed to control a conquered people. Later, the BIA was moved to the Department of the Interior, but a bureaucratic pattern had already been set. Because Native Americans were a conquered enemy, tight regulation of their internal political affairs could be justified. Only federal prison inmates, and perhaps the Confederacy in the brief period of radical Reconstruction after the Civil War, have experienced this degree of external control by government. Some kind of protective agency like the BIA was perhaps necessary when it was established in 1825, the period when genocide was at its peak. But the consequence of bureaucratic regulation has been much like that of contemporary welfare programs: It created dependency; it undermined Native American culture; it denied its clients self-respect; and it most significantly undermined the capacity for self-governance. Even today, as greater efforts are being made at encouraging self-governance, the colonized status of Native Americans on their reservations thwarts such efforts. In turn, the lack of self-governance and the dependence on the federal government is used to justify continued government intrusion, thereby perpetuating the colonized and dependent status of many Native Americans.

Much of the problem resides in the structure of the BIA itself. As a highly centralized bureaucracy with its central offices located in Washington, D.C., the bureau is too removed from its clients. From this central office, the bureau fans out into area administrative offices, then to around sixty field installations, such as boarding schools and irrigation projects, and finally into several hundred minor installations. Until recently (and even today but less so than in the past) too much authority has resided in Washington and the area offices, which are staffed primarily by nonnatives. The result is that those closest to the problems of Native Americans in the field installations have the least authority and must constantly seek higher approval by nonnative administrators.

In addition to this source of inefficiency and insensitivity to the needs and problems of its clients, the BIA bureaucracy must cope with myriad tribal rules, archaic legislative acts, recent legislation, and judicial precedents when seeking to make important decisions. For example, there are close to 400 treaties, well over 5,000 legislative statutes, hundreds upon hundreds of Interior Department and solicitor rulings, over 600 opinions submitted by the attorney general, around 100 tribal constitutions, almost that many tribal charters, and vast numbers of BIA administrative procedures. With this complex load, decisions are made slowly and given unnecessarily detailed review. Administrators become ritualists who lose sight of the goal of the BIA—to assist Native Americans—and, instead, often view the interests of the BIA and its clients as opposed. The conflict between Native Americans and the BIA is most evident in the area of economic discrimination. The BIA–administered treaties, bureaucracy, and efforts to thwart Native American self-determination have inhibited economic development on the reservations.

A recent report from the National Academy of Public Administration (1999) draws further attention to the mismanagement of the BIA, noting that "the lack of credible management of BIA appears to impair its capacity to represent Indians within the administration and before Congress." The report notes that record keeping is so incomplete and chaotic that internal auditing arms of the BIA cannot monitor the $1.7 billion budget. Indeed, the report concludes that management is so lax in the BIA that the agency currently violates federal laws governing finances. Even the current head of the BIA acknowledges that the criticisms of the report are justified. Thus, the BIA continues to be a serious problem in lives of Native Americans.

The BIA is not the only governmental agency abusing Native Americans. In 1999, government lawyers for the Treasury Department, which manages trust fund accounts worth some $500 million for 300,000 Native Americans, were found to have given false testimony to the federal judge overseeing lawsuits against Treasury for mismanagement of the fund. In a shocking report, the Treasury Department was found to have shredded 162 boxes of documents related to the case and then lied to the judge about its actions. These actions occurred while the judge was hearing testimony that the Treasury Department had also destroyed microfilm potentially pertinent to the case. Thus, other governmental agencies have conspired against the interests of Native Americans, the very group that they are supposed to be serving. It is not surprising, therefore, that the government is viewed suspiciously by Native Americans, since the same old patterns of deceit and obfuscation persist at the beginning of the twenty-first century.

Economic Discrimination   One reason European explorers ventured to the New World was to find lands they could exploit. These European explorers assumed that by conquering as many "foreign" lands as possible, the economic power of their country would increase. The settlers that came to what is now the United States also saw land as necessary for establishing their own economic base in their new surroundings. The treaties between the federal government and the Native American nations were a crucial step in colonizing the natives; these treaties, and later acts of Congress, displaced natives from their lands, making these lands accessible to white settlers. As a result, Native Americans became economically colonized—their lands were not under their control to use as an economic tool. Jaimes (1992:127) notes that the manner in which the federal government robbed Native Americans of their economic power could be highly devious:

In constricting the acknowledged size of Indian populations, the government could technically meet its obligations to receive "first rights" to water usage for Indians while simultaneously siphoning off artificial "surpluses" to non-Indian agricultural, ranching, municipal, and industrial use in the arid west. The same principle pertains to the assignment of fishing quotas in the Pacific Northwest, a matter directly related to the development of a lucrative non-Indian fishing industry there.

The loss of their lands and resources undercut Native Americans' economic infrastructure; they were unable to derive a livelihood from stock raising, herding, and agriculture. For example, in 1940, 58 percent of the Navajo reservation derived a livelihood from raising sheep and farming, but by 1958 the number had dropped to below 10 percent. Speaking for the Native Americans, Winona LaDuke (as quoted in Jaimes, 1992:128–29) states that the denial of livelihood has produced poverty and hopelessness:

> [We] have the lowest per capita income of any population group in the U.S. We have the highest rate of unemployment and the lowest level of educational attainment. We have the highest rates of malnutrition, plague disease, death by exposure and infant mortality. On the other hand, we have the shortest life-span. Now, I think this says it all. Indian wealth is going somewhere, and that somewhere is definitely not to Indians. I don't know your definition of colonialism, but this certainly fits into mine.

Unemployment and dependency on welfare are the results of economic discrimination (Tinker and Bush, 1991; Ainsworth, 1989). According to Morris (1992:70), what makes the economic condition of Native Americans unique is the amount of political and economic control as well as manipulation exercised by the BIA. The BIA often creates employment opportunities for Native Americans that keep them tied to governments. According to a report prepared by the U.S. Commission on Civil Rights in 1976, on the Navajo reservation, for example, 35 percent of the working-age population was employed year-round, leaving 65 percent of the working-age population unemployed; of the 35 percent, the majority (over 60 percent) was employed in government programs. The unemployed population is likely to depend on federal subsidies (e.g., welfare) for their livelihood, and federal programs employing only a small proportion of Navajo people assure the dependence of a larger proportion on the welfare system. Churchill and LaDuke (1992) argue that this pattern of maintaining Native Americans at a subsistence level continued through the 1980s and into the 1990s. Indeed, the budgetary cutbacks in social services during the Reagan and Bush administrations threatened even the base subsistence of Native Americans.

One effort to increase the resources available to Native Americans, and in turn to increase their degree of independence, has been to seek agreements with corporations to extract resources from reservation lands in exchange for rents and profit shares. Although the BIA has led the way in this effort, the economic condition of Native Americans (largely created by past BIA actions) places them in a poor bargaining position. Moreover, the corporations often

Casinos such as Foxwoods, in Ledyard, Connecticut, offer some hope for greater economic viability on Indian reservations. However, it will take much more than casino revenues to offset the cumulative effects of past economic, political, and legal discrimination.

gain a low-wage labor force and a nonregulated work environment, especially with respect to safety and health codes for workers.

The economic dependence of Native Americans on federal employment programs and social services increases their colonized status in the United States, even when negotiating with private corporations. Native Americans experience economic discrimination that prevents them from utilizing their central asset—land—to become economically self-sufficient. As a consequence, they remain economically dependent on government on the one side and potential victims of predatory practices of economic enterprises on the other.

The proliferation of casino-style gambling on some Indian reservations is often seen as a potential way to overcome the cumulative effects of past economic discrimination. One hundred and sixty-six of the 550 tribes had casinos in 1996, with 28 losing money and only 54 making enough money to offer $10,000 per tribal member. A report written in 1999 by the BIA concludes that "the results of shifting federal Indian policies, coupled with limited resources and investments in Indian communities and Indian people, cannot quickly be reversed by a few good years of casino revenues." Moreover, even with casino revenues, the BIA calculated that in 1998, tribes received only about one-third of what they needed for basic problems, such as child welfare, courts, land management, and assistance to the elderly. Funding fell short by at least $1.2 billion in meeting the needs of Native Americans. In asking for the BIA report, Congress wanted to consider shifting the allocation of federal monies to the poorest tribes, because some smaller and more affluent tribes get much more funding per person than larger, poorer tribes. Yet, the report cautioned against this policy, and Native American leaders are adamantly against reallocation. Their reasoning is that all Native American tribes are underfunded and that to take from one tribe to give to another is simply a way "to equalize poverty."

Educational Discrimination   Education was a key element in efforts to colonize Native Americans. In general, formal education was designed to facilitate submission; it is not surprising, therefore, that the "education" of the Native American population began very early after the arrival of the Europeans (Cross, 1999). For example, as early as 1611, French Jesuit missionaries established schools along the St. Lawrence River to educate Indians in the French manner (Mulvey, 1936). During the early 1600s, Spanish Jesuits in California developed a system of mission schools that focused on teaching Indians in Spanish as required by the Spanish government (Bishop, 1917). These early educational efforts emphasized "conversion" of the native to European culture and language, with the result that Native American languages and cultures were suppressed. Noriega (1992:373–74) has noted:

> In effect, the system by which Native Americans are purportedly "educated" by Euroamerica has from the onset been little more than a means by which to supplant indigenous cultures. This has had, or at least has been intended to have, the predictable effect of demolishing the internal cohesion of native societies, thereby destroying the ability of these societies to resist conquest and colonization.

The Educational Model   The educational model imposed on Native Americans by Europeans was rooted in the boarding school. Children were required to attend schools away from their homes, where they were rarely permitted to visit their families. The Bureau of Indian Affairs promoted the boarding schools as the best vehicle for assimilating Indian youths into American society (Trennert, 1982). As a result, Indian youths were often removed from their homes at the age of 6 and were not returned to their homes until the schooling was completed around the age of 18. When "educated" Native American children returned home, they had often lost much of their own culture and their place in this culture. As Noriega (1992:381) notes, "Altogether, the whole procedure conforms to one of the criteria—the forced transfer of children from a targeted racial, ethnic, national, or religious group to be reared and absorbed by a physically dominating group—specified as a Crime Against Humanity under the United Nations 1948 Convention on Punishment and Prevention of the Crime of Genocide."

Native American families attempted to prevent the dislocation of their children by hiding them from education authorities. Lummins (1968) documents efforts by the Hopi to prevent Mormon missionaries from sending their children to the Intermountain School in Utah. After Hopi parents refused to hand their children over to the Mormon missionaries, federal troops were called in to round up the children. The Hopi greeted the troops by showering them with rocks. The troops subdued the Hopi, rounded up the majority of their children, and sent them to a boarding school in Utah. One result of the Mormon missionaries' involvement in Indian education was the fracturing of the Hopi into two factions—*Mormon Hopi* and *traditional Hopi* (Titiev, 1944; Thompson and Joseph, 1944).

Higher Education   While boarding schools were designed to dislocate native youths from their tribes and families, higher education focused on two concerns: (1) vocational training rather than advanced academic studies and (2) the mainstreaming of Native Americans into white society (Wright and Tierney, 1991). Despite the efforts of Dartmouth and Harvard to educate select Native American students, tribal resistance to higher education was widespread. Historically, Native American tribes have regarded the higher education of their youths as a last step in their isolation from the tribe. For example, the Six Nations' response to an invitation from the College of William and Mary in 1744 to send their sons to the college was (as quoted in Wright and Tierney, 1991:13) the following:

> We love our children too well to send them so great a Way, and the Indians are not inclined to give their children learning. We allow it to be good, and we thank you for your Invitation; but our customs differing from yours, you will be so good as to excuse us.

The Indian Reorganization Act of 1934 was the U.S. government's first step in shaping higher education policy for Native Americans. Until then, religious missionaries and charities had initiated efforts in this area. The Indian Reorganization Act of 1934 attempted to increase Indian participation in higher education by establishing loan and scholarship programs, but students remained reluctant to pursue a higher education because they regarded college as a hostile and alienating environment.

It was not until the 1970s that Native Americans were able to address the issue of tribal colleges. The Indian Self-Determination and Education Assistance Act of 1975 and the Tribally Controlled Community College Assistance Act of 1978 were instrumental in shifting control of higher education from the federal government to the tribes. Native Americans could now develop a higher education system that was neither paternalistic nor assimilationist in its goals. As a result, there are now thirty-two tribally controlled colleges in twelve western and midwestern states (American Indian Higher Education Consortium, 1999). Together, these institutions service about 11,000 students and enroll about 9,200 students on a full-time basis. However, these colleges are dependent on the U.S. federal government for their financial existence. It may be that higher education for Native Americans may not survive as long as

---

Box 5.6
Problems Faced by Indian Youth

While Indian casinos attract a lot of public attention, other aspects of the American Indian community are ignored. It is often assumed by the American public that Indian gaming provides Indian communities with financial resources that allow them to live better than most Americans. It is also believed that Indian gaming results in financial gains that enable Indian communities to rid themselves of social problems.

One social problem that has been increasing in Indian communities is violent crime, especially among Indian youth. Indian youth are facing challenges that often result in violence and drug and alcohol abuse. Senator Ben Nighthorse Campbell has stated, "The greatest challenges facing American Indian youth are overcoming the obstacles to living a normal childhood, receiving a sound education, and being equipped to compete for jobs in the modern economy. Obstacles such as violence, drug and alcohol abuse, poorly funded schools, discrimination, and racism place incredible burdens on American Indian youth." Senator Campbell has identified social forces—normal childhood, a sound education, and job skills—that are important to altering the life experiences of Indian youth away from negative social outcomes. Accordingly, Senator Campbell identifies some of the social correlates that are associated with negative social outcomes for Indian youth—violence, drugs, and alcohol abuse.

VIOLENCE

There is no question that one outcome of participation in gang activities is violence. The number of Indian youth involved in gangs became more noticeable after 1990. Before 1990, less than 10 percent of Indian communities reported gang problems among youth. The Bureau of Indian Affairs noted in 1997 that 132 tribes reported 375 gangs with almost 5,000 members operating on or near Indian reservations. In 2000, 23 percent of sixty-nine Indian communities reported active youth

---

it is dependent on a government that has a history of ignoring the cultural and social rights of the tribes. As Wright and Tierney (1991:17) have observed:

> Because Indian students most often live in economically poor communities, tuition is low and local tax dollars do not offer much assistance. Congress has authorized up to $6,000 per student, but, in reality, the amount released to the colleges decreased throughout the Reagan era so that by 1989 the amount generated for each student was only $1,900. . . . One would think that if the government was serious about increasing opportunities for Indian youth, then colleges would be provided the funds necessary to aid those youth.

The history of formal education for Native Americans has been marked by deprivation of their cultural, linguistic, and social identity (Davis, 1998; Deloria and Laurence, 1991). Boarding schools were developed with a patergangs, with the majority (59 percent) of Indian communities reporting the number of gangs between one and five. The offenses that Indian youth gang members are most often involved in (by order of decreasing frequency) are: graffiti, vandalism, drug sales, aggravated assault, burglary, theft, and robbery.

DRUG AND ALCOHOL ABUSE

The alcoholism death rate for Indian youth between the ages of 15 and 24 is 5.5 deaths per 100,000 compared with 0.3 for other minorities and whites. Indian youth are arrested at twice the national average for alcohol-related crimes. The drug-related death rate for Indian youth is 3.3 deaths per 100,000 compared with a death rate of 3.0 for other minorities and 2.3 for whites.

DEATH

Indian youth are 58 percent more likely than either black or white youth to become crime victims. Indian youth account for 13 percent of all Indian deaths, compared to 4 percent for other minorities and 3 percent for whites. The suicide rate among Indian youth is 2.7 times the rates for other minorities and whites. Indian youth under the age of 15 are murdered at a rate of 2.6 per 100,000 compared with a rate of 1.8 for other minorities and 1.2 for whites.

There is increasing concern in Indian communities that the needs of Indian youth are being ignored. The preceding statistics suggest that Indian youth are at risk in American society, probably more than other minority or white youth. Tribal leaders are concerned that the increasing participation of Indian youth in criminal and deviant activities puts the Indian community at risk. In particular, the participation of Indian youth in criminal activities challenges Indian community notions of collectivism and sharing. Indian youth are vital to the continuity and strength of the Indian community. As such, American society must not lose sight of what needs to be done to help Indian youth meet the challenges they face.

Source: Arrillaga, 2001; Campbell, 2000, pp. 1–5; Major and Egley, 2002; Wound, 2000.

nalistic goal—to civilize the "savages" by having them trade in their moccasins for shoes, their language for English, and their cultural beliefs for traditional western religion (Bartlet, 1992). Overall, higher education has not created the same opportunities for self-fulfillment and advancement available to white Americans or other minority groups.

STRATIFICATION OF NATIVE AMERICANS

By almost any indicator—median income, years of schooling, job classification, housing, medical care, life expectancy—Native Americans are at or near the bottom of the resource-distribution system. Their socioeconomic position is perpetuated by the reservation system: Native Americans are isolated from the broader society in the government's effort to maintain bureaucratic control and in their own attempt to preserve what is left of their indigenous cultures. Coupled with the fact that much of their land (which could serve as an economic base for mobility within and between Native American and non–Native American class systems) has been lost, the prospect for economic development on reservations is uncertain. Those nations located on land rich in natural resources have some hope if they can secure capital and avoid nonexploitive relations with both the government and the private sector.

The impoverishment of the Native American population emerged and persisted because of the dynamic processes outlined in Chapter 2 (see especially Figure 2.3 on page 41). Native Americans were readily identifiable because of their cultural and organizational distinctiveness, and they have historically posed threats to white Americans, many of whom saw them as potentially inhibiting the growth and expansion of society (Russell, 1994). As a result, a range of negative beliefs—from "the savage" to "the fat cat"—has legitimized discriminatory practices: attempted genocide under the guise of war, continued acts of violence and murder, isolation on reservations, land grabbing, denial of voting rights, removal from traditional lands to new and unfamiliar reservations, efforts to force Native Americans to conform to European culture, stealing of mineral and resource rights, and rigid bureaucratic control by agencies of the federal government. All these forces sustained the identifiability of Native Americans while denying them resources. The result was the creation of not only a colonized population but also an ethnic caste.

To break this cycle of discrimination, individual Native Americans face difficult choices: to stay on impoverished reservations and try to preserve what is left of their culture or to enter a Eurocentric society that is not prepared to facilitate their upward mobility. In either case, the majority of Native Americans will remain isolated in either the lower socioeconomic stratum of mainstream society or the impoverished reservation system.

RESPONDING TO DISCRIMINATION

War as a Nonviable Response

The initial response of Native Americans to the European invasion of their homelands appears, on balance, to have been one of cooperation and accommodation, punctuated by acts of violence. As it became evident to Native Americans that their territories were to be occupied and that they were to be displaced, more conflict occurred. Given their numerical and technological disadvantage, however, war was not a viable response for the Native Americans. Indeed, war led to near extinction. By 1871, the remaining Native Americans and their nations had been conquered, moved to reservations, and made wards of the federal government.

Retreatism as Another Nonviable Response

One response of colonized populations is to mount retreatist social movements in the belief that supernatural powers will intervene and return the people to some idealized era. Among Native Americans such *millenarian movements* occurred frequently in the latter part of the nineteenth century and remain in some form to this day.

The most famous millenarian movement occurred in the 1870s among the Great Plains natives in *Ghost Dance groups* who were responding to a vision that Native Americans would return on a train in great numbers just as the earth swallowed up all white people. When this did not occur, the movement died down, but a decade later, a new Ghost Dance vision stimulated another movement. Although these movements did not persist, they initiated some cooperation among tribes, an initiative that would have increasing significance.

As the Ghost Dance movement receded, *peyotism* spread through the Great Plains. A mild hallucinogen, peyote gave religious ceremonies a new power because of the experiences induced. This movement sought to develop an intertribal religion, mixing some elements of Christianity and Mormonism that had been forced upon them with holdovers from their own religions. This movement was assailed, especially because drugs were involved; nonetheless, under the constitutional protection of religious freedom, it became organized as the Native American Church in 1918 and affiliated with Christian groups (Price, 1978). Over the decades, Native American criticism of Christianity has mounted, but membership continues to increase. The Native American Church was the first successful effort at *pan-Indianism,* the unification of Native American nations for explicitly political purposes (Stewart, 1987).

Pan-Indianism

In a sense, the Ghost Dance groups represented pan-Indianism; the peyote sacrament evolved into the Native American Church, which has taken on explicitly political goals. The Iroquois Confederation represented an earlier version of pan-Indianism but was confined to the Iroquois, as were a number of similar confederations dating back to the time of the first contact with Europeans.

It was only after decades of BIA domination that Native Americans began to unite in significant numbers (Snipp, 1986). The National Congress of American Indians (NCAI) was the first truly nationwide organization to represent Native Americans and to engage in active lobbying in Washington (much as the NAACP and Urban League have done for African Americans). This organization has had numerous successes in overcoming restrictive laws and abusive bureaucratic practices by the BIA. Perhaps its greatest accomplishment was to establish the Indians Claims Commission, which has been active and successful in returning land to Native Americans and in remunerating Native Americans for past abuses.

One of the more radical movements seeking to rally native Americans in pursuit of
political goals, the American Indian Movement is known for its confrontations with the
federal government and the Bureau of Indian Affairs. Here, a crowd gathers to mark
the 30th anniversary (in 2003) of AIM's standoff against the government at Wounded
Knee, South Dakota.

The *American Indian Movement (AIM)* represents a more radical movement
to organize Native American nations to pursue political goals, a movement
dominated by Plains tribes. The founders, Clyde Bellecourt and Dennis Banks,
began by using both confrontational tactics—such as patrols to monitor the
police—and more subtle strategies such as alcohol rehabilitation and school
reform. The AIM is best known for its confrontations with the federal government and the BIA. *Fish-ins* to protest government interference with traditional
Native American fishing areas, seizing Alcatraz Island in the San Francisco
Bay in 1969, and the Wounded Knee confrontation brought considerable
media notoriety to the AIM and, perhaps even more importantly, sensitized
many white Americans to the plight of the descendants of the first Americans
(Eagle, 1992).

Under President Nixon in the 1970s, some progress was made in addressing Native American grievances. But the intensity of confrontation has not
diminished; indeed, it has intensified because of the accurate perception that
the progress of the 1970s waned in the 1990s and that the government relies on
conservative tribal leaders' judgments in making policies. Moreover, infight-
ing among factions of Native American militants has escalated the violence, as
has the perception that a civil rights movement much like that among African
Americans could be more successful (Schaefer, 1990:196). Yet, the influence of

the AIM appears to be waning, and a new point of conflict has emerged: control and development of the resources on and under Native American land.

The Economic Battle

In 1975, the *Council of Energy Resource Tribes* (CERT) was formed, with the goal of forming an OPEC-like cartel to coordinate the development of, and perhaps manipulate the market for, the resources on reservation land. Vast reserves of oil and other key resources are located on Native American lands. Yet, the effort to develop and control these resources has not been highly successful. A few notable exceptions can be found, but CERT has threatened many people and mobilized large mineral and energy companies in ways that may be counterproductive to Native American economic advancement, although the long-term efforts of CERT may prove otherwise.

Other economic development programs are based on the special status of reservation lands as sovereign nations—albeit easily invaded and highly regulated nations. The use of reservations for gambling has increased over the last decade; the shift from bingo and card parlors to much more sophisticated gaming resorts has been financed and managed by hotel and gambling interests from nonreservation locations, such as Las Vegas and Atlantic City. These new kinds of enterprises provide employment and cash flow for tribes, but they rarely lead to independence from outside economic interests, who take the lion's share of profits and who maintain management control of the hotels and casinos. Moreover, gambling invites further government regulation in an effort to avoid the infiltration of organized crime and other illegal activities.

Thus, through organized protest, punctuated by sporadic violence, Native Americans have significantly reduced the government's abusive practices. Yet a basic dilemma remains: Much of Native American culture is gone, and yet assimilation into the Eurocentric mainstream is difficult and, for many, undesirable. If economic development, self-governance, and increased prosperity are to be achieved on the reservation, then new cultural traditions, new sources of start-up capital, and new relations with government and industry will have to be created. Pan-Indian organization, effective lobbying, and strategic protests offer the best hope for the future.

SUMMARY

Long before Europeans discovered the Americas, earlier immigrants from Asia had settled and established viable societies. These societies were, however, comparatively simple; though they had existed for thousands of years, they were no match for the Europeans who by 1850 had virtually eliminated the native populations of the Americas. The conquest of "American Indians" and their subsequent confinement to reservations has left a legacy of discrimination rivaled only by the treatment of African Americans, who were imported as slaves. In terms of income, access to jobs, educational attainment, rates of poverty, standards of housing, and life span, the original Americans rank at the bottom on almost all shares of valued resources in the society.

This condition has been sustained by the identifiability of Native Americans and by the embellishment of "distinctiveness" by the government's emphasis on "blood" and other biological features (rather minor ones). Such identifiability has been accompanied by derogatory stereotyping of Native Americans as savages, cigar store Indians, fodder for killing by "noble" cowboys, reservation drunks, fat cat capitalists, and many other vicious stereotypes. Only recently have these stereotypes been mitigated by some superficially more favorable portrayals of Native Americans. They still must endure the humiliation of being used as athletic team mascots and disrespect to their burial grounds via archaeological assaults. Identifiability of Native Americans has been encouraged by a system of government categories and policies, which, along with negative stereotyping, has legitimized discrimination via treaty agreements that have been routinely violated by Anglos, forced transfers of populations, mendacious practices by the Bureau of Indian Affairs, bans on voting, diminution of citizenship rights of the first Americans even on their reservations, loss of land ownership and the economic potential of these lands, bias in hiring, and inferior schools on and off the reservation. By any indicator of well-being, Native Americans are worse off than any other ethnic population in America because of discrimination.

Native Americans have fought this discrimination, first by unsuccessful wars, then by retreatism in the face of their conquest, and recently by active movements to foster a pan-Indian culture. The call of pan-Indianism engages Native Americans in political and legal protest and, most importantly, develops administrative expertise which can, perhaps, enhance the potential wealth of the remaining native lands.

POINTS OF DEBATE

Many Americans see the conquest of the native population as an outcome of war, fought fair and square. Yet no other population conquered by the Anglo-Saxon core has had to endure the discrimination experienced by Native Americans. Indeed, in this century, efforts have been made to help rebuild the conquered nations around the world and to establish friendly and mutually beneficial relations with their inhabitants. Such has not been the case for American Indians, who were displaced from their land, confined to reservations, regulated by government, and cheated at almost every turn by both government and large-scale economic enterprises. The legacy of this treatment of America's true natives now raises important points of debate.

1. Should the lands, or at least portions of them, that were taken in violation of treaties be given back to the Native Americans, or should they be compensated for the loss of their most valuable asset? Most white Americans are against any such effort; but in a society that values the principle of jus-

tice within the rule of law and order, should not past violations of the law be redressed in some way?

2. Should Native Americans be encouraged to enter the mainstream of the society or stay somewhat isolated on the reservations, preserving what is left of their cultures? To do the former would require enormous expenditures in creating new educational and job opportunities, whereas the latter, without subsidizing the economic development of the reservations, would perpetuate the current situation. How can either policy mitigate white Americans' resistance to public expenditures for welfare or their increasing fear of the development of Native American lands? Even more recent use of lands for gambling, which whites and other ethnics use and enjoy, generates protest from adjacent communities who fear a change in their lifestyle. Is such protest legitimate in light of the lifestyle adjustments forced on the first Americans over the last two centuries?

3. Is it time to dismantle the Bureau of Indian Affairs and allow Native Americans to go their own way? Or is the bureau necessary to protect Native Americans from predatory practices and to facilitate economic development? Or is some other form of government assistance needed, a form not so rooted in past patterns of exploitation?

KEY TERMS/KEY LEGISLATION

Alaska Native Claims Settlement Act (1971), 127
American Indian Movement (AIM), 140
blood quantum measure, 119
Bureau of Indian Affairs (BIA), 128
Council of Energy Resource Tribes (CERT), 141
Dawes Act of 1887 (General Allotment Act), 119
fish-ins, 140
General Allotment Act (1887), 126
Ghost Dance groups, 139
Indian Citizenship Act (1924), 126

Indian Claims Commission Act (1946), 126
Indian Removal Act (1830), 125
Indian Reorganization Act of 1934, 135
The Major Crimes Act (1885), 125
Manifest Destiny, 125
millenarian movements, 139
miscegenation laws, 124
pan-Indianism, 139
percentage of Indian blood, 119
peyotism, 139
Relocation Act (1956), 127

CHAPTER 6

Latinos

As the dominant Anglo-Saxon ethnic stock maintained the enslavement of African Americans and continued the conquest of the Native Americans, a new point of ethnic conflict emerged in the middle of the nineteenth century. This conflict was perhaps inevitable in light of the fact that Anglo-Saxon America was surrounded on its southern and western borders by Spanish-speaking populations. The Spanish had exerted their influence on the southern portions of the northern hemisphere, Central and South America, as well as the island populations off the shores of Florida and the Deep South. Inevitably the uneasy relations between the two cultures, the Anglo-Saxon core and various white ethnic groups from other European societies, on one side, and Latinos, on the other, would culminate in a clash.

The term *"Latino"* does not denote a unified ethnic population (Jones-Correa and Leal, 1996; Portes and MacLeod, 1996). While the Latino population in the United States consists of three major groups—Mexicans, Puerto Ricans, and Cubans—it also incorporates immigrants from Central and South America who immigrated in noticeable numbers during the past two decades (Munoz, 1989; Jaffe and Boswell, 1980; Johnson, Johnson-Webb, and Farrell, 1999; Lopez-Garza and Diaz, 2001).

According to the 2000 U.S. census, there are 33 million Latinos living in the United States (Guzman, 2001; Therrien and Ramirez, 2001). Mexican-origin persons make up 66 percent of all Latinos, followed by Puerto Ricans (9 percent), Central Americans (5 percent), Cubans (4 percent), and South Americans (4 percent). Despite a noticeable increase of persons from Central and South America in the United States during the past two decades, the population of Central and South Americans has yet to constitute a clearly defined and identifiable ethnic subpopulation similar to Mexicans, Puerto Ricans, or Cubans. One factor that constrains the definition and identifiability of the Central and South American populations in the United States is their regional distribution (Therrien and Ramirez, 2001). For example, the Mexican-origin population in the United States is concentrated in two regions, West (57 percent) and South (33 percent). Puerto Ricans are concentrated in the Northeast (64 percent) and Cubans are concentrated in the South (80 percent). In contrast, Central and South Americans are concentrated in three regions, South (35 percent), Northeast (32 percent), and West (28 percent). However, according to data from the 2000 U.S. Census (see Figure 6.1 on page 146), Latinos moved into more suburban areas and into states set off from traditional pathways of Latino immigration into the United States between 1980 and 2000 (Hong, 2002). For our purposes in this chapter, the focus is on the three major groups—Mexicans, Puerto Ricans, and Cubans—that constitute about 80 percent of all Latinos in the United States.

RESOURCE SHARES OF LATINOS

Poverty Levels of Latinos

As can be seen in Table 6.1, the poverty rate for Mexican Americans and Puerto Ricans is more than three times that of non-Latinos, while the poverty rate for Cuban Americans is slightly more than double the rate for non-Latinos. Most Mexican American and Puerto Rican households headed by females are in poverty, and the head of household is likely to be a non–high school graduate (Aguirre, 1990; Baca-Zinn, 1995; Enchautegui, 1997). The limited success of government-sponsored anti-poverty programs in Latino communities caused policy-makers to argue that poverty became a persistent and severe social problem in the 1990s for the Latino population (Miranda, 1991; Krueger and Orszas, 2002; Perez and Martinez, 1993; Zambrana and Dorrington, 1998). However, the economic policies implemented by President Bill Clinton in the 1990s had some effect on reducing proverty among all Americans, Latinos in particular (Pear, 1998).

Income of Latinos

The median household income of Latinos is below that of white households (see Figure 6.2 on page 147). In 2000, the median household income of Latinos was 76 percent of white median household income. The median household

TABLE 6.1 Poverty Rates for Latinos

Year	Population Living in Poverty, %			
	Non-Latino	Mexican American	Puerto Rican	Cuban American
2000	7.7%	24.1%	25.8%	17.3%
1998	9.4	27.7	33.1	12.5
1994	13.5	31.8	38.7	19.9
1990	9.2	27.7	30.4	12.5
1980	6.3	21.4	33.4	11.2
1970	7.8	26.8	28.2	13.1

Source: U.S. Bureau of the Census, 1973a, 1983a, 1991b; March 1994 CPS; CPS Annual Demographic Survey, March Supplement (Internet release date: September 28, 1999); Proctor and Dalaker, 2002.

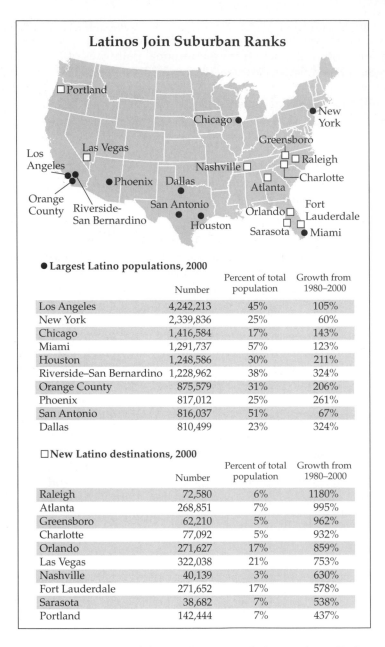

FIGURE 6.1 Areas with largest Latino populations and new Latino destinations.

Source: Hong, 2002.

FIGURE 6.2 Median household income by race and Hispanic origin: 1967 to 2000.

[1]Hispanic may be any race. Data not available prior to 1972.

Source: U.S. Census Bureau, Current Population Survey, March 1968 to 2001.

income in 2000 for Mexican Americans was $31,123, $30,129 for Puerto Ricans, and $38,312 for Cuban Americans. From another perspective, Mexican American median household income in 2000 was 70 percent, Puerto Rican median household income was 68 percent, and Cuban American median household income was 87 percent of the white median household income. The income gap between Cuban Americans and whites is smaller than for either Mexican Americans or Puerto Ricans. Interestingly, the median household income of Mexican Americans in 2000 was 81 percent and Puerto Rican median household income was 79 percent of the Cuban American household income. In addition, Table 6.2 shows that the income of both Latinos and Latinas are below those of non-Latinos.

TABLE 6.2 Latino Income Differentials Relative to Non-Latino Income

	Latinos		
Year	Total Latino Population*	Males[†]	Females[‡]
2000	0.67	0.62	0.73
1998	0.63	0.58	0.71
1993	0.62	0.63	0.77
1988	0.64	0.61	0.80
1983	0.67	0.67	0.91

*Latino income as a proportion of non-Latino income.

[†]Latino male income as a proportion of non-Latino *male* income.

[‡]Latino female income as a proportion of non-Latino *female* income.

Source: U.S. Bureau of the Census, 1994; March 1998 CPS (Internet release date: August 7, 1998); Current Population Survey 2000 (Internet release date: December 10, 2001).

Box 6.1
The Latino Marketplace

The Latino marketplace is booming! While some sectors of the U.S. marketplace may be shrinking, the growth of Latino-owned businesses is expanding in the United States. Between 1987 and 1992 the number of Latino-owned businesses increased 76 percent, from 489,973 in 1987 to 862,605 in 1992. During the same period, U.S. firms increased 26 percent, from 13.7 to 17.3 million. Receipts for Latino-owned businesses increased by 134 percent between 1987 and 1992, from $32.8 to $76.8 billion. In contrast, receipts for all U.S. firms increased 67 percent during the same time period, from $2 to $3.3 trillion.

In 1995, Latino purchasing power stood at about $220 billion. One can observe from the statistics below that Los Angeles had the largest number of Latino-owned businesses and the highest index of Latino purchasing power. However, Miami accounted for a larger share of the 1995 revenue for Latino-based businesses.

Top Five Latino Markets

	Total	Los Angeles	San Antonio	Chicago	New York	Miami
1995 Latino population	28,410,000	5,781,949	694,909	1,016,079	4,288,857	1,284,612
1995 Latino purchasing power	$220.30 b*	$48.47 b	$8.15 b	$8.37 b	$28.67 b	$13.22 b
1995 Latino TV media expenditures	$517.1 m†	$109.17 m	$11.75 m	$21.50 m	$45.28 m	$56.00 m
1995 Latino radio media expenditures	$321.2 m	$74.17 m	$15.06 m	$17.50 m	$32.25 m	$50.66 m
1995 Latino print media expenditures	$142.5 m	$55.12 m	$4.37 m	$11.71 m	$22.45 m	$22.75 m
1995 Latino-owned businesses	1,211,144	159,275	28,242	25,073	55,126	107,212
1995 Revenue of Latino-owned businesses	$127.95 b	$14.02 b	$3.01 b	$3.64 b	$6.63 b	$20.85 b

* In billions of dollars.
† In millions of dollars.

Source: www.hispanicbusiness.com.

Occupational Distribution of Latinos

Table 6.3 on page 150 shows that relatively more persons in the non-Latino population (33 percent) and in the Cuban American population (24 percent) work in managerial and professional occupations, whereas 12 percent of Mexican Americans and 17 percent of Puerto Ricans have these jobs. A noticeable number of Mexican American workers (31 percent) are farmers and laborers; 20 percent of Puerto Ricans hold such positions; and 18 percent of Cuban Americans have these jobs—a figure that approaches the 14 percent for all non-Latinos. This occupational distribution offers some insight into the reasons for differences in median earnings among the three Latino groups. The concentration of Cuban American persons in managerial, professional, technical, and sales occupations versus the percentage of Mexican Americans and Puerto Ricans in service, production, and laborer occupations accounts for the disparity in earnings among Latino populations. Managerial, professional, and technical occupations are associated with higher pay, more job security, and better fringe benefits than are service, production, and labor occupations.

Educational Attainment of Latinos

Table 6.4 on page 151 shows that the levels of education attained by Latinos are below those attained by all non-Latinos, a fact that places Latinos at an enormous disadvantage in a credential-oriented society. The education levels attained by Mexican Americans and Puerto Ricans are lower than those attained by Cuban Americans. On the college level, the number of Mexican American students who have completed four years is less than half the number of Puerto Rican college graduates and slightly less than one-third the number of Cuban American college graduates. In general, between 1970 and 2000, Cuban Americans and Puerto Ricans made larger educational gains than Mexican Americans, although all three Latino populations lag significantly behind non-Latinos.

Life Span of Latinos

Life expectancy statistics show discrepancies between the Latino and non-Latino populations. According to statistics from the Center for Disease Control (2002), Latina mothers are less likely to receive prenatal care than non-Latina mothers. The reason given by Latina mothers for their decision not to pursue prenatal care is that they do not have the money or health insurance to pay for a doctor's visit. Latina mothers are also more likely than non-Latino mothers to give birth to infants with low birth weight.

Death rates for the Latino population are little studied because death certificates identify "race" rather than ethnicity (Becerra et al., 1991). Still, an analysis of Latino death rates by the National Center for Health Statistics (2002) found that: (1) The leading cause of death for both Latino and white American children 1 to 14 years of age was unintentional injury (e.g., fires, drowning,

TABLE 6.3 Occupational Distribution among the Latino Population, 2000 through 1970*

Occupation	Non-Latino, %				Mexican American, %				Puerto Rican, %				Cuban American, %			
	2000	1990	1980	1970	2000	1990	1980	1970	2000	1990	1980	1970	2000	1990	1980	1970
Professionals, managers	33.2%	27.3%	26.4%	25.4%	11.9%	11.3%	14.2%	10.2%	17.1%	17.1%	16.6%	15.6%	23.5%	24.0%	22.6%	23.4%
Clerical workers, salespeople, craftspeople	30.3	33.2	39.7	40.2	22.4	25.3	36.9	30.4	34.9	31.4	45.3	47.8	34.0	33.9	45.3	45.2
Operatives, service workers	22.6	23.8	27.2	28.5	34.8	31.7	37.7	42.2	28.2	31.8	32.2	30.3	24.6	25.8	25.7	24.3
Farmers, laborers	13.9	15.7	6.7	5.9	30.9	31.7	11.2	17.2	19.8	19.7	5.9	6.3	17.9	16.3	6.4	7.1

*Persons 16 years old and older.

Source: U.S. Bureau of the Census, 1973a, 1983a, 1983b, 1991b; March 1994 CPS; March 1998 CPS Supplement (Internet release date: August 7, 1998); March 2000 Current Population Survey (Internet release date: March 6, 2001).

TABLE 6.4 Levels of Education Attained by Latinos and Non-Latinos*

Year	High School, %†				College, %‡			
	Non-Latino	Mexican American	Puerto Rican	Cuban American	Non-Latino	Mexican American	Puerto Rican	Cuban American
2000	88.4%	51.0%	64.3%	73.0%	28.1%	6.9%	13.0%	23.0%
1990	79.6	44.1	55.5	63.5	22.2	5.4	9.7	20.2
1980	69.6	38.1	45.9	34.6	17.4	4.9	5.6	12.2
1970	62.6	33.3	43.8	33.4	14.1	4.3	3.4	12.6

*Persons 25 years old and older with high school and college degrees.
†Four years or more of high school.
‡Four years or more of college.

Source: U.S. Bureau of the Census, 1973a, 1983a, 1983b, 1991b; March 1994 CPS; March 1998 CPS Supplement (Internet release date: July 29, 1999); March 2000 Current Population Survey (Internet release date: March 6, 2001).

motor vehicle injury); however, approximately 21 percent of Latino children ages 1 to 14 were the victims of homicide, compared to 13 percent of white children. (2) The leading cause of death for Latino and white young adults ages 15 to 24 was unintentional injury, but homicide accounted for 47 percent of Latino deaths, compared to 10 percent of deaths among white Americans. In contrast, suicide accounted for 31 percent of deaths among young white adults, and 10 percent among Latinos in this age category. (3) In Latino and white cohorts ages 25 and older, heart disease was the leading cause of death.

Another reason for the discrepancies in life expectancy between non-Latino whites and Latinos is Latinos' limited access to health care. The higher incidence of low birth weight among newborn Latino children reflects two aspects of the health care delivery system: the limited availability of affordable health care in general and prenatal care in particular (Ginzberg, 1991; LeClere, Rogers, and Peters, 1997) and the lack of affordable health care coverage for the Latino population (Treviño et al., 1991; Vitucci, 1999). These limitations

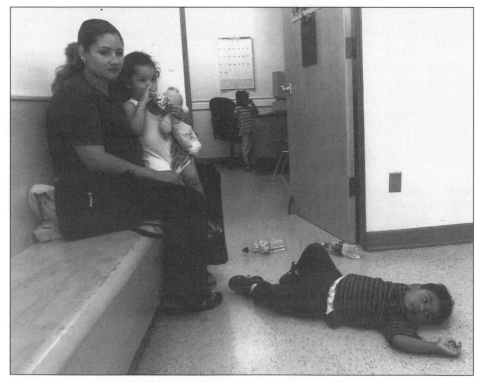

Many Latinos have limited access to health care because they lack either the money or the insurance to pay for it. Here, a young mother with two small children waits for care at a public health clinic in Los Angeles. The clinic closed its doors later that day because of budget cuts.

prevent most Latina mothers from obtaining neonatal services until the eighth or ninth month of pregnancy, when they can then utilize health care services available through social welfare programs. Less neonatal care translates into greater risks for infants.

Another reason for shorter life expectancy is violence (Martinez, 1996). The large proportion of deaths caused by homicide among Latinos in the 1 to 14 and 14 to 25 age ranges reflects the risk of living in areas with high crime rates and the presence of gang violence. For example, Latino youth are four times more likely than white youth to be the victims of gang violence (U.S. Department of Justice, 1991b and c; 2002). Latino youth are also more likely than white youth to feel unsafe or threatened while attending school (U.S. Department of Justice, 1995).

Housing of Latinos

Housing segregation limits opportunities by confining an ethnic group to areas where jobs, education, health care, and security are less available (Freeman, 2000; Wood, 2001; Santiago and Wilder, 1991). Thus, minority ethnics not living among the dominant groups in a society will have reduced access to resources (Palm, 1985; Flippen, 2001; Williams and Collins, 2001; Lopez, 1986). In their study of the Latino population in the United States, Bean and Tienda (1987) recorded the following patterns of residential segregation: (1) Puerto Ricans living in the New York City area are highly segregated residentially. This segregation pattern is based largely on racism. Since some Puerto Ricans are of African heritage, they are more likely to be relegated close to African American neighborhoods, which tend to be isolated from white American neighborhoods. (2) Mexican Americans in the Los Angeles area experience less residential segregation than Puerto Ricans in New York City. Since Mexican Americans constitute 22 percent of the Los Angeles area's population (and Latinos, in general, an even greater percentage), their large numbers increase the probability of contact in residential areas. (3) Compared with Puerto Ricans and Mexican Americans, Cuban Americans in the Miami area experience the lowest level of residential segregation and the highest rate of contact with the white population. Bean and Tienda (1987:177) concluded that the consequences of Latino segregation

> are uncertain, but probably depend on the extent to which it is voluntary or involuntary. In this regard, Puerto Ricans are clearly at greatest risk of being denied equal access to spatially determined resources like education, health, security, and employment.

Accordingly, a report on neighborhood segregation in the United States for 2000 shows that Latinos in general live in neighborhoods where they comprise almost half of the residents (Frey and Myers, 2002).

In sum, then, Latinos have less access to valued resources—income, education, health care, and housing—than white Americans, although degrees of access to these resources vary among the three Latino groups (Aponte, 1991).

Box 6.2
Latino Children at Risk

According to the National Coalition of Hispanic Health and Human Services Organization (COSSMHD), Latino children are the second largest group of children in
the United States after non-Latino white children. The majority (90 percent) of the
increase in the number of Latino children is the result of fertility and legal immigration. However, as the number of Latino children has increased, so has their risk
of becoming victims in U.S. society. For example:

- 33 percent of Latino children are uninsured compared to only 12 percent of
  white children.
- 39 percent of Latino children live in poverty compared to only 16 percent of
  white children.
- The rate of Down's syndrome per 100,000 births is 12 percent for Latino children compared to only 8 percent for white children.

Growing population

Number of children by racial, ethnic group, in millions:

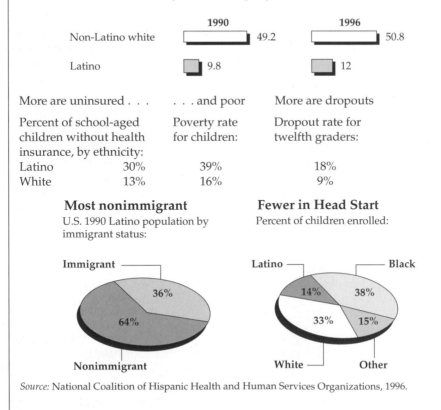

	1990	1996
Non-Latino white	49.2	50.8
Latino	9.8	12

More are uninsured . . .   . . . and poor   More are dropouts

Percent of school-aged   Poverty rate   Dropout rate for
children without health   for children: twelfth graders:
insurance, by ethnicity:

Latino	30%	39%	18%
White	13%	16%	9%

Most nonimmigrant   **Fewer in Head Start**
U.S. 1990 Latino population by   Percent of children enrolled:
immigrant status:

Immigrant — 36%
64%
Nonimmigrant

Latino — 14%   Black — 38%
White — 33%   Other — 15%

Source: National Coalition of Hispanic Health and Human Services Organizations, 1996.

Cuban Americans clearly have more access than either Puerto Ricans or Mexican Americans; and Mexican Americans have the least access of the three groups, despite the fact that they are less residentially segregated than Puerto Ricans. Let us now examine in more detail each of these three populations, in order to understand the specific forces that have determined their respective resource shares.

MEXICAN AMERICANS

Identifiability of Chicanos

Language and culture have set those of Mexican origin apart from mainstream society. The proximity of Mexico to the United States, coupled with frequent contact across the 2,000-mile border, has preserved the Spanish language as a prominent feature of social intercourse between the two cultures (Aguirre, 1980, 1984, 1988). Unlike many European immigrants who cut their ties with their homelands, Mexican Americans, or Chicanos, have had less incentive to abandon their native culture (Langley, 1988). Indeed, early Mexican American settlers regarded the Southwest as *their* homeland until the Anglo-Saxons invaded and made it part of the United States.

The maintenance of language and other features of Mexican culture have served to segregate Mexican Americans, perpetuating incentives to marry within the Latino population and to sustain traditional behavioral and social patterns (such as birth rates and family structure). Many Mexican Americans speak Spanish or speak English with an accent, have slightly darker skin than most Americans of European descent, and are overrepresented in certain occupations (see Table 6.3). Taken together, these differences create a relatively high degree of identifiability which, historically and currently, is the basis for discrimination. To understand the dynamics of this discrimination, as well as the sense of threat and prejudicial beliefs that sustain such discrimination, we need to review briefly the history of the Mexican American population. This overview tells the story of a population of conquered people (similar to Native Americans), imported menial labor (similar to African Americans, but without the extremes of slavery), and generally unwanted and illegal immigrants.

The History of Mexican Americans:
Conquest, Displacement, and Exploitation

Early History: The Conquest   By 1602, a handful of Spaniards had explored most of the southwest borderlands—from Galveston to San Diego, from Sonora to Santa Fe, and from the west coast of Mexico to Monterey. In time, the Spanish settlements in the Southwest came to consist of a fairly rooted colony in New Mexico, an easily held and fairly prosperous chain of missions in coastal California, and a number of imperiled settlements in Texas and Arizona. By 1790, the population of the Southwest, estimated at 23,000, was almost entirely Spanish-speaking (American Council of Learned Societies, 1932).

The presence of a large Spanish-speaking population in the Southwest facilitated, to a degree, the adjustment of the incoming Anglo-Saxons because they could adopt much of what was useful. For example, Spanish and Native American words were incorporated into the English vocabulary, and styles of architecture found in the Southwest—the one-story ranch house and buildings with tiled roofs, adobe walls, patios, and verandas—were adopted (Hernandez-Chavez et al., 1975).

Between the Battle of San Jacinto in 1836 and the Gadsden Purchase of 1853, the United States came to acquire most of the Southwest. A significant event in Mexican American history was the *Treaty of Guadalupe Hidalgo* in 1848, which concluded the war between the United States and Mexico (Estrada et al., 1988; Hietala, 1985). This treaty guaranteed to all Mexicans living in the "new" American territory a number of basic rights: full American citizenship, retention of Spanish as a recognized and legitimate language, political liberty, and ownership of property. The treaty was rarely enforced, however, which opened the door to social and political exploitation.

Despite the guarantees of the *Treaty of Guadalupe Hidalgo,* the Anglo-Saxons assumed the right to impose the English language on all the inhabitants of the Southwest (Villareal, 1988). Laws were written in English, leaving Spanish speakers ignorant of the law, especially laws protecting their property; Spanish was not used in the courts; and school instruction in Spanish was forbidden. As a result, Mexicans were at a disadvantage in protecting their property, in seeking redress through the courts, and in acquiring an equal education. Mexicans living in the Southwest soon became the objects of prejudice (Pitt, 1966).

For Mexican Americans, the period leading into the early nineteenth century involved loss of land, social status, culture, and language. This group became a minority in the United States by being conquered (Acuña, 1981), and as the Anglo-Saxon population settled in the Southwest, and as control of the Southwest borderlands passed into their hands, Mexican Americans became an ever-more subordinate ethnic minority.

After 1848, when the Anglo-Saxon population opened the Southwest for expansion, major economic transformations ensued. The loss of social, political, and economic status relegated Mexican Americans to a source of cheap labor. Hence, the major thrust of Anglo-Saxon economic development of the Southwest was in labor-intensive industries—agriculture, mining, and railroads (Barrera, 1979). As this development increased, more people from south of the border immigrated to U.S. territory. For example, between 1890 and 1900 the Mexican-origin population in the Southwest grew from about 75,000 to over half a million (McWilliams, 1968).

The arrival of large numbers of Mexican immigrants threatened the precarious socioeconomic status of those already living in the Southwest. Since the majority of immigrants from Mexico were illiterate and poor, they were willing to accept the lowest wages; as a consequence, the white American population tended to regard all Mexicans, including descendants of the original land holders in the Southwest, as "cheap labor." Indigenous Mexican Americans were perceived by the Anglo core as no different from poor Mexican immigrants—a perception that pushed virtually all those of Mexican extraction to the bottom rungs of the stratification system (Murguia, 1975).

Mexican Americans in the First Half of the Twentieth Century   Immigration of Mexicans into the Southwest was closely linked to the economy. On the U.S. side of the border, as labor-intensive industry expanded, the demand for cheap labor served as a "pull" factor for Mexican immigrants. On the Mexican side of the border, the revolution of 1910 to 1917 operated as a "push" factor for Mexicans seeking refuge and employment. The push out of Mexico was reinforced by the fact that employers in the United States were looking for a source of inexpensive labor to compensate for the shortage of American workers created by World War I. Soon, Mexicans became a subordinate labor force: paid less than white American laborers for the same work, concentrated in the low-paying occupations, and often indebted to their employers for food and shelter.

As the southwestern economy fluctuated, employers often had too many workers and not enough work. Ironically, the need for cheap labor to run the labor-intensive industries of the Southwest also created the need to eliminate the presence of surplus labor during economic downturns. For example, between 1870 and 1930 immigration policy was relatively unrestricted for Mexican immigrants, who were allowed to enter the United States on an open-door policy to fill the need for labor. But the Great Depression of the 1930s changed immigration policy dramatically. As white Americans lost jobs and homes, anti-Mexican feelings emerged; and as whites increasingly competed with those of Mexican origin for low-wage jobs and welfare benefits, white resentment toward "Mexicans" grew. The result was a repatriation movement for Mexicans, a movement that included both indigenous Mexican Americans and those who had more recently immigrated. Between 1929 and 1935 over a half million Mexicans were repatriated (Hoffman, 1974; Humphrey, 1941; Chavira, 1977).

While immigration initiatives such as Operation Wetback were deterrents to illegal immigration, they were not effective in stemming the demand for inexpensive labor. An interesting feature of immigration reform in the 1980s was its focus on employers; rather than continuing to fixate on the number of Mexicans crossing the border, the U.S. Congress placed the burden on employers (Bean, Vernez, and Keeley, 1989; Bean et al., 1990). For example, in 1986 Congress implemented the *Immigration Reform and Control Act (IRCA)* to prohibit employers from hiring illegal immigrants and to establish a monitoring system for employer compliance. Yet, a study to examine the progress of the IRCA found that the enforcement of employer sanctions is weak, that few criminal and civil fines have been assessed against employers, and that a low degree of cooperation between employers and the Immigration and Naturalization Service prevails (Fix and Hill, 1990).

Box 6.4
Chicano Farmworkers and Pesticides

Chicano farmworkers who pick and harvest America's agricultural crops face tremendous risks from the pesticides sprayed on the crops. In particular, since children make up a large share of the farmworker pool, the risks of cancer and/or learning disability that might result from exposure to pesticides for them are of national concern (Taylor, 1973; Benavides, 1981; and Moses, 1993). In an attempt to discuss the health danger of pesticide exposure to farmworkers, the House of Representatives Select Committee on Aging (1992) held a series of hearings. Maria Gomez spoke before the Select Committee on Aging (1992:10–11) regarding her experience as a farmworker:

> My name is Maria Gomez. I live in Pharr, Texas. I have been a worker in the field for twenty years.
> First of all, I would like to talk about pesticides in work. Little by little they have been killing us because there is no regulation for these pesticides. Back in 1985, they were already using planes to spray the fields, and I was in my home asleep when one of these planes flew over my home and sprayed, and the spray came into my house.
> The doctors are not trained as to what reaction the pesticide has on the body and what other complications you could have with the medication. The medication that was given to me produced high blood pressure. This was also complicated by the fact that I was picking cantaloupe melon in the field; it is in the heat of the day and the sun also caused some of these side-effects.

The occupational health of Chicano farm workers is an important concern in large agriculture-producing states like California and Texas. There are various resources on the Internet that inform interested students about legislation at the state and federal level regarding farm worker safety, and organizations that focus on the health issues of Chicano farm workers. For example, some of the Internet resources available are:

1. Occupational health issues of farm workers: http://www.lib.berkeley.edu/PUBL/guide13.html.
2. News stories on farm workers: http://news.pacificnews.org.
3. Organizations focused on farm worker issues: http://www.americaspolicy.org/borderlines; and http://www.sfsu.edu/~cecipp/chavez&farmworkers.htm.

Negative Beliefs about Chicanos

As the process of subordinating the indigenous Mexican population in the Southwest began, Mexicans were portrayed in highly negative and stereotyped terms (Reisler, 1996). Many slaveholders, and former slaveholders, who had settled in the Southwest in the second half of the nineteenth century, portrayed Mexicans as an inferior "race," biologically tainted by Indian blood. The early perception of Mexicans as "greasers" (presumably because some once greased wagon wheels) and as cowardly originated after the defeats of the Mexican Army in the 1880s (Meyer, 1978; Ortego, 1973; Keller, 1985). Those who insisted that Mexicans constituted a distinctive "race" thus based their negative stereotypes on perceived biological traits. As a result, during the first decades of the twentieth century, fear was expressed in Congress and in diatribes by white nativists that the "white race" would be "mongrelized" because of excessive contact with Mexicans, who many regarded as lazy, shiftless, lawless, and potentially violent (Stoddard, 1973; Almaguer, 1994).

These stereotypes persisted in the second half of the twentieth century (Duran and Bernard, 1973) and still exist today. Males of Mexican origin have been portrayed as "banditos" (fat, lazy, thieving, and immoral) or as overly "macho" and violent street criminals. Mexican American women have been viewed as young seductresses or as passive mothers of violent gang youth and wives of lazy husbands (Simmons, 1973; Mazon, 1984; Paredes, 1977). Consequently, "Mexican-looking" people, Spanish-speaking people, or individuals who speak English with a Spanish accent must endure prejudice about their character, honesty, work ethic, and reliability (Martinez, 1969). These beliefs have justified past discrimination; now they legitimize current treatment of Mexican Americans. Negative beliefs about Mexican-origin persons in the United States are reinforced by the depiction of Mexicans as deviants—especially as criminals or drug dealers—in the mass media (Keller, 1985; Robinson, 1963). The focus by the television and newspaper media, for example, on Mexican Americans and Mexicans carrying the Mexican flag in protests against Proposition 187 in California fueled nativist sentiments in the Anglo population, sentiments that supported the discrimination against Mexican Americans (Aguirre, 1995a).

The Dynamics of Discrimination against Mexican Americans

Economic Discrimination   Despite the anti-Mexican sentiment of the 1930s and the resulting repatriation movement, the United States sought assistance from Mexico during the 1940s to fill labor shortages in agriculture created by World War II. In 1942 the United States and Mexico established a labor contract system known as the "Bracero Program." Participating Mexican workers were granted temporary visas and labeled *braceros* (hired hands). The Bracero Program operated from 1942 to 1964. During its existence about five million Mexican workers entered the U.S. labor force as legal seasonal workers (Garcia, 1980).

The U.S. Congress used the Bracero Program as a way of reducing the number of illegal immigrants from Mexico. By extending the Bracero Program beyond World War II, Congress sought to provide some relief for the struggling U.S. Border Patrol, which had been relatively ineffective in its control of illegal immigration. In 1954, for example, Congress allowed the Border Patrol to launch *Operation Wetback*, which targeted Mexican immigrants who did not have papers identifying them as braceros. Congress gave the Border Patrol blanket authority to stop and search any "Mexican-looking" person. Between 1954 and 1959, the patrol returned 3.8 million people to Mexico (Grebler, Moore, and Guzman, 1970). Operation Wetback reinforced the perception among Mexican Americans that their presence in the United States would always be marginal and tenuous.

Mexican Americans in the Second Half of the Twentieth Century Comparatively speaking, Mexican immigration between 1970 and 1990 was overshadowed by immigration from Central and South American countries. In contrast, most of the growth of the Mexican American population between 1970 and 1990 was the result of high birthrates of those already living in the United States (McCarthy and Valdez, 1986).

The identification of Mexican Americans as a colonized people has perpetuated discriminatory economic practices. One source of discrimination was built into the wage structure of the Southwest. The availability of Mexican workers created a depressed labor market, providing only limited menial jobs with very few economic rewards and benefits (Romo, 1989).

Economic discrimination against Mexican Americans has been aggravated by a number of circumstances. First, until the 1960s, many labor unions actively discriminated against Mexican Americans (Grebler, Moore, and Guzman, 1970). As a consequence, Mexican American workers were prevented from moving to higher-wage and skill positions which, in turn, could serve as the springboard for further mobility by subsequent generations—much as union jobs had done for white European immigrants. Today, although institutionalized discrimination has declined, the economy has shifted away from industrial work, thereby reducing the number of better-paying jobs and forcing many Mexican Americans onto the welfare rolls or into service, agriculture, and light-industrial jobs with low wages, little security, and no benefits. Second, the existence of a large unemployed Mexican American labor pool, either just across the border or in urban areas, has depressed wages and kept workers from demanding new benefits—lest they be fired and replaced by more eager and pliant workers. Third, the undocumented citizenship status of many Mexicans has driven down wages because undocumented aliens will rarely protest wages and working conditions—unless they wish to run the risk of being deported.

The imposition of the English language on Mexican Americans not only contradicted the intent of the Treaty of Guadalupe Hidalgo but also caused a form of economic discrimination (Falcon and Campbell, 1991): Because laws were changed from Spanish to English and court proceedings were conducted only in English, land grants written in Spanish were deemed worthless, and Mexican Americans were forced to rent their own land (Aguirre, 1982). In the Southwest, where land ownership became a measure of power, Mexican Americans soon became second-class citizens, displaced from their land and forced into the low-wage labor market.

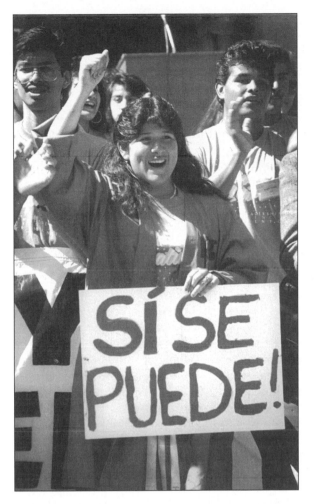

Chicano pride rally in Sacramento, California, focuses
attention on the need to eliminate negative stereotypes
about Chicanos.

Chicanos, however, did not always accept economic domination passively.
"Social banditry" emerged, a phenomenon that reinforced prejudicial beliefs.
For example, Las Gorras Blancas (the White Caps) was a group of Mexican
American social bandits around 1887 who protested their loss of land by cutting down fences and burning property acquired by white ranchers—
especially those who had obtained land through manipulation of the English-
speaking court system (Barrera, 1985). Las Gorras Blancas received widespread support in the Mexican-origin community, but this support was not
strong enough to sustain a major challenge to the erosion of Mexican American land rights. Today, protest has diminished in the wave of undocumented

workers and illegal aliens. Indeed, all protest invites harsh response in a political climate that is highly receptive to mass deportation of Mexicans who have recently come to the United States.

Some Mexican American protests against economic discrimination have been remarkably effective, however. In the 1960s, Cesar Chavez unionized the farmworkers. Through the use of media, personal charisma, and well-organized boycotts and strikes, Chavez and his colleagues greatly improved the working conditions and wages of agricultural workers. To this day, United Farm Workers of America operates effectively to improve wages and working conditions—most recently extending its lines of battle to include the dangers of chemical pesticides to both workers and consumers. Yet, the limited success of the Mexican American farmworkers has not been matched by Mexican Americans living in cities. Urban Chicanos remain vulnerable to an oversupply of undocumented labor and the actions of law enforcement agencies.

Legal Discrimination   The use of English by the Anglo core as the language of the courts, despite guarantees to the contrary in the Treaty of Guadalupe Hidalgo, has been a crucial step in depriving Chicanos of justice. For example, in an analysis of Mexican American prisoners who had been executed between 1890 and 1986, Aguirre and Baker (1989) note that Mexican American prisoners given capital sentences had lower rates of appeal than either white American or African American prisoners because either they did not understand the legal rights communicated to them in English or they were unable to communicate in English with the court. The inadequate defense of Mexican American prisoners increases their number in the prison population, thus reinforcing prejudicial beliefs that they are criminally prone, or natural "hardcore criminals."

Perhaps more significantly, because many Mexican Americans are subjected constantly to questions about their citizenship, they have been abused by those enforcement agencies—first the *Texas Rangers* and later the *Immigration and Naturalization Service* (INS), *U.S. Border Patrol,* and state highway police—designed to detect, capture, and deport "Mexicans." Special law enforcement agencies charged with the task of targeting a particular ethnic subpopulation are often a license for discriminatory abuse.

The strain between the Mexican American population and the mainstream legal system was established early with the creation of the Texas Rangers. According to Grebler, Moore, and Guzman (1970), the Texas Rangers were created in 1835 as a symbol of white American control over the social progress of the Mexican American. Though their primary purpose was to protect the Texas Republic from the Mexicans, the Texas Rangers spread their law enforcement presence throughout the Southwest. The rangers were given wide latitude in their treatment of Mexicans and Mexican Americans; and, as a consequence, beatings, lynchings, firing squads, and dismemberment were common (McWilliams, 1968). In fact, the general view of many Chicanos and Mexicans is that "every Texas Ranger has some Mexican blood. He has it on his boots" (Murguia, 1975).

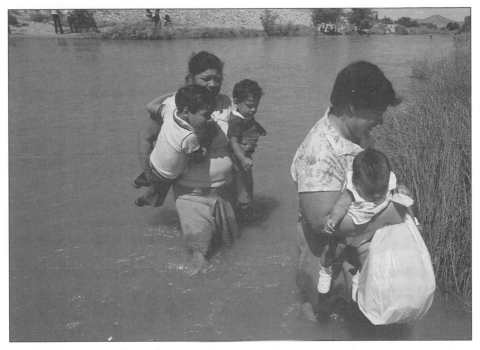

Despite local and federal government efforts to stem the tide of illegal immigration from Mexico, many Mexicans are willing to risk their lives for what they see as a better life in America. Here, a Mexican family crosses the Rio Grande in pursuit of that dream.

Similar to the Texas Rangers, the U.S. Border Patrol was created in 1924 to protect the United States from Mexican infiltration. Congress gave the patrol the authority to apprehend those suspected of illegal entry into the United States and to search persons and property within 25 miles of the U.S.–Mexico border (Grebler, Moore, and Guzman, 1970). The primary target of the Border Patrol became the "wetbacks"—Mexicans who crossed over to the United States by swimming across the Rio Grande River. The patrol became ever more oppressive in its efforts to apprehend illegal aliens, cruising the streets in Mexican American neighborhoods and stopping any "Mexican-looking" person who acted in a suspicious manner (McWilliams, 1968). Through its actions the Border Patrol communicated to the Mexican American community their tenuous place in American society.

Two major efforts of the Border Patrol had a significant impact on the Mexican American population. First, the Border Patrol deployed enforcement procedures during the great depression of the 1930s to deport Mexicans who were identified as burdens to U.S. society. Second, as noted earlier, they initiated Operation Wetback in 1954 to combat the "wetback invasion" of illegal aliens, allowing as many as 3.8 million Mexicans to be deported without due legal process (Grebler, Moore, and Guzman, 1970). These two efforts by the

Border Patrol resulted in the deportation of longtime Mexican American residents of the United States, Mexican American parents and their children born in the United States, along with immigrant Mexicans. These massive efforts served to brand the remaining Chicanos wrongfully as second-class citizens.

Studies of police tactics in small communities have shown that Mexican Americans are victims of prejudiced attitudes, indiscriminate searches and detentions, and high arrest-conviction rates (Aguirre and Baker, 1994; Morales, 1972, 1973; Welch et al., 1984). The 1970 report of the U.S. Commission on Civil Rights, *Mexican Americans and the Administration of Justice in the Southwest*, identified several discriminatory police actions: use of excessive force, verbal abuse, discriminatory treatment of juveniles arising from the nonnotification of parents, and random stops and searches. A decade later, the papers presented at the National Latino Conference on Law Enforcement and Criminal Justice documented similar patterns of police abuse in the Chicano community (U.S. Department of Justice, 1980). This same pattern of abuse persists today.

Fears about the enforcement of laws regarding citizenship status were demonstrated dramatically in the response to the amnesty provision of the 1986 Immigration Reform and Control Act (IRCA). This provision allowed many undocumented immigrants to apply for legal residence. While over 1.7 million undocumented aliens did apply, this figure was far below the estimated 3 million who were eligible for amnesty. At the same time that amnesty was offered, new restrictions on immigration were imposed, including penalties (not strictly enforced thus far) on employers who give jobs to undocumented workers and screening of welfare applicants for migration and citizenship status. The effectiveness of the IRCA now seems questionable; undocumented Mexicans continue to enter the Southwest, and documented workers and legal citizens are subject to abuse by law enforcement agencies targeting "Mexican-looking" people.

Educational Discrimination   When the Mexican American population was employed primarily as agricultural workers in the early 1900s, virtually no formal education was offered to children; and it was well into the 1930s before the lack of schools for Mexican American children was considered a problem. As schools were built, segregation prevailed as a result of housing segregation, local ordinances, and gerrymandering of school and district lines. Even as integration increased in the 1970s and 1980s, Mexican American teachers, administrators, and counselors were dramatically underrepresented in school systems.

This virtual absence of Mexican American school personnel, coupled with powerful local pressure exerted by white Americans, created an Anglo-Saxon American school culture, even in predominantly Mexican American neighborhoods and districts. Mexican American children were thus placed in a school system that was alien to their culture. Although children in European ethnic groups often had the same experience in school, they did not have to experience the constant conflict between the Anglo culture of schools and the culture of their homeland just across the border. Chicano children sometimes experience ambivalence at home because of their parents' close ties to their Mexican homeland and custom. They are torn between two cultures—the Mexican culture of their family and the American culture of the school and broader society. Moreover, because the school system has always been designed to "Americanize" immigrants, students living in the two cultures—that of the Mexican homeland across the border and that of their new or temporary place of residence—have often become alienated in schools. Because many Mexican American schoolchildren resisted heavy-handed efforts at Americanization, they were placed in segregated schools, under constant pressure to become "American" (Grebler, Moore, and Guzman, 1970; Sanchez, 1951; Rubel, 1966; San Miguel, 1987). For example, Mexican American children who spoke Spanish in school were often the victims of corporal punishment from teachers (for example, spanking with a paddle); Mexican American children were ridiculed by teachers if they brought burritos or tacos to school for their lunch. In the end, "good" American citizens were those Mexican American children who rejected their ethnic identity and culture.

In the only other major study conducted on the education of Mexican Americans in the Southwest, the U.S. Commission on Civil Rights (1972) found that teachers tended to ridicule Mexican American students who spoke English with an accent, exclude them from classroom discussion, refrain from asking them questions during classroom lessons, and punish them corporally for speaking Spanish in the classroom or on the school playground. The commission (1972:48) concluded its report by stating:

> The basic finding of the Commission's study is that school systems of the southwest have not recognized the rich culture and tradition of the Mexican American students and have not adopted policies and programs which would enable the students to participate fully in the benefits of the educational process.

Contributing to the sense of alienation in the school was the belief that Mexican American children needed only a rudimentary education before they dropped out and entered the low-wage labor pool. This belief, in turn, became a self-fulfilling prophecy: Schools imposing mainstream American culture on Mexican American children, with little sensitivity to or appreciation of their place in two active cultures, caused children to become unhappy in school, which led them to drop out.

The Elementary and Secondary Education Act passed by Congress in 1968 allocated some funds for bilingual education. The hope was that, if Spanish-speaking children could be sensitively introduced to English and the dominant Anglo-Saxon-European culture, their education would prove more effective, thereby reducing dropout rates. Yet very little bilingual education actually ensued in the early 1970s, and only with a 1974 Supreme Court decision (*Lau v. Nichols*) prohibiting schools from ignoring the language difficulties of national-origin minority groups did bilingual education increase. Currently, bilingualism in schools is not universal (Aguirre, 1995b; Macias, 1993). More recent political movements for "English only" as the official language of all Americans, culminating in the passing of formal laws in several states, have slowed the progress of bilingual education (Adams and Brink, 1990; Califa, 1989; Juarez, 1995). For example, in November 1986, voters in California approved Proposition 63 declaring English the official language of the state. The importance of Proposition 63 is that it was approved by the voters in a state with a sizable population of non-English speakers. Other states that have approved English-only amendments and that have large numbers of non-English speakers in the state's population are Arizona, Colorado, and Florida. Moreover, the effectiveness of bilingual education in helping Mexican American children is the subject of intense debate (Padilla and Benavides, 1992; Imhoff, 1990).

As a result of these discriminatory factors, many Mexican American children leave school early. Today only about 50 percent graduate from high school (Aguirre and Martinez, 1993). Without an education in a society that values it, the economic prospects of Mexican American youth are indeed dim (Aguirre and Martinez, 1984).

Political Discrimination   With the signing of the Treaty of Guadalupe Hidalgo in 1848, Mexicans living in the Southwest became citizens of the United States. However, the disregard for the rights granted to Mexicans in the treaty placed the latter in a relatively powerless position. At times, Mexicans responded to their colonization—for example, the mobilization of Las Gorras Blancas, mentioned earlier—but the majority of the Mexican population did not develop a cohesive political identity with which to challenge the Anglo population. By the 1920s, however, Mexican Americans were awakening to the reality that they would be politically powerless as long as the mainstream white population perceived them as foreigners. Thus, first attempts to create a political identity focused on integration into mainstream American society (Garcia and de la Garza, 1977). For example, in 1921 in San Antonio, Texas, middle-class Mexican Americans formed the *Orden Hijos de America* as a signal to the white population that they were interested in participating in U.S. society—even at the expense of accepting negative stereotypes for their behavior. In 1929, the *League of United Latin American Citizens (LULAC)* was founded in Corpus Christi, Texas, by Mexican Americans who chose to refer to themselves as "Latins" in order to reinforce their loyalty, in the eyes of white Americans, to the United States (Marquez, 1993).

Later, Mexican American veterans returning from World War II encouraged increased political activity in their communities. These war veterans saw that they were returning to a country in which they were regarded as second-class citizens. Two of the most significant political organizations arising out of the efforts of these war veterans during the 1940s and 1950s were the *G.I. Forum* and the *Community Service Organization* (Hero, 1992). The G.I. Forum advocated the rights of Mexican American war veterans, sought representation in Congress, encouraged voter registration, and focused attention on the segregation of schoolchildren. The Community Service Organization was formed in Los Angeles as a community-based organization to encourage Mexican American participation in local, state, and national elections.

Despite these efforts to increase political participation, Mexican Americans remained politically underrepresented in the 1960s. Yet, this was a period of awakening in the Mexican American community, as political events stimulated political awareness. For example, the "Viva Kennedy" movement in the 1960s presidential campaign, the land rights movement led by Reyes Tijerina to reclaim land in northern New Mexico, the farmworkers' movement led by Cesar Chavez, and the rise of *La Raza Unida* as a political party in Texas were all manifestations of a newfound political awareness.

The post-1970s signaled a period of political decline among Chicanos, although various radical political parties, such as the La Raza Unida in Texas, formed to wage local political campaigns. As Hero (1992) has noted, most of the political organizations formed before 1970 became involved in moderate political activities—voter registration, legal challenges to redistricting, and lobbying efforts at the local and state levels. As a result, political efforts within the Chicano population have shifted to the development of traditional political techniques with which to forge a unified social, economic, and political identity.

In the 1990s, Mexican Americans were politically underrepresented at all levels of political life: at the local level (mayors, city council members, school board members, county supervisors, sheriffs), at the state level (state legislators, court judges and justices, and governors), and at the national level (congressional representatives, senators, federal judges, and high-level executive appointees) (Hero, 1990). During the 1980s and early 1990s, the Republican White House had little incentive to initiate efforts to redress this imbalance of power because Mexican Americans traditionally vote overwhelmingly for the Democratic party. Some progress has since been made at the local and state levels in those cities and districts where Mexican Americans outnumber non-Latinos, but even here progress is slow. For example, Los Angeles, which is now close to 50 percent Latino, elected its first Chicano representative, Gloria Molina, to the Los Angeles Board of Supervisors in only 1991. Without political power proportionate to their numbers or their needs, Mexican Americans have found it difficult to address other forms of discrimination (Garcia, 1996).

Stratification of the Mexican-Origin Population

As a consequence of the long history of economic, legal, educational, and political discrimination against individuals of Mexican origin, Chicanos are disproportionately overrepresented in lower socioeconomic positions in American society. As a population, they tend to be more successful than African Americans and Native Americans, but they remain disproportionately locked into agricultural labor, urban barrios with high crime and little hope, and jobs that have few benefits and no future.

The negative beliefs about Mexican Americans—prone to criminality, lazy, un-American, uneducable, overly macho or seductive, welfare burdens, gang-oriented and violent—have legitimized discrimination and aroused fears among non-Latinos. Like all institutionalized patterns of discrimination, those against Mexican Americans are an outcome of perceptions that this population is a threat. At one time Europeans saw Mexicans as a military enemy. More recently, those of Mexican origin have posed a series of threats: as a low-wage labor pool that could potentially undercut higher-wage labor, as a political threat to European American ways of speaking and thinking; as a threat to social order arising from criminality and gang activity, and, most recently, as a numerical threat in the Southwest, where they are rapidly becoming a numerical majority. In turn, as the number of Mexican Americans has increased, new threats have emerged and old ones have been intensified. For example, fears about the schools' being overrun, about loss of white control of local politics, about burdens on the welfare and health care systems, about lost jobs for non-Latinos, and about the loss of white mainstream cultural hegemony have all escalated. These fears fuel discrimination, even in an age when antidiscrimination laws are well established. This discrimination can be subtle—housing discrimination, low educational expectations, biased hiring practices—or it can be blatant—English-only political movements and attacks on bilingualism. The result is a population disproportionately stuck in the lower stratum of American society.

PUERTO RICANS

The forces that created the minority population of Puerto Ricans stand in marked contrast to those that forged the Mexican American community. Puerto Ricans became U.S. citizens in 1898, when the United States annexed Puerto Rico, and the Jones Act of 1917 allowed Puerto Ricans free access to the U.S. mainland long before the island became a commonwealth in 1952. By the 1940s, the U.S. census indicated that 70,000 Puerto Ricans had settled on the mainland, but during the 1950s, almost 20 percent of the island's population migrated to the United States (Fitzpatrick, 1987). By 1970, over 800,000 Puerto Ricans were living on the U.S. mainland, 57 percent of whom were island-born. In 1993, the Puerto Rican population on the U.S. mainland was estimated at 2.4 million (U.S. Bureau of the Census, 1994) and, today, it continues to grow.

Both "push" and "pull" factors have affected the Puerto Rican migration. First, the island's size, 35 miles wide by 100 miles long, has generated problems of overpopulation; many island residents view the United States as a place to improve their living standard—especially the opportunity for adequate housing and employment (Maldonado-Denis, 1972). Second, conferring full U.S. citizenship rights on island residents meant that Puerto Ricans could enter the United States without having to confront restrictive immigration quotas and harassment by enforcement agencies such as the Border Patrol and the INS. Third, lowered costs for air travel between San Juan and New York City have encouraged movement to and from Puerto Rico.

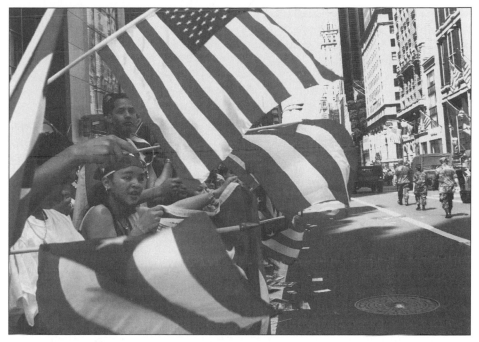

Puerto Ricans celebrate patriotism and ethnic pride during the annual National Puerto Rican Day Parade along New York's Fifth Avenue.

Identifiability of Puerto Ricans

As with other Latinos, Puerto Ricans are identifiable by their language, although they are far more likely to be bilingual than Mexican Americans. Puerto Ricans are also frequently visible in terms of their skin color, categorized by some as "black" if they are particularly dark or as Latino if they have a lighter skin tone. In fact, because the island of Puerto Rico has been a U.S. colony since the late 1800s, the cultural differences between Puerto Ricans and white Europeans are less critical than are perceived biological differences—a situation that is the reverse for Mexican Americans. Because some perceive Puerto Ricans as members of a distinct "race," discrimination can become intense.

Negative Beliefs about Puerto Ricans

Like Mexican Americans, Puerto Ricans are at times considered lazy, submissive, and immoral, with propensities for crime and gang violence (Wagenheim, 1973; Lopez, 1973; Díaz-Cotto, 1996). Because poor Puerto Ricans are concentrated in a few cities, and mostly in the New York City area, they are viewed as a drain on the welfare system and social services. Much like African

Americans, they are stigmatized on the basis of their welfare dependency, large families, and lack of stable employment. These beliefs create a sense of threat among some in the white population and legitimize the resulting patterns of discrimination.

The Dynamics of Discrimination against Puerto Ricans

Economic Discrimination   As is the case with Mexican migrants, the timing of Puerto Rican migration to the United States has been related to cycles in the U.S. economy. During the 1950s job recruiters would go to the island of Puerto Rico to recruit workers for the increasing number of sweatshops in the garment industry (Morales, 1986). The targets of these recruiting efforts were farmworkers in the sugar cane industry; the inability of Puerto Rico to offer these farmworkers urban jobs caused many to migrate to the United States in hopes of increasing their economic well-being (Ayala, 1996). Despite increased industrialization in Puerto Rico during the 1960s, people continued to leave the island because the Puerto Rican economy failed to absorb the growing population of unemployed farmworkers (Maldonado, 1976; U.S. Commission on Civil Rights, 1976).

Increasing unemployment and factory closings in the United States during the 1970s did not stem the tide of migration from Puerto Rico. At the same time, however, a pattern of return migration from the United States emerged, despite an unemployment rate of 20 percent in Puerto Rico (Morales, 1986). As Bean and Tienda (1987:25) summarize:

> The persistent inability of many island migrants to secure steady employment on the mainland, coupled with the displacement of Puerto Rican workers from declining textile and garment industries in the northeast during the decade of the 1970s, set in motion a return migration process whose scale and duration cannot be predicted.

Puerto Ricans have experienced job discrimination in much the same form as both Mexican Americans and African Americans. Those who lack fluency in English have not performed well on occupational screening tests, even for menial manual jobs. Those with darker skin color have often been excluded from skilled trade and craft unions, which, today, remain predominantly white. Specifically in New York City, Puerto Ricans have been negatively affected by structural changes in the city's economy away from the kinds of blue-collar jobs that provided an economic and social springboard for white ethnic groups. Similarly, Puerto Ricans who have moved to other northeastern cities have experienced the same shift in occupational structure, resulting in limited job opportunities. Unlike Mexican Americans, who are widely dispersed across urban and rural areas of the Southwest, Puerto Ricans, like urban African Americans, are concentrated in cities with a declining industrial and union base, forcing them to take temporary and low-wage jobs. Moreover, informal discrimination operates, much as it does for urban African Americans, to block Puerto Ricans from higher-wage occupations and to keep them in a large, oversupplied labor pool sustained by the welfare system. Housing discrimination almost equal to that experienced by African Americans (indeed, African American and Puerto Rican neighborhoods are often contiguous or overlapping) and inadequate public transportation limit access to jobs far from their neighborhoods (Mendoza Report, 1978).

Poverty rates for Puerto Ricans exceed those for Mexican Americans; many return to Puerto Rico, even though job prospects are dim there. This mobility creates the same problem for Puerto Ricans as it does for Mexican migrants: Movement back and forth disrupts family life, reduces the chances for building a stable employment history, and inhibits full integration into mainstream American culture, all of which further limit economic opportunities for Puerto Ricans.

Legal Discrimination   Puerto Ricans face a U.S. criminal justice system in which "the police are often seen as oppressors who do not speak the language, do not understand the culture, and lack empathy and sensitivity when acting in what otherwise would be a minor or routine situation" (Carro, 1980:369). In 1965, Chicago's Puerto Rican community rioted for three days to protest against police brutality (Cruz, 1995). The Puerto Rican community felt that they had been the victims of police brutality since their arrival in Chicago in the 1950s (Padilla, 1987). A detailed study (Sissons, 1979) of how U.S. criminal justice organizations treat Puerto Ricans found the following: Puerto Ricans are victims of language discrimination in the courts; Puerto Ricans are persecuted for some activities that are legal in Puerto Rico, such as playing the numbers and cockfighting; Puerto Ricans are more likely to be institutionalized than placed on probation; and, compared with white Americans, Puerto Ricans receive longer sentences for the same criminal acts.

Educational Discrimination   The regulation of Puerto Ricans to low-wage occupations, along with rampant housing discrimination, has limited their ability to move both within and out of urban environments, especially in New York City. Consequently, many Puerto Rican children attend schools in which they are the majority; this de facto segregation limits educational opportunity (Fitzpatrick, 1987).

The concentration of a large portion of the Puerto Rican population in low-wage seasonal jobs, along with movement to and from the island of Puerto Rico, creates waves of unemployment, thereby increasing the chances that Puerto Rican youth will drop out of school in order to help the family by obtaining a job in the low-wage seasonal sector. As a consequence, only about 65 percent of Puerto Ricans have completed high school and only about 13 percent have completed college.

Within the schools, language skills are an issue for many Puerto Rican children. Relatively few teachers and administrators are Latino, and so the culture of the school system is unfamiliar. Spanish speakers often are labeled as "learning disabled" on account of their limited English-speaking skills and their understanding of Euro-American cultural traditions. Language barriers, movement to and from the island, and the need to help support the family in temporary jobs all contribute to a high dropout rate among Puerto Rican youth, and to marginal career opportunities for many.

Political Discrimination   Puerto Ricans are underrepresented in local, state, and national politics. Even in New York City, where it could be expected that their numbers would translate into political power, Puerto Ricans are not prominent in city government, the judicial system, state legislatures, or Congress (Falcon, 1984, 1988). Part of the problem is that only about 20 percent of registered Puerto Ricans vote, a pattern that reflects deeper problems.

One reason for political disempowerment, as Hero (1992:40) notes, is that "Puerto Ricans often do not see themselves as permanent residents on the U.S. mainland—that is, they feel that they will someday return to the island—they do not develop deep political attachments on the mainland." As a consequence, they do not mobilize effective and stable bases of power, despite their large numbers in key cities. A second source of apparent political apathy is that big-city political machines traditionally have paid little attention to the Puerto Rican population. These machines tended to be dominated by white Americans of European origin who saw little need to respond to a sojourning ethnic group. Moreover, Puerto Ricans traditionally have been more politically radical and left-wing than politicians in entrenched city machines found acceptable; these politicians typically do not feel the need to respond to extremist political voices. Consequently, as networks of power were being constructed in large cities during the 1930s and 1940s, Puerto Ricans were excluded, and the legacy of this exclusion persists today, even as many political machines are being dismantled (Hardy-Fanta, 1993). Without an established network of patronage appointments and informal ties, it is difficult for Puerto Ricans to exert power proportionate to their numbers. Without political power, it is almost impossible to attack other forms of discrimination in housing, schools, the workplace, and the courts.

Puerto Ricans have reacted to their relative powerlessness, on both the island and the mainland. A nationalist movement on the island seeks separation from the United States, but the majority want statehood or the current status quo. While the platforms of the Republican and Democratic parties advocate statehood for Puerto Rico, the fact that it has not been achieved says a great deal about the reluctance of Congress to incorporate formally a Spanish-speaking population into the Union. On the mainland, a number of community service organizations have sought to organize legal services, family counseling, voter registration, political debate, and women's consciousness within the Puerto Rican community. Efforts have also been made to increase attendance in the city school systems (Fitzpatrick, 1987).

In contrast to these quiet organizational efforts, some strategies have been more aggressive. Perhaps fueled by President Johnson's effort in the 1960s to reduce poverty, political militancy grew among Puerto Ricans. One manifestation of this militancy was the emergence of the Young Lords, who used community services such as providing hot lunches and patrolling schools for drug dealers to focus attention on the plight of the Puerto Ricans in New York City (Baver, 1984; National Puerto Rican Coalition, 1985). The Young Lords also became involved in nationalist politics that advocated the severing of ties with the island of Puerto Rico.

Despite some of the strides Puerto Ricans have made, they remain politically isolated, even in areas where their numbers are great. Without political power, the ability to overcome social and economic stratification is limited.

Stratification of Puerto Ricans

Discriminatory practices against Puerto Ricans are legitimized by highly prejudicial beliefs. These practices and beliefs are ultimately fueled by a sense of threat among non-Latinos in the cities where Puerto Ricans are concentrated. Some white Americans fear that Puerto Ricans will "dilute" white European culture, that they will have to pay for increased social services to Puerto Ricans who are unemployed and have too many babies, that they will lose their jobs to Puerto Ricans who will work for less, that they will have to share local political power, that they will lose control over the Eurocentric curriculum in schools, and that they will become the victims of gang violence and crime.

Aside from the barriers created by prejudice, Puerto Ricans must battle an economic system that fails to accommodate them. They cannot easily move into middleman minority niches; their numbers are too large in key cities and their entrepreneurial skills are lacking. Without a firm foothold in the economy, the educational system, or the political arena, most Puerto Ricans living in the United States have fallen to the lower stratum of American society, although a sizable minority has been mobile to the middle and upper-middle classes.

CUBAN AMERICANS

Fewer than 50,000 Cubans lived in the United States before Fidel Castro overthrew the regime of Fulgencio Batista in 1959 (Perez, 1980). This coup led to an exodus of Cubans seeking political asylum during the 1960s. By 1970, over a half million Cubans resided in the United States (Massey, 1983); and by the end of the 1970s, Cuban American communities were firmly established in south Florida. Although the Cuban population grew to slightly over one million persons by 1993, it is the smallest segment of the Latino population relative to the Mexican American and Puerto Rican segments. Its relatively small size and concentration in Florida, especially Miami, has created a Cuban American ethnic enclave with an economic base in small business (Wilson and Portes, 1980).

Several factors differentiate the arrival of Cubans in the United States from that of Mexicans and Puerto Ricans. First, the Cubans came to the United States as political refugees from communism; hence, they were perceived as desirable in light of the politics of the cold war. Their arrival stimulated the

U.S. Congress to enact legislation creating a resettlement program for Cubans that provided job training, employment assistance, small-business loans, mortgage assistance for home purchases, educational services (such as bilingual instruction), and reimbursement for school districts educating Cuban children (Rogg, 1974).

Second, the majority of early Cuban refugees were from the upper and middle classes, with professional and technical training as well as entrepreneurial skills and resources; these attributes could shield them from menial work and low-status occupations. Although many Cuban refugees did have to accept low-paying jobs on their arrival, the legislation approved by Congress allowed them to retrain so that they could pursue business and professional options. This opportunity enabled many refugees to transpose their occupations and professions in Cuba to the United States.

The opportunity for Cuban Americans to gain upward mobility has had visible results: Cuban-owned enterprises in Miami increased from 919 in 1967 to more than 8,000 in 1980; close to one-third of all businesses in Miami are Cuban-owned; 75 percent of the workforce in construction is Cuban, and 40 percent of the industry is Cuban-owned; Cubans control 20 percent of the banks in Miami, accounting for 16 out of 62 bank presidents and 250 vice presidents (Wilson and Portes, 1980; Bach, 1980). In 1988, five of the ten largest Latino businesses were located in Dade County, Florida (Shorris, 1992).

In 1980, Fidel Castro emptied Cuban prisons and mental hospitals, declaring that "all" who wished to leave Cuba could do so. Thus began the *Mariel boatlifts,* from the Cuban port of Mariel to south Florida. An entirely different population of Cubans entered the United States, a predominantly darker skinned, poorer, and often unemployable population. The composition of the Cuban population in the United States thus began to shift. Many of these more recent refugees created problems for the U.S. government and the Cuban community in south Florida in the areas of employment, crime, housing, and welfare services (Boswell, 1985).

Negative Beliefs about Cuban Americans

Cubans were not faced with the level or kind of stereotyping and discrimination as was encountered by Mexican Americans in the Southwest or Puerto Ricans in the cities of the Northeast. For example, the appropriation of funds by Congress to create bilingual multicultural public instruction in Dade County, Florida, guaranteed that Spanish-speaking Cuban children could maintain their Spanish-language skills while acquiring English-language facility (Pedraza-Bailey and Sullivan, 1979). As a result, Cuban children were not perceived as foreigners in public instruction, as Mexican Americans were in the Southwest.

Cubans were welcome in the United States because they were anti-Castro and anticommunist. Whereas Mexican Americans and Puerto Ricans were treated as territorial minority groups, Cubans were regarded as refugees waiting for the removal of Castro from power. Although many Americans did not

Some of the participants in the 1980 Mariel boatlifts who set sail from the port of Mariel, Cuba, to south Florida when Fidel Castro declared that anyone who wished to leave Cuba could do so.

initially expect Cubans to remain in the United States, as the Cubans assimilated into American society, they were perceived as industrious, intelligent, and law-abiding (Bryce-Laporte, 1982).

The Mariel boatlift in 1980, along with growing recognition that most Cubans are here to stay, has altered many Americans' perceptions of Cubans. Hostility toward Cubans has escalated (Portes and Rumbaut, 1990). Moreover, African Americans in south Florida have begun to discriminate against Cubans in reaction to their own increasingly subordinate economic status. Many African Americans living in this region are now competing with low-wage labor from Cuba. As the welfare and social services burden of the Mariel boatlifts has reduced benefits for African Americans, the latter's intolerance has increased, culminating in a series of riots in Liberty City and Overtown, Florida.

The Mariel experience may have triggered latent white and manifest African American resentment toward Cubans. Then, as Miami has expanded its image as a bilingual–bicultural community, resentment from the non-Latino community has increased. In November 1980 voters in Dade County approved an English-only ordinance that reversed the policy of official bilingualism established by the Board of County Commissioners in 1973 with the official support of Congress. An analysis of the voting patterns showed that non-Latino white citizens voted overwhelmingly for the English-only ordinance because they wanted to limit the increasing Latinoization of south Florida. Positive perceptions of Cubans as anticommunist refugees have shifted to a more negative belief based on their language as well as their Latino cultural roots, their more recent criminality and violence, and their success in "Latinoizing" south Florida.

The Dynamics of Discrimination against Cuban Americans

Economic Discrimination   The arrival of Cubans as political refugees triggered a response from the federal government that insulated them from many of the economic obstacles faced by Mexican Americans and Puerto Ricans. To the government, the comparatively small numbers of Cubans meant that social and educational programs could focus on mainstreaming Cuban refugees into the U.S. economy. As a result, the Cuban American population has been overrepresented in white-collar professions and businesses, while being underrepresented in agricultural and blue-collar occupations (Boswell, 1985).

The entrepreneurial skills of many Cuban refugees allowed for the creation of an ethnic enclave—"Little Havana" in Florida—that facilitated the economic transition of newly arrived Cuban refugees (Wilson and Portes, 1980). The emergence of Cuban-owned firms, especially in Dade County, Florida, provided employment opportunities for other Cuban refugees. These opportunities made it possible to stratify Cuban refugees as employers or low-wage earners, with the result that Cuban-owned firms reproduced in microcosm the stratification evident in pre-Castro Cuba. Indeed, as in the pre-Castro era, Cubans in lower-paying jobs have been subject to the exploitive economic practices of entrepreneurial Cuban business owners.

The arrival of the *Marielitos* in the United States in 1980 added a new stratum to the socioeconomic structure of the Cuban American population. The majority of the Marielitos were single, black, adult males with a criminal background. The arrival of the Marielitos in Dade County was so dramatic that the county's unemployment rate jumped from 5 percent to 13 percent (Boswell, 1985). The unwelcome reception given to the Marielitos by the American public was reinforced by the Cuban American community in Miami as well. Like other dark-skinned minority groups in the United States, the Marielitos were exploited as a cheap-labor pool that could be hired and fired at will.

Legal Discrimination   The comparatively high socioeconomic status of the early Cuban migrants, the relative recency of their arrival in the United States, and their image as anti-Castro, anticommunist political refugees have limited their involvement with the U.S. legal system. The majority of the Cuban American population resides in an economic and social niche that insulates them from unnecessary contact with law enforcement agencies. There are, however, two exceptions to this situation, both centering on the Marielitos.

First, the 1980 Mariel boatlifts created a logistical problem: Where were an estimated 125,000 Cuban refugees to be housed? The Carter administration responded by using Eglin Air Force Base as a processing center for the Marielitos (Boswell, 1985). The majority of the Marielitos regarded their move to Eglin as an attempt by the president to institutionalize them, a reminder of their status as prisoners in Cuba. As a result, soon after their arrival in Eglin, the Marielitos rioted and federal troops were called in. The Marielitos were the first segment of the Cuban American population to come into conflict with U.S. law enforcement agents in much the same way as the unwanted Mexican immigrants.

Second, the arrival of the Marielitos in Miami brought unexpected social problems to the Cuban community. A large number of the Marielitos had been Cuban prisoners because they were drug addicts (Page, 1980). Not surprisingly, their arrival increased the incidence of drug use in Miami's Cuban population. Since the majority of the Marielitos were black, the African American community in Miami perceived them as a threat to the positive relationship it had forged with law enforcement agencies; if crime-prone and drug-using Marielitos were mistaken for African Americans, the latter would suffer at the hands of law enforcement agencies. As a result, African Americans pushed for a distinction between Marielitos and themselves in treatment by the law—a pressure that only increased discrimination against newly arrived Marielitos.

Educational Discrimination   In contrast to the prejudice and discrimination experienced by Mexican Americans and Puerto Ricans in the educational system, Cubans were offered educational programs as a vehicle for assimilation into U.S. society. Hence, the education of Cubans in the United States has not been associated with the production and perpetuation of inequality. Indeed, the average level of education attained by the Cuban American population is closer to that of the non-Latino white population.

The recent *"English as the official language" movement* has been particularly strong in south Florida, and it has changed the receptiveness of schools to bilingual and special programs for Cubans at the very time that the most needy members of this population—the Marielitos—entered the educational system (Castro, Haun, and Roca, 1990; Dyste, 1990). Consequently, more recent, poor, and black Cuban immigrants will be more likely to experience the same types of educational discrimination as other Latino migrants.

Political Discrimination   The initial waves of Cuban refugees to the United States were members of the professional, entrepreneurial, and/or upper classes in Cuba, who, like most people in affluent social strata, were politically conservative. Their self-perception as "exiles" and their commitment to preserving the class distinctions eliminated by Fidel Castro caused a majority to align themselves with the conservative politics of the Republican party (Torres, 1988). According to Hero (1992), the Reagan administration was instrumental in promoting conservative politics in the Cuban American population. For example, the Cuban community lobbied for the creation of Radio Jose Marti and for aid to the Nicaraguan contras. The Cuban community has also exhibited its ability to serve as a voting bloc for Republican party candidates to the Florida state legislature. Moreover, in local community politics, Cubans have been highly successful in securing seats on city councils and school boards. Such success, however, has caused political backlash from African Americans, who overwhelmingly vote against Cuban candidates, and, increasingly, from white Americans who are also threatened by Cuban political success.

With the fall of communism as a cold war threat, and with the social and economic problems associated with more recent Cuban immigrants, the success of Cuban Americans in politics may begin to level off. Also, African and white Americans may feel threatened by Cuban politicians as national politics moves away from its forty-year obsession with containing communism. Thus, despite the success of Cubans in the political arena, political discrimination against them may well increase over the next decade.

Stratification of Cuban Americans

If there is a success story among the Latino population it is Cuban Americans. Their entry into this country was a positive one. The U.S. government created social, educational, and occupational programs that allowed them to transfer their social and economic positions in Cuba to the United States. They lead other Latinos in educational, economic, and occupational attainment. In some cases, the Cuban American population has outpaced the non-Latino white population. Despite the recency of their arrival in the United States, most Cuban Americans enjoy a privileged position in U.S. society relative to other Latinos (Nelson and Tienda, 1985; Rodriguez, 1992). Stratification is more evident *within* the Cuban community, however. Recent immigrants are more likely to be black, less skilled, poor, unemployable, drug-addicted, and criminal; like their counterparts within the African American community, they may eventually constitute a volatile subpopulation. Those who are willing and able to work may be exploited by their employers, as is the case with many other Latinos and African Americans. Thus, while Cubans as an aggregate are highly successful, considerable inequality and stratification within the Cuban population exist (Perez, 1986).

As African Americans and white Americans feel more threatened by the Cuban American presence, discrimination against, and stratification of, Cubans are likely to increase. The English-only movement in Dade County, Florida, is perhaps a harbinger of a new, more intense wave of institutionalized discrimination.

SUMMARY

With the Spanish conquest of Mexico, Central and South America, and parts of the Caribbean islands, Spanish-speaking populations surrounded the English-speaking Anglo-Saxon core in the United States. Inevitably they were to come into conflict, with the Anglo-Saxon core winning all of the important confrontations. The consolidation of formerly Spanish territories as part of the United States (or at least as part of its sphere of influence), coupled with subsequent patterns of immigration and settlement from formerly Spanish-controlled areas, has created a highly dynamic and fluid situation in which the Latino population will soon be America's largest minority. Most of this large Latino minority will be of Mexican origin, with significant numbers of Puerto Ricans, Cubans, and both Central and South Americans.

The largest group in the Latino population, Mexican Americans, lags behind Puerto Ricans and Cuban Americans in educational attainment, income, and occupational status. Chicanos are thus at the bottom of the Latino population, whereas Cubans are at the top and Puerto Ricans somewhere in between. Rank in resource distribution and stratification is the result of intense and institutionalized discrimination against those of Mexican origin, somewhat less severe discrimination against those from the island of Puerto Rico, and more favorable treatment of those early anti-Castro Cuban refugees, with growing discrimination against those who have immigrated recently.

Among Mexican Americans, the retention of the Spanish language, as well as other cultural traits, sustains their identifiability, making them easy targets of discrimination since the Mexican-American War. Continued immigration, both legal and illegal, from Mexico has maintained this identifiability, which has been codified into negative stereotypes ranging from portrayals of males as "banditos" and, later, as macho and violent street criminals to images of young women as seductresses and of mature women as overbreeding, passive mothers of street gang members, and the accepting wives of lazy husbands or macho men. These beliefs help to sustain discrimination in jobs and wages in both rural and urban settings in every facet of life. They have legitimated maltreatment by the legal system since the early betrayals of the Treaty of Guadalupe Hidalgo by Anglos. The educational system fails to recognize the special learning problems of Spanish-speaking youths who are members of a culture that has not fully abandoned its original home or accepted its new home. In politics a wide variety of tactics, from gerrymandering to intimidation by the Immigration and Naturalization Service and the Border Patrol, have kept Mexican Americans disenfranchised relative to their numbers in the population. Such patterns of discrimination are sustained by widespread fears among non-Latinos about the rapidly growing size of the Spanish-speaking population and what this will mean for Anglo culture and institutions.

For Puerto Ricans, who became U.S. citizens through the annexation of Puerto Rico and the Jones Act, which gave them free access to the mainland, discrimination has taken a pattern somewhat different from the discrimination against the Mexican-origin population. Puerto Ricans are visible not only because of their language and culture but also because a significant portion of the population bears the dark skin of their African origins. For both segments of the Puerto Rican population, negative stereotypes of them as lazy, sneaky, clannish, crime-prone, violent, and welfare-dependent have been used to justify discrimination in jobs, in treatment by law enforcement, and in schools. At least 35 percent of the over-25 age groups have not completed high school. In politics they are underrepresented even in those areas with very high numbers and concentrations of Puerto Ricans. In housing they are victimized by high segregation. Because Puerto Ricans continue to be concentrated in the urban

Northeast, they are perceived as a threat to non-Latino whites in this region of the country, thereby guaranteeing continued patterns of discrimination.

For Cuban Americans, who have been treated as desirable anticommunist refugees of the Castro regime in Cuba rather than as undesirable immigrants, discrimination has been much less intense. Since the early waves of Cubans were upper and middle class with technical, professional, and business skills, they were not subjected to the same intense stereotypes as were other Latinos. However, the more recent waves of poor and often criminal Cubans, many of whom are black, to the mainland have escalated the level of discrimination. With the recognition by many, especially those in south Florida, that Cubans are here to stay, negative stereotyping much like that experienced by Puerto Ricans is beginning to accelerate, foretelling of future discrimination.

Until the last decade, Cubans were able to prosper economically, often with the help of programs sponsored by the federal government, and to become politically successful and powerful in south Florida. Their success and refugee status shielded them from entanglement in the legal or law enforcement system. Educationally they achieve at a rate higher than non-Latino whites. But as poorer Cubans have entered the country, they have brought many of the problems of the poor—from crime to drug abuse—and this shift will change the perception of Cubans in the future.

Increasingly, all Latinos are seen as a threat because their numbers are increasing relative to the European-American stock. This threat has reinvigorated old prejudicial beliefs against Latinos and legitimated new patterns of discrimination in schools, in the activities of law enforcement agencies, in politics, and in the job markets for low-skilled workers. Mexican-origin people suffer the most discrimination and prejudice because they are the largest, fastest-growing, and, hence, the most threatening of the Latino ethnic groups. But recent Cuban refugees still suffer a great deal of discrimination and prejudice within and outside the Cuban community; and unskilled Puerto Ricans have a difficult struggle in the financially burdened cities of the Northeast. In the near future, then, Latinos will come to rival African Americans for the dilemma they pose to the Anglo-Saxon core in a free and democratic society that values equality of opportunity.

POINTS OF DEBATE

As the size of the Latino population grows and as white ethnic Americans approach being a bare majority of the total population, the sense of threat among non-Latino Americans will increase, potentially setting into motion new and intense forms of discrimination. On the other hand, the very size of the Latino population by the midpoint of the twenty-first century will serve the Latinos as a resource for economic and political power against the discrimination that ensues from the threat. In any case, the next fifty years will pose a number of volatile points of debate.

1. Can English be maintained as the ascendant language, or are parts of the country to become bilingual? Non-Latino Americans feel intensely that all immigrants must learn English, but because Latino immigrants remain close to their country of origin, Spanish remains the language of everyday use among large numbers of Latinos. Should this use of language and other non-Anglo cultural traits be suppressed? Or are Americans going to have to change their views about bilingualism in America? In either case, debate and action will be intense.

2. Because the Latino population will be so large and a clear majority of the population in the Southwest, the patterns of assimilation evident for other minority populations may not occur. Latinos may be able to carve out a social niche within the Anglo-Saxon core, maintaining their own economic, cultural, educational, and religious institutions. The intensity of feeling in the Southwest about language will thus be magnified many times over, as Anglos seek to stop this potential subsociety in America. What will happen? Violence? Mass exodus of non-Latinos? Adjustment and accommodation of non-Latinos to a dual culture and society? Or will this confrontation of lifestyle and culture be avoided? There is no clear answer to these questions, indicating that ferment and debate will be intense—as is already evident.

3. Americans do not feel that they "owe" Latinos compensation for past acts of discrimination in the same way that they owe African and Native Americans. This lack of "collective guilt," coupled with rising fears about the Latinoization of American culture, will pose a real problem for non-Latino Americans who resent with ever greater intensity the invasion of their territory, institutions, and cultural patterns. How is this resentment to be mitigated? Can it be reduced? Or are non-Latino Americans and Latinos on a collision course? And what will be the outcome of this collision as it intensifies from the political posturing of today to the dramatically escalated rhetoric and potential Latino political empowerment of tomorrow?

KEY TERMS/KEY LEGISLATION

braceros, 159
Community Service Organization, 166
"English as the official language" movement, 177
G.I. Forum, 166
Immigration and Naturalization Service (INS), 162
Immigration Reform and Control Act (IRCA), 157
La Raza Unida, 167

Latino, 144
League of United Latin American Citizens (LULAC), 166
Mariel boatlifts/Marielitos, 174, 176
Operation Wetback, 159
Texas Rangers, 162
Treaty of Guadalupe Hidalgo (1848), 156
U.S. Border Patrol, 162

CHAPTER 7

Asian Americans

*P*raised for their industriousness, heralded for their educational attainments, and lauded for their economic success, Asian Americans are often viewed as the *model minority*. Indeed, most Americans believe that the success of Asian Americans stems from a combination of industriousness and avoidance of discrimination (McQueen, 1991). But the history of Asian immigration tells a very different story, and the persistence of negative stereotypes and acts of discrimination reflect past patterns that persist today, though in more subtle and muted form (Takaki, 1989; Matthaei and Amott, 1990).

The first Asians to arrive in the United States in significant numbers were the Chinese, who initially worked in the gold mines of California in the 1850s and, later, in building the transcontinental railroad. By the early twentieth century, the Chinese were joined by increasing numbers of Japanese, Filipinos, Koreans, and Asian Indians. By the 1920s, this immigration decreased dramatically in reaction to a series of highly restrictive immigration laws enacted by the U.S. Congress and targeted at immigrants from Asian countries. Later, in the period after World War II, these laws were liberalized, opening the door to a new wave of Asian immigration (Hing, 1993).

Asians made up 1.5 percent of the U.S. population in 1980 and 4.2 percent in 2000, indicating that their numbers have increased by 180 percent over the last twenty-four years (U.S. Bureau of the Census, 1995, 1999b, 2002). Over 40 percent of the Asian American population is composed of Chinese and Filipinos, followed respectively by Asian Indians, Vietnamese, and Koreans (U.S. Bureau of the Census, 2002). The growth of the Asian American population between 1980 and 2000 is summarized in Table 7.1. According to the data in the table, the Vietnamese population has grown the most, while the Japanese population has grown the least. Figure 7.1 shows the cities in California with the highest percentage of Asians in their populations.

People tend to lump Asians together because of their physical appearance, but each subpopulation has a distinct language, culture, and organizational pattern. Indeed, much of the subtle discrimination against Asians comes from the failure to recognize and appreciate their differences. Yet, for our purposes it is useful to consider Asian Americans together in order to describe what they

TABLE 7.1 Growth of the Asian American Population by Major Ethnic Group, 1980 through 2000

Asian Ethnic Groups	Number (thousands)		Percent change between 1980 and 2000
	1980	2000[1]	
Total Asians	3,466	10,019	+189%
Chinese	812	2,315	+185
Filipino	782	1,850	+137
Japanese	716	797	+11
Asian Indian	387	1,679	+334
Korean	357	1,077	+202
Vietnamese	245	1,123	+359
Other Southeast Asian[2]	69	510	+639
Other Asian[3]	97	557	+474

[1]Asian alone category.
[2]Cambodian, Hmong, Laotian.
[3]All other Asian American ethnic groups.

Source: Lee, 1998; U.S. Bureau of the Census, 2002.

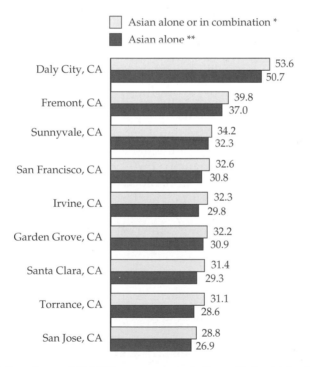

FIGURE 7.1 Ten places of 100,000 or more population with the highest percentage of Asians: 2000.

*Persons reporting Asian and at least one other race.
†Persons reporting only Asian.

Source: U.S. Bureau of the Census. The Asian Population: 2000. Washington, DC: U.S. Census Bureau, 2002.

all have in common—the experience of being victims of negative stereotyping, prejudice, and discriminatory practices directed at Asians living in America.

RESOURCE SHARES OF ASIAN AMERICANS

Impoverishment of Asian Americans

Table 7.2 summarizes poverty statistics for both the white American and Asian American populations. From 1970 to 2000, poverty rates for both populations were roughly similar. Between 1990 and 2000, however, the poverty rate decreased by 5 percent for white Americans and 30 percent for Asian Americans.

Income of Asian Americans

Table 7.3 shows that the median household income of Asian Americans is higher than that for white Americans. The net gain in income between 1990 and 2000 was 22 percent for white Americans and 26 percent for Asian Americans. Interestingly, comparing the data in Table 7.2 and Table 7.3 shows that the decrease in poverty between 1990 and 2000 for white Americans and Asian Americans, 5 percent and 30 percent, respectively, coupled with the increase in income between 1990 and 2000 for white Americans and Asian Americans, 22 percent and 26 percent, respectively, suggests that Asian Americans had a noticeable improvement in their quality of life between 1990 and 2000. According to Wellner (2002), Asian Americans have become the wealthiest ethnic group in the United States with an estimated spending power of over $300 billion.

Three main factors contribute to the higher incomes of Asian Americans (Cabezas, Shinagawa, and Kawaguchi, 1990). First, both spouses work in a larger proportion of Asian American families. Second, because Asian American children tend to live with their parents for a longer period than do white American children, they become contributors to the household income. Third, Asian families are larger on average, thus more wage earners live in each

TABLE 7.2 Poverty Rates among White Americans and Asian Americans

Year	White Americans, %	Asian Americans, %
2000	9.5%	9.9%
1990	10.0	14.1
1980	9.4	9.0
1970	10.9	11.5

Source: U.S. Commission on Civil Rights, 1988, 1992; U.S. Bureau of the Census, 1992a; March 1994 CPS; March 1998 CPS; Proctor and Dalaker, 2002.

TABLE 7.3 Median Household Income and Number of Workers per Household for White Americans and Asian Americans: 1980, 1990, and 2000

	White Americans			Asian Americans		
	1980	1990	2000	1980	1990	2000
Median household income	$20,835	$36,915	$45,904	$22,713	$42,245	$55,521
Number of workers in each household, %						
0		12.3%	13.9%	*	7.8%	10.4%	*
1		32.9	26.5	*	29.2	26.5	*
2 or more		54.9	59.7	*	63.0	63.1	*

*Not reported.

Source: U.S. Bureau of the Census, 1999a; U.S. Commission on Civil Rights, 1992; March 1994 CPS; March 1998 CPS; DeNavas-Walt et al., 2001.

household (Suzuki, 1989; U.S. Commission on Civil Rights, 1980, 1988). Thus, the income figures for Asian American families do not reflect the fact that it takes more Asian American wage earners per household to attain the income level of the average white American household.

Occupational Distribution of Asian Americans

Statistically, it is undeniable that Asian Americans are successful in the employment arena. According to the figures in Table 7.4, Asian Americans outnumber white Americans in several desirable occupations. For example, the percentage increase between 1980 and 2000 of Asian Americans in executive, managerial, and administrative occupations was greater than that of white Americans; 67.4 percent of the Asian American population is now employed in executive, managerial, administrative, technical, sales, and administrative support occupations compared to 63.5 percent of the white population.

The occupational success of the Asian American population, especially compared to other minority groups such as African Americans and Latinos, needs to be qualified, however. Hurk and Kim (1989) argue that the occupational accomplishments of Asian Americans create a "false consciousness" among Asian Americans that disguises their patterns of underemployment. That is, Asian Americans accept, to a degree, the stereotype that they are successful in light of their visibility in high-status occupations (doctors, engineers, scientists, entrepreneurs, etc.). As a result, they develop a false consciousness in believing that Asian Americans are more successful than they are unsuccessful (Gee, 1993; Wong et al., 1998). Yet, despite their representation in high-status occupations, most Asian Americans hold jobs in the *lower levels* of these professions (Osako, 1984; Duleep and Sanders, 1992; Sue, Zane, and Sue, 1985; Cabezas et al., 1989). For example, the placement of Asian Americans at lower

TABLE 7.4 Occupational Categories for White Americans and Asian
Americans* Age 16 and Over: 1980, 1990, and 2000

Occupational	White Americans, %			Asian Americans, %		
Category	1980	1990	2000	1980	1990	2000
Managerial and professional specialty	24.3%	27.4%	33.2%	24.8%	31.9%	39.3%
Technical, sales, and administrative support	31.3	33.2	30.3	30.3	33.8	28.1
Service	11.5	12.5	11.8	15.9	15.2	14.9
Farming, forestry, fishing	2.9	2.6	2.3	1.9	0.7	0.6
Precision production, craft, and repair	13.4	11.0	10.9	9.9	7.7	5.7
Operators, fabricators, laborers	16.6	13.3	11.6	17.3	10.8	11.3

*Includes Japanese, Chinese, Koreans, and Filipinos.

Source: U.S. Commission on Civil Rights, 1986; U.S. Bureau of the Census, 1992a, 1992b; March 1994 CPS; March 1998 CPS; Current Population Survey, March 2000 (Internet release date: June 28, 2001).

levels in their professions has resulted in a noticeable pattern according to Ronald Takaki (1996:43):

> This very image can produce a reinforcing pattern: Asian-American professionals often find they "top out," reaching a promotional ceiling early in their careers.

For example, in a study of Asian workers in management positions in local, state, and federal government agencies in the San Francisco area, Amado Cabezas found that most of the Asian American workers were at the bottom of the managerial tier, indicating that Asian Americans had lower salaries than their white counterparts (U.S. Commission on Civil Rights, 1979). Similarly, in a study of managers in U.S. corporations, "Asian descent" was found to have a negative effect on becoming a manager (Chiu, 1994:1089):

> The probability that an Asian man will become a manager is seven to eleven percentage points lower than for a white man. The study was adjusted for English-proficiency and was limited to American-born Asian Americans, so that language proficiency and cultural barriers could not account for these findings.

Thus, because of a "glass" or "bamboo" ceiling, many Asian Americans have not fully benefited from their mobility into the professional and management ranks (Equal Employment Opportunity Commission, 1985). Pat Chew (1996:37) has noted that even in occupations, such as law school faculty, where Asian Americans are relatively invisible, they find themselves channeled into certain professional roles because they are perceived as "foreigners, inarticulate, and nonadversarial."

Asian Americans have achieved visibility in high-status occupations (e.g., as doctors, engineers, scientists, and entrepreneurs), creating the stereotype of success. However, most Asian Americans hold jobs in the lower levels of these professions, held back by a *glass* or *bamboo* ceiling.

The notion of a *glass or bamboo ceiling* refers to the perception held by Asian Americans that, because of negative stereotypes about them, they are limited, despite being qualified, for advancement in professional occupations. Some of these negative stereotypes are rooted in the perceptions that Asian Americans are unaggressive, have poor and/or limited communication skills in English, and are too technical to be effective managers (Nguyen, 1993). As Chiu (1994:1090) has noted: "Asian Americans continue to be denied employment opportunities simply because they speak English with a foreign accent."

The overall occupational success of the Asian American population has reinforced the image of them as the model minority, an image that belies their difficulty in integrating fully in the professional world, especially its upper echelons (Thomas, 1995; Kang, 1996). Acceptance of the image by both Asian Americans and white Americans also creates the illusion that the entire Asian American population is not subject to social problems and does not need help from either the state or federal government (Hu, 1989; Lee, 1993). As Crystal (1989:405) has noted:

> In reality, the "model minority" myth has obscured many serious problems in the Asian community and has been used to justify omitting Asian Americans from federal funding and some special minority programs. Moreover, the Asian-American success story has been turned into a weapon against other minorities by persons who deny the existence of racism in America.

Educational Attainment of Asian Americans

The Asian American population is regarded as the most educated group in U.S. society (Grove and Wu, 1991; Hirschman and Wong, 1986). A review of the data in Table 7.5 shows that the high school graduation rate is similar for Asian Americans and white Americans. However, the college completion rate for Asian Americans is noticeably greater than that of white Americans, 43.9 percent and 28.1 percent, respectively. Despite the difference in college completion rates between Asian Americans and white Americans in Table 7.5, the percentage of white Americans completing four years or more of college increased noticeably between 1990 and 2000, in contrast to a slight decrease for Asian Americans.

In 2000, 43.9 percent of Asian Americans had completed four years of college or more, compared to 28.1 percent of white Americans, a figure that accounts for their occupational success. The college completion figures in Table 7.5 often are utilized to argue that there are no barriers to higher education for Asian American students. These numbers do not reflect, however, the existence of restrictive admission policies against Asian American college applicants. Asian American student activists argue that although college applications submitted by Asian American students increased by over 70 percent between 1980 and 1990, while the number of Asian American students accepted decreased by almost 80 percent (U.S. Commission on Civil Rights, 1992).

At Harvard, Brown, Princeton, Yale, Stanford, and the University of California, a pattern of lower admission rates for Asian American applicants was discovered, even though those applicants had academic qualifications equal to those of white applicants (Bunzel and Au, 1987; Nakanishi, 1988; and Takagi, 1990). Interestingly, some college admission officers have contended that restrictive admission policies for Asian American applicants are important "because Asian American college admits would overshadow white college admits" (Takagi, 1990). This pattern of underadmitting qualified Asians has been justified as a way of overcoming "reverse discrimination" that would hurt qualified white applicants; in fact, it is a form of direct discrimination against Asian Americans, for whom "quotas" *limiting* (not increasing) their numbers apparently exist (Kang, 1996).

TABLE 7.5 Educational Outcomes for White Americans and Asian Americans, Age 25 and Older: 1980, 1990, and 2000

	High School Graduates, %			Completed 4 or More Years of College, %		
	1980	1990	2000	1980	1990	2000
White Americans	68.9%	79.1%	88.4%	17.3%	24.8%	28.1%
Asian Americans	75.1	80.6	85.6	33.4	44.3	43.9

Source: U.S. Bureau of the Census, 1983a, 1983b, 1983c, 1992a; March 1994 CPS; March 1998 CPS; Current Population Survey, March 2000 (Internet release date: December 19, 2000).

Interestingly, according to data from the 2000 U.S. Census, Asian Americans are concentrated in towns that have a major university (Wellner, 2002). For example, Asian Americans tend to be concentrated in the following college towns:

University	Percent Asian in the State	Percent Asian in the College Town
Cornell University (Ithaca, NY)	5.5%	13.7%
Penn State University (State College, PA)	1.8	8.8
University of Indiana (Bloomington, IN)	1.0	5.3
University of Wisconsin (Madison, WI)	1.7	5.8
Dartmouth College (Hanover, NH)	1.3	6.8
University of North Carolina (Chapel Hill, NC)	1.4	7.2
Texas A&M University (College Station, TX)	2.7	7.3

The preceding data show that Asians are overrepresented in college town populations relative to their representation in the state's population. One interpretation of the data is that Asians locate to areas where they are barely noticeable in a state's population simply to pursue their college education (Wellner, 2002). As such, Asians bring diversity to both the college town and campus.

Housing of Asian Americans

The existence of "Koreatowns," "Little Tokyos," "Chinatowns," "Little Saigons," and "Little Manilas" indicates patterns of residential segregation among Asian American populations. Many Asian Americans have chosen to settle in large metropolitan areas in order to enhance their social, cultural, and economic development in U.S. society (Wong, 1976; Lyman, 1986; Cabezas, Shinagawa, and Kawaguchi, 1986–87); and as a consequence, their concentration in these areas produces a high degree of residential segregation (U.S. Bureau of the Census, 2002b).

Using a *segregation index* based on the percentage of the population that would need to move into white neighborhoods to achieve complete desegregation, the U.S. Commission on Civil Rights (1992) listed the results for five groups in the Asian Americans: Japanese (42 percent), Chinese (52 percent), Filipino (55 percent), Korean (55 percent), and Vietnamese (69 percent). Based on the segregation index for each group, then, Japanese Americans are the least segregated, whereas Vietnamese Americans are the most segregated. Researchers

Box 7.1

Earnings and Education: A Dilemma
for the Model Minority

One of the indicators used to gauge the success of a population is "returns of education." The table below shows that across all categories of educational attainment the median earnings of the Asian American population are lower than the median earnings of equivalently educated white Americans. The discrepancy is more apparent for the category "4 or more years of college." While the proportion of the Asian American population in this category is greater than the proportion of the white population, the median earnings of the latter are 10 percent greater than the median earnings of the former. For Asian Americans, then, the returns of education are not comparable to those for white Americans.

	Less than High School		4 Years of High School		1–3 Years of College		4 or More Years of College	
	White Americans	Asian Americans	White Americans	Asian Americans	White Americans	Asian Americans	White Americans	Asian Americans
Median earnings*	$23,263	$18,615	$26,936	$23,016	$31,652	$30,117	$45,896	$41,755

*1998 year-round, full-time workers 25 years old and older.

Source: March 1998 Current Population Survey.

have suggested that the segregation index also reflects the groups' country of origin and length of residence in the United States (Langberg and Farley, 1985; Montero, 1981). Japanese Americans have a lower segregation index because they tend to be American-born and have resided longer in the United States. In contrast, Vietnamese Americans have a higher segregation index because the majority are foreign-born and have resided in the United States for a shorter period of time. Moreover, some of the separation of whites and Asians may be self-segregation by Asians. Yet, the separation of Asian and white Americans cannot be fully explained in terms of self-selection, nativity, and length of residence. Discrimination is also involved, as we will see shortly.

Life Span of Asian Americans

There are negligible differences between Asians and whites on factors associated with life and death (Lauderdale and Kestenbaum, 2002). According to the National Center for Health Statistics (1991), Asian Americans have a lower death rate from accidents and homicides than do white Americans. For example, in 1990 the death rate per 100,000 population by accidents was 22 for Asians and 40 for whites, while the rate per 100,000 population for homicide was 29 for Asians and 49 for whites.

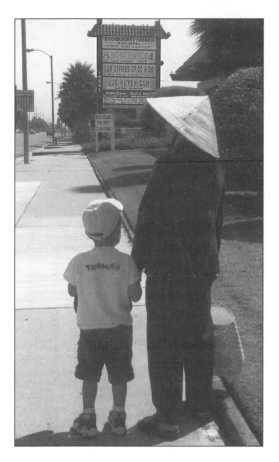

The "Little Saigon" area of West-minster, California, is home to an ethnic Vietnamese community of 300,000 residents, demonstrating the residential segregation among Asian Americans. Here, a woman and her grandson wait for a bus on a street with signs in Vietnamese clearly visible.

THE DYNAMICS OF DISCRIMINATION AGAINST ASIAN AMERICANS

Like other ethnic subpopulations in the United States, Asian Americans are victims of inaccurate perceptions by others (Lo, 2001; Thornton and Taylor, 1988; Stephan and Stephan, 1989; Sodowsky et al., 1991). Stewart Kwoh, director of the Asian American Legal Center, has observed:

> Asian Americans have been viewed as non-citizens. . . . Historically, we (Asians) have all been considered immigrants, temporary visitors, or foreigners. Even though we are not immigrants, Asian Americans, when they move out of Asian neighborhoods, are seen as new immigrants (U.S. Commission on Civil Rights, 1986:31–32).

As the number of Asian immigrants to the United States increases in the next decades, so will the perception that all Asians are recent arrivals to the United States. The perception that all Asian Americans are foreigners increases their visibility in U.S. society and reinforces negative beliefs and stereotypes that are used to legitimize discrimination (Thrupkaew, 2002).

Box 7.2
A Note on Pacific Islanders

In 2000, Pacific Islanders made up about 4 percent of the Asian population in the United States or about 399,000 persons. While the Pacific Islander population increased by 9 percent between 1990 and 2000, their proportion of the Asian–Pacific Islander population actually decreased because other Asian populations experienced even greater numerical increases—especially, Southeast Asian populations. The Pacific Islander population is divided into three groups based on region of origin: Polynesians, Micronesians, and Melanesians. Hawaiians are the largest segment in the Polynesian population followed by Samoans and Tongans. Guamanians are the largest segment in the Micronesian population, and Fijians are the largest segment in the Melanesian population.

An examination of Table 7.6 on page 193 shows that the majority (60 percent) of Hawaiians live in the state of Hawaii and the majority of Fijians (74 percent) live in California. In addition to Fijians, large percentages of Tongans (41 percent), Samoans (37 percent), and Guamanians or Chamorros (36 percent) live in California. Comparatively speaking, then, a large proportion of the Pacific Islander population residing in the United States is found in the state of California—a not unexpected finding given California's proximity to countries in the Pacific Rim.

In general, the Pacific Islander population is relatively youthful compared to the median age of the U.S. population, 21 years of age versus 30 years of age. Educational outcomes for the Pacific Islander population show that the population is enrolled at comparable levels in secondary schools (26 percent) and college (17 percent) with the U.S. population as a whole (at 25 percent and 20 percent, respectively). Since most Pacific Islanders enter the U.S. labor market as immigrants, they tend to be clustered in blue-collar occupations; and because of this fact, Pacific Islanders are underrepresented in managerial and professional occupations. Poverty in the Pacific Islander population varies by group. Tongans (22 percent), Samoans (30 percent), and Micronesians (38 percent) have a higher rate of poverty than the total U.S. population (with 13.5 percent being poor). Hawaiians (16 percent) and Guamanians (14 percent) have a slightly lower rate of poverty than other Pacific Islanders, but still a rate that is higher than the national average.

Source: Current Population Survey. Native Hawaiian and Other Pacific Islander Population 2000 (Issued September 2001).

Identifiability of Asian Americans

In the United States, Asians are unique in their physical appearance. Their skin and hair color, as well as facial characteristics (especially the epicanthic fold), make Asian Americans very noticeable in American society. This identifiability, coupled with the misconception that Asian Americans are recent immigrants, has resulted in an anti-Asian climate in the United States. For example, according to the U.S. Commission on Civil Rights (1992), anti-Asian slogans, signs, and slurs are widespread:

TABLE 7.6 Pacific Islanders in Selected States by Group, 2000

Group	Size of Various Pacific Islander Populations in 2000	Hawaii	California	Washington	Texas	Utah
Hawaiian	401,920	60%	15%	3%	2%	1%
Samoan	133,680	21	37	8	3	5
Guamanian or Chamorro	92,845	5	36	9	6	*
Tongan	36,846	16	41	3	4	23
Fijian	13,581	3	74	8	1	1

*Less than 1 percent.

Source: http://factfinder.census.gov/servlet/BasicFactsServlet.

- In California, the word "JAP" was spray-painted on the door of a Japanese American state legislator.
- In Houston, Texas, public health officials harassed Chinese and Vietnamese restaurant owners for not adopting "American" standards of cleanliness.
- A car constructed as a caricature of a Japanese face dropping a bomb on Detroit was displayed at an automobile exhibit in Flint, Michigan.
- Bumper stickers have appeared on cars in Los Angeles with the following messages: "Toyota-Datsun-Honda and Pearl Harbor," and "Unemployment Made in Japan."

Anti-Asian sentiment in the United States has targeted Asian Americans as scapegoats for many of the social ills facing the U.S. economy.

Negative Beliefs about Asian Americans

Stereotypes of Asian Americans have shifted from those stereotypes characterizing them as sneaky, obsequious, or inscrutable to the stereotype of the model minority (Chun, 1980; Hurk and Kim, 1989). According to this stereotype, all Asian Americans are hardworking, intelligent, and successful. Although this stereotype appears to be positive, it can also have negative implications, the most important of which is the perception that Asian Americans do not experience the same social and economic problems of other populations. Consequently, homelessness, poverty, unemployment, crime, and other problems of the Asian American population are often ignored (Crystal, 1989).

Another negative belief about Asian Americans is that many are recent immigrants (Hosokawa, 1982). For example, Asians are commonly asked, "Where did you learn English?" Diane C. Yu, a member of the California Commission on Racial, Ethnic, Religious, and Minority Violence, has noted that when acquaintances ask her where she was born, they are reluctant to accept "the United States" as a response; they are appeased when she mentions that her parents came from China (U.S. Commission on Civil Rights, 1986).

Portrayals in movies and television have also created persistent stereotypes (Delgado and Stefancic, 1992; Wong, 1978). Early on, Asians were portrayed in movies as cunning and savage. As anti-Asian sentiment grew, especially after the bombing of Pearl Harbor, they were depicted as tricky and devious (Wong, 1978). During World War II, most movies promoted anti-Japanese sentiment by depicting Japanese as master criminals (ironically, the role of master criminal was usually played by a white actor in makeup). These stereotypes built upon those created in 1919 by William Randolph Hearst who began an anti-Asian film serial that promoted the image of Asians as the "yellow peril."

In the public mind, Asian Americans often are regarded as "foreigners" because their status in U.S. society is often associated with foreign policy between Asia and the United States (Takaki, 1993; Schrieke, 1936). As relations between Asia and America fluctuate, so does public sentiment in the United States toward Asian Americans. For example, when the Japanese automaking industry increased its share in the United States, in certain segments of the population living in certain locations sentiment became anti-Asian. In some cases, anti-Asian sentiment has produced violent and tragic results. For example, the 1982 killing of Vincent Chin, a Chinese American, in Detroit was the result of his killers' resentment of Japanese automobile exports to the United States. As Asian automobile plants have been established in the United States, much of this intensity has receded, but the potential for a new wave of anti-Asian sentiment remains, as industries export jobs to lower-priced labor in Asian countries.

Even as excessively negative beliefs have moved some to violence against Asian Americans, a series of more subtle and invidious beliefs has emerged (Sodowsky et al., 1991). For example, the model minority becomes the "yellow peril" when Asian Americans are accused of taking jobs from white Americans, African Americans, and Latinos (Chang, 1993). Also, tensions between Japan and the United States have created various waves of "Japan bashing." Another negative belief stems from "Buy American" campaigns, which contain subtle anti-Asian messages, despite the fact that two of America's three biggest trading partners are European.

Finally, Asians' occupational niche as a middleman minority group that sells to non-Asians has created the same kinds of negative beliefs that emerge against all middleman minority groups—that they are clannish, secretive, dishonest, and devious. The Chinese were labeled with these negative epithets early on, but in recent decades these beliefs have been revived with a new intensity as Asian Americans have established small businesses in the neighborhoods of other disadvantaged minority groups, particularly African Americans and Latinos. These beliefs have created a sometimes volatile mix of resentment that erupts into violence, as the Korean merchants learned in the Los Angeles riots of 1992.

Institutionalized Discrimination against Asian Americans

The model minority stereotype has obscured the issue of discrimination against Asian Americans. This stereotype, as with so many other stereotypes, runs counter to the fact that prejudice and discrimination have been very much a part of the Asian experience in America.

Legal Discrimination Legalized discrimination against Asian Americans is best exemplified by immigration legislation, most of which was designed to exclude Asian immigrants from competing with white Europeans and, at the same time, to perpetuate negative stereotypes about Asians.

Chinese Immigration In 1848, the arrival of two men and one woman from China began a flow of Chinese immigrants that spanned three decades (Zo, 1978). The majority of Chinese immigrants were recruited as labor for the mining industry in the western United States and, later, for the building of railroads that would connect the West and East coasts. This massive immigration, however, produced a series of efforts to constrain social mobility and occupational opportunities (McKenzie, 1928; Miller, 1969):

- In 1855, California passed a law placing a fifty-five-dollar head tax on every Chinese immigrant. In 1858, a law was passed forbidding Chinese immigration into the state. In 1876 the U.S. Supreme Court ruled both laws unconstitutional.
- The U.S. Congress passed the *Chinese Exclusion Act of 1882*. The act suspended the immigration of Chinese laborers to the United States for ten years and prohibited persons of Chinese ancestry residing in the United States from obtaining U.S. citizenship after the effective date of the act. An 1888 amendment to the act applied the exclusion to all Chinese immigrants except merchants, students, teachers, tourists, and government officials. The act was extended for ten years in 1892, for two years in 1902, and indefinitely in 1904. The act was repealed in 1943 by Congress and replaced by a legislative agenda that established a quota system for Chinese immigrants.

Japanese Immigration The Japanese began arriving in the United States, especially on the West Coast, at the turn of the twentieth century. Immediately upon their arrival, they were accused of taking jobs away from U.S. citizens, of working for very low wages, and of displacing white domestic and factory workers. Anti-Japanese sentiment quickly gained supporters from participants in the Chinese exclusion movement (Penrose, 1973; Fukuda, 1980). As the number of Japanese immigrants grew, the demand for a national policy restricting Japanese immigration increased. The United States tried to avoid enacting immigration legislation against the Japanese by reaching an accord with Japan called the *"Gentleman's Agreement of 1907."* Under this compact, Japan agreed not to issue passports to skilled or unskilled workers, except for those already in the United States, or to wives or children of these workers. However, the agreement did not stem the tide of anti-Japanese sentiment:

- *The 1917 Immigration Act* was enacted in order to stop Japanese immigration as well as immigration from other Asian countries. The act barred

Chinese immigrants in San Francisco during the late 1890s.

admission of any person from "islands not possessed by the United States adjacent to the Continent of Asia" or the continent of Asia (excluding Persia and parts of Afghanistan and Russia).

- *The 1924 National Origins Act* was passed in order to stop the flow of Japanese immigrants. The act barred the immigration of Japanese wives even if their husbands were U.S. citizens, and prohibited the immigration of Japanese aliens ineligible for U.S. citizenship. The act reinforced the legal decision in *Ozawa v. United States* (1922) that persons of Japanese ancestry could not become naturalized citizens.

Filipino and Korean Immigration   While immigration from Japan and China accounted for the bulk of Asian immigration to the United States prior to the 1920s, other Asian groups came in smaller numbers. Two of these groups were Filipinos and Koreans. Since the Philippine Islands were a territory of the United States in the 1920s, they were exempt from the 1917 Immigration Act and the 1924 National Origins Act. As a result, Filipinos were free to immigrate to the United States; they are now the second largest Asian ethnic population in the United States. Filipinos were recruited to work on sugar plantations in Hawaii and as field laborers in the California agricultural industry (Knoll, 1982; Kitano, 1980). However, as the number of Filipinos grew in California, riots between Filipinos and white Americans took place. The white rioters saw the Filipinos as another part of the "Asian horde" attempting to enter the United States. Partly in response to tensions between Filipinos and white Americans on the West Coast, the U.S. Congress passed, in 1934, an act granting deferred independence to the Philippine Islands and imposing an annual quota of fifty Filipino immigrants to the U.S. mainland per year.

As early as 1885, Korean political exiles came to the United States (Kitano and Daniels, 1988). The first sizable wave of Korean immigrants went to Hawaii; between 1903 and 1905, approximately 7,000 Koreans immigrated there (Choy, 1979). By 1905, one thousand Koreans were living in California. These immigrants expected to find better working and living conditions; instead, they found low wages and substandard housing. In an attempt to protect its citizens, the Korean government banned the entry of Koreans to the United States; as a consequence, Korean immigration did not reach noticeable proportions again until the passage of the Immigration and Naturalization Act of 1965.

The Internment of Japanese Americans   Besides the use of immigration legislation to both exclude and control Asian immigrants to and within the United States, the U.S. government manipulated the legal system to discriminate against Japanese Americans by placing them in *internment* camps after the bombing of Pearl Harbor on December 7, 1941. Immediately after the bombing, the FBI rounded up over 2,000 Japanese Americans suspected of aiding Japan's war effort. Not satisfied with the small numbers of incarcerated Japanese Americans, the Hearst press, through the column of Henry McLemore, rallied the cry of "Japs Must Go" (cited in Kitano, 1980:216):

> I am for the immediate removal of every Japanese on the West Coast to a point deep in the interior . . . let 'em be pinched, hurt, and hungry. Personally, I hate Japanese. And that goes for all of them.

Responding to mounting demands for anti-Japanese legislation, on February 19, 1942, President Franklin D. Roosevelt signed Executive Order 9066, which established restricted military areas and authorized the building of relocation camps. These camps were located in California, Arizona, Idaho, Wyoming, Colorado, Utah, and Arkansas. Interestingly, even though Executive Order 9066 did not specify that it applied to persons of Japanese descent, it was applied to them exclusively. The U.S. government argued that the relocation camps were vital to the national security of the United States.

The movement of Japanese Americans to the relocation camps began in March 1942. Anyone at least one-eighth Japanese was relocated. Of the approximately 127,000 Americans of Japanese descent living in the United States in 1940, 110,000 were placed in relocation camps (Peterson, 1971; Tsuchida, 1990). Japanese Americans were forced to sell property and businesses at a fraction of their value—usually 5 cents on the dollar—and were

The identifiability of Asians has made it easy for white persons to exclude them from their neighborhoods.

allowed to bring to the camps only what they could carry. The relocation of Japanese Americans to the camps was generally smooth as a result of Japanese American cooperation; they responded to posted notices, gathered at designated departure areas, and boarded trains or buses for the trip to the camps.

Although things may have looked calm on the surface, there was turbulence underneath. Japanese Americans regarded the relocation camps as concentration camps (Daniels, 1971). At some camps, there were riots; at others, there were periods of silence between the Japanese Americans and the white guards; and in some camps anti-American slogans were painted on banners and buildings. In the cases of *Korematsu v. United States* (1944) and *Hirabayashi v. United States* (1943), Japanese Americans used the U.S. court system to question the legal status of the relocation camps. The U.S. Supreme Court upheld Executive Order 9066 in both cases (Bell, 1973).

Japanese Americans were officially released from the relocation camps on January 2, 1945. As might be expected, they wanted to know how the United States was going to redress their losses. According to the Commission on Wartime Relocation and Internment of Civilians (1983), the losses suffered by Japanese Americans interned in the camps—personal wealth, residences, businesses, and farms—were between $185 million and $400 million. In 1948, the U.S. Congress passed the Japanese American Evacuation Claims Act, which limited claims to a maximum amount of $2,500, with all claims to be submitted within eighteen months of the act's passage. The $131 million Congress appropriated for the act paid ten cents for every dollar of actual loss. It took the federal government seventeen years to process all the claims submitted; in the end, the federal government paid out $38 million (in 1942 dollars, without interest) of the $131 million allocated by Congress.

In 1976, President Gerald Ford issued Presidential Proclamation 4417, which rescinded Executive Order 9066 and apologized to the Japanese American community. This proclamation created a new concern that victimization of Japanese Americans was being perpetuated by the government's failure to fully redress their losses during the internment period. In 1980, Congress created the Commission on Wartime Relocation and Internment of Civilians (1983) in order to examine the issue of uncompensated loss of income and property to Japanese Americans during the internment period. In 1983, the commission made the following recommendations:

1. The U.S. government must offer an "official apology" to Japanese Americans.
2. The U.S. government should pardon Japanese Americans convicted of violating Executive Order 9066.
3. The U.S. government should establish a $1.5 billion fund, from which $20,000 would be paid to each of the approximately 60,000 survivors of the relocation camps.

Prompted by the commission's recommendation, Congress passed the Civil Liberties Act of 1988, authorizing the $20,000 compensation payment for living survivors of the relocation camps.

The internment itself and the reluctance in its aftermath to apologize for suspending Americans' civil rights and to compensate for obvious damages afterward sent a clear message to all Asians: This can happen to you. Though this seemed implausible, it remained a subtle threat. More significantly, the willingness to suspend Asians' (but not Germans') civil rights reflected, and at the same time contributed to, a willingness to use the law to restrict Asian immigration and to threaten those who were already here with deportation or harassment. This legal threat persists today; although it is not as blatant as the one faced by Latinos, it is just as real, especially in a period when economic tensions between the United States and its Asian trading partners are high.

Economic Discrimination   Legal discrimination against Asian immigrants limits their economic opportunities. The driving force behind anti-Asian sentiment and negative beliefs is, and has been, fear that Asian immigrants would displace white workers. The ability of Asian immigrants to create economic opportunities for themselves through small business activities was curtailed in the early decades of the twentieth century by stereotypes portraying them as dirty, immoral, unassimilable, sly, sneaky, and cheap. Such negative beliefs are typically applied to middleman minority groups, but they have been particularly intense when applied to Asian Americans because many white Americans, African Americans, and Latinos now believe that Asians want their jobs (Takaki, 1989).

These fears are codified into a set of social beliefs portraying Asians as a threat to the social and economic fabric of U.S. society. For example, according

Box 7.3
Asian Gangs and Legal Discrimination

Gangs are a part of the organizational structure of many Asian societies, linked to Asian organized crime (narcotics trafficking, prostitution, gambling, extortion, loan sharking, and other illegal activities). Elements of this activity have been imported into the United States and adapted to ghetto life. Among the Chinese, for example, violent street gangs are linked to *tongs,* fraternal societies (sometimes called "clans") that control much of the internal activity in large urban Chinese enclaves in order to secure large profits from illegal activities. The gangs control territories, typically for one of the tongs.

The result of this gang activity is that all citizens in the affected areas feel threatened by gang violence. Many complain bitterly that the police do not attack this problem with the same zeal as they attack, say, Mafia activities in other ethnic enclaves. Few federal resources—FBI and special investigators and prosecutors—or local resources—organized crime units or drug enforcement units—are devoted to Asian ghettos, where it is presumed that residents "can take care of themselves." Inattention to gangs and organized crime in Asian communities represents a form of legal discrimination against the model minority.

to the U.S. Commission on Civil Rights (1992), even though Asian Americans are represented in greater numbers than other ethnic minorities in white-collar occupations in the United States, they suffer from discrimination that limits their mobility within these occupations. They eventually confront the glass ceiling: They are in, but they can go only so far. The glass ceiling is partially attributed to stereotypical notions of Asian Americans—unaggressive, poor communicators in English, and unassimilated. Asian Americans in white-collar, especially management, occupations express their concerns as follows (U.S. Commission on Civil Rights, 1992:132):

- I am of the opinion that most Asian Americans are facing an insurmountable glass wall in the corporate world. As a matter of fact, most of us have given up hope of advancing up the corporate ladder. The more we think about it, the more frustrated, discouraged, and depressed we become. . . .
- I suspect that the minds of many corporate managers and the senior staff members who have direct control . . . are still in the 1960s. As a consequence, for most of them we Asians are a suspect class, and we usually have to prove that we are better in order to be equal. . . .
- Most of us have proved our technical capability. However, many major corporations tend to overlook the nontechnical side of many Asian Americans. Corporations pick pigeon holes for us. And what is worse, they believe that we are quite content staying in those technologically airtight pigeon holes.

Many Asian Americans perceive the glass ceiling as the product of attitudes held by white Americans. In a survey of Asian American professionals and managers in the San Francisco Bay area, Cabezas et al. (1989) found that respondents regarded prejudice as the factor that limited their upward mobility. In particular, Asian respondents blamed prejudicial attitudes for excluding them from corporate network structures, creating an environment of management insensitivity, and inhibiting mentoring opportunities for them within the corporate organization. One economic result of these attitudes is income inequality for Asian American professionals and managers (see Box 7.1) caused by limited upward mobility (Cabezas and Kawaguchi, 1990).

How real is the glass ceiling for Asian Americans? According to the U.S. Commission on Civil Rights (1988), Asian American men are less likely to be in management positions than white men with the same qualifications. In a study of the aerospace industry, the U.S. General Accounting Office (1989) found that Asian Americans were less successful in moving from professional to managerial positions than were either white Americans or other ethnic minority groups. A study of Asian American engineers found that they were less likely to be in management positions or to be promoted to management positions than were white engineers with the same qualifications (Tang, 1991). An analysis of managers in the aerospace industry also showed that while Asian Americans constituted a higher percentage of aerospace professionals than either African Americans or Latinos, they constituted the lowest percentage of managers (Chiu, 1994). A study of San Francisco's civil service found that because Asian Americans lacked opportunities for promotion, they tended to cluster in technical jobs (Der and Lye, 1989). Not only are Asian Americans clustered in some jobs in San Francisco's civil service, they are also underrepresented (13 percent) in the civil service relative to their number (28 percent) in San Francisco's population (Moore and Gunnison, 1994). This evidence affirms the existence of a glass ceiling for Asian Americans.

One result of the glass ceiling is that Asian Americans who have white-collar management and professional positions earn less than white Americans in similar positions (Cabezas and Kawaguchi, 1988). Limited upward mobility becomes a subtle but widespread form of economic discrimination, which reflects and reinforces negative beliefs held by top-level management in American corporations.

The arrest of Wen Ho Lee, a research scientist at the Los Alamos National Laboratory, on December 10, 1999, sent ripples throughout the Asian American community because it reinforced negative images of Asians in American society. The ripples merged into a tidal wave as the U.S. government increased its accusations that Lee was a spy for communist China (Loeb and Pincus, 2000). Lee's arrest portrayed Asian scientists as tools for the Chinese government's interest in stealing nuclear secrets from the United States (Bromwich, 1999). As such, the government's portrayal of Lee as a spy reinforced the stereotypic perception that Asians are sneaky and sly. A positive outcome of Lee's arrest, however, is that it caused Asian research scientists at the Lawrence Livermore National Laboratory to file bias complaints that they were paid less than white scientists and subject to racial harassment from white scientists (Kim, 1999). On September 13, 2000, Lee was released from custody when the U.S. government dropped its case against him. In dropping its case, the government admitted that 99 percent of the information Lee was accused of stealing was already available to the public and that the government's principal witness offered deceptive testimony (Locke, 2000).

Political Discrimination   Despite their increasing numbers in the last two decades, Asian Americans are relatively absent from political offices and activities. Outside the state of Hawaii, few Asian Americans have been elected to political office. According to the U.S. Commission on Civil Rights, 10 percent of the California population is Asian American; yet, only a few Asian Americans serve in Congress, only one has been elected to a state position, and Asian Americans rarely serve in the California legislature. Political offices at the local level have also evaded Asian Americans (Tamayo, Toma, and Koh, 1991; Karnow, 1992). For example, in Daly City, California, where Asian Americans constitute over 42 percent of the population, no Asian American had ever been elected to the city council by the mid-1990s; in New York City, with an Asian American population of over a half million, no Asian American has ever been elected to the city council; and in Los Angeles, only recently have Asian Americans been elected to the city council. The relative absence of Asian Americans from the political scene has resulted in some embarrassing moments. For example, Senator Daniel Inouye of Hawaii was born in the United States and was a decorated soldier, having earned the Distinguished Service Cross during World War II. During the Iran-Contra hearings in the 1980s, however, he became the target of telephone calls and telegrams, often containing racial slurs, that told him to return to Japan.

The political underrepresentation of the Asian American population is largely the result of discriminatory political practices. Bai (1991:733–34) has identified the model minority stereotype as contributing to the political underrepresentation of the Asian American population:

> This popular preconception of Asian Pacific Americans as a politically silent "model minority" is just one of the many barriers facing Asian Pacific Americans who desire to enter the political process. . . . Obscured by the popular type which labels them as the "successful" minority, however, Asian Pacific Americans are viewed either as not warranting special protection from official discriminatory practices or as already participating greatly in the political process.

What are some of the other barriers to the political participation and representation of Asian Americans? They are discussed below.

Apportionment Policies   The potential political power of Asian Americans has been diluted by gerrymandering policies that split the Asian population of a community into several districts. In a study of how apportionment policies affect the political power of the Asian American population, Tamayo, Toma, and Koh (1991) have noted that Senate district boundaries split the

Asian American community in San Francisco; and in Los Angeles, Koreatown, Chinatown, and Filipinotown each are split into several city council districts. As a result of gerrymandering, Asian Americans are not able to elect representatives from their own ranks because their voting power has been diluted.

Bilingual Election Materials   According to a provision of the Voting Rights Act of 1982, if 5 percent of a district's voting-age population is identifiable as a "single-language minority," then bilingual voting materials (that is, ballots) must be made available in the language of that minority. The linguistic diversity among Asian American populations and their lack of residential concentration prevent them from constituting 5 percent of a district's voting-age population (U.S. Commission on Civil Rights, 1992). As a result, the unavailability of bilingual election materials makes limited proficiency in English a barrier to the political participation of Asian Americans. For example, by 1980 over 100,000 Chinese Americans were of voting age in New York City, but the size of New York's population prevented this number from constituting the necessary 5 percent cutoff point for bilingual election materials. In an effort to incorporate Chinese Americans into the electoral process, federal legislation was passed in 1992 requiring bilingual ballots for Chinese American voters in parts of Manhattan, Brooklyn, and Queens (Dunn, 1994). However, two problems emerged in the effort to provide bilingual ballots: It is difficult to provide a transliteration of English names in Chinese characters, and ballot slots on voting machines are not big enough to accommodate both Chinese and English characters on the same ballot. Margaret Fung, executive director of the Asian American Legal Defense and Education Fund (quoted in U.S. Commission on Civil Rights, 1992:161), notes that:

> In Chinatown, four out of five voters have language difficulties. These voters stated . . . that they would vote more often if bilingual assistance were provided. Similarly in Queens, four out of every five limited–English proficient Asian American voters indicated that they would vote more if bilingual assistance were provided.

Political Party Snobbery   Both the Democratic and Republican parties have ignored the Asian American population, creating a lack of political party identification among Asian Americans (Bai, 1991). In turn, Asian American candidates for political office have encountered difficulties in attracting support from the major political parties. In addition, these parties have failed to create agendas that incorporate Asian American concerns. For example, in a 1989 *Washington Post* article, Joel Kotkin and Bill Bradley (1989) chastised the Democratic party for not creating a political agenda that responds to Asian American concerns and for promoting anti-Asian political rhetoric: "Yet to date, the Democrats have been remarkably resistant . . . to the idea of a less Eurocentric foreign policy. Perhaps the most ominous is the increasingly anti-Asian tone of Democratic rhetoric, all too clearly demonstrated in the 'Japan-bashing' and

---

Box 7.4
Does a Glass Ceiling Exist for Asian Americans?

- An Asian American sales professional with an MBA in marketing and sales had worked with the same Fortune 500 company for well over a decade and received many sales achievement awards when he was promoted to be the regional sales manager for the San Francisco Bay Area. He had been working in that position for three years when a new management group came in. His new boss frequently used racial slurs against him. For instance, one time, when he was speaking to his boss, his boss said, "Slow down, I cannot write as fast as a Chinaman." Eventually he was demoted and transferred to a sales territory. When he asked his boss why he had been demoted, his boss told him that it was his "gut feeling" that he [the sales professional] was not a good manager and that he did not exhibit leadership qualities. The man subsequently filed a discrimination suit against his employer at the California Fair Employment and Housing Commission and was issued a right-to-sue letter. The suit was eventually settled out of court. He still works for the same company, but he has not been reinstated to his old position.
- A woman of Asian Indian descent was hired as the personnel manager for a midwestern city. She was the first woman and the first minority member ever to be hired in a managerial position by that city. As soon as she arrived at her job, she began encountering resistance from her staff, and when she brought their behavior to the attention of her boss, he told her that her staff was insubordinate because she was a woman of color. Almost a year after she started the job, despite receiving an above-average performance appraisal, she was abruptly fired without severance pay. A subsequent investigation by the city's human relations commission found that "substantial evidence exists to show that the Complainant was discriminated against because of her sex, female, and her

---

'Korea-bashing' campaign ads." As preparation for the 1992 presidential election, Republicans established an outreach office in GOP national headquarters that targeted the recruitment of voters in the Asian American community (Awanohara, 1990). Republicans used the themes of anticommunism, antiwelfarism, and entrepreneurship to appeal to Asian American voters.

Educational Discrimination   The high levels of educational attainment by Asian Americans are often interpreted to mean that this ethnic group does not experience discrimination in education (Peng, 1990; Hsia, 1988; Wang, 1988). Yet, considerable discrimination exists, especially in institutions of higher education. The higher level of Asian American enrollment in colleges and universities has resulted in strong anti-Asian sentiments (Chiu, 1994: 1093):

> White college students rework college acronyms into biting commentary on Asian American presence. MIT becomes "Made in Taiwan," UCLA becomes

face, Asian; her national origin, India; and her color, non-white, in the manner in which she was terminated/suspended and in the conditions under which she performed her job." Despite the human relations commission finding, the city did nothing to rectify the situation. In fact, city employees repeatedly told the woman's professional colleagues and others who called that she was under suspension for not performing up to par. As a result, the woman could not find another comparable job, suffered considerable mental anguish, and did not have the financial resources necessary to pursue her case in court.

- In early 1988, Angelo Tom, a fifth-generation Chinese American who had worked at the U.S. Department of Housing and Urban Development's (HUD) San Francisco Regional office for nine years and become nationally recognized as the leading community planning and development analyst in the Bay Area, was turned down for promotion to the position of supervisor of his unit. The woman chosen to fill the job had less experience than Mr. Tom. At the time of Mr. Tom's rejection there were only three Asian Americans in middle-management positions at HUD's San Francisco office and none in upper management, and several qualified Asian Americans had repeatedly been rejected for management positions. After Mr. Tom filed a complaint, a HUD investigation found that he had been rejected for the position because he did not have leadership or interpersonal skills and was too technical for the job. Mr. Tom then requested and received a formal hearing in front of the U.S. Equal Employment Opportunity Commission (EEOC). At that hearing, witnesses refuted the HUD contention that he had poor leadership and interpersonal skills, and the EEOC administrative law judge agreed. He also held that a white man who was highly technically skilled would have been promoted with the confidence that he could develop the general outlook necessary to perform the management job. Mr. Tom was awarded back pay, a retroactive promotion, and attorney's fees.

Source: U.S. Commission on Civil Rights, 1992, pp. 134–35.

"University of Caucasians Living Among Asians," and U.C. Irvine (UCI) becomes "University of Chinese Immigrants."

Let us review a couple of prominent cases that highlight the problem.

Brown University   Between 1980 and 1983 the Asian American admission rate at Brown University fell below the overall admission rate, even though the admission rate of Asian Americans had been historically higher than the overall admission rates. As a result, the Asian American Student Association of Brown University produced a report; its analysis of admission rates between 1979 and 1983 found the following:

- The Asian American admission rate dropped from 46 percent to 26 percent, while the overall admission rate declined from 27 percent to 24 percent.

- An analysis of academic qualifications between Asian American and white American applicants did not show significant changes for Asian Americans that would justify the decrease in their admission rate.
- The acceptance of the model minority stereotype by the university administration and admissions office resulted in reduced efforts to recruit Asian American students.

Brown University responded to the report's findings by establishing the Brown University Corporation Committee on Minority Affairs. After a review of the Asian American Student Association report, this committee admitted that Asian American applicants had been treated unfairly in the admissions process. The committee recommended that in order to rectify injustices against Asian American applicants, and minority applicants in general, the admission rate of minority applicants with academic qualifications comparable to those of nonminority applicants should be equal to the admission rate of nonminority applicants.

Berkeley   The Asian American Task Force on University of California Admissions was formed in 1984 to examine a decline in Asian American freshman enrollment. In particular, the task force was concerned about the fact that as the pool of Asian American applicants grew between 1979 and 1984, the proportion of Asian American freshmen declined (Takagi, 1990). As the controversy intensified and attracted the attention of the California legislature, the auditor general of California (1987) completed a review of freshman admissions policies at Berkeley. The auditor general's report concluded that Asian American freshman applicants had been admitted at a lower rate than white American applicants despite a larger increase in the grade point average (GPA) of Asian American applicants than of white American applicants.

In 1989, the academic senate at Berkeley moved to examine the controversy surrounding Asian American freshman admissions by forming the Special Committee on Asian American Admissions. The committee reviewed admission policies, interviewed admissions personnel, and read application files. After its lengthy investigation, the committee produced a report that listed three factors responsible for the drop in Asian American freshman admissions:

1. The university's decision not to guarantee admission to applicants under the Educational Opportunity Program (EOP), and to exclude them from affirmative action initiatives (that is, applicants from economically disadvantaged backgrounds but who are not members of underrepresented groups), had a significant effect on Asian American freshman admissions because the majority (90 percent) of EOP applicants were found to be Asian Americans.
2. In the fall of 1984 the College of Letters and Science decided to raise the minimum GPA for admission but not the minimum scores on college entrance exams (for example, SATs). Applicants to Berkeley, at the time, could meet either the minimum GPA or the minimum test score for admission. Since Asian American applicants were more likely to gain admission

to Berkeley on the basis of their GPA and white students on the basis of their test scores, the change in the minimum GPA discriminated against Asian American applicants. That is, Asian American applicants had to meet higher standards than white applicants.

3. The Office of Admissions and Records announced on December 28, 1983, that applicants of "permanent alien" status not meeting a minimum SAT verbal score would be redirected to another UC campus. Even though this decision was reversed ten days later, the admissions office established a minimum score of 400 on the verbal part of the SAT for immigrant applicants only. The implementation of a minimum SAT verbal score was an obstacle to Asian American immigrant applicants.

Harvard   In 1988 the U.S. Office for Civil Rights, in response to concerns raised by the Asian American community at Harvard University, initiated a review of undergraduate admissions there. After two years of investigating undergraduate admissions, the Office for Civil Rights did not find discriminatory policies or procedures regarding Asian American applicants. Although the Office for Civil Rights cleared Harvard of discrimination charges, the review of applicant folders uncovered practices that some would deem discriminatory. In its review of applicant folders, the Office for Civil Rights found:

- Inequitable use of "ethnic readers" for Asian American applicant folders. Members of ethnic groups were used in the undergraduate admissions process to control for special cultural or ethnic factors. The Office for Civil Rights found that only a small number of Asian American applicant folders were read by Asian Americans. Consequently, it was possible that special cultural or ethnic factors were overlooked regarding Asian American applicants.
- Written comments stereotyping Asian American applicants. Some of these comments were: soft-spoken, math oriented, English-speaking difficulty, shy, and reserved. The Office for Civil Rights suggested that while the comments did not affect negatively the admission rate of Asian American applicants, they did reflect the operation of stereotypical beliefs about Asian Americans.

Housing Discrimination   A 1980 poll of white American attitudes toward Asian Americans found that the majority of white respondents (1) were against Asians moving into their neighborhoods, (2) believed that there were "too many" Asians in the United States, and (3) felt that Asians should have settled in other Asian countries (U.S. Commission on Civil Rights, 1986). At that time, in 1980, many white residents did not welcome Asian Americans into their neighborhoods, a situation that persists today. The U.S. Commission on Civil Rights (1986) documented the following examples of acts by white Americans who sought to discourage Asian Americans from living in their predominantly white neighborhoods:

- In San Francisco, white neighbors painted anti-Asian graffiti on the car of the only Asian American resident in the neighborhood.
- In Seattle, Washington, white neighbors fired gunshots at a home occupied by an Asian American family while the family was in the house.
- In Providence, Rhode Island, white neighbors painted "No Nips" on a house the day after an Asian family moved in.
- In 1987, anti-Asian flyers were distributed to mailboxes in the Bensonhurst and Gravesend neighborhoods of Brooklyn. These flyers urged the boycotting of Asian businesses and demanded that real estate agents not sell property to Asians in the neighborhoods. As a result of the flyers, Asian businesses and real estate offices that had sold property to Asians were vandalized (Giordano, 1987a and b).
- In 1981, a Cambodian family that had bought a home in a white neighborhood in Maine was the target of racial bigotry. As the father played with his children in the snow, one of his white neighbors threw a snowball at him, a snowball containing a rock. The Cambodian man approached his neighbors, blood streaming down his face, to ask why they had hurt him. His neighbors responded: "Go back where ya came from, gook" (U.S. Commission on Civil Rights, 1989).
- In Massachusetts, arsonists set fire to an apartment building that left thirty-one Cambodians homeless (Yen, 1988).

Thus, the popular belief that Asians prefer to live "with their own kind" is weakened by the discrimination Asian Americans experience when entering non-Asian neighborhoods.

Typically, the model minority does not protest as loudly as others to discriminatory treatment, but this treatment is a fact of life for Asian Americans today, over 100 years since they began immigrating to the United States. Chinatowns, Little Tokyos, Koreatowns, Little Manilas, and similar Asian enclaves exist for reasons other than the desire to live with "their own kind."

STRATIFICATION OF ASIAN AMERICANS

White American workers regarded early Asian immigrants as a threat to their jobs. In contrast, large-scale employers in agriculture and in the railroad industry viewed Asians as an inexpensive source of productive labor. Nevertheless, despite employers' views, when a majority of the working population sees a minority as a threat, negative beliefs are codified which, ironically, intensify the sense of threat. Such beliefs also legitimize discrimination. In the case of Asian immigrants, acts of violence and legal restrictions initially prevented them from fully realizing economic opportunities and gaining political power. Ghettoization ensued as a response to hostility in the host society. Yet, Asian Americans made significant gains in education, which, in turn, opened opportunities in jobs, especially after the early fears of the *yellow peril* faded and the panic of Pearl Harbor abated with the victory over Japan in World War II. Education credentials coupled with middleman entrepreneurial skills enabled the descendants of these early immigrants to enter the middle classes but with restrictions on where they could live and how high on the corporate ladder they could climb. More recent tensions with Asian trading partners, along with a new wave of Asian immigrants, have rekindled old fears, intensified negative beliefs, and generated sporadic acts of discrimination against both newly arrived and established Asian American groups.

All these factors have sustained the subtle restrictions on this disproportionately middle-class minority. In time, these restrictions may diminish, but as long as Asian Americans remain readily identifiable in tight domestic job markets and in the context of tension-filled international trade with Asian nations, the potential for sustaining or even increasing barriers to full economic and political participation remains.

RESPONDING TO DISCRIMINATION

The Asian populations discussed in this chapter—Chinese, Japanese, Korean, and Filipino—are much more successful economically than the ethnic populations explored in other chapters of this text. A much higher percentage of Asian Americans are middle class and white collar than these other populations; as a consequence, their "success" has made Asian Americans the model minority. However, the success of these established Asian immigrant groups has not been fully matched by newer immigrants. The hostility toward these new migrants creates a climate of prejudice and antagonism for the Asian American community as a whole.

Historically Asians have not mounted highly visible or violent protests against those who discriminate against them. Indeed, part of the reason why Asian Americans are considered the model minority is, no doubt, their relatively low-key protests against discrimination. For example, the internment of Japanese Americans did not generate confrontation, except in the court system. Earlier laws that restricted the rights of Chinese and Japanese Americans were often accepted, and only later challenged in court. Asian American middleman minorities in inner-city neighborhoods have countered violence with civil protests (marches and court actions) but not confrontation. The harassment and, at times, violence against Asian Americans who enter white neighborhoods usually go uncontested. The clear discrimination in college admissions patterns has been challenged, in a quiet and legal way.

The lack of effective political organization in many Asian American communities has also hindered protests against discrimination. Indeed, not until 1986 was a pan-Asian organization—the Asian-American Voters Coalition—formed to consolidate diverse Asian subpopulations into an effective voting bloc. Potentially this bloc could affect elections in states such as California, Texas, New York, and Illinois, where significant numbers of Asian Americans reside, but at this time, there is little evidence to indicate the influence of this bloc.

The subtlety of much discrimination—for example, college admissions practices, corporate glass or "bamboo" ceilings, and gerrymandering of voting

---

Box 7.5
Violence against Asian Americans

Two murders of Asian Americans in the 1980s have been etched into the national consciousness as examples of the potential intensity of discrimination against Asian Americans: the murder of Vincent Chin in 1982 and the murder of Jim (Ming Hai) Loo in 1989. These killings are prominent examples, but they are not isolated incidents. Violence against Asians leading to injury and sometimes death occurs with disturbing frequency across the country and affects many different Asian groups.

VINCENT CHIN

The racially motivated murder of Vincent Chin and the inability of the American judicial system to bring his murderers to justice became a vivid symbol and source of outrage during the mid-1980s. The facts of the case are as follows.

On the evening of June 19, 1982, Vincent Chin, a 27-year-old Chinese American, met with some friends in a Detroit bar to celebrate his upcoming wedding. He was accosted by Ronald Ebens and Michael Nitz, two white automobile factory workers, who reportedly called him a "Jap" and blamed him for the loss of jobs in the automobile industry. Ebens and Nitz chased Chin out of the bar, and, when they caught up with him, Nitz held Chin while Ebens beat him "numerous times in the knee, the chest, and the head" with a baseball bat. Chin died of his injuries four days later.

Ebens and Nitz were initially charged with second-degree murder but subsequently were allowed to plead guilty to manslaughter. In March 1983 the defendants were each sentenced to three years' probation and fined $3,780 by Wayne Circuit County Judge Charles Kaufman, who reasoned that the defendants had no previous history of violence and were unlikely to violate probation.

The U.S. Department of Justice brought federal civil rights charges against Ebens and Nitz to a federal grand jury, which indicted them on November 2, 1982. On June 18, 1984, Ebens was found guilty of interfering with Chin's civil rights, and on September 18, 1984, he was sentenced to twenty-five years in prison. However, Nitz was acquitted of the federal civil rights charges.

Ebens's conviction was overturned by the Sixth Circuit Court of Appeals in September 1986 for technical reasons, including issues pertaining to the admissibility of audiotapes and prosecutorial misconduct (overzealousness) in preparing witnesses. When Ebens came up for retrial in the Eastern District of Michigan, the defense moved for a change of venue on the grounds that Ebens could not get a fair trial in Detroit. The defense motion was granted, and the trial was moved to Cincinnati. The case was retried during the month of April 1987, and this time Ebens was acquitted.

The acquittal of Ebens in the second federal trial means that neither Ebens nor Nitz ever went to prison for Vincent Chin's killing. Some have speculated that the main reason the Cincinnati jury acquitted Ebens is that the jury could not comprehend the reality of anti-Asian bias. Whereas Detroit in the early 1980s was the scene of a massive media campaign against foreign imports, especially those from Japan, a campaign that inflamed anti-Asian sentiments in that city, there had not been the same type of campaign in Cincinnati. Also, there were very few Asians in Cincinnati, and anti-Asian sentiments were not widespread.

Box 7.5
Violence against Asian Americans (continued)

Others contend that the Cincinnati jury's acquittal of Ebens reflects a fundamental problem with current federal civil rights laws. Ebens was charged under federal criminal civil rights law Section 245(b), which prohibits (among other things) the racially motivated interference by force or threat of force with a person's use of public facilities, such as restaurants and bars. Some experts argue that the jury may have been confused about what had to be shown for there to be a civil rights violation under Section 245(b); even though the jury may have felt that the attack was indeed racially motivated, it might not have thought that Ebens specifically intended to interfere with Chin's use of a public facility (the bar).

JIM (MING HAI) LOO

Seven years after Vincent Chin's killing, another Chinese American was killed in Raleigh, North Carolina, under similar circumstances. Jim (Ming Hai) Loo, 24, had immigrated to the United States from China thirteen years before, was working in a Chinese restaurant, and was saving money so that he could attend college. On the evening of Saturday, July 29, 1989, during an altercation that began in a nearby pool hall, Loo was hit on the back of the head by a handgun held by Robert Piche. He fell into a broken beer bottle, which pierced his eye and caused a bone fragment to enter his brain, resulting in his death on July 31.

Loo and several Vietnamese friends had been playing pool in the pool hall, when Robert Piche, 35, and his brother, Lloyd Piche, 29, began calling them "gooks" and "chinks" and blaming them for American deaths in Vietnam. Lloyd Piche said, "I don't like you because you're Vietnamese. Our brothers went over to Vietnam, and they never came back," and "I'm gonna finish you tonight." Although the manager forced the Piche brothers to leave the pool hall, they waited outside for Loo and his friends, and attacked them as they left the pool hall. Robert Piche and his brother first attacked one of Loo's friends, Lahn Tang, with a shotgun, but when Tang escaped, Robert swung a pistol at another of Loo's friends, Jim Ta. He missed his intended victim and hit Loo on the head instead.

Although Lloyd Piche made most of the racial remarks, he did not strike the fatal blow. He was sentenced to six months in prison for disorderly conduct and simple assault (on Tang), both of which are misdemeanors. In March 1990, Robert Piche was found guilty of second-degree murder and assault with a deadly weapon and sentenced to a total of thirty-seven years in prison. Although Judge Howard E. Manning, Jr., gave Piche a stiff lecture, the sentence was less than he could have meted out: Under North Carolina law, Piche could have been given life in prison.

Many Asian American community leaders, struck by the similarities between Loo's murder and Chin's, pressed the U.S. Department of Justice to bring federal civil rights charges against Robert and Lloyd Piche. They were particularly anxious to see a prosecution of Lloyd Piche, who received a minimal sentence despite being the chief instigator of the incident. After a lengthy investigation, the Justice Department announced on March 29, 1991, that it had indicted Lloyd Piche on federal civil rights charges, but it did not indict Robert Piche.

Box 7.5
Violence against Asian Americans (concluded)

Lloyd Piche was indicted on eight counts of violating federal civil rights laws. On July 15, 1991, in a federal district court in Wilmington, North Carolina, Lloyd Piche was found guilty on all eight counts. On October 15, 1991, Lloyd Piche was sentenced to four years in prison and ordered to pay over $28,000 in restitution to the Loo family. Although the Justice Department had sought the maximum sentence under federal sentencing guidelines, Piche's sentence was less than the minimum sentence (six to seven and one-half years) under federal guidelines.

There are many similarities between the Loo and the Chin murders. In each case, the victim was a young man spending an evening relaxing with friends in a public facility (a bar in Chin's case, a pool hall in Loo's). In each case, an altercation began inside the public facility, and violence leading to murder erupted outside of the facility. In each case, the victim was killed after being mistaken for or associated with Asians of other nationalities. In Chin's case, his killers were venting hostility against foreign Japanese, and in Loo's case, his murderers apparently mistook him for a Vietnamese. Thus, both Chin and Loo became victims simply because they were of Asian descent.

Together, the Chin and Loo murders underscore the harsh reality of ethnically motivated violence against Asians. They also signal in different ways the general public's lack of awareness of and to some extent indifference to anti-Asian discrimination. The three-year probation and almost nominal fines imposed by Judge Kaufman on Chin's murderers are suggestive of very little value being placed on an Asian American life. The ultimate failure of the American justice system to convict Ebens of civil rights charges, perhaps partly because of the Cincinnati jury's difficulty in believing in the existence of anti-Asian hatred, also implies that many Americans view racial hatred purely as a black–white problem and are unaware that Asian Americans are also frequently targets of hate crimes. Finally, neither murder was given much national prominence. Chin's killing did receive some national attention, but Loo's killing (in stark contrast to the murder of a young black man in Bensonhurst that occurred at roughly the same time) was hardly covered by the national media and raised no national sense of outrage.

Unlike the Vincent Chin case, Loo's murder resulted in a successful federal prosecution—the first ever successful federal civil rights prosecution in which the victim was Asian American. If given sufficient attention, the federal civil rights trial of Lloyd Piche could do much to highlight the racial aspect of Loo's killing and would send a message that anti-Asian racism will not be tolerated by the U.S. government.

Source: U.S. Commission on Civil Rights, 1992, pp. 25–28.

districts—along with the sporadic nature of acts of violence against Asian Americans by angry whites and disadvantaged minorities makes it difficult to mount a concerted corrective effort, especially by a largely politically passive model minority that is not perceived to have problems. Especially as we enter the twenty-first century when considerable effort has been made by governmental and legal agencies to be more conscious of, and to correct for, past and present discrimination against African Americans, Latinos, and Native Americans, we must view with some wonder the comparatively little effort that has been made on behalf of, or by, Asian Americans. Without protests and political mobilization by Asians, it is not likely that much will be done in the future—another cost of being the quiet, model minority.

THE PRECARIOUS SITUATION
FOR ASIAN AMERICANS

Are Asian Americans really the model minority in the United States? On the surface, one could argue that their educational, occupational, and economic status is an indicator of success, especially in light of efforts to limit Asian American presence in, and assimilation into, mainstream American society. Asian Americans thus fit the model minority stereotype because many have overcome the odds and succeeded. Beneath the surface, however, the model minority image has negative repercussions for not only Asian Americans but other ethnic groups as well. For other ethnics, Hurk and Kim (1989:530) have noted:

> The dominant group's stereotype of Asian Americans as a model minority also affects negatively other minorities. Since the Asian Americans' "success" may be considered by the dominant group as a proof of openness in the American opportunity structure, there is a constant danger that other less successful minorities could be regarded as "inferior" and/or "lazy." These less achieving minorities may be blamed for their own failure and become victims of scapegoating ("Japanese have made it. Why can't they?").

The dominant group (that is, white society) can thus use the model minority image of Asian Americans as an ideological tool to maintain a pattern of unequal access to valued resources. To overstate the case in order to emphasize our point: Asian Americans succeed because they represent a small (though growing) percentage of the total population and, hence, pose less threat to the majority; other minority populations, such as African Americans and Latinos, are much larger and consequently pose more threat, which leads to more intense discrimination (Blumstein, 1982; Aguirre and Baker, 1988). With the model minority as a basis for comparison, these larger populations appear less successful—an unfair comparison because of the greater degree of discrimination experienced by these larger minority groups. Members of larger minority groups grow to resent Asian Americans whose success is used to highlight their failure. As the success of the model minority stereotype is used by white society to illustrate the "openness" of the American opportunity

Many African Americans and Latinos resent Asian Americans, evidenced by the loot-
ing and destruction suffered by Korean American store owners in South Central Los
Angeles during the riots that broke out in 1992 after four white police officers were
acquitted in the beating of Rodney King. While relations between Korean American
store owners and their black and Latino customers have improved, this Korean
American store owner works from behind protective glass.

structure, other minority populations, which have experienced far more discrimination, will be blamed for their inability to take advantage of imagined
opportunities. Yu (1980) has noted that many African Americans and Latinos
resent Asian Americans because they believe that Asian Americans are the first
to receive assistance in the United States. Similarly, Thornton and Taylor (1988)
have found that many African Americans feel distant from Asian American
populations and do not perceive Asian Americans as a minority group.

The model minority stereotype creates problems for Asian Americans as
well, perpetuating the perception that poverty, homelessness, mental illness,
crime, and other social problems do not exist among Asian Americans. As
Crystal (1989:406) has noted:

> Rather than the "yellow peril" of the past, Asian Americans are currently
> viewed as an exemplary group of honest and hardworking citizens with low
> rates of juvenile delinquency and divorce. They are perceived as having few, if
> any, mental health problems and are thought to live in homogeneous commu-
> nities composed of stable, close-knit families that "take care of their own"
> with little need of outside social services.

In reality, the lower rates of return on education, especially at the postsecondary level, and the existence of a glass ceiling in the job sector indicate that Asian Americans do indeed experience institutionalized discrimination and prejudice.

SUMMARY

The first Asians came to America beginning in the 1850s and were instrumental in the development of the commercial, industrial, and agricultural infrastructure of the West. For many years, Asian immigration was restricted, but over the last decade these restrictions have been relaxed, and the Asian population has doubled in size since 1980, although it is still quite small compared to the African American and Latino populations.

Asian Americans match or exceed white Americans in terms of average family income, educational attainment, incumbency in managerial and professional occupations, and life span. Yet, the signs of discrimination are evident along a number of fronts: Asian poverty rates exceed those of whites; returns on education to Asians are less than those for whites; and many Asians still remain segregated from non-Asians.

Asians are readily identifiable because of their distinctive eye fold and, to a lesser extent, color tones of their skin; hence, they are easy targets of discrimination. Although their success gives them the title of a "model minority" that has succeeded in spite of obstacles, lurking beneath the surface of this portrayal is a more sinister revival of the old "yellow peril" stereotype in which Asians are seen as foreigners who take jobs, admission slots in higher education, and business opportunities away from non-Asians. In the past, such perceived threats and their codification into negative stereotypes have propagated considerable violence against Asians, but more significant has been the long legacy of open legal and political discrimination against Asians, which has abated only over the last few decades. Yet, Asians still are subject to considerable violence against them from other minorities and whites. As the Asian population has increased over the last decade, more subtle forms of discrimination have been evident: Asians frequently run up against a glass ceiling, keeping their careers in check despite obvious performance and other qualifications. Asians rarely get elected to political office because of gerrymandering of their neighborhoods and because non-Asians are reluctant to vote for Asians. Asians are underrepresented in governmental appointments despite the fact that their educational credentials qualify them for these appointments in disproportionate numbers. Asians have been subjected to a quota system by elite colleges and universities, thereby denying opportunity to many qualified Asian students. And informal housing discrimination, often punctuated with white violence, is still evident in many communities. Historically, Asians have not been prone to visible protests, but in more recent years, legal and political challenges to all of these discriminatory practices have been mounted, indicating that Asians will no longer passively accept discrimination.

POINTS OF DEBATE

Asian Americans are caught in a difficult bind: Their success engenders white
hostility and, at the same time, is also used to condemn less successful minorities, thereby arousing increased hostility from disadvantaged minorities.
Asians are caught in the middle of all manner of ethnic hostility, and as the
percentage of Asians in the population increases, many intensely debated
issues will surface:

1. Considering that they are so successful, especially relative to other large
   minorities, should Asian complaints about subtle forms of discrimination
   limiting their further success be given the same attention as those from
   more disadvantaged minorities? Should programs to help Asians be of the
   same intensity as those to help less successful minorities? Should efforts at
   reducing ethnic discrimination be calibrated along a sliding scale, with
   those who are worse off getting most of the attention? The law would say
   no as an answer to all of these questions, but the policies of government
   always involve interpretations and selective implementations of the law. Is
   this desirable? Necessary? Inevitable in light of political realities?
2. As the Asian population grows in size and occupies many economic
   niches desired not only by whites but more significantly by other minorities, can hostility toward Asians be reduced, or will this tension, as mani-
   fested in the hostility of African Americans and Latinos toward Asian-
   owned businesses in their communities, become a chronic feature of the
   American landscape? If so, what is to be done to reduce this hostility?
3. Is American society in danger of hardening the lines of hostility among
   Asians, whites, Latinos, and blacks? If all are competing for the same
   scarce resources—jobs, income, education, housing—how is the tension to
   be mitigated? If America is on the path toward tension-provoking ethnic
   pluralism with each subpopulation viewing the other with considerable
   hostility, is this what most Americans want? If not, what is to be done?

KEY TERMS/KEY LEGISLATION

CHAPTER 8

White Ethnic Americans

It is often noted that America is a land of immigrants. The largest waves of immigration occurred in the nineteenth and early twentieth centuries when vast numbers of non-Protestant white Europeans entered the United States. The southern Irish were the first non-Protestants to enter in significant numbers in the early 1800s. In the final decades of the nineteenth century and the first two decades of the twentieth century, additional masses of Catholic Italians and Poles as well as Jews immigrated. This influx posed a threat to the Anglo-Saxon Protestant core, setting in motion the dynamics of discrimination.

These white ethnic populations eventually overcame Anglo-Saxon Protestant discrimination and moved up the socioeconomic ladder, and their success—often used to condemn Native Americans, African Americans, and Latinos for not doing as well—has ironically contributed to present-day negative stereotypes about other ethnic groups and to persistent patterns of discrimination against them. Although the history of these white subpopulations does provide an example of what is possible for other ethnic groups, the greater identifiability of the currently unassimilated makes them targets of prejudice and discrimination that typically inhibit full movement into the American mainstream made up of the Anglos plus the white immigrants who overcame discrimination.

RESOURCE SHARES
OF WHITE ETHNIC GROUPS

Table 8.1 on page 218 lists the occupations of prominent European-origin ethnics in 1980 and, then again, in 1990. At the bottom of the table, the occupations of non-European ethnic subpopulations are presented as a basis for comparison. Reading down, the table reports the percentage of each ethnic subpopulation in the various occupations listed across the top of the table. In a rough sense, the occupations on the left in the table generate higher incomes and prestige than those on the right side.

A person's occupation can say a great deal about access to scarce resources; and while we might also like to have income data for this detailed list of white ethnics, the only data available from the census bureau (and these data had to be hand-calculated from the raw census figures) are on the occupations of

Table 8.1 Occupations of Prominent Ethnic Groups, 1980 and 1990

Ethnic Subpopulations by Ancestry	Percentage in Managerial and Professional Specialty Occupations		Percentage in Technical, Sales, and Administrative Support Occupations		Percentage in Service Occupations		Percentage in Precision Production, Craft, and Repair Occupations		Percentage in Operators, Fabricators, and Laborers		Percentage in Farming, Forestry, and Fishing Occupations	
	1980	1990	1980	1990	1980	1990	1980	1990	1980	1990	1980	1990
EUROPEAN ETHNIC GROUPS												
British Isles												
English	30%	40%	32%	36%	10%	7%	12%	7%	14%	8%	2%	2%
Irish	28	33	33	39	11	9	12	8	14	10	2	1
Scottish	35	43	34	34	9	7	10	7	10	7	2	2
Welsh	36	43	33	34	8	7	11	8	10	7	2	1
German	28	33	32	37	10	9	12	9	15	10	3	2
Italian	27	33	36	41	11	9	12	8	13	8	1	1
Polish	28	35	34	39	10	8	12	8	14	9	2	1
Dutch	24	31	30	37	12	9	13	10	18	11	3	2
French	26	31	33	39	11	10	13	9	15	10	2	1
Swedish	31	38	33	37	10	8	12	7	11	8	3	3
Norwegian	30	36	32	36	10	9	11	8	12	8	5	3
Russian	46	57	36	33	5	4	6	3	6	3	1	*
Czech	30	35	34	36	9	8	12	9	11	9	4	3
Hungarian	32	40	34	37	9	7	11	8	13	7	1	1
Danish	32	39	33	36	9	8	11	7	11	7	4	3
Portuguese	22	23	31	36	12	11	12	11	20	16	3	3
NON-EUROPEAN ETHNIC GROUPS												
African Americans	15	20	21	30	23	19	10	9	28	21	3	1
Latinos	16	14	27	26	16	17	13	14	25	23	3	6
Native Americans	17	20	26	29	15	17	16	15	23	15	3	4
Asians	28	31	31	33	14	14	11	8	13	13	3	1

*< 1 percent.

Source: U.S. Bureau of the Census, 1983e, 1993c.

Families await processing at Ellis Island, through
which most European immigrants of the nineteenth
and early twentieth centuries had to pass.

European-origin ethnics. Thus, we will simply have to assume that the occupations listed across the top of the table are a reasonable proxy for resource shares.
Since occupation is related to educational credentials, to income, and, hence, to
living standards, the inferences to be drawn from these data are appropriate.

What, then, do these data say? European-origin white ethnics are more
likely to be in managerial and professional occupations than African Americans, Latinos, Native Americans, and, to somewhat varying degrees, Asians.
Except for Russians, who have the highest percentage in managerial and professional occupations (and those listed under Russian are predominately Jewish immigrants), and for Irish, who lag slightly behind some white ethnics, the
British Isle–origin ethnics occupy more favored occupations than non-British
Isle ethnics. And if we compare 1980 and 1990, we can see that the gap between
British Isle–origin ethnics and other Europeans has not closed. In general, data
from the 2000 U.S. census regarding occupations of the foreign-born by world
region of birth (Europe, Asia, and Latin America) show that: 1) persons born in
Europe (38%) and Asia (39%) are the highest percentage in managerial and professional occupations; 2) persons born in Asia (27%) are the highest percentage
in technical, sales, and administrative support occupations; and 3) persons born
in Latin America are the highest percentage in service occupations (23%), in
precision production, craft and repair occupations (16%), in operator, fabricator,
and laborer occupations (25%), and in farming, forestry, and fishing occupations (8%) (data can be found at www.census.gov/foreignborn/March2000).

By following any particular white ethnic's percentages across the table, it is evident that all the European-origin ethnics do better than all other non-European ethnics, except Asians who do the best among non-Europeans in securing managerial and professional positions but not as well as most white ethnics. Yet, except for Latinos, all ethnics appear to have been somewhat upwardly mobile in securing managerial and professional occupations (the Latino drop between 1980 and 1990 can be attributed to the massive immigration of the poor and uneducated Latinos, coupled with very high dropout rates from high school among Latinos).

Reading down the second column of Table 8.1 where percentages of ethnics in technical, sales, and administrative support occupations are listed, all ethnic subpopulations have improved their representation in these types of occupations, again except for Latinos, who reveal about the same percentage as in 1980. Much of this shift is the result of changes in the occupational structure of the society toward white-collar occupations, but some of this change is the result of real improvement in living standards.

The service occupations listed in the middle of the table represent a good indicator of mobility patterns; those ethnics who see their percentage decline in service occupations will generally experience an increase in their percentage in managerial, professional, technical, sales, and administrative positions. At the same time that their numbers increase in these higher-paying jobs, their percentages in the manual occupations on the right side of the table decline. Indeed, all ethnics see their percentage in manual occupations decline, or remain about the same—again, signaling the shift of the broader occupational structure away from manual jobs. Yet, some ethnics see a greater decline in their percentages in manual occupations than others, which is another indicator of upward mobility among ethnics between the 1980s and 1990s.

Thus, in a very rough sense, as we can see from the percentages of various ethnic groups in basic types of occupations (as reported by the census bureau), European-origin ethnics do well in securing occupations that bring income and prestige. In Table 8.2, we pull from the census figures another basis for comparing the resource shares of white ethnics as a whole to Latinos, Asians, blacks, and Native Americans. By education, median earnings, poverty status, and, once again, occupations, it is clear that white ethnics do better than all other ethnics, except Asians who evidence a higher percentage of college graduates than whites and, as a result, have higher median incomes than all other ethnics.

Thus, on some measures of success, Asian Americans have achieved parity with, or exceeded, white Europeans in access to particular resources. Yet Asian American poverty rates are higher than those for white ethnics (indicating that not all Asian Americans are succeeding, as the model minority stereotype would suggest). With respect to occupational distribution, white ethnic groups and Asian Americans are far more likely to have higher-income jobs than other ethnic groups.

These tables show that successive waves of white European immigrants and their descendants have been able to overcome the effects of initial discrimination. To understand how white ethnic groups have assimilated with the

TABLE 8.2 Resource Shares of Prominent Ethnic Groups, 2000

	White Americans	African Americans	Latinos	Asian Americans	Native Americans*
Education (25 years old and older)					
Less than 9th grade	4.2%	6.7%	27.3%	8.5%	14.0%
Four years or more of high school	88.4	78.9	57.0	85.6	49.5
Four years or more of college	26.6	16.6	10.6	43.9	9.3
Median earnings					
Persons 25 years old and older	$28,372	$23,446	$19,113	$29,844	$14,428
Poverty status					
Families below poverty level	5.5%	21.2%	20.3%	8.1%	36.1%
Persons below poverty level	7.4	22.5	21.5	9.9	38.7
Occupations					
Managerial and professional	33.2	21.7	17.5	39.3	16.9
Sales, clerical	30.3	29.0	30.4	28.1	25.3
Service	11.8	22.6	29.2	14.9	16.2
Farmers	11.6	0.8	22.9	11.9	—
Laborers	—	—	—	—	3.6

*1990 Census data.

Sources: 1990 Census Detailed Occupation Characteristics from the EEO File; 1990 Census of Population and Housing Summary Table File 3c; Educational Attainment: March 2000 (Internet release date: December 19, 2000); U.S. Bureau of the Census, 2002.

Anglo-Saxon core of American society, we should examine particular European-origin subpopulations in more detail. What is true for these illustrative cases has been, in general, true for other white ethnics who migrated to America.

IRISH AMERICANS

Irish Americans constitute approximately 18 percent of the population in the United States, which makes them the third largest ethnic group behind the English and Germans (Lieberson and Waters, 1988:34). The first major wave of Irish immigrants arrived in the 1700s, but the exact national heritage of these immigrants is a subject of debate. Most were Protestant Scots-Irish, who had immigrated to northern Ireland after the British conquest of Ireland (Leyburn, 1962), but many southern and Catholic Irish also immigrated—perhaps as many as a third of the total in this first large influx (Dickson, 1966:60–70). Because of prejudice against *Papists,* many of these Catholics were forced to convert to some form of Protestantism in order to avoid persecution. By the end of the Revolutionary War, 10 percent of the colonial population was Irish (signaling that the American legacy of the Irish coincided with American society at its founding).

The next wave of immigration began in the 1830s owing to several factors (Shrier, 1958): the potato famine of the 1840s, persistent British persecution of poor Irish, and British encouragement of emigration as a solution to their "Irish problem." Unlike the earlier wave of immigrants who came in search of more opportunities, many of these southern and Catholic migrants saw themselves as banished to America by the British, which perhaps accounts for their intense loyalty to their homeland (Miller, 1985).

As the first of the non-Protestant white ethnic groups to immigrate to America in large numbers, the Irish were targets of vicious prejudice and sustained discrimination. Two generations later, however, most Irish Americans had overcome these disadvantages.

Identifiability of Irish Americans

As with all white ethnic groups, the identifiability of the Irish could be made only in terms of distinctive cultural, behavioral, and organizational patterns. In the nineteenth century, very conscious efforts were undertaken to portray mainly southern Catholic Irish as a distinct "race," thereby imputing biological differences where none existed. During this time "Scots-Irish" became a popular label, as Protestant northern Irish sought to distance themselves from southern Catholics. Before the efforts to identify southern Catholics, Scots-Irish simply had considered themselves Irish, but with the emerging hostility toward the southern Irish, these northerners sought to differentiate themselves in order to avoid discrimination.

Underlying prejudicial stereotypes of the southern Irish were objections to their Catholicism, their poverty, and their willingness to work for wages lower

than those accepted by earlier immigrants. Prejudicial stereotypes perpetuated
the perception of the southern Irish as identifiably different and, hence, legitimate targets of discrimination.

Negative Beliefs about Irish Americans

As early as the eighteenth century, southern Irish were subject to negative
stereotyping because of their Catholicism. This religious stereotyping became
the basis on which some questioned Irish American political loyalty. Indeed,
the suspicion that an Irish American politician would be governed by the Pope
was articulated as recently as 1960 when John F. Kennedy—an Irish Catholic—
ran for president.

The most vicious stereotypes emerged with the large-scale Irish immigra-
tions of the nineteenth century. Fueled by the threat of so many non-Protestant,
low-wage workers, white Protestants stereotyped the Irish as immoral and
unintelligent, and Irish Catholics in particular as wicked, ignorant, and tem-
peramental (Knobel, 1986:27). All subsequent waves of Catholic white ethnic
groups were similarly stereotyped, especially those, such as the Italians and
Poles, who immigrated in large numbers to the United States.

In particular, stereotypes of the Irish were perhaps as vicious as against
blacks, that is, they were portrayed as less than human. English prejudice
against the Irish was imported to America and intensified; and in the context
of evolutionary theories and the plight of African Americans, the English prejudice against the Irish imported to America amplified into vicious stereotypes
of the Irish as subhuman, apelike, drunk, hostile, and immoral (Curtis, 1971).
The Irish were described as a "missing link" between apes, Africans, and the
English. Today these extreme stereotypes have diminished, but at times the
Irish are viewed as tending toward drunkenness, pugnaciousness, and corruption. Thus, although the Irish have largely overcome prejudice and discrimination, muted forms of the old stereotypes persist.

The Dynamics of Discrimination against Irish Americans

Economic Discrimination　As with most white non-Protestant ethnic groups
who migrated to the United States in the nineteenth century, the Catholic Irish
were forced to take low-wage jobs. Earlier Protestant Irish, most of whom were
"Scots-Irish," had penetrated business and professional positions, but those who
came later were less educated and skilled; as a result, they began their experience in America with jobs in manufacturing, mining, construction (of railroads,
canals), textiles, and domestic service. Because many women immigrated alone,
domestic service offered these women a place to live. Earlier pre-Revolutionary
northern Irish had also done much of the menial and domestic labor, often as
indentured servants, but by the 1830s and 1840s, when the southern Irish began
to come in large numbers, the Scots-Irish had begun to be economically mobile.

The economic discrimination, the exclusion of the migrating Catholic
Irish workers from anything but unskilled work by Protestant employers,

was legitimated by beliefs in their "racial" inferiority, low intelligence, general pugnaciousness, and unreliability. Employers used even lower-wage black workers to threaten the job security of Irish workers, generating black–Irish tension that persists to this day in many northeastern cities (Roediger, 1991; Bonacich, 1976). Because Irish children were forced to go to work early in life, the second generation frequently did not acquire the educational credentials necessary for mobility out of low-wage jobs.

By the turn of the twentieth century, however, both the northern and southern Irish were becoming economically mobile (Dinnerstein and Reimers, 1988). The industrial expansion in the East and Midwest created new opportunities for more skilled workers, and since the Irish had arrived several decades before the large influx of Italians, Poles, and other white ethnic groups, they were more assimilated and advantaged. Economic mobility also came through political success. In many cities, Irish Americans created and controlled the "big-city political machine." For all their corruption, political machines could provide government jobs to individuals and contracts to Irish-owned businesses. During this time, many Irish American workers overcame discrimination by unionizing; their efforts were so successful that they dominated many local unions, especially in mining, construction, and dock work. Although Irish Americans remained dramatically underrepresented in high-skill and professional jobs, they were establishing a more secure economic base from which subsequent generations could move into higher-skill blue-collar jobs, white-collar positions, and an expanding array of professions. Today many Irish Americans have overcome earlier discrimination as revealed by their higher incomes, jobs, and educational credentials (Lieberson and Waters, 1988).

Political Discrimination   One of the enduring stereotypes about Irish Americans is their involvement in corrupt big-city political machines. Political machines in large cities had, of course, emerged and prospered before the Irish were able to penetrate them, but the massive immigration of southern Catholic Irish to the cities created a new constituency for these corrupt political machines. Large pools of poor, ill-housed, and unemployed individuals sustained the machines, and despite the graft and corruption, the machines provided food, jobs, and housing to people in desperate straits in a national political and economic climate where the role of the federal government in addressing urban problems was minimal.

Not only did the political machines provide needed services, but they became an early path to upward mobility for many Irish Americans as well as for large numbers of Italian, Polish, and Jewish immigrants. The corrupt letting of city contracts to private businesses created jobs in a government-supported private sector. Moreover, the machines generated networks of ties among political, business, religious, and philanthropic leaders who, in turn, controlled vast arrays of employment opportunities for poor immigrants. Although the machines in Brooklyn, New York, Boston, New Haven, Philadelphia, Chicago, and various smaller cities in the Northeast and upper Midwest often extracted a high price in misuse of tax revenues and in subsidies for unneeded or inefficient workers, early generations of white immigrants would have suffered even more without them.

Big political machines could not endure forever, since their corruption and inefficiency were all too obvious. As white ethnic groups became more secure, the need for these corrupt networks diminished, leading to a series of reform movements that established new structures of city government. However, it was not until the 1970s that the Chicago political machine began to fall apart, which shows how a network of power can exist long past the time it serves useful functions.

Success at the local level of politics did not translate into positions of power for Irish Americans at the national level, however. Prejudicial attitudes toward Catholics in an Anglo-Saxon Protestant society excluded Irish Americans from appointments in the judiciary and executive branches of government, and limited their success in statewide and national electoral politics. Only in the 1920s did the Catholic Irish begin to enjoy some success in national politics when Alfred E. Smith became the Democratic candidate for president. It was not until the administration of President Roosevelt in the 1930s that Irish Americans were appointed to visible positions in the judiciary, the White House, and other executive branches of government. President Truman continued Roosevelt's pattern of appointing Irish Americans to powerful government positions. When John F. Kennedy ran for president in the 1960s, many of the old fears about Papists were revived, although Kennedy's subsequent election appears to have broken the last discriminatory barriers to full political participation by Irish Americans. Today, the fact that a political candidate is Catholic or Irish is not important, unless it influences that candidate's views on such emotionally charged issues as abortion.

Educational Discrimination   Irish Americans have educational achievement scores above the national average. Most Irish American children are educated in Catholic schools, many of which were created in reaction to discrimination in the mid-1800s as well as to retain Irish ethnicity in the face of intense efforts of the public schools to "Americanize" Irish Catholics. A vast system of Catholic primary and secondary schools, Catholic universities, hospitals, charities, and community service organizations emerged as a result.

The Catholic school system enabled early generations of Irish (and eventually other Catholic immigrants like Italians and Poles) to overcome discrimination against all non-Protestants in the public schools and to sustain important elements of their ethnicity. As this system of education has evolved, it has provided opportunities for Irish Americans to acquire credentials that have facilitated the movement of the last two generations of Irish Americans into higher economic, political, social, and educational positions. Today the educational component of Catholic parochial schools serves many non-Irish Catholics, such as Mexican Americans, Italian Americans, and significant numbers of African Americans. These schools are no longer sustained by reaction to discrimination in public schools, as in the 1880s, but by the desire to maintain or promote religious affiliation and, simultaneously, to ameliorate the problems of decaying public school systems in many urban areas.

The Stratification of Irish Americans

Because the Irish were the first non-Protestant population to immigrate to Protestant America, conflict with the Anglo-Saxon core was inevitable. Large numbers of very poor Catholics, willing to work for low wages and settling in cities where their numbers upset old balances of power and social mores, were threatening to indigenous, Protestant residents. The resulting conflict occurred on several fronts: between higher-wage English workers and lower-wage Irish, between Anglo-Saxon employers in industry who tried to destroy unions and Irish workers who sought the protection of unions, between Anglo-Saxon incumbents in political machines and Irish aspirants to power, and between residents of Anglo-Saxon Protestant neighborhoods and Irish Catholics who desperately needed housing. Conflict led to discrimination; education levels, employment profiles, and residence patterns of the first two generations of Irish Catholics indicate that this discrimination was effective (Lieberson and Waters, 1988). For these early immigrants, poor housing, low-wage employment, and low levels of education were typical.

When Irish Americans gained local political power, as the Catholic system of schools and service organizations developed, and as patronage jobs to workers and contracts to Irish-run businesses increased, Irish Americans began to move forward economically, educationally, and socially by the turn of the century. Today, Irish Americans are highly assimilated, retaining their ethnicity through Saint Patrick's Day celebrations, expressions of loyalty toward their homeland, and vestiges of their old neighborhoods and local political power.

When Irish Americans moved up the socioeconomic ladder, they came into conflict with more recent white immigrants and with African Americans as they migrated northward in the first two decades of this century. These new immigrants began to pose a threat not only to the Anglo-Saxon core but also to the more established Irish Americans. In particular, African Americans were viewed as a threat because industrialists used them as strikebreakers in efforts to destroy the unions of the Irish and other white ethnic groups. Today, African Americans still suffer from the legacy of this hostility (Bonacich, 1976).

Because they are white, those Irish who immigrated to the United States were more easily assimilated into the mainstream of American society. Today, Irish Americans are virtually indistinguishable from the descendants of the Anglo-Saxon core in terms of their place in the American socioeconomic hierarchy.

ITALIAN AMERICANS

In the early decades of the nineteenth century, some northern Italians began to migrate to South and North America in a steady trickle that continued for the rest of the century (Schiavo, 1934; U.S. Bureau of the Census, 1975a). The large-scale immigration of southern Italians began in the 1860s and peaked in the first decade of the twentieth century. In contrast to earlier northern Italians, who tended to be more educated, affluent, and able to enter professions and

Italian immigrants work on a railroad project in Lebanon Springs, New York, circa 1900. It was common in the late nineteenth and early twentieth centuries for Italian immigrants, many from southern Italy and Sicily, to take on relatively unskilled jobs in public works projects.

small businesses, the southern Italians were more likely to be poor, uneducated, and agrarian peasants. Moreover, southern Italians tended to sojourn: staying for short periods, making some money, and returning to Italy. Indeed, perhaps as many as one-third of these later Italian immigrants did return to their homeland, a rate of repatriation that far surpasses any other ethnic group during this period (Learsi, 1954). In all, some four million Italian migrants poured into the United States between 1880 and 1920, with close to 90 percent coming from southern Italy or the island of Sicily (U.S. Bureau of the Census, 1975a). These peasant immigrants were fleeing poverty, low wages, unemployment, economic and political domination by elites, governmental neglect, and declining agricultural productivity (Lopreato, 1970). Soon after entering the United States, they formed "Little Italys" in various cities, primarily in the Northeast but also in the Midwest and somewhat later in the West. From these locations they sought relatively unskilled jobs in public works projects, such as building of canals, sewer systems, and roadways, and in similar labor-intensive sectors of the economy.

Identifiability of Italian Americans

As with the Irish, southern Europeans were portrayed as a distinct "race" that was inferior intellectually and morally. Both the media and intellectuals depicted Italians as incapable of assimilating into Anglo-Saxon society. Fear of their intermarriage with Anglo-Saxons was expressed routinely. Underlying these attitudes were Protestant prejudices against Catholics, as well as other cultural differences between northern and southern European ethnic groups (Gambino, 1974; Higham, 1963). Moreover, because Mediterranean Italians have somewhat darker skin tones than northern Europeans, their identifiability by skin color made them seem a different "race" to northern Europeans.

Negative Beliefs about Italian Americans

The early use of intelligence tests was particularly harmful to Italian Americans because the tests were highly biased against people who were unacculturated and uneducated (Tomasi and Engel, 1970). Italian American schoolchildren (and other newly arrived white ethnic children as well) and enlisted personnel in the army tended to score poorly on these tests, which was used as "scientific proof" of Italians' inferior intellect (Kamin, 1974:1–20). When a group is portrayed as inferior in any way, discrimination follows.

Along with early portrayals of intellectual inferiority came a more persistent "mafia" stereotype portraying Italians as people involved with crime and having little integrity. Up to the prohibition period, Irish and Jewish Americans controlled most organized criminal syndicates. When a number of visible and infamous Italians moved into these criminal syndicates, the Italian gangster stereotype emerged and stuck. For Italian Americans, crime was a means of upward mobility in a hostile society, but the general crime rates for Italians during this period were actually low (Lopreato, 1970:124–26). The mafia stereotype remains today in American culture—defined, and perhaps perpetuated, by movies such as *The Godfather* trilogy, *The Untouchables, Prizzi's Honor,* and many others, often produced by Italians themselves as if the stereotype were being reversed, glamorized, and exploited for economic gain.

Perhaps even more pernicious are media portrayals of Italian males as somewhat ingratiating but tough, dim-witted, and oversexed womanizers ("The Fonz" in television reruns of *Happy Days*). Italian jokes are still uttered with relative impunity, along with ethnic labels such as "dago" and "wop." Images of Italian Americans as overly emotional, jealous, oversexed when young, fat mammas when old, physical, tough, racist hard hats persist (Gambino, 1974:352). Thus, far more than the Irish and Poles, Italian Americans still suffer from negative stereotyping, despite their success in fighting the effects of economic, political, and educational discrimination for over two generations.

The Dynamics of Discrimination against Italian Americans

Economic Discrimination   Today, Italian Americans have incomes and employment histories approximating those for other whites. Yet, despite the high visibility of a few individuals, Italians are still underrepresented in top administrative positions of government and private industry, even as Italian American workers occupy rank-and-file positions proportionate to their numbers in the general population. Italian Americans are thus just beginning to reach full economic mobility, as their levels of educational attainment and income have surpassed national averages.

The previous 100 years have seen considerable economic discrimination against Italians. From the beginning, many came as indentured workers to bosses who provided low-wage work, overpriced food, and expensive slum housing. Under such a system it was difficult for migrants to escape poverty, but eventually this system began to collapse. Even under less oppressive conditions, early Italian immigrants faced a number of barriers: language, few vocational skills, little education, and isolation in Italian ghettos away from job networks. Blatant discrimination also hindered upward mobility for these immigrants who were paid lower wages and excluded from unions. These practices subsided by the turn of the century, when Italian Americans became very active in the union movement.

Southern Italian immigrants became upwardly mobile during the first decades of this century. Union involvement provided jobs of increasing skill; the sons of many unskilled and semiskilled workers moved into higher-skill craft occupations; and entrepreneurial activity among Italian businessmen increased, with many achieving considerable economic success. The great depression curtailed some of this progress, but the post–World War II period saw continued Italian American upward mobility into white-collar jobs, professions, and businesses (Greeley, 1977). Some scholars predict that fourth-generation Italians may achieve parity with British and German ethnic groups in levels of education, income, and employment (Alba, 1985).

Political Discrimination   Early Italian immigrants had relatively low voter participation rates, a pattern attributed to the distrust that many southern Italians felt toward government and to the dampening effects of low socioeconomic status on political activity (Lopreato, 1970). At the local political level, Italian Americans became allied with the Democratic political machines in northeastern and midwestern cities. Later, anti-Catholic prejudices among the broader population prevented Italian Americans from holding national political office. It was not until 1950 that an Italian American was elected to the Senate. As late as the 1940s, fewer than a dozen Italian Americans served in the House of Representatives. Only in 1962 did an Italian American hold a cabinet post in the federal government. The first Italian American vice presidential candidate was nominated in 1984; two years later the first Italian American was appointed to the Supreme Court.

Although the Protestant reform movements that curtailed the activities of big-city political machines temporarily loosened the Italian American foothold in the halls of local power, upward mobility and a declining distrust of government increased Italian American voter participation to a point where many cities with significant Italian American communities elected Italian mayors and city council members. Thus, even before World War II Italian Americans exhibited a significant presence in local politics, despite the fact that anti-Catholic prejudice prevented Protestant voters from voting for Italian Americans as state and national candidates.

Box 8.1
What's Up with The Sopranos?

The Sopranos is an HBO (Home Box Office) cable television series that depicts the life and times of a modern-day organized crime (Mafia) family living in New Jersey. The series focuses on "boss" Tony Soprano and his "family" as they maneuver their way through an underworld thriving on drugs, prostitution, extortion, violence, and murder. It has won numerous awards for being a "critical" and "realistic" view of organized crime in the United States. However, the show has enraged some members of the Italian American community who argue that it portrays Italian Americans as uneducated, low-life brutes, and criminals. There is also some concern that the series' success might encourage young people to see the Mafia lifestyle as positive and rewarding.

New York City Mayor Michael Bloomberg's decision to invite two cast members from *The Sopranos*—Dominic Chianese, who plays Tony Soprano's Uncle Junior, and Lorraine Bracco, who plays Tony Soprano's psychiatrist—to march in the 2002 Columbus Day Parade drew immediate criticism from the Columbus Citizens Foundation, which plans the annual event. The Foundation has turned down requests in the past for *Sopranos* cast members to march in the parade because it regards *The Sopranos* as a negative portrayal of Italian Americans. Parade organizers went to court in an attempt to exclude the cast members from the parade. Asked about the controversy, former New York City mayor Rudolph Giuliani said, "I'm a big *Sopranos* fan. The show is a terrific show, and I would urge some Italian Americans to be less sensitive. You could spend your whole life wanting to be insulted. . . . Why? Why do you want to be insulted?"

So, how do viewers respond to *The Sopranos*? Do viewers think the show stereotypes Italian Americans as criminals? Do viewers think *The Sopranos* glorifies the Mafia lifestyle?

An opinion poll conducted by Fairleigh Dickinson University's PublicMind (www.publicmind.fdu.edu) found that half of adult TV viewers in New Jersey

---

By the 1970s, the political barriers to state and national politics were rapidly coming down. Italian mayors, governors, congressional representatives, and senators became increasingly common. Today, Italian Americans hold office in local, state, and congressional political arenas in numbers approximately proportionate to their numbers in the general population. Third- and fourth-generation Italian Americans have moved rapidly into politics, proving that they have overcome anti-Italian and anti-Catholic prejudice and discrimination.

Educational Discrimination   The first wave of southern Italian migrants to the United States tended to be illiterate and impoverished. Their children went to school for short periods of time in order to acquire basic skills, then dropped out to help support the family. The high dropout rates were also caused by the pervasive culture in the public schools, which sought to "Americanize" Italians.

watched *The Sopranos* at least occasionally, compared with about one-third of adult viewers in other states. Both in New Jersey and in other states, viewers of *The Sopranos* were most likely to be men. A comparison of viewers of *The Sopranos* with non-viewers indicates that viewers are more likely to believe that New Jersey has more crime, dishonest politicians, and pollution than other states, and that New Jersey is a worse place to live than other states. In general, it appears that viewers of *The Sopranos* are more likely than nonviewers to have negative opinions of New Jersey.

The majority (63 percent) of poll respondents living in New Jersey knew that *The Sopranos* took place in New Jersey, whereas the majority (57 percent) of poll respondents living in other states did not know, or were unsure. The majority (62 percent) of poll respondents think of *The Sopranos* as "just a story," whereas only 26 percent of respondents think the show "tells the truth." The majority of poll respondents disagreed with the criticism that *The Sopranos* "glorifies organized crime" and that it "portrays Italian Americans in a negative way" (57 percent versus 65 percent, respectively).

There appears to be a good news/bad news context for *The Sopranos*. The good news is that it is not regarded as portraying Italian Americans in a negative light nor is it seen as glorifying organized crime. Enhancing the good news is the poll result that *The Sopranos* is more likely to be regarded as "just a story" instead of "telling the truth." The bad news is that viewers of *The Sopranos* are more likely than nonviewers to have negative views of New Jersey; negative views that suggest that viewers may think New Jersey serves as an opportunistic context for the Mafia lifestyle. What do you think?

Sources: "New Jersey and The Sopranos: Perfect Together?" (available at: www.publicmind.fdu. edu/badabing/index.html); Michael Regan, "Sopranos Raises Curiosity about Real-Life N.J. Mob" (January 15, 2000), available at www.beachbrowser.com; Jennifer Steinhauer, "Object to 'Sopranos' Actors in Parade? What Are You Gonna Do?" *New York Times,* October 10, 2002, p. C16; Jennifer Steinhauer and Robert Worth, "His 'Sopranos' Guests Excluded, Mayor Will Skip Columbus Day Parade," *New York Times,* October 12, 2002, p. B16; Michael Wilson, "Columbus Day Parade Goes On, as Mayor and Sopranos Dine in the Bronx," *New York Times,* October 15, 2002, p. C16.

Children were put under enormous pressure to change their look, their speech, their dress, and their demeanor to conform with a more Anglo-Saxon profile.

The Catholic school system was not a readily available alternative to the first waves of southern Italian immigrants because of conflict with Irish Americans, who dominated this system, and because of their inability to pay for tuition and books. As a consequence, Italian youth either endured the public schools or dropped out. These high dropout rates hindered the second generation's economic mobility.

By the 1920s, Italian Americans began to make significant progress in education, a trend that has continued into the present. Today, the average number of years of education completed by Italian Americans surpasses that of many other white ethnic groups, and that of the white population as a whole. Thus, third and fourth generations of Italian American immigrants have overcome the effects of discrimination against the first and second generations; as levels of education have increased, upward economic and political mobility has ensued.

Legal Discrimination   The passage of the Immigration Act of 1924 limited immigration to the United States, especially for eastern and southern Europeans. The quota set for Italians was over ten times lower than the quota for the British and five times lower than the quota for Germans. Clearly the intent was to favor Anglo-Saxons and northern Europeans over all other ethnic groups, with the result that many Italians were prevented from immigrating to the United States. Although the laws were changed several times, only the new Immigration Law of 1965 enabled more Italians to immigrate by using the unfilled quotas of other ethnic groups from northern Europe. However, the earlier restrictions on immigration sent a not-too-subtle message to Italian Americans: You are inferior and undesirable. Such messages supported existing negative beliefs about Italians in the United States and, no doubt, perpetuated discriminatory practices up to World War II.

Stratification of Italian Americans

As the second-largest Catholic population to enter the United States, Italian immigrants threatened the Anglo-Saxon Protestant core. This threat was reinforced by other large influxes of Catholic Poles and of Jews. Nativist sentiments ran high within the Protestant white community. Much like the Irish, Italians were portrayed as an inferior "race" that could potentially "mongrelize" America through intermarriage. Italians constituted the first wave of immigrants from southern Europe to the United States, which made them seem doubly different and, hence, threatening.

In addition to white Protestant hostility, Italians faced, at least initially, Irish fears about the presence of yet another disadvantaged immigrant population. Such fears were aggravated when employers used Italians as strikebreakers against unions heavily populated by Irish workers. The problems that Italians initially had in enrolling their children in Catholic schools attest to the tension between Irish and Italians—a tension that was aggravated by the wave of poor Catholic Polish immigrants.

Their lack of education and job skills, coupled with Protestant and Irish discrimination, ensured that first- and most second-generation Italian Americans would be at the bottom of the socioeconomic ladder. Similar to all white ethnic groups, however, Italians had some distinct advantages: They were white and possessed organizational resources in family and church; over time these resources could be used to penetrate unions, skilled workplaces, white-collar jobs, professions, and schools. By the third generation, rapid upward mobility was occurring. Today, Italian Americans are above the national average in educational attainment and income. Lingering stereotypes and informal discrimination against Italian Americans persist. The final phase of assimilation is yet to be completed, although it is imminent.

JEWISH AMERICANS

Jews have been the most persistently persecuted minority group in history. Massacres of Jews have occurred since Rome's occupation of present-day Israel in the period before and after the birth of Christ. The intensity of this persecution is etched in the modern conscience by the death camps of Nazi Germany. Indeed, many American Jews are the descendants of those who sought refuge from more recent persecution. The first Jewish immigrants to the United States, the Sephardic Jews, arrived in the 1640s to escape massacres and expulsion from Spain and Portugal; their numbers did not exceed a few thousand. The second group of Jewish immigrants began to enter the United States in the 1840s in an effort to escape widening persecution in Europe. Most of these immigrants came from what is now Germany and settled in the Midwest, causing the Jewish population to grow from 15,000 to more than 250,000 in the early 1880s (Herberg, 1960:176). The third wave of immigration, beginning in the 1880s and lasting until the 1920s, led to the significant presence of Jews in America. Coming from areas of eastern Europe controlled by the Russian Czar (and later the communists of the former Soviet Union), some two million Jews settled in the United States, primarily in urban areas of the Northeast (Lestschinsky, 1955:56). While many sought refuge from persecution, the vast majority came voluntarily in search of opportunities in a new land (Sklare, 1971; Learsi, 1954). Yet, even as the Immigration Act of 1924 curtailed the mass immigration of all ethnic groups to the United States, some 400,000 more Jews immigrated, in most cases to escape Nazi persecution. By the eve of World War II, however, immigration policy had become so strict that many hundreds of thousands of Jews who desperately sought refuge in America were forced to stay and suffer the consequences of Hitler's death camps. Some 150,000 were able to enter the United States as political refugees; among these were many of the great scientists and intellectuals of modern times—Albert Einstein, Edward Teller, Eric Fromm, Herbert Marcuse, and Bruno Bettelheim.

In more recent decades, immigration statistics for the American Jewish population are inaccurate because the Immigration and Naturalization Service no longer identifies immigrants by religion; estimates run as high as 500,000 recent immigrants. Today, around six million Jews live in America, a figure that comes close to 50 percent of the world's Jewish population. The rest live primarily in Israel, the recently independent states of the former Soviet Union, and various European and South American countries. The majority of Jewish Americans live in the Northeast, although the number residing in the West and South is increasing rapidly—mirroring the trend in the general population. Jewish Americans represent about 3 percent of the American population; yet their massive immigration in the 1880s activated the same dynamics of discrimination experienced by other white ethnic groups, such as the Irish, Italians, and Poles.

Identifiability of Jewish Americans

Throughout history, Jews have been considered a "race," but the basis for this designation is social and cultural, not biological. Those who have persecuted Jews in the United States and around the world have used the spurious belief that Jews are biologically different as the basis for extreme forms of discrimination. In reality, there is no distinguishing physical trait that makes it easy to designate someone as a "Jew."

Jews are defined by their religious beliefs, which are based on the texts of the Torah, or the first five books of the Bible. *Orthodox Jews* adhere to the Torah in strict terms—ritual, food preparation and consumption, and synagogue attendance. About one-fifth of all American Jews are Orthodox. At the other extreme are *Reform Jews*, who represent perhaps one-third of the American Jewish population and who have modernized and secularized their religious activity. Between these extremes are *Conservative Jews*, who represent from one-third to one-half of all American Jews.

Being Jewish in a Protestant society makes one different, but many Jews are not outwardly religious. Moreover, synagogue attendance rates tend to be low, rendering this particular indicator of religious affiliation relatively useless (except for some Orthodox Jews, who may be easily identified by dress, demeanor, and ritual practices). Thus, religion does not outwardly distinguish Jews from gentiles.

In many respects, the source of Jewish identifiability is the awareness of a shared history of persecution and the sense among Jews that they constitute a community with a unique set of traditions. Because Jews have historically been treated as a distinct community rather than as a nationality, they have developed organizations, networks, and shared beliefs that have provided them with a sense of identity and that, during historical episodes of extreme discrimination, have allowed them to survive in hostile environments. Thus, unlike other white ethnic groups living in the United States whose identity is tied to their country of origin, Jews have maintained a sense of being a community that has sustained itself within many countries. Consequently, Jews have been able to mobilize resources—primarily organizational but also economic and educational—that make them somewhat distinguishable, *to themselves*, and that enable them to rank high in terms of education and income in America (Goldschneider, 1986).

Negative Beliefs about Jewish Americans

Because Jews have persisted as a cohesive and successful community within hostile societies, negative beliefs about them have evolved over time and, under conditions of extreme persecution, have intensified. These beliefs have been reinforced by the *middleman minority* positions Jews have historically occupied; as we noted in Chapter 2, middleman minority groups are traditionally targets of hostility.

From the Middle Ages to the present, Jews have been the subjects of persistent prejudicial beliefs and stereotypes. Although Christ was crucified by the Romans, some people believe that Jews were the culprits. In a Christian society like the United States, this belief undergirds hostility toward Jews. In fact, some Catholic and Protestant ministers have in the past promoted this idea, conveniently ignoring all the pertinent historical facts. Jews are also stereotyped as shrewd, crafty, cheap, money-grubbing, materialistic, and sly (Glock and Stark, 1966; Gordon, 1988). Another set of beliefs is based on the "Jewish conspiracy." In the 1920s and 1930s in America, people such as Henry Ford actively propagated the idea that Jews were involved in an international conspiracy to control all governments. The Ku Klux Klan, the German-American Bund, media personalities such as the Catholic priest Charles E. Coughlin, and even Charles Lindbergh saw Jews as conspiring to control the world. Even as late as the 1970s, a member of the Joint Chiefs of Staff could be heard arguing that Jews "own, you know, the banks in the country, the newspapers" (Selzer, 1972). More recent debates over the threat of Zionism and the *Jewish lobby* in Congress have revived elements of the Jewish conspiracy theory.

Most surveys and polls report dramatic drops in negative stereotypes about Jews over the last sixty years (Lipset, 1987). Many Americans hold very positive views of Jews as intelligent, educated, and industrious. Yet, often lurking beneath the surface are subtle condemnations of Jews as being *too* bright, hardworking, and ambitious. Many of the older stereotypes—from "Christ killers" to "money grubbers"—still prevail. People know that it is unacceptable in most public situations, including surveys and polls, to utter these negative beliefs, but the recent increase in acts of vandalism at Jewish cemeteries and synagogues indicates that below the polite surface lurk powerful prejudices against Jews. These beliefs often legitimate discriminatory practices against Jews in America.

The Dynamics of Discrimination against Jewish Americans

The comparatively high incomes and levels of education among Jewish Americans are a tribute to their ability to overcome open discrimination in jobs, politics, housing, and education, as well as more covert discrimination in clubs, fraternal organizations, and other social groups. Yet, despite a record of economic and academic success, Jews are underrepresented in many occupations, professions, and high-level positions of power.

Economic Discrimination   Early Jewish immigrants assumed middleman minority positions. Although most Jews of German origin arrived with little money, they had entrepreneurial skills that enabled them to start small businesses (primarily in the garment, jewelry, meat, and leather trades) as well as trading and financial positions. By the 1890s, census data report that almost 60 percent of Jews were in trade and finance, 20 percent were in office work, and only 6 percent were in the professions. With centuries of experience in finding economic niches in the hostile environments of Europe, Jews were able to find such niches in the United States (Glazer, 1957).

The eastern European Jews who began to immigrate to the United States in the 1880s tended to be less educated and skilled than earlier German immigrants; as a result, they established an economic foothold in unskilled manufacturing jobs, as did other white immigrants. Men and women worked long hours for low wages in sweatshops; many women did sewing and laundry in the home to help make ends meet. Those eastern European immigrants who had small-business experience were able to find middleman minority niches, as had earlier German migrants. Because education and study have always been highly valued in the Jewish community, considerable upward mobility was possible for the sons and daughters of these Jewish immigrants. For example, by the early 1900s, Jews in the Northeast were moving into law, medicine, and other professions, while assuming middle-level clerical positions in businesses and government.

Immigration was cut off in the 1920s, and those who had made it to the United States continued their economic mobility. When the Great Depression hit in the 1930s, however, this mobility was curtailed by economic discrimination. The success of Jewish Americans was now intensely resented in a tightening job market; signs reading "No Jews need apply" were common. Jews were excluded from many professional positions in banking, teaching, medicine, law, and engineering, as well as more skilled blue-collar and clerical jobs. Jews began to experience systematic, institutionalized discrimination, which forced them to find economic opportunities in risky sectors such as media and small business, and in professional and clerical jobs for which they were overqualified. The legacy of economic discrimination remains today, for Jews are underrepresented in high-level positions in banking, in management positions at savings and loans, utilities, and insurance companies, and the top levels of management in almost all industries. The two exceptions to this pattern are the media and plastics, in which Jews took the early risks.

On average, Jewish Americans are wealthier than non-Jews. This wealth is the result of taking risks in a narrow range of businesses such as clothing, mass communications, jewelry, and merchandising, while overcoming quotas and outright bans in professions such as law and medicine. Jewish Americans exist in what is termed a "golden ghetto," but it is nonetheless a ghetto. In the present, however, the pattern of informal exclusion appears to be diminishing; it is likely that Jewish Americans will move into a broader range of management positions commensurate with their education and skill.

Open exclusion (or token representation) of Jews in country clubs, some fraternal and community organizations, and many elite social circles indicates that informal discrimination and quotas persist even today at the beginning of the new millennium. Because these organizational affiliations are often crucial to the development of informal contacts and networks necessary for economic success and mobility, Jewish Americans will continue to feel the effects of this form of exclusion.

Political Discrimination   Unlike many minority groups who have established themselves in economic middlemen positions, Jewish Americans have been politically active, voting in large numbers and engaging in volunteer political activity. Yet, despite their economic and academic success, this involvement has not translated into significant political power until recent decades. Jews have become governors of a few northeastern states over the years, and they have been successful in local politics where there is a substantial community of Jewish Americans. Yet, Jewish Americans did not gain access to higher-level administrative positions in the federal government until the 1930s; they have had only a handful of Supreme Court appointments, despite the fact that a high proportion of lawyers and law professors are Jewish Americans, and they reached proportionate representation in Congress only in the 1970s. Jewish Americans are now overrepresented in Congress, holding 8 percent of Senate seats and constituting 7 percent of the House membership.

Although Jewish Americans have become increasingly prominent in politics, their underrepresentation in top management positions in industry and manufacturing limits their ability to use informal economic power to secure top-level appointments in those governmental posts where experience as a corporate manager is considered important (Zweigenhaft and Domhoff, 1982; Alba and Moore, 1982). Yet, 90 percent of Americans say that they would vote for a qualified Jewish presidential candidate, whereas less than 50 percent would have done so five decades ago (Marger, 2000:211). Such shifts in attitudes indicate that Jewish Americans will become increasingly assimilated in the political arena.

Legal Discrimination   Unlike many other societies, the United States never legally institutionalized *anti-Semitism*. Before the signing of the Constitution, most states had established "Christian-only" restrictions for public office. Indeed, it is possible that some signatories to the Constitution were anti-Semitic (or anti-non-Christian); yet these prejudices are not reflected in law or in government policy. The closest instances approaching legal discrimination against Jews have been the *blue laws* of many communities that require businesses to close on Sunday—a day when many Jewish businesses could remain open.

Discrimination against Jewish Americans has been largely informal. Jews have had to overcome informal restrictive quotas in jobs and education, informal restrictive housing practices, and informal restrictive memberships in clubs and social organizations. The law has rarely supported these practices, except in the area of housing, where written restrictive covenants were enforced until the 1960s. Yet, legal tolerance of informal discrimination is, in fact, a form of legalized discrimination. Indeed, until passage of the various civil rights acts in the 1960s, the legal system did not attack the injustices of such informal practices of discrimination.

Educational Discrimination   It may seem absurd, on the surface, to consider educational discrimination against the most educated ethnic subpopulation in the United States. The long tradition of respect for learning and education in the Jewish community is so powerful that it has been possible to overcome clear patterns of discrimination. One of these patterns was established at the turn of the century, when Jewish American children were segregated in many of the public schools in the Northeast. Despite this segregation, however, Jewish students completed high school in much higher numbers than did non-Jews. Another discriminatory pattern was the informal, but often articulated, quota system for Jewish American high school graduates in American colleges and universities. Particularly in private schools, this system of limiting Jewish enrollment existed well into the 1960s. Also, on college campuses, discrimination in membership to fraternities and sororities was, and is, rampant. Jewish students have responded by forming their own fraternities and sororities. In private elite schools, the informal contacts and networks formed socially can be crucial to future occupational placement in mainstream corporate America; in this respect, many Jewish Americans are at a disadvantage. However, the magnitude of Jewish academic achievement in a society valuing educational credentials has enabled Jewish Americans to find business and professional niches and, increasingly in recent decades, to penetrate large, elite corporations. Despite their obvious economic success, Jewish graduates still encounter invisible barriers and must endure the subtle favoritism given to less educated and skilled non-Jews.

The Stratification of Jewish Americans

Because many Jewish Americans have been enormously successful, the fact that many Jews live below the poverty line (but in low percentages compared to the rest of the population) is often overlooked. In spite of their qualifications and credentials, because of language and professional barriers, many recently arrived Russian Jews make their livings as cab drivers, cooks, and waiters. Success has come for Jews despite sometimes intense informal discrimination, legitimized by prejudicial beliefs. Such discrimination has been fueled by perceptions of threat in the minds of non-Jews, perceptions which have by no means disappeared. All immigrants once competed for industrial jobs, especially when the depression diminished the job market. Jewish American skill in running small businesses, in education, and in the professions posed a threat to gentiles. Coupled with long-standing and inaccurate European beliefs (imported to America) that Jews are shrewd and conspiratorial, this sense of threat increased and, in turn, intensified informal discrimination.

Jewish Americans are concentrated in the middle and upper middle strata, and are underrepresented in both lower socioeconomic positions and elite political and economic spheres. However, because movement into more elite positions has become increasingly possible, Jewish Americans are likely to penetrate and achieve parity in this sphere.

SUMMARY

The 100 years from the early nineteenth century to the first decades of the twentieth century are the bookends for the mass immigration of non-Protestant Europeans to America. Their religion and eagerness to work threatened the existing Anglo-Saxon core. The non-Protestant southern Irish came in the early years of the nineteenth century, followed in the second half of the century by large influxes of Italians, Poles, and Jews. Because these migrants were white and European, their early experiences with discrimination were more readily overcome than those who are more readily identified by surface biological features.

The advantages of white skin in overcoming discrimination in America are revealed in the resource shares of white ethnics today. They secure better jobs, earn more money, attain more education, and live in less segregated neighborhoods than most non-European ethnics. Thus, while the legacy of negative stereotyping persists and discrimination is still evident, these forces have not prevented white ethnic groups from gaining their share of the resources available in America.

The Irish, who today represent the third-largest ethnic population after those from the British Isles and Germany, were the first of the white ethnics to come to America after the Anglo-Saxon core. The Protestant Irish had arrived in the 1700s, but it was the Catholic Irish immigration beginning in the 1830s that escalated discrimination against the Irish. These non-Protestant migrants came from the heart of rural poverty and were desperate for any work—thereby representing a threat not only to Protestantism as the dominant religion but to the wages and economic security of those already settled in America. These perceived threats fueled prejudicial stereotypes of Irish Catholics as a distinct "race" who were wicked, ignorant, and less than human. Efforts to exclude them from better jobs, centers of political power, public schools, and adequate housing were, in the long run, unsuccessful as the Catholic Irish worked their way up the occupational system. They captured or created the big-city political machines, utilized the Catholic school system to overcome discrimination in public schools, and used their financial and political clout to move into better neighborhoods. This mobility threatened other whites, but it also led to considerable assimilation of the Catholic Irish into the societal mainstream, which reduced the threat experienced by the descendants of earlier immigrants. Indeed, the more successful Catholic Irish became, the more they began to fear the new waves of European immigrants who would threaten their hard-won gains.

Small numbers of northern Italians immigrated to the United States during the early decades of the nineteenth century, but beginning in 1860 large numbers of poor, less educated, rural southern Italians entered the country. As with the Irish, systematic efforts were made to identify these Italians as a separate "race" because of their Catholicism, southern European ways, and

Mediterranean skin tones. These characteristics made them different from the Anglo-Saxon core and subject to prejudicial beliefs and blatant discrimination. Initial negative stereotypes of Italian Americans branded them as lacking intelligence and, somewhat later, as having loose morals and a propensity toward violence as well as crime. More recent stereotyping focuses on the presumed emotionality, sexuality, bigotry, and hotheadedness of Italian Americans. Such negative stereotyping was initially used to bolster discrimination in jobs, schools, and politics. Laws were passed to restrict immigration from southern Europe. Yet, as with other white ethnics, Italians' white skin, strong family structures, commitment to church, and effective use of unions enabled second- and third-generation Italians to move up the stratification system so that today they are above most other ethnics in the shares of resources. Still, there are lingering stereotypes about Italians, often highlighted in the media. These may still serve to support informal patterns of discrimination.

Jews have been persecuted all over the world. As their numbers increased during the 1840s in America and especially when immigration accelerated in the 1880s, discrimination against Jews became as obvious here as elsewhere in the world. Later, in the years preceding and during World War II, more Jews came to escape the ravages of Nazism. Today, a steady stream of Jews still migrates to America, making the United States the place of residence for almost half of the world's Jewish population. Like other white ethnic minorities, Jews were distinguished as a peculiar "race," which made them just "different" enough to justify discrimination. Negative stereotypes could be brutal, such as those portraying Jews as "Christ killers" (an erroneous charge since the Romans performed the execution). More subtle and age-old stereotypes of Jews as cheap, sly, and clannish, coupled with more blatant and paranoid visions of a world Jewish conspiracy, still haunt Jewish Americans, as well as Jews all over the world. Out of necessity, Jews have had to sustain a strong sense of ethnic identity, hence their need to establish a viable set of institutions in a discriminating world. As they have done so, they developed the organizational and financial resources to succeed in educational attainment, business, and professional activity. Yet, this success is circumscribed by the exclusionary practices in almost all spheres of American life. Ordinary jobs, many professions, business opportunities, and top management positions still remain somewhat closed to the Jewish population. Significant inroads into politics and government jobs have been made by Jews only in recent decades, but informal discrimination persists in housing, social clubs, and non-Jewish businesses.

For all white ethnics—Jews, Italians, Irish, and many others—white skin has made a big difference in their overcoming discrimination. By simply adopting the culture, speech, values, and other characteristics of the Anglo-Saxon core, white ethnics could blend with the general population and move up the educational and occupational ladder. They have realized the "American dream." Many of the descendants of the white ethnic immigrants who blazed an upwardly mobile trail have forgotten—perhaps gratefully—the legacy of discrimination in words like "wop," "Paddy," or "Polack." The descendants of the white ethnic immigrants are often the perpetuators of big-otry and discrimination against people of color.

Their own tenuous economic standing has contributed to the tradition of racism among white ethnics. Discrimination against African Americans emerged full-blown in the early decades of the twentieth century when black workers were used as strikebreakers (Bonacich, 1976; Olzak, 1992). Early Asian immigrants experienced considerable resistance when they were perceived as a threat to the hard-won gains of white ethnics. And Latinos were also viewed as a potential labor pool that would take away the jobs of white ethnic labor-ers. Recent patterns of increased immigration by Latinos and Asians, coupled with old prejudices against African Americans, sustain the sense of threat among white ethnics over their jobs and culture. Such threats are magnified by global corporate systems that pull jobs overseas. As we have seen, threat is the fuel behind prejudice and discrimination. Competition with empowered peo-ple of color makes the success of some white ethnics seem uncertain. The movement of manual labor into the world economy, coupled with the propor-tional decline of members of the original Anglo-Saxon core and their white converts, has increased ethnic tensions in America and now represents a major problem for peaceful ethnic relations in the next century.

POINTS OF DEBATE

Caucasians or people with European-looking features are at an advantage in American society. They are able to overcome discrimination by simply assimi-lating into the Anglo-Saxon core, while retaining a few of their old ethnic tra-ditions that do not threaten this core. By contrast, people of color and those with non-European features must face constant reminders from others about their "distinctiveness." Even with social assimilation into much of the core, they still stand out physically. The unwillingness of white ethnics to accept the efforts at social mobility of members of other ethnic groups toward realizing the American dream makes for many points of debate:

1. Given their different history in America, is it possible for white people to understand what it is like to "stand out" and to be vulnerable to the preju-dicial beliefs and acts of discrimination nonwhites encounter? Can whites recognize the enormous psychic costs for members of readily identifiable minority populations? What can be done about this situation? Should cur-rent efforts to impose a "political correctness" ideology on all others be allowed to continue? If so, who is to decide what is correct? Or, alterna-tively, is the introduction of sensitivity training in the workplace, school, or community a better path? If so, who decides what will be taught, from what perspective, and *by* whom *to* whom? Or is it best to let the forces involved take a natural course? If so, should a society that values equal opportunity allow the inevitable discrimination that results from a "hands-off" policy to continue?

2. Can white Americans fully understand that the playing field has not been, and is not today, level in a society that values equality of opportunity? The legacy of slavery, Jim Crow, conquest and annexation, reservation life, and many other patterns of discrimination makes it difficult for many, though not all, nonwhites to have the same chance in the society as whites. White Americans tend to be fixated on, and angry over, the reverse discrimination that inevitably accompanies efforts at inclusive affirmative action. Must white Americans suffer the same frustration and anger that many members of minorities have endured over the decades? Is it the same? Or, is it possible for white Americans to accept a certain amount of reverse discrimination in order to compensate for past discrimination against specific ethnics? If not, then what is to be done by white America to curb the pathologies inherent in decades, if not centuries, of discrimination—the pathologies of racism, violence, crime, drug use, welfare dependency, and other problems that accompany long-term discrimination?

KEY TERMS

anti-Semitism, 237
blue laws, 237
Conservative Jews, 234
Jewish lobby, 235

middleman minority, 234
Orthodox Jews, 234
Papists, 222
Reform Jews, 234

CHAPTER 9

The Future of Ethnicity in America

Changes in the ethnic composition of a society are always accompanied by tensions between declining populations and those that are growing. In the nineteenth and early twentieth centuries, dramatic changes in the composition of white ethnics occurred, the first wave of Asian immigration arrived, and African Americans migrated from the South to the North. These demographic transformations were highlighted by extreme prejudice and discrimination. Today, as the twenty-first century begins, America is experiencing a similar transformation of the population. The numbers of Latinos are dramatically increasing, whites are moving toward minority status, and Asian populations are beginning to grow again. In Table 9.1, the U.S. Bureau of the Census's projections for the first fifty years of the twenty-first century are summarized. As is evident, the non-Latino white population is declining and will constitute a bare majority at the century's midpoint, while both black and white Hispanics' numbers are growing and will reach over 30 percent of the population. Asian and Pacific Islanders are also increasing their numbers, but not nearly to the degree of Latinos. The two most victimized minorities in America, African and Native Americans, will grow very little or not at all as a percentage of the total population. Thus, the demographic fuel is there for escalation of prejudice and discrimination by those who are threatened, although a century of dealing with ethnic relations and enactment of civil rights laws may diminish the conflict so evident in the last century. The fuel for ethnic fires will become potentially more volatile as the century progresses to its midpoint.

Much as in the nineteenth century and the first decade of the twentieth century, immigration is the engine of change. With the exception of Native Americans, who were already here, and African Americans, who were brought as slaves, the population of the United States has been built by immigrants. The ever-changing ethnic makeup of the United States—past, present, and future—is the result of immigration patterns and relative birthrates among immigrant populations (Portes and Rumbaut, 1990). Legal immigration, for example, steadily increased after World War II, then dramatically escalated to a peak of 1,827,167 in 1991 as seen in Figure 9.1 on page 245. Of course, this

TABLE 9.1 The Changing Ethnic Composition of the American Population

Ethnic Population	Projected Percentage of Population in Selected Years			
	2010	2035	2045	2050
Non-Latino whites	68.0%	58.6%	54.7%	52.8%
Latino*	13.8	20.3	30.7	31.0
Non-Latino blacks	12.6	13.2	13.5	13.6
Asian/Pacific Islanders	4.8	7.1	7.9	8.2
Native Americans	0.8	0.9	0.9	0.9

*Includes black Latinos.

Source: U.S. Bureau of the Census (1999): "Population of the United States by Age, Sex, Race, and Hispanic Origins: 1995–2050."

figure accounts for only legal immigration; considerable illegal immigration has occurred, primarily from Latin America. By 1993, legal immigration rates had fallen to 904,300 under the impact of the 1990 Immigration Act (discussed shortly); however, this drop probably was more than compensated for by illegal immigration rates (Vernez and McCarthy, 1990; Fernandez and Robinson, 1994).

THE NEW IMMIGRANTS

Countries of Origin

Table 9.2 reports the area of origin of those who immigrated to the United States between 1951 and 2000; the post–World War II period of escalating immigration saw a dramatic change in the national origins of immigrants (Rolph, 1992; U.S. Department of Justice, 1991a). In 1951, almost 68 percent of immigrants came from Europe and Canada, slightly over 6 percent from Asia, and about 25 percent from Latin America and the Caribbean. Over the last five decades, however, the percentage of immigrants from Europe and Canada has dropped dramatically, while the Asian and the combined Latin American and

TABLE 9.2 The Shifting Profile of Immigrants to the United States, 1951 through 1997

Area of Origin	1951–60	1961–70	1971–80	1981–90	1991–93	1997	2000
Europe and Canada	67.7%	46.3%	21.6%	12.5%	13.1%	18.4%	17.8%
Asia	6.1	12.9	35.5	37.5	30.0	26.5	25.5
Latin America and the Caribbean	24.6	39.2	40.3	47.1	49.9	61.5	51.0

Sources: Elizabeth Rolph, *Immigration Policies: Legacy from the 1980s and Issues for the 1990s* (Santa Monica, CA: The RAND Corporation, 1992); U.S. Department of Justice, 1991a; U.S. Bureau of the Census, 1995; U.S. Bureau of the Census, March 1997 Current Population Survey (Internet release date: October 15, 1999); U.S. Bureau of the Census, 2001.

Thousands

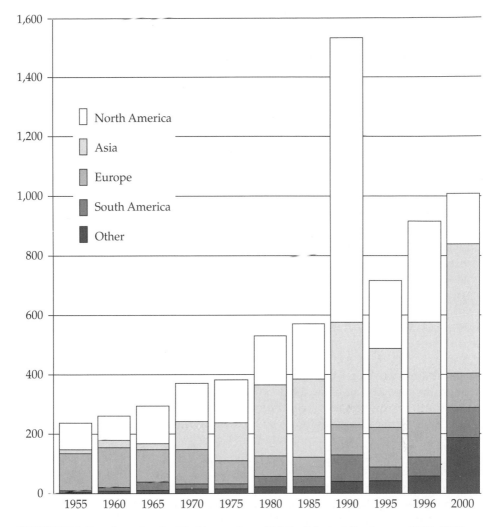

FIGURE 9.1 Immigrants admitted by region of birth: Selected fiscal years 1955–2000.

Source: 1996 Statistical Yearbook of the Immigration and Naturalization Service. Washington, D.C.: U.S. Department of Justice, Immigration and Naturalization Service, 1997; U.S. Bureau of the Census, 2001.

Caribbean percentages have increased. As of 2000, 51 percent of all immigrants came from Latin American or Caribbean countries and 25.5 percent from Asian countries. If illegal immigrants could be counted, of course, these percentages would be much higher.

An Immigration and Naturalization Service (INS) report offers a more complete breakdown of the area of origin of immigrants from 1955 to 2000. In Figure 9.1 one can note that legal immigration peaked in 1990, declined in 1995, but started increasing in 1996. Figure 9.2 shows that the majority of legal

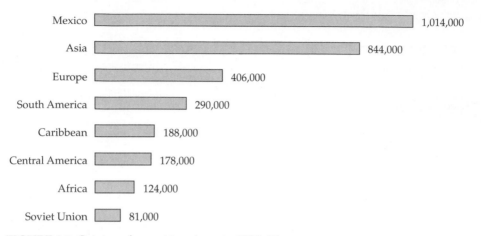

FIGURE 9.2 Origins of recent immigrants, 2000–02.

Source: Camarota (2002).

immigrants came from Mexico, the next largest number came from Asia, then Europe, followed by the Caribbean, South America, Central America, Africa, and the former Soviet Union. Because all the immigrants from Mexico, Central America, and South America constitute the Latino population in the United States, Latinos are by far the largest immigrant ethnic group (Mozo and Vasquez, 1988; Camarillo and Bonilla, 2001). Since a significant portion of the Caribbean immigrant population is black, the combined African and Caribbean figure exceeds the white European figure by almost a 1.5-to-1 margin (see Figure 9.2).

Consequences of the New Immigration Patterns

The most recent census data on immigration trends, coupled with past immigration rates and birthrates, form the ethnic profile of America reported in Table 9.2. Today, 75 percent of the U.S. population is white, 12 percent is black, almost 13 percent is Latino, close to 4 percent is Asian–Pacific Islander, and less than 1 percent is Native American (Grieco and Cassidy, 2001). By the year 2050, the white population will decrease to a slight majority—from 52 to 53 percent. Latinos will make up 21 to 24 percent of the population, blacks 13 to 16 percent, Asians (including Pacific Islanders) 11 to 13 percent, and Native Americans less than 1 percent. We can, of course, see these trends around us each day in terms of whom we encounter in school, work, neighborhood, and public places. For a comparison of immigrant persons by ethnicity in the United States, see Box 9.2 on page 248.

Ethnic diversity accompanied by rapid shifts in the relative numbers of diverse ethnic subpopulations makes ethnicity a salient issue and, for many, an unsettling one. Members of all ethnic populations must accommodate one

---

Box 9.1
Why Do Mexicans Come to the United States?

Why do Mexicans come to the United States? Is it the promise of riches or fame? Is it the perception of the United States as a paradise? The historical survey of Mexican immigration to the United States in Chapter 6 (p. 160) identified social conditions in Mexico and the need for cheap labor in the United States as the "push-pull" factors behind Mexican immigration to the United States. Although these socioeconomic indicators may explain the circumstances behind Mexican immigration, do we know what reasons Mexicans offer for Mexican immigration to the United States?

In a study conducted by Aguirre (1993) regarding the association between English-language and U.S.-origin communication media and how Mexicans perceive Mexican social issues, Aguirre found that Mexicans have definite perceptions as to why Mexicans immigrate to the United States. By order of decreasing importance, Aguirre found that Mexicans believe that Mexicans immigrate to the United States for the following reasons:

1. There is no employment in Mexico (59 percent).
2. Mexicans want to earn more money (38 percent).
3. The standard of living is higher in the United States (36 percent).
4. There are better employers in the United States (32 percent).
5. Mexicans like adventure (28 percent).

Source: Aguirre, 1993.

---

another, a task that may prove difficult and, when unsuccessful, may create the same dynamic of discrimination experienced by past generations of immigrants.

Reasons for the Shift in Immigration Patterns

This shift in immigration patterns is, to a great extent, the result of changes in immigration laws over the last three decades. Rolph (1992) has suggested that much of the shift is due to the *Immigration Act of 1965*, which eliminated country-specific quotas that had favored European countries and, simultaneously, allowed immediate family members of U.S. citizens the opportunity to enter the country without numerical restriction. In addition, prior to 1965, immigrants from European countries had entered the United States largely through a program that gave visas to persons in professions and occupations that were in short supply. The Immigration Act of 1965 placed a 20 percent ceiling on these visas. Thus, as Rolph (1992:10) notes: "Removal of country-specific quotas and the new preference system designed to facilitate family reunification had been . . . responsible for substantial changes in the ethnic composition and skill level of the immigrant pool over the years."

Box 9.2
Immigrant Persons by Ethnicity in the United States: 2000

Table 9.3, on page 249, summarizes selected characteristics of the U.S. immigrant population by ethnicity.

EDUCATIONAL ATTAINMENT

- Black immigrants and Asian immigrants have a higher rate of college completion than white and Latino immigrants. In contrast, Latino immigrants have the highest rate of non–high school completion.

HOUSING

- In general, the majority of white, black, and Latino immigrants live in owner-occupied housing. In contrast, the majority of Asian immigrants live in renter-occupied housing.

POVERTY STATUS

- Latino immigrants have the highest poverty rate, while white immigrants have the lowest poverty rate. Asian and black immigrants have similar poverty rates.

INCOME

- Asian immigrants have higher median household incomes than other immigrant households. White immigrants have higher median household incomes than blacks and Latinos, and black immigrants have higher median household incomes than Latinos.

UNEMPLOYMENT

- White immigrants have a lower unemployment rate than Asian and Latino immigrants. By comparison, the unemployment rate for Latino immigrants is more than three times the white rate and almost double the Asian rate.

TABLE 9.3 Selected Characteristics by Percentage of the Immigrant Populations in the United States, 1994, 1997, and 2000.

Characteristic	White, %			Blacks, %			Latinos, %			Asians, %		
	2000	1997	1994	2000	1997	1994	2000	1997	1994	2000	1997	1994
Educational Attainment												
Not a high school graduate	19%	21%	42%	5%	12%	23%	50%	65%	17%	16%	17%	57%
High school graduate or some college	49	50	40	45	39	56	39	30	40	39	39	34
College graduate	33*	17	11	49*	33	14	11*	4	30	45*	28	6
Graduate/professional degree	—	12	7	—	19	7	—	1	13	—	16	3
Housing												
Owner-occupied unit	64	63	47	62	33	30	59	36	51	48	50	35
Renter-occupied unit	36	37	53	38	67	70	41	64	49	52	50	65
Poverty Status												
In poverty	9	13	24	13	17	23	22	32	18	13	15	32
Income												
Less than $10,000		5	43		4	36		14	35		5	47
$10,000–$34,999		47	45		61	54		76	44		52	46
$35,000–$49,999		22	6		21	6		7	10		18	4
$50,000 or more		26	6		14	4		3	11		25	3
Median Household Income (2000)	$41,733			$36,371			$29,388			$51,363		
Employment status												
Unemployed	2	6	9	NA	7	12	7	9	7	4	4	11

*Bachelor's degree or more.

Source: March 1994 CPS: The Foreign-Born Population: 1994; March 1997 Current Population Survey (Internet release date: Oct. 15, 1999); Schmidley, 2001; U.S. Statistical Abstract 2001.

The growth of immigrant populations from Asia and combined Latin American and Caribbean countries between 1981 and the present is related to two additional pieces of immigration legislation. The first, the Refugee Act of 1980, encouraged immigration from Asian countries—especially from Vietnam, Laos, and Cambodia. In the aftermath of the Vietnam War, Congress enacted the Refugee Act in an attempt to regulate the flow and number of refugees that qualified for admission to the United States. A *refugee* was defined as anyone who held a "well-founded fear of persecution in their home country." At the same time, *asylees* (persons who petition for legal status in the United States because they fear persecution in their country of origin) were given the same statutory recognition as a refugee. The Refugee Act of 1980 resulted in the arrival of large numbers of immigrants from Vietnam, Laos, and Cambodia as either refugees or asylees.

The second piece of legislation, the *Immigration Reform and Control Act (IRCA) of 1986,* targeted two immigrant groups: *long-term undocumented residents (LTUR)* and *special categories of agricultural workers (SCAW)* who had entered the United States illegally. While the primary purpose of the IRCA was to curb undocumented immigration, it also sought to protect those persons already in the United States from being uprooted and deported. The implementation component of the IRCA was an amnesty program that offered legal status to (1) persons who had resided continuously in the United States since January 1, 1982, and (2) persons who could demonstrate that they had worked ninety days or more in designated agricultural labor between May 1985 and May 1986. Since the vast majority of immigrants from Latin America were most likely to enter the agricultural labor force in the United States, the IRCA resulted in an increase of immigration from Latin America in the 1986 to 1990 period (Hollmann, 1992; Vernez, 1990).

The effects of immigration policy on the ethnic composition of the U.S. population are summarized in Table 9.4 on page 251. The largest percentage of refugees entering the United States in 2000 were from Eastern Europe and the Soviet Union. In contrast, the smallest percentage of refugees in 2000 were from Africa.

In response to public pressure and to a mixture of lobbying interests, the 1990 Immigration Act allowed immigration to increase substantially. The act encouraged immigration of more skilled workers and those from Europe, but it also sought to limit numbers of immigrants in the future. The full effect of this law is hard to estimate, but, as reported above, the reality for the next half century is that the U.S. population will include more Latinos and more Asians because of the continued effects of the 1965 and 1986 acts.

Settlement Patterns of the New Immigrants

Where do recent immigrants live? Table 9.5, on page 252, reports where immigrants have settled, by state and region. California is the state most heavily populated by immigrants; in 2000–02, 27 percent of immigrants settled there, especially in southern California along the Long Beach–Los Angeles and

TABLE 9.4 Percentage of Total Refugee Arrivals in the United States by Geographic Area, 1990 through 2000

Refugee Arrivals by Geographic Area (% of total)	1990	1991	1992	1993	1994	1995	1996	1997	2000
Total numbers	109,078	96,587	114,498	107,926	109,593	98,520	74,791	69,276	65,941
Africa	3%	5%	5%	6%	5%	5%	10%	9%	3%
East Asia	35	39	30	36	37	36	25	11	11
Eastern Europe and Soviet Union (former)	52	47	56	48	46	46	55	70	41.9
Latin America and Caribbean	5	4	3	4	6	8	5	4	23.6
Near East	5	5	6	6	6	5	5	6	6.7

Source: U.S. Department of Justice, 1999b; 2000 Statistical Yearbook of the Immigration and Naturalization Service.

TABLE 9.5 Patterns of Immigrant Settlement by Selected States and Metropolitan Areas, 1995 through 2002

	1995	1996	1997	1998	2000–02
State					
California	23%	22%	26%	26%	26.4%*
New York	18	17	16	15	21.0
Florida	9	9	10	9	18.5
Texas	7	9	7	7	14.2
New Jersey	6	7	5	5	18.6
Metropolitan Area					
New York, NY	16%	15%	14%	12%	13.9%
Los Angeles–					
Long Beach, CA	8	7	8	9	11.3
Chicago, IL	4	4	4	5	3.4
Miami, FL	4	5	6	4	5.0
Washington, DC–					
MD–VA	4	4	4	4	5.3

*Percent of state's population made up of immigrants.

Source: U.S. Department of Justice, 1999a; Camarota, 2002.

Anaheim–Santa Ana metropolitan corridors. Currently, states where immigrants locate are forced to carry the financial burden of managing these immigrants' transition into U.S. society (Vernez and McCarthy, 1996).

Other Characteristics of the New Immigrants

Table 9.6, on page 254, summarizes some of the characteristics of the immigrants who came to the United States after 1983. Regarding educational attainment, several differences are evident. First, compared to other populations, a noticeable proportion of Latinos have not graduated from high school. Second, on average, almost one-fourth of Latinos and Europeans have completed four years of high school. Third, more than one-third of the Asian population has completed four years or more of college. In 2000, the college completion rate of the Asian population was four times that of the Latino population. In general, the data in Table 9.6 support observations by researchers that Asian and Latino immigrants in the United States have high educational aspirations and outcomes (Gray et al., 1996; Vernez and Abrahamse, 1996).

In general, according to Table 9.6 the majority of foreign-born Asians, Latinos, and Europeans are employed in the United States. Interestingly, both Asians and Latinos have higher employment rates than Europeans. Latinos tend to have a higher unemployment rate, followed by Asians and Europeans, respectively. The vast majority of Asians, Latinos, and Europeans live in nonpoverty areas. Latinos have a higher rate of living in poverty areas than either Asians or Europeans.

Finally, among the three populations, the group born in Europe has generally had the highest naturalization rate. This statistic is consistent with Rolph's

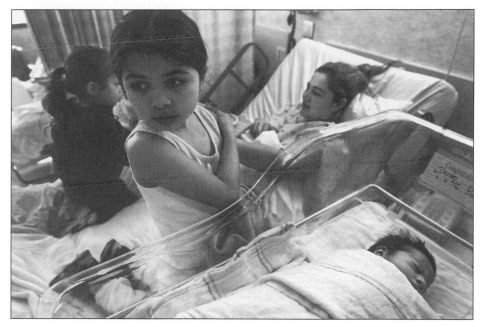

Latino births fueled the explosive growth of the Latino population in the 1990s. By the end of the decade, for the first time since the late 1850s, Latino births accounted for more than half of the births in California.

(1992) suggestion that U.S. immigration policies have historically favored persons of European origins. The larger proportion of noncitizens among the Asian and especially the Latino populations may suggest something about their accommodation in U.S. society. Asians and Latinos tend to locate within residential or geographical areas where they are the majority population. For example, many settle in areas where their native language is dominant—in the neighborhood, the workplace, and the home (Wilson and Portes, 1980; Portes and Rumbaut, 1990; and Wallace, 1989). Settlement within areas of shared ethnic identity may curtail interest in becoming naturalized citizens (see Chavez, Flores, and Lopez-Garza, 1990; Greenwell, DeVanzo, and Valdez, 1993; and Jaret, 1991). In a sense, the structural accommodation of Asians and Latinos in the United States may facilitate their participation in, but not their absorption into, mainstream social institutions (see Box 9.3, p. 256, on the economic progress of immigrants).

THE IMMIGRATION DILEMMA

Despite the fact that most Americans are the descendants of immigrants, recent immigrants are not welcomed by a majority of the American public (Morganthau, 1993). These immigrants have sparked debate over such questions as who

TABLE 9.6 Characteristics of Foreign-Born Persons* in the United States, 1983 through 2000

Characteristics	Asian, %						Latino, %						European, %					
	1983	1986	1988	1994	1997	2000	1983	1986	1988	1994	1997	2000	1983	1986	1988	1994	1997	2000
Educational Attainment																		
Not high school graduate	26.5%	26.6%	23.9%	12.9%	16.0%	16.2%	60.1%	58.0%	58.8%	40.9%	64.6%	50.4%	40.2%	33.3%	30.5%	33.0%	34.7%	18.7%
4 years of high school	20.5	23.6	21.5	30.8	26.2	21.8	22.8	23.4	23.6	24.3	36.1	24.9	31.7	34.1	35.3	31.4	34.3	25.0
4 years or more of college	36.6	34.7	36.3	34.0	44.5	44.9	7.8	7.8	6.7	6.1	5.6	11.2	15.2	18.3	19.1	13.6	24.5	25.8
Labor Force Status																		
Employed	55.2	56.4	60.7	53.6	65.1	64.0	54.0	60.9	63.4	52.2	63.0	64.9	44.7	48.9	49.9	50.6	52.5	55.8
Unemployed	5.7	4.9	3.1	4.0	4.4	3.5	10.1	6.3	4.5	6.4	8.6	7.3	4.0	2.3	1.5	5.2	5.9	2.3
Residence																		
In poverty area	7.2	10.5	16.5	18.0	15.0	12.8	18.8	27.5	37.0	31.7	32.0	21.9	5.5	4.0	6.0	24.1	13.0	9.3
Not in poverty area	92.8	89.5	83.6	82.0	85.0	87.2	81.2	72.5	62.9	68.3	68.0	78.1	94.5	96.0	94.0	75.9	87.0	90.7
Citizenship Status																		
Naturalized	39.3	41.2	45.4	51.7	44.3	47.1	30.0	29.7	31.4	38.3	15.7	28.3	71.1	65.1	66.4	69.2	53.3	52.0
Not a citizen	58.7	57.6	52.1	48.3	55.7	52.9	68.3	67.6	66.2	61.7	84.3	71.7	27.0	31.7	31.4	30.8	46.7	48.0

*Persons 14 years old and older.

Source: U.S. Bureau of the Census, 1991d; March 1994 CPS: *The Foreign-born Population: 1994*; U.S. Census Bureau, "Profile of the Foreign-Born Population in the United States, 1997"; Schmidley, 2001.

can come; how many can come; who is to pay for their needs; how can institutions like the schools and the economy absorb them; and will they adopt the tenets of the Anglo-Saxon core culture (Trueba, 1989; Valdez et al., 1993; and Vernez, 1993). Table 9.7 illustrates the changes in public opinion concerning immigration, to the United States in general and to heavily populated states such as California and Florida in particular. Over 50 percent of Americans—up from one-third in 1965—now want immigration reduced; the number of those who want immigration to remain "about the same" has decreased noticeably between 1965 and 2000; the percentage of those who have "no opinion" dropped by 75 percent. These data indicate that immigration is now a priority issue on the American agenda. The tragic events of September 11th may have increased anti-immigrant sentiment in the United States (see Box 9.4 on page 264).

Part of the reason for this hardening of public opinion is, no doubt, the result of the recent shift in composition of the immigrant population from mostly European to mostly Latin American, Caribbean, and Asian. This shift has aroused the suspicion and fears not only of those of European ancestry but also among those of Latino ancestry. The Latino National Political Survey—the most extensive effort to date to measure Latino attitudes—found considerable

TABLE 9.7 Public Opinion on Appropriate Levels of Immigration to the United States

Survey Year and Scope	IMMIGRATION LEVELS SHOULD BE:			
	Increased, %	Kept the Same, %	Reduced, %	No Opinion, %
1965 (U.S.)[a]	8%	39%	33%	20%
1977 (U.S.)[b]	7	37	42	14
1982 (Calif.)[c]	5	31	62	2
1984 (U.S.)[d]	8	38	40	14
1987 (Calif.)[e]	8	38	40	14
1988 (Fla.)[f]	6	24	67	3
1990 (U.S.)[g]	9	29	48	14
1992 (U.S.)[h]	5	28	59	8
1992 (Calif.)[h]	8	18	63	11
1999 (U.S.)[i]	10	41	44	5
2000 (U.S.)[j]	17	26	54	3

[a]George H. Gallup, *The Gallup Poll: Public Opinion, 1935–1971*, vol. 3 (New York: Random House, 1972), p. 1953.
[b]George H. Gallup, *The Gallup Poll: Public Opinion, 1972–1977*, vol. 2 (Wilmington, DE: Scholarly Resources, Inc., 1979), p. 1050.
[c]California Opinion Index, "Immigration" (mimeo), Field Institute, San Francisco, June 1982.
[d]Jonathan Alter and Joseph Contreras, "Closing the Door?" *Newsweek*, June 25, 1984, p. 18. Average of responses to immigration level.
[e]California Opinion Index, "Immigration" (mimeo), Field Institute, San Francisco, October 1987.
[f]*Atlanta Journal*, January 31, 1988.
[g]*Los Angeles Times*, June 5, 1990, p. A23 (Roper Organization poll).
[h]*American Attitudes toward Immigration* (New York: The Roper Organization, April 1992).
[i] Gallup Poll (March 8, 1999 release).
[j]Gallup Poll (September 6, 2002 release).

Box 9.3
Economic Progress of Immigrants

How do immigrants fare in the economic marketplace? How has the economic progress of immigrants changed between 1970 and 1990? The data presented in Table 9.8, on page 257 are helpful in answering these two questions. Table 9.8 compares the median weekly earnings of immigrant workers with those of native-born workers in order to derive a measure of how immigrant workers fare relative to native-born workers. For example, in 1970, early arrivals in the United States from Mexico earned 63 percent of the median weekly earnings of native-born workers. Some of the more salient characteristics of the data in Table 9.8 are the following:

MEXICO

- Early arrivals have done better than late arrivals in narrowing the earning gap between immigrants and native-born workers.
- Regardless of arrival date, the earning gap between immigrants and native-born workers has widened between 1970 and 1990.

EUROPE

- The earning gap between immigrant and native-born workers has exceeded parity.
- Regardless of arrival date, immigrants reach or exceed parity in earnings within the first ten years.

ASIA

- Early arrivals have made greater gains than late arrivals in narrowing the earning gap between immigrant and native-born workers.
- Similar to European immigrant workers, Asians have reached or exceeded parity with the earnings of native-born workers within ten years.

---

hostility toward new immigrants, who represent economic competition for those already here (de la Garza et al., 1992). Perhaps the growing sentiment against immigrants extends to many ethnic subpopulations who perceive the same threat.

Much of the energy and vitality of the United States lies in its immigrant subpopulations. If the American public now wants to close the borders, will such restrictions damage the engine that has driven America? In some respects this question is rhetorical because, legally or illegally, immigrants will continue to arrive in the United States.

The dilemma is this: Will the inevitable influx of immigrants set in motion a dynamic of discrimination and ethnic antagonism that will undermine the structure and integrity of American society? Could this relatively recent broad-based resentment of non-European immigrants escalate the intensity of

TABLE 9.8 Relative Median Weekly Earnings of Immigrant and Native-Born Workers for Earlier versus More Recent Arrivals by Country of Origin, 1970 to 1990

Country of Origin, Date of Arrival	1970, %	1980, %	1990, %
Mexico			
Early arrivals: 1965–69	63%	61%	57%
Late arrivals: 1975–79	—	52	50
Europe			
Early arrivals: 1965–69	94	101	105
Late arrivals: 1975–79	—	90	110
Asia			
Early arrivals: 1965–69	74	120	141
Late arrivals: 1975–79	—	78	115

Source: Schoeni et al., 1996.

In general, the data above suggest that, given the earning gap, immigrant workers from Mexico are not assimilating to the U.S. labor market. If Mexican immigrant workers were assimilating to the U.S. labor market, then the earning gap between them and native-born workers would have narrowed between 1970 and 1990. In contrast, immigrant workers from Europe and Asia have reached or exceeded parity in earnings with native-born workers because they have assimilated successfully to the U.S. labor market. In addition, the widening earning gap for Mexican immigrant workers between 1970 and 1990 suggests that they may be disproportionately segmented in low-skill and low-wage jobs in the United States.

the dynamic to a new, disintegrative level? As we close our review of American ethnicity, these questions are worth consideration.

THE FUTURE DYNAMIC OF DISCRIMINATION

The shift in the ethnic composition of American society over the next fifty years will increase the Latino, Asian, and African American subpopulations. Most of the Latino population will consist of Mexican Americans, with significant numbers of Puerto Ricans, Central and South Americans, and Spanish-speaking Caribbean Islanders (Mahler, 1995; Pessar, 1995). The Asian population will be of diverse origins; Filipinos are likely to be the most numerous, followed by Chinese, Vietnamese, Koreans, and Asian Indians (Lessinger, 1995; Freeman,

1995). The predominant segment of the African American population will
be the descendants of slaves, supplemented by some recent Caribbean and
African immigrants.

If we refer to the theoretical model presented in Chapter 2 and delineated
in Figures 2.1 and 2.3, on pages 36 and 41, we can make some predictions
about the future of ethnic relations in the United States. The key variables in
the model are the following:

1. The size of an ethnic population
2. The entrepreneurial and educational resources of a population
3. The distinctiveness and identifiability of a population
4. The sense of threat experienced by other ethnic groups, especially the
   dominant ethnic subpopulations
5. The intensity of negative and prejudicial stereotypes
6. The degree of discrimination against a subpopulation
7. The resource shares of a subpopulation
8. The level of stratification, or confinement to a particular social class
9. The salience of egalitarian values and beliefs

We have seen how these variables have structured the lives of ethnic groups
discussed in Chapters 4 through 8; let us now assess how these variables will
influence the lives of recent immigrants within these groups.

Latinos and the American Future

As the largest minority in the future, Latinos will not be able to fill middleman
minority niches and positions. The sheer size of this subpopulation, along
with its average lower levels of education, job skills, and financial resources,
will continue to limit the entrepreneurial opportunities for most Latinos. The
sense of threat generated by the growing size of the Latino population will
increase and generate considerable negative stereotyping. The movement of
many Latinos back and forth to their country of origin will ensure the survival
of barrios, patterns of intragroup marriage and reproduction, native language
use, and other cultural traditions. These cultural ties will not only sustain
identifiability but also increase the sense of threat to a diminishing white
majority and an African American population who will have to compete with
Latinos for jobs.

These negative effects of increasing numbers and low socioeconomic position eventually will be neutralized by a number of factors: (1) Most Latinos are
less physically identifiable than either Asian Americans or African Americans;
(2) Latinos are likely to intermarry with other ethnic groups in relatively large
numbers because of their physical and cultural similarities with the white population; (3) the Latino population will continue to concentrate in the Southwest
and, by virtue of their numbers, will acquire access to political power; (4) Latinos will obtain academic credentials in significant numbers and, hence, will
have access to nonmenial jobs and higher incomes. Coupled with these factors
are the effects of civil rights laws, which can, and will, be used to redress many

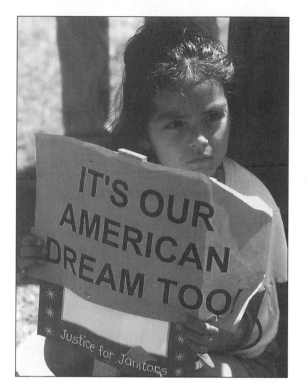

A young girl protests the arrests of Latino immigrant workers at airports in southern California. After the events of September 11, the Bush administration pushed for stricter security measures at the nation's airports. One result was the displacement of Latino immigrant workers from minimum-wage jobs, such as baggage handlers, screeners, and janitors.

of the law enforcement abuses of the past. Moreover, affirmative action extensions of these laws—or those that survive current efforts to eliminate them—will also be used to facilitate educational attainment and job placement. These large numbers of Latinos will continue to infiltrate the Anglo mainstream, even as a large mass remains ghettoized in barrios.

Despite these mitigating factors, the large size of the Latino population and its concentration in the Southwest as well as in the larger cities of the Northeast and south Florida will continue to fuel the hostility and resentment of white Americans who believe that their majority status is threatened and who feel forced to accommodate a "foreign culture" in ways never before experienced in America. Such hostility will translate into discrimination. If economic pressures continue to limit the number of available jobs and the flow of tax revenues to schools and other institutional structures, then considerable conflict and antagonism will ensue. The flash points will be symbolic issues such as bilingual education, and language use in general, or highly visible stratification issues such as gang violence. The underlying tension will emanate from the threat that a large Latino population poses to the integrity of white American culture, job security, education, public services, and control of political power. As we saw in Chapter 6, the antagonism has been great as Latinos approached 8 percent of the U.S. population; as the Latino population surpasses 20 percent of the general population and over 50 percent in much of the Southwest, the antagonism will increase.

Asian Americans in the Future

The Asian population is highly diverse, immigrating from many different societies and cultures. Currently the largest Asian American population is the Chinese (2.3 million), followed by Filipinos (1.8 million), Asian Indians (1.7 million), Vietnamese (1.1 million), Koreans (1.1 million), and Japanese (0.80 million) (U.S. Bureau of the Census, 2002). Except for the Japanese, these populations have been growing rapidly over the last decade. Individually, no Asian subpopulation will ever constitute more than 1 to 1.5 percent of the total population, but as a whole and adding Cambodians, Hmong, Laotians, Thailanders, Indonesians, Malaysians, Okinawans, Pakistanis, Sri Lankans, and a dozen or so Pacific Islander subpopulations to this list, Asians may constitute as much as 11 to 12 percent of the U.S. population.

This increase in the aggregate numbers of Asian Americans may pose an increased threat to white Americans, especially if world competition with Japan and emerging Asian economic powers creates economic hardships for non-Asian workers. Most Asian Americans are likely to move into middleman minority and professional niches because many bring with them education (or an education ethic), entrepreneurial skills, and systems for pooling capital. Different Asian ethnic groups may seek somewhat different middleman minority niches, although considerable competition among Asians may occur in certain metropolitan areas (Whitmore, Trautmann, and Caplan, 1989). Equally likely, younger Asians will secure those academic credentials that will place them in middle- and upper-middle-class professions and occupations. Their growing numbers in higher education and occupations formerly dominated by white Americans will cause considerable hostility and discrimination. Moreover, Latinos and African Americans will resent Asians who take advantage of opportunities in small business, higher education, and middle-class professions and positions. As a result, negative stereotypes about Asians will be propagated and used to justify discrimination, primarily of the informal and subtle kind that Asian Americans experience today (see Chapter 7).

Mitigating these discriminatory forces are counterforces: (1) Significant numbers of Asian Americans will intermarry with white Americans, thereby blurring the lines of physical distinction; (2) Asian American communities will continue to use their resources to promote success in business and education, two arenas in which positive interaction with white Americans frequently occurs; (3) large numbers of Asian Americans living in the metropolitan areas will use their financial resources to mobilize political and legal resources to combat discrimination; and (4) young Asian Americans will use their academic credentials to penetrate all types of middle-class economic positions, thereby breaking the cycle of Asian confinement to middleman minority activity.

Asian American success will generate hostility among those who are less successful. Asian Americans who do not have academic credentials or other resources will remain in menial jobs within Asian ghettos or will enter the labor market and compete with Latinos and African Americans in a declining pool of lower-skilled and semiskilled jobs.

It is likely that Asian Americans will continue to use their resources to overcome discrimination. History has shown that when broad-based anti-Asian sentiments emerge, Asian Americans tend to come out of their "cultural shell" and fight discrimination aggressively. Yet, we predict that within the next fifty years, relatively peaceful relations will prevail among diverse Asian subpopulations and mainstream America.

African Americans in the Future

As African Americans approach 16 percent of the population in the future, many of the problems that confront this population today will persist. The size of the population prevents it from filling only middleman minority niches, unless Asian Americans abandon these niches because of African American and, to a lesser extent, Latino hostility and violence. Negative stereotypes will perpetuate hostility from as well as toward African Americans. Moreover, as poorer African Americans and Latinos compete for the decreasing number of low-skilled and semiskilled jobs, tensions, mutual stereotyping, and hostility between these populations may increase (Graham, 1990).

The economic future of the African American population will be both bitter and sweet. As a result of affirmative action and other programs, many African Americans have escaped poverty, and the proportion of African Americans in the middle class will continue to increase. African Americans have increased their average years of education, violent crime in slums has decreased, literacy skills have increased, and drug use has declined (Jencks, 1991:5). However, the drop in male college enrollment may hinder further upward mobility for many males. Also, trends toward a dramatically expanded black middle class will emphasize the socioeconomic differences within the black population. Many poor black families are headed by single mothers and their relatives; these caretakers must raise children without benefit of a father at home, often in substandard housing located in violent and crime-infested neighborhoods. Under these conditions, the jobless rate for young males has increased; many have simply withdrawn from the labor market and some have drifted into gangs. Those who do not join the expanding middle class are likely to find it harder to rise above poverty, and their offspring will carry the legacy of poverty into adulthood. This scenario will become reality if the national economy declines and if the American public does not address the social problems with dollars from both the public and private sectors. In the future, African Americans will be overrepresented in the lowest socioeconomic strata without enough resources to correct this imbalance. Tension between poor African Americans and other ethnic groups will persist as a result of a combination of factors: competition for jobs and government resources, resentment over long-term poverty and discrimination, and the incursion of other ethnic groups into entry-level, menial jobs.

Although black culture and its icons—celebrities in sports, music, movies, and television—will continue to penetrate the Anglo-Saxon cultural core, the general population of blacks will experience discrimination owing to skin color and other cultural differences. In most cases this discrimination will be informal and subtle, but very real. Moreover, despite a growing African American middle class becoming more integrated with white and Asian Americans in jobs, housing, and education—with a concomitant reduction in the intensity of established stereotypes and blatant forms of discrimination—the problems of those left behind will foster new levels of threat, new negative stereotypes, and new forms of discrimination.

These predictions are based on attributes shown in the discrimination model, which apply to African Americans living in poverty: large in number, easy to identify, threatening to other populations, negatively stereotyped, low on the socioeconomic ladder, lacking in resources, and persistent targets of discrimination. The white Americans' sense of threat in the perception that affirmative action programs as well as government aid programs diminish their own well-being will discourage many from making resources available to the black community and, thereby, from redressing this long-standing American dilemma.

THE PROBLEMATIC NATURE OF A MULTICULTURAL AMERICA

No large-scale society has ever successfully integrated all of its ethnic subpopulations, nor has any ever eliminated the tensions among ethnic populations. The United States has done better than most societies along these lines, primarily because it was created through immigration to a land where genocide had been practiced on the indigenous population, thereby opening the land for settlement (Takaki, 1993). The most enduring problems are the plight of African Americans who cannot escape the legacy of slavery and Native Americans who have not overcome the effects of their conquest and attempted genocide. The most visible new problem in the future is the growth of the Latino population and the challenges this poses to the Anglo-Saxon cultural core.

As our speculative scenario has emphasized, the enduring problems of a large black population and the explosive growth of the Latino population ensure tension in the future. Added to these two fault lines are the growth of diverse Asian ethnics, the continued plight of Native Americans, and the declining size of white ethnics relative to other ethnic subpopulations. Just how these points of cleavage will play out cannot be known for sure, but the salience of ethnicity will increase in the next decades.

Some celebrate ethnic diversity, but it should be noted that no large-scale society with highly diverse and entrenched ethnic subpopulations has been stable (Gold, 1995). Historically, ethnic tensions have torn societies apart. The collapse of the Soviet empire along roughly ethnic lines, the brutality of hostility in what was once Yugoslavia, the festering conflicts in the "United" Kingdom over Northern Ireland, the ethnic hostilities among diverse Muslim sects in most countries of the Middle East, the state of tension between Indians and

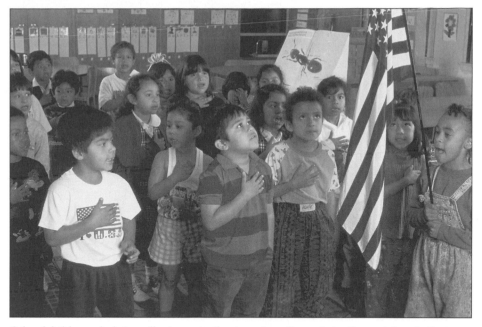

Schoolchildren pledging allegiance to the American flag mirror the racial and ethnic diversity in American society.

Pakistanis, and the "wars" of ethnic liberation all over the world today illustrate that when ethnicity runs deep, conflict becomes intense.

Thus, ethnic pluralism must revolve around relatively weak ethnic identification, or otherwise it becomes a focal point for societal disintegration (Trueba, 1993). It is now politically *in*correct to question pluralism or, worse, to extol the virtues of integration of ethnics into an Anglo-Saxon cultural core—at least within academia. But if there is no cultural core to which each wave of immigrants adjusts, or if ethnic populations of any size refuse or cannot adjust, then societal integration will be tenuous. It is for this reason that discrimination is such a harmful force: It often forces ethnics to sustain deep-seated ethnic patterns at odds with the cultural core. Discrimination is, of course, inevitable when some feel threatened by the presence of other ethnics, but if the discrimination can be only temporary and, in fact, serve to decrease differences between ethnics as its victims seek to reduce their identifiability and, hence, their vulnerability to discrimination, then something positive comes of discrimination. But when discrimination is intense, long-term, and inhibits assimilation, then it creates cleavages along ethnic lines, and such cleavages are among the most volatile forces of human organization. And so, if discrimination over the next decades prevents African Americans, Latinos, and Asian Americans from adopting the cultural core and from fully participating in the society, and at the same time heightens their ethnic identity, it

---

Box 9.4

Hate Crimes against Arabs and Muslims
after September 11th

British sociologist Frank Furedi argues that the image of the half-crazed third-world terrorist with a bomb in hand, ready to die for some incomprehensible cause, has taken hold of the Western imagination. The terrorist attacks of September 11, 2001, on the World Trade Center in New York City served as a catalyst for reinforcing negative stereotypes in popular thinking of Arab Americans and Muslims as *terrorists*. According to Human Rights Watch, Arabs and Muslims in the United States—including persons perceived to be Arab or Muslim—became victims of a severe wave of backlash violence after September 11 that included murder, beatings, arson, vandalizing mosques, shootings, and verbal threats. According to Human Rights Watch, more than 2,000 September 11 hate crimes were committed against Arabs, Muslims, and those perceived to be either Arab or Muslim. Hate crimes committed against Arabs and Muslims increased seventeenfold after September 11.

Human Rights Watch has documented at least seven murders resulting from anti-Arab and anti-Muslim hatred after September 11. More than 300 assaults occurred between September 11 and the first week of February that were related to anti-Arab and anti-Muslim hatred. During the first week after September 11, over 100 bias incidents were reported regarding vandalism and arson of mosques, and worshippers being threatened with violence. Some examples of the reported bias incidents are the following:

- On September 29, 2001, Abdo Ali Ahmed, a 51-year-old Yemini Arab and Muslim, and father of eight, was shot and killed while working at his convenience store in Reedley, California. The cash in two registers was left untouched.

---

will increase the level of ethnic tension in America, perhaps to the point of societal disintegration.

Such is not likely to be the case because of powerful values and beliefs emphasizing equality and because these cultural tenets have been codified into laws and enforcement procedures. These can be used to mitigate discrimination and to weaken the intensity of people's diverse ethnic identities. At the same time, the reality of a declining proportion of the population from Anglo-Saxon European stock can, perhaps, force some changes in the Anglo-Saxon cultural core, not to the point of its destruction, which would only deepen ethnic boundaries, but to the point of inclusion of new cultural elements from African, Latino, and Asian cultures. Such inclusion has always occurred, but the ethnics involved were white and European. In particular, just whether the same inclusion can occur for the descendants of black slaves and the returning descendants of those who were pushed off their land in the Southwest is the real problem of the future. These are the most volatile cleavages; others also exist but the populations involved are too small to disintegrate the society. If

---

- On September 15, 2001, Adel Karas, a 48-year-old Arab and Coptic Christian, and a father of three, was shot and killed at his convenience store in San Gabriel, California. Again, no money was taken from the cash register.
- On November 19, 2001, four teenagers burned down the Gobind Sadan, a multi-faith worship center in Oswego, New York, because they believed the worshippers to be supporters of Osama Bin Laden. On September 23, 2001, the St. John's Assyrian American Church was set on fire in Chicago. The church's pastor said that the person whom he believed to have set the fire had asked a local resident whether the church was a mosque.
- On August 24, 2002, federal authorities in Tampa Bay discovered a plan by a doctor to bomb and destroy approximately 50 mosques and Islamic cultural centers in south Florida.

The preceding are examples of the types of bias experienced by Arabs and Muslims in the United States. While it is difficult to document all of the hate crimes committed against Arabs and Muslims, it is clear that they became identifiable targets for hatred and violence as a result of September 11. More importantly, the context of hatred and violence that developed after September 11 is indicative of a long-standing problem in American society—the persistence of hate crimes in the social fabric. The anti-Arab and anti-Muslim hatred expressed after September 11 has its roots in a historical context of hate—the Rodney King beating, the burning of African American churches, the murders of James Byrd, Yusef Hawkins, and Matthew Shepard, and the 1993 Long Island Railroad shooting spree.

Source: Furedi, 1994; Human Rights Watch, 2002.

---

these points of antagonism among whites, blacks, and browns in America can be reduced in the next century, then the United States will have been unique in the history of the world.

CONCLUSION: THE STRUGGLE FOR SOCIAL JUSTICE IN TWENTY-FIRST CENTURY U.S. SOCIETY

U.S. society portrays itself as rooted in a pluralist framework that promotes access of opportunity to all its citizens. However, previous chapters in this book have documented how racial and ethnic populations do not have equal access to resources in American society. As the chapters have shown, unequal resource shares create contexts of inequality that often enhance the saliency of race and ethnicity in determining quality of life in society. Ironically, as U.S. society crosses the threshold into the twenty-first century, it does so cloaked

---

Box 9.5
Where Multiculturalism Succeeds

To the east of Los Angeles a series of ethnic suburbs are emerging. Previously all-white in profile, minorities are now moving in. Walnut, California, is perhaps the most unique of these communities, because it has undergone two dramatic transformations in the last few decades: (1) from agriculture to suburban and (2) from predominately white to multiethnic. At the high school prom couples of very different ethnic backgrounds can be found on the dance floor together. "Race" and ethnicity do not seem to matter so much as they do in other communities; indeed, African Americans dance with Asians, Anglos with Latinos, Latinos with African Americans, Anglos with African Americans and Asians, and just about any combination possible in light of the demographics of Walnut, which has become 36 percent Asian and Pacific Islander; 34 percent non-Latino white; 24 percent Latino; and 7 percent African American. The city has had African American, Anglo, and Asian mayors; and neighborhoods are, for the most part, fully integrated.

Is Walnut a harbinger of America's future? By 2050, the U.S. Bureau of the Census estimates that non-Latino whites will constitute only 52 percent of the U.S. population; and in California, there will be no majority. Indeed, such is the case now or in the very near future for California, as the 2000 Census reported. Thus, California and much of the nation will be multiethnic, and the real question is, Can communities be like Walnut or will they degenerate into patterns of residential segregation, hate crimes, and ethnic anxiety?

The transition to a peaceful multiethnic community was not always smooth in Walnut. There was a backlash as whites saw that they were soon to become just another minority. Many left. Others sought to protect themselves through subtle practices of discrimination, as when realtors would guide blacks away from white neighborhoods or when a now disbanded Anglo-American club was formed. Yet, other factors worked in favor of not just ethnic tolerance, but real ethnic diversity

---

with institutionalized forms of discrimination that limit the life chances of racial and ethnic minority populations.

We noted earlier in Chapter 4 that the social struggles of the 1960s served as an opportunity for the formalization of social policy interventions intended to promote equal opportunity for socially oppressed groups. These social interventions were designed to alter societal contexts of inequality that restricted the access of racial and ethnic minorities to resource shares in U.S. society. For example, income maintenance programs were utilized to alleviate the economic hardships of the working poor; Head Start programs were introduced as vehicles for improving access to education opportunity among poor—especially minority—households; and affirmative action was designed and mutual understanding; and perhaps when these same conditions exist in other changing communities, these too can become like Walnut.

What were these factors? First, Walnut evolved into a community with ethnic balance among diverse groups, not just a dominant majority and a few minority populations. Second, Walnut is an affluent suburb; its residents have common economic aspirations, shared values, and similar orientations to housing standards and neighborhood quality. Third, people had a choice of whether or not to settle in Walnut; residence was not determined by history or a dominant industry, and in fact, many have moved to Walnut because of its multicultural profile and reputation for tolerance. Fourth, individuals are not in economic competition for jobs, as is the case in many urban communities, and as a result, they do not see in each other an economic threat to their well-being. Fifth, Walnut is a relatively new suburb and, hence, had little of the negative baggage of communities with longer histories of ethnic competition, ethnic politics, and ethnic neighborhoods.

The schools have also been particularly important in fostering ethnic tolerance. There are many ethnic clubs in the high school, but these do not seem to impose barriers. Moreover, there does not appear to be the same rigid hierarchy of social status typical of most American high schools, enabling all students to feel that they are "in" rather than "out"; and without the hostility that such hierarchies generate, students feel free to move about and mix, getting to know each other. Parents appear more worried about ethnic heritage than do their children, often encouraging study and participation in narrow ethnic activities, but such efforts tend to fail in the multi-ethnic mix of student friendships. The students' common orientation is more to youth culture than to ethnic heritage.

Thus, when ethnics do not see each other as threats, in an environment in which they can interact as equals, the engine of ethnic fear and discrimination is shut down. Not all communities can be Walnut; but in Walnut there is at least a demonstration that many of the typical patterns of ethnic tension in America can be broken down.

Source: O'Connor (1999).

to increase the changes that racial and ethnic minority populations could compete for resource shares. Interestingly, the most controversial social policy initiative from the 1960s, and the one that continues to pose a serious challenge to the distribution of resource shares in American society, is affirmative action.

Discussions of affirmative action quite often result in moral arguments about who "merits" access to resource shares or technical discussions of "who" determines access to resource shares (Aguirre, 2000). We noted in Box 2.1 in Chapter 2 that the American public is ambivalent in their thinking of how affirmative action can be practiced without challenging general notions of equality, merit, and opportunity. Can affirmative action serve as an intervention strategy for increasing the access of underserved populations to resource shares in U.S. society without challenging ideological notions of equality? As an intervention strategy, affirmative action is controversial because it challenges the social production of *merit* by trying to "close the gap" between the privileged and underprivileged in U.S. society (Greenberg, 2002). Affirmative action is also controversial because it attacks unequal access to opportunity in order to remove the "lingering effects" of discrimination against minority (nonwhite) persons (Cunningham, Loury, and Skrentny, 2002).

The controversy surrounding affirmative action has unfortunately *racialized* affirmative action in the minds of the American public as a social policy that seeks to give racial and ethnic minorities resource shares by taking them away from white persons. Not surprisingly, affirmative action is viewed by white Americans as a policy of *reverse racism* that victimizes them in initiatives to redress the unequal access of racial and ethnic minorities to resource shares in U.S. society (Platt, 1997). Affirmative action is perceived as a social policy of reverse racism by white Americans because they regard it as an excuse for racial and ethnic minorities to avoid playing by the rules that "hard work, assimilation, and virtue can overcome any adversity, including racism" (Vargas, 1998:1502).

Caught in the vortex of the Civil Rights movement of the 1960s, affirmative action continues to challenge the principles about equality and opportunity that operate as the ideological framework for U.S. society (Delgado, 1995; Morris, 1984). Supporters of affirmative action argue that it is vital to increasing the representation of racial and ethnic minorities in the social fabric of American society, especially within societal institutions that structure pathways to resource shares. Supporters of affirmative action also argue that it is vital to a society whose social fabric is becoming increasingly diverse in its racial and ethnic composition (Bell, 1997). In a sense, affirmative action is a vehicle for including racial and ethnic minorities in mainstream social institutions and for enhancing their participation within those institutions.

The United States Supreme Court is in a position to determine the utility of affirmative action for including racial and ethnic minorities in the structure of opportunity in American society. The Supreme Court is expected to rule sometime in the summer of 2003 on the use of affirmative action policies at the University of Michigan. The Supreme Court will review the university's use of affirmative action in its admissions process as a strategy for leveling the playing field between white persons and racial and ethnic minorities. Specifically, the Supreme Court will decide whether the *diversity rationale* advanced by Justice Powell in his opinion regarding *Bakke* (see the following box summarizing historic cases) is an appropriate and legal means for diversifying institutions of higher eduction by using race as one factor in the admissions process. The decision handed down by the Supreme Court in the *Michigan* cases regarding affirmative action will either affirm that affirmative action is an appropriate vehicle for accommodating an increasingly diverse and multicultural population within societal institutions in the United States; or, it will deny affirmative action the opportunity to redress the social injustices faced by racial and ethnic minorities in American society.

Affirmative Action at the Crossroads

Justice Lewis Powell, Jr.'s opinion in *University of California v. Bakke* [438 U.S. 265 (1978)] noted that ethnic diversity could be one factor in a range of factors that a university might consider in attaining a diverse student body. Justice Powell's opinion in *Bakke* was interpreted by institutions of higher eduction as identifying a diversity rationale that allows the use of race as a selective factor in admissions as long as racial quotas are not promoted. Unsurprisingly, institutions of higher education adopted admission policies that utilized race as one factor in determining an applicant's qualifications for admission and for diversifying the student body.

Twenty-five years later, the diversity rationale noted in Justice Powell's opinion has placed affirmative action at the crossroads. The U.S. Supreme Court is poised to settle the debate about the diversity rationale in university admissions, and more important, perhaps bring closure to the acrimonious debates about affirmative action in public life. The U.S. Supreme Court is expected to settle the constitutionality question of a *diversity rationale* by reviewing the use of affirmative action in university admissions at the University of Michigan's main undergraduate college and its law school.

Starting with the Michigan cases, we outline a series of court cases that have challenged the use of diversity measures in higher education and that frame the legal context regarding the diversity rationale in higher education under review by the U.S. Supreme Court.

GRATZ V. BOLLINGER (THE UNIVERSITY OF MICHIGAN— THE UNDERGRADUATE CASE)

In 1997, Jennifer Gratz and Patrick Hamacher filed a class action suit on behalf of themselves and all others similarly situated against the University of Michigan, alleging that the university's College of Literature, Science and the Arts had violated Title VI of the Civil Rights Act and the Equal Protection Clause of the Fourteenth Amendment by using race as a factor in admissions decisions. The court ruled in favor of the plaintiffs and declared the admissions programs in existence from 1995 through 1998 unconstitutional on the basis that they were not narrowly tailored to meet the interest of diversity under the standard of strict scrutiny. However, the court found the admissions programs in existence in 1999 and 2000 to be constitutional [*Gratz v. Bollinger,* 122 F. Supp. 2d 811 (E.D. Mich. 2000)].

GRUTTER V. BOLLINGER (THE UNIVERSITY OF MICHIGAN— THE LAW SCHOOL CASE)

In 1997, Barbara Gutter filed suit against the University of Michigan Law School after having been denied admission in June of that year. Grutter alleged that she was discriminated against on the basis of her race (Caucasian—"a disfavored racial group") and that the law school violated the Fourteenth Amendment and Title VI of the Civil Rights Act of 1964, which prohibits recipients of federal funds from discriminating on the basis of race [*Grutter v. Bollinger,* 137 F. Supp. 2d 821 (U.S. Dist. 2001)]. In 1998, the University of Michigan sought to have this case designated as a companion to *Gratz v. Bollinger.* However, in a series of odd

Affirmative Action at the Crossroads (continued)

procedures involving an Order of Disqualification and Transfer by the Chief Judge of the District Court and the nullification of an opinion by a two-judge panel, the cases were ultimately deemed not to be companion cases [16 F. Supp. 2d 797 (E.D. Mich. 1998)].

In *Grutter*, the district court found in favor of the plaintiff and against the law school. The court declared that the law school's use of race in its admissions decisions violated the Equal Protection Clause of the Fourteenth Amendment and Title VI of the Civil Rights Act of 1964, and prohibited the law school from using race as a factor in its admissions decisions. The University of Michigan requested a stay of injunction and was denied by the district court. On May 14, 2002, a sharply divided Sixth Circuit Court of Appeals voted 5 to 4 to overturn the lower court's ruling that the admissions policy used by the University of Michigan's law school illegally discriminated against white applicants.

JOHNSON V. UNIVERSITY OF GEORGIA

In 1999, Jennifer Johnson filed suit against the University of Georgia after she was denied admission to the freshman class for Fall 1999. Her complaint was later consolidated with the complaints of Aimee Bogrow and Molly Ann Beckenhauer, who were also denied admission in 1999. Johnson was offered admission to the University of Georgia after she had filed her lawsuit, but she declined to enroll at that time. The plaintiffs alleged that they were denied admission on the bases of race (Title VI) and gender (Title IX). The University of Georgia gave automatic preference in admissions to male applicants. The U.S. District Court for the Southern District of Georgia ruled in favor of the plaintiffs [*Johnson v. University of Georgia*, 106 F. Supp. 2d 1362 (S.D. Ga. 2000)]. The decision was upheld by the U.S. Court of Appeals for the 11th Circuit [263 F. 3d 1234 (U.S. App. 2001)].

SMITH V. UNIVERSITY OF WASHINGTON

In 1997, Katuria Smith, Angela Rock, and Michael Pyle (collectively Smith) filed a class-action suit against the University of Washington Law School alleging that they and other white applicants had been denied admission on the basis of racially discriminatory admissions policies [*Smith v. Univ. of Washington*, 2000 WL 177045 (2000)]. In this case, the court followed the majority opinion rendered in *Bakke* and held that the law school's admissions program could consider race in the promotion of educational diversity, a compelling governmental interest, and that it met the demands of strict scrutiny of race-conscious measures. In 2001, the Supreme Court declined to hear the appeal despite the contradiction between this ruling and that in *Hopwood*. The court held that the issue was moot, since the University of Washington had discontinued using race, ethnicity, and national origin as factors in the admissions process following passage of Initiative 200. Initiative 200, the Washington State Civil Rights Initiative, was approved by voters in 1998. Modeled after California's Proposition 209, Initiative 200 prohibited the state from granting preferential treatment on the basis of race, sex, or national origin in the areas of public eduction, public contracting, and public employment.

Affirmative Action at the Crossroads (concluded)

HOPWOOD V. UNIVERSITY OF TEXAS

In 1992, Cheryl J. Hopwood and three other white plaintiffs filed suit against the University of Texas Law School alleging that they were denied admission as a result of procedures granting preferences to black and Mexican American applicants. The court paid deference to the Supreme Court precedent in *Bakke* and declined to declare the school's use of racial preferences in its admissions process unconstitutional [*Hopwood v. State of Texas*, 861 F. Supp. 551 (W.D. Tex. 1994)]. Instead, the court applied strict scrutiny to the law school's admissions process and found that the use of racial preferences for the purpose of achieving a diverse student body served a compelling state interest under the Fourteenth Amendment. The court also found that the use of racial classifications for overcoming the present effects of past discrimination served a compelling government interest. However, the court ultimately found that the law school's use of separate admissions procedures for minorities and nonminorities prevented any meaningful comparative evaluation among applicants of different races and was not narrowly tailored to achieve those compelling interests. Consequently, the court declared that the law school's 1992 admissions procedures violated the Fourteenth Amendment. In effect, the court ruled that the admissions procedures favored only black and Mexican American applicants.

The Fifth Circuit Court reversed and remanded the court's decision in part. It declared that the law school's use of racial preferences served no compelling state interests under the Fourteenth Amendment and directed the law school not to use race as a factor in admissions. The remanded part of the decision had to do with whether or not the plaintiffs would have been admitted to the law school in the absence of admissions procedures that take into account an applicant's race or ethnicity. The U.S. Supreme Court declined to hear appeals of the circuit court's decision, acknowledging that the 1992 admissions program had been discontinued and would not be reinstated.

UNIVERSITY OF CALIFORNIA V. BAKKE

Alan Bakke, a white male, challenged the validity of a special admissions program at the University of California at Davis School of Medicine after having twice been denied admission. The medical school filled 16 of its 100 slots in its entering class through a special admissions program open only to minority applicants who were compared among themselves and not with the overall applicant pool. Bakke's college grade point average and MCAT score were among the highest of all the applicants, and higher than those of all of the minority applicants admitted into the medical school through the special admissions program. In *Bakke*, the U.S. Supreme Court affirmed the California Supreme Court's decision that the special admissions program had violated the equal protection clause of the Fourteenth Amendment, directed that the plaintiff be admitted to the School of Medicine, and reversed the judgment prohibiting the defendant from considering race in its future admissions [*University of California v. Bakke*, 438 U.S. 265 (1978)].

POINTS OF DEBATE

As the United States becomes more pluralistic, and as lines of ethnic distinction harden, tensions will escalate. Such tensions and the conflicts that they generate will force all Americans to think seriously about a number of debatable issues:

1. Can any society remain integrated when ethnic identifications are strong, when the cultural core has eroded, and when ethnic conflicts are frequent? No society has yet to do so; hence, all Americans need to consider whether America is on the road to permanent partitions and the conflicts that these divisions generate. Liberal ideologies preach the virtues of diversity, conveniently ignoring the conflictive reality that they cause, whereas conservative ideologies demand rigid conformity to the cultural core and propose tension-producing, repressive means to ensure this conformity. Is there not some middle way—as exemplified by the case of past immigrants—to open the avenues of opportunity to the new immigrants, absorb portions of the immigrant culture into the cultural core, and eventually generate a revised core of old and new citizens? If this seems politically incorrect, or naive, or impossible, then what is the fate of America? Are we locked into an inexorable and destructive path of ethnic conflict?

2. Can illegal immigration be stopped? This is the immigration that bothers and threatens Americans the most. Most discussions of this problem involve political and ideological posturing rather than concrete solutions to the problem. Thus far, simply adding border patrol agents, using new high-tech means of detection, massive deportations, and other procedures have not been particularly effective. Do we try more of the same thing? Do we dare entertain solutions that, historically, have proved effective, such as shooting those who cross a border? Or do we admit that repressive means are unacceptable to society and seek alternatives, such as the economic development of Mexico, Latin America, and the Caribbean, thus reducing incentives to immigrate? If the latter, how do we pay for such actions?

3. In a society where the unskilled, entry-level jobs are fast disappearing to labor markets overseas and to labor-reducing technologies, how are the new poor and unskilled immigrants to find work and to become part of the American mainstream? If there is no clear track for the unskilled to make it in America—as their predecessors did in the past—then what is to be done? Who will support them? How are the pathologies of despair—crime, drug use, gangs, welfare dependency—to be avoided?

4. Can the United States cut off immigration without destroying its ultimate source of energy and vitality? Can it encourage limited and selective immigration in the face of rampant illegal immigration? If the answer is no to both questions, then what does this mean for America's future?

KEY TERMS/KEY LEGISLATION

References

Acuña, Rodolfo. 1981. *Occupied America: A History of Chicanos*, 2d edition. New York: Harper & Row.

Adams, Karen, and Daniel Brink (eds.). 1990. *Perspectives on Official English: The Campaign for English as the Official Language of the USA*. Berlin: Mouton de Gruyter.

Aguirre, Adalberto, Jr. 1973. "Communication Media and Mexican Social Issues: A Focus on English-language and U.S.-origin Communication Media." *International Journal of Comparative Sociology* 34:231–43.

———. 1980. "The Sociolinguistic Situation of Chicano Adolescents in a California Border Town." *AZTLAN: International Journal of Chicano Studies Research* 10:55–67.

———. 1982. "The Political Economy Context of Language in Social Service Delivery for Hispanics." In *Ethnicity and Public Policy*, edited by Winston Van Horne, pp. 89–104. Madison: University of Wisconsin Press.

———. 1984. "Language Use in Bilingual Mexican American Households." *Social Science Quarterly* 65:565–72.

———. 1988. "Language Use and Media Orientations in Bilingual Mexican-Origin Households in Southern California." *Mexican Studies/Estudios Mexicanos* 4:115–30.

———. 1990. "Poverty in the United States: Race, Ethnic, and Gender Differentials." In *Income and Status Differences between White and Minority Americans: A Persistent Inequality*, edited by Sucheng Chan, pp. 101–12. Lewiston, NY: Edwin Mellen Press.

———. 1993. "Communication Media and Mexican Social Issues: A Focus on English-language and U.S.-origin Communication Media." *International Journal of Comparative Sociology* 34:231–43.

———. 1995a. "Nativist Feeling and Immigrant Workers: An Interpretive Note." *Latino Studies Journal* 6:48–62.

———. 1995b. "Ethnolinguistic Populations in California: A Focus on LEP Students and Public Education." *The Journal of Educational Issues of Language Minority Students* 15:77–91.

———. 2000. "Academic Storytelling: A Critical Race Theory Story of Affirmative Action." *Sociological Perspectives* 43:319–39.

Aguirre, Adalberto, Jr., and David Baker. 1988. "A Descriptive Profile of the Hispanic Penal Population: Conceptual and Reliability Limitations in Public Use Data." *The Justice Professional* 3:189–200.

———. 1989. "The Execution of Mexican American Prisoners in the Southwest." *Social Justice* 16:150–61.

———. 1991. *Race, Racism and the Death Penalty in the United States.* Berrien Spring, MI: Vande Vere.

———. 1993. "Racial Prejudice and the Death Penalty: A Research Note." *Social Justice* 20:150–55.

———. 1994. *Perspectives on Race and Ethnicity in American Criminal Justice.* New York: West.

———. 1999. "Slave Executions in the United States: A Description Profile of Social and Historical Factors." *Social Science Journal* 36:1–31.

Aguirre, Adalberto, Jr., and Ruben Martinez. 1984. "Hispanics and the U.S. Occupational Structure: A Focus on Vocational Education." *The International Journal of Sociology and Social Policy* 4:50–59.

———. 1993. *Chicanos In Higher Education: Issues and Dilemmas for the 21st Century.* ASHE-ERIC Higher Education Report No. 3. Washington, DC: The George Washington University, School of Education and Human Development.

Ainsworth, Robert. 1989. *An Overview of the Labor Market Problems of Indians and Native Americans.* Research Report No. 89-02. Washington, DC: National Commission for Employment Policy.

Alba, Richard. 1985. *Italian Americans: Into the Twilight of Ethnicity.* Englewood Cliffs, NJ: Prentice-Hall.

Alba, Richard, and Gwen Moore. 1982. "Ethnicity in the American Elite." *American Sociological Review* 47:373–83.

Almaguer, Tomas. 1994. *Racial Fault Lines: The Historical Origins of White Supremacy in California.* Berkeley: University of California Press.

Ambler, Marjane. 1990. *Breaking the Iron Bonds: Indian Control of Energy Development.* Lawrence: University Press of Kansas.

American Council of Learned Societies. 1932. *Report of the Committee of Linguistic and National Stocks in the Population of the United States.* Washington, DC: American Council of Learned Societies.

American Historical Association. 1932. *Annual Report on Proceedings,* Volume 1. Washington, DC: U.S. Government Printing Office.

American Indian Higher Education Consortium. 1999. *Tribal Colleges: An Introduction.* Alexandria, VA: American Indian Higher Education Consortium, The Institute for Higher Education Policy.

American Jewish Committee. 1991. *American Jewish Yearbook.* New York: American Jewish Committee.

Anderson, Terry (ed.). 1992. *Property Rights and Indian Economics.* Landham, MD: Rowman Littlefield.

Andrews, William. 1994. "The Black Male in American Literature." In *The American Black Male,* edited by Richard Majors and Jacob Gordon, pp. 59–68. Chicago: Nelson-Hall.

Aponte, Robert. 1991. "Urban Hispanic Poverty: Disaggregations and Explanations." *Social Problems* 38:516–28.

Arrilaga, Pauline. 2001. "Stuck between Cultures, Indian Youth Struggle with Violence, Dependency, Depression." Available at: www.montanaforum.com.

Auditor General of California. 1987. *A Review of First-Year Admissions of Asians and Caucasians at the University of California at Berkeley.* Sacramento, CA: Auditor General's Office.

Auletta, Ken. 1982. *The Underclass.* New York: Random House.

Awanohara, Susumu. 1990. "Spicier Melting Pot: Asian Americans Come of Age Politically." *Far Eastern Economic Review* (Nov. 22): 30, 32–36.

Ayala, Cesar. 1996. "The Decline of the Plantation Economy and the Puerto Rican Migration of the 1950s." *Latino Studies Journal* 7:62–90.

Baca-Zinn, Maxine. 1989. "Family, Race, and Poverty in the Eighties." *Signs: Journal of Women in Culture and Society* 14:856–74.

———. 1995. "Family, Race, and Poverty in the Eighties." In *Sources: Notable Selections in Race and Ethnicity*, edited by A. Aguirre, Jr. and D. Baker, pp. 297–306. Guilford, CT: Dushkin.

Bach, Robert. 1980. "The New Cuban Immigrants: Their Background and Prospects." *Monthly Labor Review* 103:39–46.

Bai, Su. 1991. "Affirmative Pursuit of Political Equality for Asian Pacific Americans: Reclaiming the Voting Rights Act." *University of Pennsylvania Law Review* 139:731–67.

Barlett, Donald, and James Steele. 2002. "Wheel of Misfortune." *Time* (Dec. 16): 44–57.

Barlett, Donald, James Steele, Laura Karmatz, Joan Levinstein, Mitch Frank, and Nadia Mustafa. "Playing the Political Slots." *Time*, Dec. 23, 2002, pp. 52–61.

Barrera, Mario. 1979. *Race and Class in the Southwest: A Theory of Racial Inequality.* South Bend, IN: University of Notre Dame Press.

———. 1985. "The Historical Evolution of Chicano Ethnic Goals: A Bibliographic Essay." *Sage Race Relations Abstracts* 10:1–48.

Barringer, Herbert, Robert Gardner, and Michael Lewis. 1993. *Asian and Pacific Islanders in the United States.* New York: Russell Sage Foundation.

Bartelt, H. Guillermo. 1992. "Boarding School Language Policy and the Spread of English among Indians of the American Southwest." In *Native Americans and Public Policy*, edited by Fremont J. Lyden and Lyman H. Legters, pp. 137–46. Pittsburgh: University of Pittsburgh Press.

Bates, Timothy. 1995. "Rising Skill Levels and Declining Labor Force Status Among African American Males." *Journal of Negro Education* 64:373–83.

Baver, S. 1984. "Puerto Rican Politics in New York City: The Post–World War II Period." In *Puerto Rican Politics in Urban America*, edited by James Jennings and Monte Rivera, pp. 43–60. New York: Greenwood Press.

Bean, Frank, Barry Edmonston, and Jeffery Passel (eds.). 1990. *Undocumented Migration to the United States: IRCA and the Experience of the 1980s.* Santa Monica, CA: RAND Corporation and the Urban Institute.

Bean, Frank, and Marta Tienda. 1987. *The Hispanic Population of the United States.* New York: Russell Sage Foundation.

Bean, Frank, Georges Vernez, and Charles Keeley. 1989. *Opening and Closing the Doors: Evaluating Immigration Reform and Control.* Santa Monica, CA: RAND Corporation and the Urban Institute.

Becerra, Jose, Carol Hogue, Hani Atrash, and Nilsa Perez. 1991. "Infant Mortality among Hispanics: A Portrait of Heterogeneity." *Journal of the American Medical Association* 265:217–21.

Bell, Derrick, Jr. 1973. *Race, Racism and American Law.* Boston: Little, Brown.

———. 1997. "California's Proposition 209: A Temporary Diversion on the Road to Racial Disaster." *Loyola of Los Angeles Law Review* 30:1447–64.

Benavides, Alfredo. 1981. "Education and the Environment: Pesticide Contamination and Children's Learning." *Social Studies Teacher* 2:5, 13.

Bieder, Robert. 1980. "Scientific Attitudes toward Indian Mixed-Bloods in Early Nineteenth Century America." *Journal of Ethnic Studies* 8:17–30.

Biles, Roger. 2000. "Public Housing on the Reservation." *American Indian Culture and Research Journal* 24:49–50.

Bishop, Herbert. 1917. "The Mission as a Frontier Institution in the Spanish-American Colonies." *American Historical Review* 23:42–61.

Blalock, Hubert M., Jr. 1967. *Toward a Theory of Minority-Group Relations.* New York: Wiley.

Blauner, Robert. 1969. "Internal Colonialism and Ghetto Revolt." *Social Problems* 16:393–408.

———. 1972. *Racial Oppression in America.* New York: Harper and Row.

———. 1989. *Black Lives, White Lives: Three Decades of Race Relations in America.* Berkeley: University of California Press.

Blumstein, Alfred. 1982. "On the Racial Disproportionality of United States' Prison Populations." *Journal of Criminal Law & Criminology* 73:1259–81.

Bonacich, Edna. 1972. "A Theory of Ethnic Antagonism: The Split Labor Market." *American Sociological Review* 37:547–59.

———. 1973. "A Theory of Middleman Minorities." *American Sociological Review* 38:583–94.

———. 1976. "Advanced Capitalism and Black-White Race Relations in the United States: A Split Labor Market Interpretation." *American Sociological Review* 41:34–51.

Boozer, Michael, Alan Krueger, and Shari Wolkon. 1992. "Race and School Quality Since *Brown v. Board of Education.*" In *Brookings Papers in Economic Activity: Microeconomics 1992,* edited by Martin Baily and Clifford Winston, pp. 169–326. Washington, DC: Brookings Institution.

Boskin, Joseph. 1986. *Sambo: The Rise and Demise of an American Jester.* New York: Oxford University Press.

Boswell, Thomas. 1985. "The Cuban Americans." In *Ethnicity in Contemporary America: A Geographical Appraisal,* edited by Jesse McKee, pp. 95–116. Dubuque, IA: Kendall/Hunt.

Bromwich, Michael. 1999. "The Pawn: Politics Colors Pursuit of Wen Ho Lee." *Tulsa World,* Dec. 26, 1999, p. A1.

Brown, Dee. 1970. *Bury My Heart at Wounded Knee: An Indian History of the American West.* New York: Holt, Rinehart and Winston.

Bryce-Laporte, Roy. 1982. "The New Immigration: Its Origin, Visibility, and Implications for Public Policy." In *Ethnicity and Public Policy,* edited by Winston Van Horne, pp. 62–88. Madison: University of Wisconsin Press.

Bullard, Robert. 1991. "Housing Problems and Prospects for Blacks in Houston." *Review of Black Political Economy* 19:175–94.

———. 1993. "Race and Environmental Justice in the United States." *The Yale Journal of International Law* 18:319–35.

———. 2000. *Dumping in Dixie: Race, Class, and Environmental Quality.* Boulder, CO: Westview Press.

Bullock, Henry A. 1967. *A History of Negro Education in the South.* New York: Praeger.

Bunzel, John, and Jeffrey Au. 1987. "Diversity or Discrimination?—Asian Americans in College." *The Public Interest* 87:49–62.

Cabezas, Amado, and Gary Kawaguchi. 1988. "Empirical Evidence for Continuing Asian American Income Inequality." In *Reflections on Shattered Windows: Promises and Prospects for Asian American Studies,* edited by Gary Okihiro, Shirley Hume, Arthur Hansen, and John Liu, pp. 144–64. Pullman: Washington State University Press.

———. 1990. "Industrial Sectorization in California in 1980: The Continuing Significance of Race/Ethnicity, Gender, and Nativity." In *Income and Status Differences between White and Minority Americans: A Persistent Inequality,* edited by Sucheny Chan, pp. 57–99. Lewiston, NY: Edwin Mellen Press.

Cabezas, Amado, Larry Shinagawa, and Gary Kawaguchi. 1986–87. "New Inquiries into the Socioeconomic Status of Filipino Americans in California." *Amerasia Journal* 13:1–21.

————. 1990. "Income Differentials between Asian Americans and White Americans in California, 1980." In *Income and Status Differences between White and Minority Americans: A Persistent Inequality*, edited by Sucheny Chan, pp. 181–201. Lewiston, NY: Edwin Mellen Press.

Cabezas, Amado, Tse Tam, Brenda Lowe, Anna Wong, and Kathy Turner. 1989. "Empirical Study of Barriers to Upward Mobility of Asian Americans in the San Francisco Bay Area." In *Frontiers of Asian American Studies: Writing, Research and Commentary*, edited by Gail Nomura, Russell Endo, Stephen Sumida, and Russell Leong, pp. 93–115. Pullman: Washington State University Press.

Califa, Antonio. 1989. "Declaring English the Official Language: Prejudice Spoken Here." *Harvard Civil Rights–Civil Liberties Law Review* 24:293–348.

Calmore, John. 1993. "Spatial Equality and the Kerner Commission Report: A Back-to-the-Future Essay." *North Carolina Law Review* 71:1487–1518.

Camarillo, Albert, and Frank Bonilla. 2001. In *America Becoming: Racial Trends and Their Consequences* (Vol. I), edited by Neil Smelser, William Wilson, and Baith Mitchel, pp. 103–34. Washington, DC: National Academy Press.

Camarota, Steven. 2002. *Immigrants in the United States—2002: A Snapshot of America's Foreign-Born Population*. Washington, DC: Center for Immigration Studies.

Campbell, Ben Nighthorse. 2000. "Challenges Facing American Indian Youth: On the Front Lines with Senator Ben Nighthorse Campbell." *Juvenile Justice Journal* 7:1–5.

Caputo, Richard. 1993. "Family, Poverty, Unemployment Rates, and AFDC Payments: Trends among Black and Whites." *Families in Society: The Journal of Contemporary Human Services* 74:515–26.

Carro, John. 1980. "Impact of the Criminal Justice System on Hispanics." In *National Conference on Law Enforcement and Criminal Justice*, pp. 361–82. Washington, DC: U.S. Department of Justice Law Enforcement Assistance Administration.

Cash, W. J. 1941. *The Mind of the South*. New York: Vintage Books.

Castro, Max, Margaret Haun, and Ana Roca. 1990. "The Official English Movement in Florida." In *Perspectives on Official English: The Campaign for English as the Official Language of the USA*, edited by Karen Adams and Daniel Brink, pp. 150–60. New York: Mouton de Gruyter.

Cella, John. 1982. *The Highest Stage of White Supremacy: The Origins of Segregation in the South*. New York: Cambridge University Press.

Centers for Disease Control. 2002. "Entry Into Prenatal Care—United States, 1989–1997." *Morbidity and Mortality Weekly Report*, May 12.

Chang, Robert. 1993. "Toward an Asian American Legal Scholarship: Critical Race Theory, Post-Structuralism, and Narrative Space." *California Law Review* 81:1243–1323.

Chavez, Leo, Estevan Flores, and Marta Lopez-Garza. 1990. "Here Today, Gone Tomorrow? Undocumented Settlers and Immigration Reform." *Human Organization* 49:193–205.

Chavira, Ricardo. 1977. "A Case Study: Reporting of Mexican Emigration and Deportation." *Journalism History* 4:59–61.

Chew, Pat. 1996. "Asian Americans in the Legal Academy: An Empirical and Narrative Profile." *Asian Law Journal* 3:7–38.

Chiu, Daina. 1994. "The Cultural Defense: Beyond Exclusion, Assimilation, and Guilty Liberalism." *California Law Review* 82(4):1053–1125.

Choy, Bong-youn. 1979. *Koreans in America*. Chicago: Nelson-Hall.

Chronicle of Higher Education. 2002. Almanac 2002–3. *The Chronicle of Higher Education* (Aug. 30).

Chun, Ki-Taek. 1980. "The Myth of Asian American Success and Its Educational Ramifications." *IRCO Bulletin* 15:1–12.

Churchill, Ward. 1992. *Fantasies of the Master Race: Literature, Cinema, and the Colonization of American Indians.* Marroe, ME: Common Courage Press.

———. 1993. "Crimes Against Humanity." *Z Magazine* (March):43–47.

Churchill, Ward, and Winona LaDuke. 1992. "Native North America: The Political Economy of Radioactive Colonialism." In *The State of Native America: Genocide, Colonization, and Resistance,* edited by M. Annette Jaimes, pp. 241–66. Boston: South End Press.

Churchill, Ward, and Glenn Morris. 1992. "Key Indian Laws and Cases." In *The State of Native America: Genocide, Colonization, and Resistance,* edited by M. Annette Jaimes, pp. 13–21. Boston: South End Press.

Clifton, James (ed.). 1989. *Being and Becoming Indian: Biographical Studies of North American Frontiers.* Chicago: Dorsey.

Commission on Wartime Relocation and Internment of Civilians. 1983. *Personal Justice Denied.* Washington, DC: U.S. Government Printing Office.

Coughlin, Ellen. 1994. "Returning Indian Remains." *The Chronicle of Higher Education* (March 16), pp. A8, A9, A16.

Cox, Oliver. 1948. *Caste, Class, and Race.* Garden City, NY: Doubleday.

Crosby, Alfred. 1976. "Virgin Soil Epidemics as a Factor in Aboriginal Depopulation in America." *William and Mary Quarterly* 33:289–99.

Cross, Raymond. 1999. "American Indian Education: The Terror of History and the Nation's Debt to the Indian People." *University of Arkansas Little Rock Law Review* 21:941–88.

Cruz, Wilfredo. 1995. "Police Brutality in African American and Latino Communities." *Latino Studies Journal* 6:30–47.

Crystal, David. 1989. "Asian Americans and the Myth of the Model Minority." *Social Casework* 70:405–13.

Cunningham, Clark, Glenn Loury, and John Skrentny. 2002. "Passing Strict Scrutiny: Using Social Science to Design Affirmative Action Programs." *Georgetown Law Journal* 90:835–82.

Curtis, Lewis P. 1971. *Apes and Angels: The Irish Victorian Caricature.* Washington, DC: Smithsonian Institution Press.

Daniel, Pete. 1973. *The Shadow of Slavery: Peonage in the South 1901–69.* London: Oxford University Press.

Daniels, Roger. 1971. *Concentration Camps USA: Japanese Americans and World War II.* Hinsdale, IL: Dryden Press.

Darby, John. 1976. *Conflict in Northern Ireland: The Development of a Polarized Community.* Dublin: Gill and Macmillan.

Darity, William, and Samuel Myers. 2001. "Racial Economic Inequality in the USA." In *The Blackwell Companion to Sociology,* edited by Judith Blau, pp. 178–95. Malden, MA: Blackwell.

Davis, Jerry. 1998. "Re-Mythologizing Poor Lo: American Indians and Higher Education in the Southwest, 1945–1995." *Journal of the West* 37:99–107.

de la Garza, Rodolfo O., Louis DeSipio, F. Chris Garcia, John Garcia, and Angelo Falcon. 1992. *Latino Voices: Mexican, Puerto Rican, and Cuban Perspectives on American Politics.* Boulder, CO: Westview Press.

Delgado, Richard. 1995. "Affirmative Action as a Majoritarian Device: Or, Do You Really Want to Be a Role Model?" In *Critical Race Theory: The Cutting Edge,* edited by R. Delgado, pp. 355–61. Philadelphia: Temple University Press.

Delgado, Richard, and Jean Stefancic. 1992. "Images of the Outsider in American Law and Culture: Can Free Expression Remedy Systemic Social Ills?" *Cornell Law Review* 77:1258–97.

Deloria, Vine, Jr. 1969. *Custer Died for Your Sins.* New York: Macmillan.

———. 1976. "The Place of Indians in Contemporary Education." *American Indian Journal* 2:2.

———. 1992. "Trouble in High Places: Erosion of American Indian Rights to Religious Freedom in the United States." In *The State of Native America: Genocide, Colonization, and Resistance,* edited by M. Annette Jaimes, pp. 267–90. Boston: South End Press.

Deloria, Vine, Jr., and Clifford Lytle. 1983. *American Indians, American Justice.* Austin: University of Texas Press.

Deloria, P., and Robert Laurence. 1991. "What's An Indian: A Conversation about Law School Admissions, Indian Tribal Sovereignty, and Affirmative Action." *Arkansas Law Review* 44:1107–35.

DeNavas-Walt, Carmen, and Robert Cleveland. 2002. *Money Income in the United States: 2001.* Washington, DC: U.S. Bureau of the Census.

DeNavas-Walt, Carmen, Robert Cleveland, and Marc Roemer. 2001. *Money Income in the United States: 2000.* Washington, DC: U.S. Bureau of the Census.

Der, Henry, and Colleen Lye. 1989. *The Broken Ladder '89: Asian Americans in City Government.* San Francisco: Chinese for Affirmative Action.

Díaz-Cotto, Juanita. 1996. *Gender, Ethnicity, and the State: Latina and Latino Prison Politics.* Albany: State University of New York Press.

Dickson, Robert J. 1966. *Ulster Immigration to Colonial America, 1718–73.* London: Routledge & Kegan Paul.

Dinnerstein, Leonard, and David M. Reimers. 1988. *Ethnic Americans: A History of Immigration,* 3d edition. New York: Harper & Row.

Domenech, Emmanuel. 1860. *Seven Years Residence in the Great Deserts of North America.* London: Longmans.

Duleep, Harriet, and Seth Sanders. 1992. "Discrimination at the Top: American-born Asian and White Men." *Industrial Relations* 31:416–32.

Dunn, Ashley. 1994. "Bilingual Ballot Law Fails to Help Chinese American Voters." *The New York Times* (August 14):34.

Duran, Livie, and H. Russell Bernard (eds.). 1973. *Introduction to Chicano Studies.* New York: Macmillan.

Durham, Jimmie. 1992. "Cowboys and Notes on Art, Literature, and American Indians in the Modern American Mind." In *The State of Native America: Genocide, Colonization, and Resistance,* edited by M. Annette Jaimes, pp. 423–38. Boston: South End Press.

Eagle, Adam. 1992. *Alcatraz! Alcatraz!: The Indian Occupation of 1969–71.* Berkeley, CA: Heyday Books.

Edmunds, R. David. 1983. "Tecumseh, the Shawnee Prophet, and American History: A Reassessment." *Western Historical Quarterly* 14:261–76.

Eggers, Mitchell, and Douglas Massey. 1992. "A Longitudinal Analysis of Urban Poverty: Blacks in U.S. Metropolitan Areas between 1970 and 1980." *Social Science Research* 21:175–203.

Enchautegui, Maria. 1997. "Latino Neighborhoods and Latino Neighborhood Poverty." *Journal of Urban Affairs* 19:445–67.

Equal Employment Opportunity Commission. 1985. *Equal Employment Opportunity Report—1983: Job Patterns of Minorities and Women in Private Industry.* Washington, DC: U.S. Government Printing Office.

Estrada, Leo, F. Chris Garcia, Reynaldo Macias, and Lionel Maldonado. 1988. "Chicanos in the United States: A History of Exploitation and Resistance." In *Latinos and the Political System*, edited by F. Chris Garcia, pp. 28–64. Notre Dame, IN: University of Notre Dame Press.

Fainstein, Norman. 1993. "Race, Class and Segregation: Discourses about African Americans." *International Journal of Urban and Regional Research* 17: 384–403.

Falcon, Angelo. 1984. "Puerto Rican Politics in New York City: 1860s to 1945." In *Puerto Rican Politics in Urban America*, edited by James Jennings and Monte Rivera, pp. 15–42. New York: Greenwood Press.

———. 1988. "Black and Latino Politics: Race and Ethnicity in a Changing Urban Context." In *Latinos and the Political System*, edited by F. Chris Garcia, pp. 171–94. Notre Dame, IN: University of Notre Dame Press.

Falcon, Priscilla, and Patricia J. Campbell. 1991. "The Politics of Language and the Mexican American: The English Only Movement and Bilingual Education." In *Racism and the Underclass: State Policy and Discrimination against Minorities*, edited by George W. Shepherd, Jr., and David Penna, pp. 145–58. New York: Greenwood Press.

Farhat, Sarah. 2002. "Environmental Racism: The PIBBY Principle." *McGeorge Law Review* 33:295–304.

Farley, John. 1987. "Disproportionate Black and Hispanic Unemployment in U.S. Metropolitan Areas: The Roles of Racial Inequality, Segregation and Discrimination and Male Joblessness." *American Journal of Economics and Sociology* 46:129–50.

———. 1995. "Race Still Matters: The Minimal Role of Income and Housing Cost as Causes of Housing Segregation in St. Louis, 1990." *Urban Affairs Review* 31:244–54.

Farley, Reynolds. 1990. "Blacks, Hispanics, and White Ethnic Groups: Are Blacks Uniquely Disadvantaged?" *American Economic Review* 80:237–41.

Farley, Reynolds, and Walter R. Allen. 1987. *The Color Line and the Quality of Life in America*. New York: Russell Sage Foundation.

Farley, Reynolds, and William H. Frey. 1994. "Changes in the Segregation of Whites from Blacks during the 1980s: Small Steps towards a More Integrated Society." *American Sociological Review* 59:23–45.

Feagin, Joe R. 1989. *Racial and Ethnic Relations*, 3d edition. Englewood Cliffs, NJ: Prentice-Hall.

———. 1991. "The Continuing Significance of Race: Antiblack Discrimination in Public Places." *American Sociological Review* 56:101–16.

Feagins, Ken. 1990. "Affirmative Action or the Same Sin?" *Denver University Law Review* 67:442–51.

Fernandez, Edward, and J. Gregory Robinson. 1994. *Illustrative Ranges of the Distribution of Undocumented Immigrants by State* (Technical Working Paper No. 8). Washington, DC: U.S. Bureau of the Census.

Fitzpatrick, Joseph. 1987. *Puerto Rican Americans: The Meaning of Migration to the Mainland*, 2d edition. Englewood Cliffs, NJ: Prentice-Hall.

Fix, Michael, and Paul Hill. 1990. *Enforcing Employer Sanctions: Challenges and Strategies.* Santa Monica, CA: The RAND Corporation.

Flippen, Chenoa. 2001. "Residential Segregation and Minority Home Ownership." *Social Science Research* 30:337–63.

Fogel, Robert, and Stanley Engerman. 1974. *Time on the Cross.* Boston: Little, Brown.

Fost, Dan. 1991. "American Indians in the 1990s." *American Demographics* (Dec.): 26–34.

Fredrickson, George M. 1971. *The Black Image in the White Mind.* New York: Harper & Row.

———. 1981. *White Supremacy: A Comparative Study in American and South African History.* New York: Oxford University Press.

———. 1988. *The Arrogance of Race.* Middletown, CT: Wesleyan University Press.

Freeman, James. 1995. *Changing Identities: Vietnamese Americans 1975–95.* Boston: Allyn and Bacon.

Freeman, Lance. 2000. "Minority Housing Segregation: A Test of Three Perspectives." *Journal of Urban Affairs* 22:15–36.

Frey, William H., and Dowell Myers. 2002. *Neighborhood Segregation in Single-Race and Multirace America: A Census 2000 Study of Cities and Metropolitan Areas.* Washington, DC: Fannie Mae Corporation.

Fukuda, Moritoshi. 1980. *Legal Problems of Japanese Americans.* Tokyo: Keio Tsushin.

Furedi, Frank. 1994. *The New Ideology of Imperialism: Renewing the Moral Imperative.* London: Pluto Press.

Gabriel, Paul E., Donald R. Williams, and Susanne Schmitz. 1990. "The Relative Occupational Attainment of Young Blacks, Whites, and Hispanics." *Southern Economic Journal* 57:35–46.

Gambino, Richard. 1974. *Blood of My Blood: The Dilemma of Italian-Americans.* Garden City, NY: Doubleday.

Garcia, F. Chris, and Rodolfo de la Garza. 1977. *The Chicano Political Experience: Three Perspectives.* North Scituate, MA: Duxbury Press.

Garcia, Ignacio. 1996. "Backwards from Aztlan: Politics in the Age of Hispanics." In *Chicanas and Chicanos in Contemporary Society,* edited by Robert M. De Anda, pp. 191–204. Boston: Allyn and Bacon.

Garcia, Juan. 1980. *Operation Wetback.* Westport, CT: Greenwood Press.

Gee, Harry. 1993. "Employment Issues for Asians in Texas." In *Meeting the Challenge: Critical Issues in Education, Health, and Employment in Texas,* pp. 39–46. College Station: Texas A&M University Institute for Race and Ethnic Studies.

Genovese, Eugene D. 1965. *The Political Economy of Slavery.* New York: Vintage Books.

Geshwender, James, and Rita Carroll-Seguin. 1990. "Exploding the Myth of African-American Progress." *Signs* 15:285–99.

Ginzberg, Eli. 1991. "Access to Health Care for Hispanics." *Journal of the American Medical Association* 265:238–41.

Giordano, Rita. 1987a. "Anti-Asian Fliers' Origin a Mystery." *Newsday* (Nov. 4).

———. 1987b. "Bensonhurst: Anti-Asian Bias Linked to Incidents." *Newsday* (Dec. 15).

Glazer, Nathan. 1957. *American Judaism.* Chicago: University of Chicago Press.

Glazer, Nathan, and Daniel P. Moynihan. 1970. *Beyond the Melting Pot,* 2d edition. Cambridge: MIT Press.

Glock, Charles Y., and Rodney Stark. 1966. *Christian Beliefs and Anti-Semitism.* New York: Harper & Row.

Gold, Steven. 1995. *From the Workers' State to the Golden State: Jews from the Former Soviet Union in California.* Boston: Allyn and Bacon.

Goldschneider, Calvin. 1986. *Jewish Continuity and Change: Emerging Patterns in America.* Bloomington: Indiana University Press.

Gomes, Ralph C., and Linda Faye Williams. 1990. "Race and Crime: The Role of the Media in Perpetuating Racism and Classism in America." *The Urban League Review* 14:57–69.

Gordon, Milton. 1964. *Assimilation in American Life: The Role of Race, Religion, and National Origins.* New York: Oxford University Press.

———. 1981. "Models of Pluralism: The New American Dilemma." *Annals of the American Academy of Political and Social Science* 454:178–88.

————. 1988. *The Scope of Sociology.* New York: Oxford University Press.

Graham, Hugh D. 1990. "Race, Language, and Social Policy: Comparing the Black and Hispanic Experience in the U.S." *Population and Environment* 12:43–58.

Gray, Maryann, Elizabeth Rolph, and Elan Melamid. 1996. *Immigration and Higher Education: Institutional Responses to Changing Demographics.* Santa Monica, CA: RAND Corporation.

Grebler, Leo, Joan Moore, and Ralph Guzman. 1970. *The Mexican-American People: The Nation's Second Largest Minority.* New York: Free Press.

Greeley, Andrew M. 1971. *Why Can't They Be Like Us?* New York: Dutton.

————. 1974. *Ethnicity in the United States: A Preliminary Reconnaissance.* New York: Wiley.

————. 1977. *The American Catholic: A Social Portrait.* New York: Harper and Row.

————. 1981. *The Irish Americans.* New York: Harper and Row.

Greenberg, Jack. 2002. "Affirmative Action in Higher Education: Confronting the Condition and Theory." *Boston College Law Review* 43:521–619.

Greenwell, Lisa, Julie DaVanzo, and R. Burciage Valdez. 1993. "Social Ties, Wages, and Gender among Salvadorean and Filipino Immigrants in Los Angeles." Santa Monica, CA: RAND Program for Research on Immigration Policy DRU-213-PRIP.

Grieco, Elizabeth, and Rachel Cassidy. 2001. *Overview of Race and Hispanic Origin.* Washington, DC: U.S. Bureau of the Census.

Grove, John, and Jiping Wu. 1991. "Who Benefitted from the Gains of Asian-Americans, 1940–1980?" In *Racism and the Underclass: State Policy and Discrimination against Minorities,* edited by George Shepherd and David Penna, pp. 99–117. New York: Greenwood Press.

Guzman, Betsy. 2001. The *Hispanic Population: Census 2000 Brief.* Washington, DC: U.S. Census Bureau.

Hamilton, Horace C. 1964. "The Negro Leaves the South." *Demography* 1:273–95.

Hardy-Fanta, Carol. 1993. *Latina Politics, Latino Politics: Gender, Culture, and Political Participation in Boston.* Philadelphia: Temple University Press.

Harmon, Alexandra. 1990. "When Is an Indian Not an Indian? `Friends of the Indian' and the Problems of Indian Identity." *Journal of Ethnic Studies* 18:95–123.

Harrison, Roderick J., and Daniel H. Weinberg. 1992. "Changes in Racial and Ethic Residential Segregation, 1980–1990." Paper presented at the American Statistical Association Meeting, Boston, August.

Herberg, Will. 1960. *Protestant-Catholic-Jew.* Garden City, NY: Doubleday.

Hernandez-Chavez, Eduardo, Andrew Cohen, and Anthony Beltramo (eds.). 1975. *El Lenguaje de los Chicanos: Regional and Social Characteristics of Language Used by Mexican Americans.* Arlington, VA: Center for Applied Linguistics.

Hero, Rodney. 1990. "Hispanics in Urban Government and Politics: Some Findings, Comparisons and Implications." *Western Political Quarterly* 43:403–14.

————. 1992. *Latinos and the U.S. Political System: Two-Tiered Pluralism.* Philadelphia: Temple University Press.

Hietala, Thomas. 1985. *Manifest Density: Anxious Aggrandizement in Late Jacksonian America.* Ithaca, NY: Cornell University Press.

Higham, John. 1963. *Strangers in the Land: Patterns of American Nativism 1860–1925,* 2d edition. New York: Atheneum.

Hillard, David, and Lewis Cole. 1993. *This Side of Glory: The Autobiography of David Hillard and the Story of the Black Panther Party.* New York: Little, Brown.

Hilliard, Asa G. 1988. "Conceptual Confusion and the Persistence of Group Oppression through Education." *Equity and Excellence* 24:36–43.

Hing, Bill Ong. 1993. *Making and Remaking Asian America through Immigration Policy 1850–1990*. Stanford, CA: Stanford University Press.

Hirschman, Charles, and Morrison Wong. 1986. "The Extraordinary Educational Attainment of Asian Americans: A Search for Historical Evidence and Explanations." *Social Forces* 65:1–27.

Hoffman, Abraham. 1974. *Unwanted Mexican Americans in the Great Depression: Repatriation Pressures, 1929–1939*. Tucson: University of Arizona Press.

Hollmann, Frederick. 1992. "National Population Trends." In *Population Trends in the 1980's*, pp. 1–11. Washington, DC: U.S. Bureau of the Census Special Studies P-23-No. 175.

Hong, Peter. 2002. "Latinos Finding New Home in Suburbs, Study Shows." *Los Angeles Times* (July 31): B1.

Horowitz, Harold, and Kenneth Karst. 1969. *Law, Lawyers and Social Change: Cases and Materials on the Abolition of Slavery, Racial Segregation and Inequality of Educational Opportunity*. New York: Bobbs-Merrill.

Hosokawa, Bill. 1982. "Accentuating the American in Japanese American." *Perspectives: The Civil Rights Quarterly* 14:40–44.

House Committee on Indian Affairs. 1934. U.S. Department of the Interior Hearings on HR7902, 73rd Congress, 2d Session. Washington, DC: U.S. Government Printing Office.

Hsia, Jayjia. 1988. *Asian Americans in Higher Education and at Work*. Hillsdale, NJ: Lawrence Erlbaum Associates.

Hu, Arthur. 1989. "Asian Americans: Model Minority or Double Minority?" *AMERASIA* 15:243–57.

Hughes, Mark, and Janice Madden. 1991. "Residential Segregation and the Economic Status of Black Workers: New Evidence for an Old Debate." *Journal of Urban Economics* 29:28–49.

Human Rights Watch. 2002. *We Are Not the Enemy: Hate Crimes against Arabs, Muslims, and Those Perceived to Be Arab or Muslim after September 11*. New York: Human Rights Watch.

Humphrey, Norman. 1941. "Mexican Repatriation from Michigan: Public Assistance in Historical Perspective." *Social Service Review* 15:497–513.

Hunnington, Samuel P. 1966. "Political Modernization: America vs. Europe." *World Politics* 18:147–48.

Hurk, Won, and Kwang Kim. 1989. "The 'Success' Image of Asian Americans: Its Validity, and Its Practical and Theoretical Implications." *Ethnic and Racial Studies* 12:512–38.

Hurtado, Albert. 1982. "Hardly a Farm House—A Kitchen without Them: Indian and White Households on the California Borderland Frontier in 1860." *Western Historical Quarterly* 13:245–70.

Hurtado, Albert, and Peter Iverson (eds.). 1994. *Major Problems in American Indian History: Documents and Essays*. Lexington, MA: D.C. Heath.

Huskisson, Gregory. 1988. "Enough Is Enough: Blacks Protest Redlining." *Black Enterprise* (October): 22.

Imhoff, Gary. 1990. "The Position of U.S. English on Bilingual Education." *The Annals* 508:48–61.

Jackson, Aurora. 1993. "Black, Single, Working Mothers in Poverty: Preferences for Employment, Well-Being, and Perceptions of Preschool-age Children." *Social Work* 38:26–35.

Jaffe, A., Ruth Cullen, and Thomas Boswell. 1980. *The Changing Demography of Spanish Americans*. New York: Academic Press.

Jaimes, M. Annette. 1992. "Federal Indian Identification Policy: A Usurpation of Indige-
    nous Sovereignty in North America." In *Native Americans and Public Policy*, edited
    by Fremont Lyden and Lyman Legters, pp. 113–35. Pittsburgh: University of Pitts-
    burgh Press.
Jaret, Charles. 1991. "Recent Structural Change and U.S. Urban Ethnic Minorities." *Jour-
    nal of Urban Affairs* 13:307–36.
Jarvenpa, Robert. 1985. "The Political Economy and Political Ethnicity of American
    Indian Adaptations and Identities." In *Ethnicity and Race in the U.S.A.: Toward the
    Twenty-First Century*, edited by Richard D. Alba, pp. 29–48. New York: Routledge.
Jaynes, Gerald David, and Robin Williams (eds.). 1989. *A Common Destiny: Blacks and
    American Society*. Washington, DC: National Academy Press.
Jencks, Christopher. 1991. "Is the American Underclass Growing?" In *The Urban Under-
    class*, edited by C. Jencks and P. E. Peterson, pp. 28–102. Washington, DC: The
    Brookings Institution.
Jet. 2000. "Annual poll shows that most people believe racial profiling by cops is com-
    mon." *JET* (Jan 10): 6.
Johnson, James, Karen Johnson-Webb, and Walter Farrell. 1999. "Newly Emerging Com-
    munities in the United States: A Spatial Analysis of Settlement Patterns." In *Immigra-
    tion and Opportunity: Race, Ethnicity, and Employment in the United States*, edited by
    Frank Bean and Stephanie Bell-Rose, pp. 263–310. New York: Russell Sage Foundation.
Johnson, Kevin. 2000. "The Case against Racial Profiling in Immigration Enforcement."
    Washington University Law Quarterly 78:675–736.
Joint Center for Political Studies. 1977. *Profiles of Black Mayors in America*. Washing-
    ton, DC.
———. 1996. *Blacks and the 1996 Elections: A Preliminary Analysis*. Washington, DC.
Jones, Eugene. 1988. *Native Americans as Shown on the Stage, 1753–1916*. Metuchen, NJ:
    Scarecrow Press.
Jones-Correa, Michael, and David Leal. 1996. "Becoming 'Hispanic': Secondary Paneth-
    nic Identification among Latin American-Origin Populations in the United States."
    Hispanic Journal of Behavioral Sciences 18:214–54.
Jordan, Winthrop D. 1962. "Modern Tensions and the Origins of American Slavery."
    Journal of Southern History 28:18–30.
———. 1968. *White Over Black: American Attitudes Toward the Negro, 1550–1812*. Chapel
    Hill: University of North Carolina Press.
Juarez, José. 1995. "The American Tradition of Language Rights: The Forgotten Right to
    Government in a 'Known Tongue.'" *Law and Inequality* 13:443–642.
Kamin, Leon J. 1974. *The Science and Politics of I.Q.* New York: Wiley.
Kang, Jerry. 1996. "Negative Action against Asian Americans: The Internal Instability of
    Dworkin's Defense of Affirmative Action." *Harvard Civil Rights–Civil Liberties Law
    Review* 31:1–47.
Karnow, Stanley. 1992. *Asian Americans in Transition*. New York: Asia Society.
Keller, Gary. 1985. "The Image of the Chicano in Mexican, United States, and Chicano
    Cinema: An Overview." In *Chicano Cinema: Research, Reviews and Resources*, edited
    by Gary Keller, pp. 13–58. Binghamton, NY: Bilingual Review Press.
Keller, Gary (ed.). 1985. *Chicano Cinema: Research, Reviews, and Resources*. Binghamton,
    NY: Bilingual Review Press.
Kelly, Lawrence. 1975. "The Indian Reorganization Act: The Dream and the Reality."
    Pacific Historical Review 44:291–312.
Kim, Ryan. 1999. "Livermore Scientists File Bias Claims." *San Francisco Examiner* (Dec.
    24): A1.

Kinder, Donald, and Lynn Sanders. 1990. "Mimicking Political Debate with Survey Questions: The Case of White Opinion on Affirmative Action for Blacks." *Social Cognition* 8:73–103.

Kitano, Harry. 1980. *Race Relations*. Englewood Cliffs, NJ: Prentice-Hall.

Kitano, Harry, and Roger Daniels. 1988. *Asian Americans: Emerging Minorities*. Englewood Cliffs, NJ: Prentice-Hall.

Kluegel, James R., and Lawrence Bobo. 1993. "Opposition to Race-Targeting: Self-Interest, Stratification Ideology, or Racial Attitudes?" *American Sociological Review* 58:443–64.

Kluegel, James R., and Eliot R. Smith. 1986. *Beliefs about Inequality in America*. Hawthorne, NY: Aldine de Gruyter.

Kluger, Richard. 1975. *Simple Justice: The History of Brown v. Board of Education and Black America's Struggle for Equality*. New York: Vintage Books.

Knobel, Dale T. 1986. *Paddy and the Republic*. Middletown, CT: Wesleyan University Press.

Knoll, Tricia. 1982. *Becoming Americans: Asian Sojourners, Immigrants, and Refugees in the Western United States*. Portland, OR: Coast to Coast Books.

Kotkin, Joel, and Bill Bradley. 1989. "Democrats and Demographics; Asians, Hispanics and Small Business Are the Party's Future." *Washington Post*, February 26.

Kousser, J. Morgan. 1974. *The Shaping of Southern Politics: Suffrage Restrictions and the Establishment of the One-Party South, 1880–1910*. New Haven, CT: Yale University Press.

Krueger, Alan, and Jonathan Orszag. 2002. "Hispanics and the Current Economic Downturn: Will the Receding Tide Sink Hispanics?" Washington, DC: PEW Hispanic Center.

Kunitz, Stephen. 1971. "The Social Philosophy of John Collier." *Ethnohistory* 18:213–39.

LaDuke, Winona. 1981. "Indian Land Claims and Treaty Areas of North America: Succeeding into Native North America." *CoEvolution Quarterly* 32:64–65.

Lander, Ernest McPherson. 1969. *The Textile Industry in Antebellum South Carolina*. Baton Rouge: Louisiana State University Press.

Langberg, Mark, and Reynolds Farley. 1985. "Residential Segregation of Asian Americans in 1980." *Sociology and Social Research* 70:71–75.

Langley, Lester. 1988. *MexAmerica: Two Countries, One Future*. New York: Crown.

La Piere, Richard T. 1934. "Attitudes vs. Actions." *Social Forces* 13:230–37.

Lauderdale, Diane, and Bert Kestenbaum. 2002. "Mortality Rates of Elderly Asian American Populations Based on Medicare and Social Security Data." *Demography* 39:529–41.

Learsi, Rufus. 1954. *The Jews in America: A History*. Cleveland, OH: World.

LeClere, Felicia, Richard Rogers, and Kimberly Peters. 1997. "Ethnicity and Mortality in the United States: Individual and Community Correlates." *Social Forces* 76:169–99.

Lee, Moon. 1993. "Asian Americans Don't Fit Their Monochrome Image." *Christian Science Monitor* (July 27): 9, 10.

Lee, Sharon. 1998. "Asian Americans: Diverse and Growing." Population Bulletin vol. 53, no. 2. Washington, DC: Population Reference Bureau.

Lessinger, Johanna. 1995. *From the Ganges to the Hudson: Indian Immigrants in New York City*. Boston: Allyn and Bacon.

Lestschinsky, Jacob. 1955. "Economic Development of American Jewry." In *The Jewish People*, vol. 4, pp. 131–56. New York: Jewish Encyclopedic Handbooks.

Lewis, Ronald L. 1979. *Coal, Iron and Slaves: Industrial Slavery in Maryland and Virginia 1715–1865*. Westport, CT: Greenwood Press.

———. 1989. *Black Workers: A Documentary History from Colonial Times to the Present*, edited by Philip S. Foner and R. L. Lewis. Philadelphia: Temple University Press.

Leyburn, James G. 1962. *The Scotch-Irish*. Chapel Hill: University of North Carolina Press.

Li, Peter S. (ed.). 1990. *Race and Ethnic Relations in Canada.* Toronto: Oxford University Press.

Lieberson, Stanley, and Mary C. Waters. 1988. *From Many Strands: Racial and Ethnic Groups in Contemporary America.* New York: Russell Sage Foundation.

Lipset, Seymour Martin. 1987. "Blacks and Jews: How Much Bias?" *Public Opinion* 10 (July/August): 4–5, 57–58.

———. 1991. *Equality and the American Creed: Understanding the Affirmative Action Debate* (Washington, DC: Progressive Policy Institute, 1991).

Litwack, Leon F. 1961. *North of Slavery: The Negro in the Free States, 1790–1860.* Chicago: University of Chicago Press.

Lo, Kwai-Cheung. 2001. "Double Negations: Hong Kong Cultural Identity in Hollywood's Transnational Representations." *Cultural Studies* 15:4–26.

Locke, Michelle. 2000. "Scientist Celebrates Turning 61 as a Free Man." *Associated Press Wire* (Dec. 21).

Loeb, Vernon, and Walter Pincus. 2000. "Judge: Lee Can Be Freed on Bail." *Washington Post* (Aug. 25): A1.

Lopez, Alfred. 1973. *The Puerto Rican Papers.* Indianapolis, IN: Bobbs-Merrill.

Lopez, Manuel. 1986. "Su Casa No Es Mi Casa: Hispanic Housing Conditions in Contemporary America, 1949–1980." In *Race, Ethnicity, and Minority Housing in the United States,* edited by Jamshid Momeni, pp. 127–45. New York: Greenwood Press.

Lopez-Garza, Marta, and David Diaz (eds.). 2001. *Asian and Latino Immigrants in a Restructuring Economy: The Metamorphosis of Southern California.* Stanford, CA: Stanford University Press.

Lopreato, Joseph. 1970. *Italian Americans.* New York: Random House.

Lummins, Charles. 1968. *Bullying the Hopi.* Prescott, AZ: Prescott College Press.

Lyman, Stanford. 1986. *Chinatown and Little Tokyo: Power, Conflict, and Community among Chinese and Japanese Immigrants in America.* Milwood, NY: Associated Faculty Press.

———. 1990. "Race, Sex, and Servitude: Images of Blacks in American Cinema." *International Journal of Politics, Culture and Society* 4:49–77.

Macias, Reynaldo. 1993. "Language and Ethnic Classification of Language Minorities: Chicano and Latino Students in the 1990s." *Hispanic Journal of Behavioral Sciences* 15:230–57.

Mahler, Sarah. 1995. *Salvadorans in Suburbia: Symbiosis and Conflict.* Boston: Allyn and Bacon.

Major, Aline, and Arien Egley. 2002. "2000 Survey of Youth Gangs in Indian Country." *National Youth Gang Center Fact Sheet #01* (June).

Maldonado, Rita. 1976. "Why Puerto Ricans Migrated to the United States in 1947–1973." *Monthly Labor Review* 9:7–18.

Maldonado-Denis, Manuel. 1972. *Puerto Rico, A Socio-historic Interpretation,* translated by E. Vialo. New York: Random House.

Marger, Martin. 2000. *Race and Ethnic Relations: American and Global Perspectives,* 5th edition. Belmont, CA: Wadsworth.

Marquez, Benjamin. 1993. *LULAC: The Evolution of a Mexican American Political Organization.* Austin: University of Texas Press.

Martinez, Ramiro, Jr. 1996. "Latinos and Lethal Violence: The Impact of Poverty and Inequality." *Social Problems* 43:131–46.

Martinez, Tomás. 1969. "Advertising and Racism: The Case of Mexican Americans." *El Grito* 2 (Summer): 13–31.

Massey, Douglas. 1983. *The Demographic and Economic Position of Hispanics in the United States: The Decade of the 1970s.* Washington, DC: National Commission for Employment Policy.

Matthaei, Julie, and Teresa Amott. 1990. "Race, Gender, Work: The History of Asian and Asian-American Women." *Race and Class* 31:61–80.

Mazon, Mauricio. 1984. *The Zoot-Suit Riots: The Psychology of Symbolic Annihilation.* Austin: University of Texas Press.

McAdam, Doug. 1982. *Political Processes and the Development of Black Insurgency, 1930–1970.* Chicago: University of Chicago Press.

———. 1988. *Freedom Summer.* New York: Oxford University Press.

McCarthy, Cameron. 1990. *Race and Curriculum.* New York: Falmer Press.

McCarthy, Kevin, and R. Valdez. 1986. *Current and Future Effects of Mexican Immigration in California.* Santa Monica, CA: The RAND Corporation.

McDonnell, Janet. 1991. *The Dispossession of the American Indian 1887–1934.* Bloomington: Indiana University Press.

McKenzie, R. 1928. *Oriental Exclusion.* Chicago: University of Chicago Press.

McKinney, Scott, and Ann B. Schnare. 1989. "Trends in Residential Segregation by Race: 1960–1980." *Journal of Urban Economics* 26:269–80.

McQueen, Michel. 1991. "Voters' Responses to Poll Disclose Huge Chasm between Social Attitudes of Blacks." *Wall Street Journal* (May 17): A16.

McWilliams, Carey. 1968. *North from Mexico: The Spanish-Speaking People of the United States.* New York: Greenwood Press.

Medina, Marcell, Jr. 1988. "Hispanic Apartheid in American Public Education." *Educational Administration Quarterly* 24:336–49.

Mendoza Report. 1978. *Access of Non or Limited English Speaking Persons of Hispanic Origin to the New York City Department of Social Services.* Washington, DC: U.S. Department of Health, Education, and Welfare.

Merrell, James. 1984. "The Indians' New World: The Catawba Experience." *William and Mary Quarterly* 41:537–65.

Merton, Robert K. 1949. "Discrimination and the American Creed." In *Discrimination and National Welfare,* edited by R. H. MacIver, pp. 99–126. New York: Harper and Row.

Meyer, Doris. 1978. "Early Mexican-American Responses to Negative Stereotyping." *New Mexico Historical Review* 53:75–91.

Meyer, Melissa. 1991. " 'We Can Not Get a Living As We Used To': Dispossession and the White Earth Anishinaabeg, 1889–1920." *American Historical Review* 96:386–94.

Miller, Kerby A. 1985. *Emigrants and Exiles.* New York: Oxford University Press.

Miller, Stuart. 1969. *The Unwelcome Immigrant: The American Image of the Chinese, 1785–1882.* Berkeley: University of California Press.

Minerbrook, Scott. 1993. "Blacks Locked Out of the American Dream." *Business and Society Review* 87:23–28.

Miranda, Leticia. 1991. *Latino Child Poverty in the United States.* Washington, DC: Children's Defense Fund.

Montero, Darrel. 1981. "The Japanese Americans: Changing Patterns of Assimilation over Three Generations." *American Sociological Review* 46:829–39.

Mooney, James. 1928. *The Aboriginal Population of America North of Mexico.* Washington, DC: Smithsonian Institution Miscellaneous Collections, vol. 80, no. 7.

Moore, Theresa, and Robert Gunnison. 1994. "Blacks and Asians Say the System Is Insensitive." *San Francisco Chronicle* (Mar. 3): A4.

Morales, Armando. 1972. *Ando Sangrando (I am Bleeding): A Study of Mexican American-Police Conflict.* La Puente, CA: Perspectiva Publications.

———. 1973. "Police Deployment Theories." In *Voices: Readings from El Grito,* edited by Octavio Ignacio Romano-V., pp. 167–80. Berkeley, CA: Quinto Sol Publications.

Morales, Julio. 1986. *Puerto Rican Poverty and Migration: We Just Had to Try Elsewhere.* New York: Praeger.

Morganthau, Tom. 1993. "America: Still a Melting Pot?" *Newsweek* (Aug. 9): 16–23.

Morris, Aldon. 1984. *The Origins of the Civil Rights Movement: Black Communities Organizing for Change.* New York: Free Press.

Morris, Glenn. 1992. "International Law and Politics: Toward a Right to Self-Determination for Indigenous People." In *The State of Native America: Genocide, Colonization, and Resistance,* edited by M. Annette Jaimes, pp. 55–86. Boston: South End Press.

Moses, Marion. 1993. "Farmworkers and Pesticides." In *Confronting Environmental Racism: Voices from the Grassroots,* edited by Robert Bullard, pp. 161–78. Boston: South End Press.

Mozo, S. Montes, and J. Garcia Vasquez. 1988. *Salvadorian Migration to the United States: An Exploratory Study.* Washington, DC: Georgetown University Center for Immigration Policy and Refugee Assistance.

Muller, Thomas. 1993. *Immigrants and the American City.* New York: New York University Press.

Mulvey, Sister Mary. 1936. *French Catholic Missionaries in the Present United States, 1604–1791.* Washington, DC: Catholic University of America Press.

Munoz, Carlos, Jr. 1989. *Youth, Identity, Power: The Chicano Movement.* New York: Verso.

Murguia, Edward. 1975. *Assimilation, Colonialism, and the Mexican American People.* Monograph Series No. 1. Austin: University of Texas at Austin Center for Mexican American Studies.

Nakanishi, Don. 1988. "Asian Pacific Americans and Selective Undergraduate Admissions." *Journal of College Admissions* 118:17–26.

National Academy of Public Administration. 1999. *A Study of Management and Administration: The Bureau of Indian Affairs.* Washington, DC: Author.

National Center for Health Statistics. 1991. *Health: United States, 1990.* Hyattsville, MD: Public Health Service.

———. 2002. *Deaths: Final Data for 2000.* Washington, DC: U.S. Government Printing Office.

National Puerto Rican Coalition. 1985. *Puerto Ricans in the Mid '80s: An American Challenge.* Washington, DC: National Puerto Rican Coalition.

National Vital Statistics Reports. 2002. Volume 50, no. 15. "Deaths: Final Data for 2001." Washington, DC: Department of Health and Human Services.

Nelson, Candace, and Marta Tienda. 1985. "The Structuring of Hispanic Ethnicity: Historical and Contemporary Perspectives." *Ethnic and Racial Studies* 8:49–74.

Newton, James E., and R. L. Lewis (eds.). 1978. *The Other Slaves: Mechanics, Artisans and Craftsmen.* Boston: G. K. Hall.

Nguyen, Beatrice Bich-Dao. 1993. "Accent Discrimination and the Test of Spoken English: A Call for an Objective Assessment of the Comprehensibility of Nonnative Speakers." *California Law Review* 81:1325–61.

Noriega, Jorge. 1992. "American Indian Education in the United States: Indoctrination for Subordination to Colonialism." In *The State of Native America: Genocide, Colonization, and Resistance,* edited by M. Annette Jaimes, pp. 371–402. Boston: South End Press.

O'Connor, Anne-Marie. 1999. "Learning to Look Past Race." *Los Angeles Times* (Aug 25): A1.

O'Connor, John. 1980. *The Hollywood Indian: Stereotypes of Native Americans in Film.* Trenton, NJ: New Jersey State Museum.

O'Hare, W., and J. Felt. 1991. *Asian Americans: America's Fastest Growing Minority Group.* Report No. 19. Washington, DC: Population Reference Bureau.

Olzak, Susan. 1986. "A Competition Model of Collective Action in American Cities." In *Competitive Ethnic Relations,* edited by S. Olzak and J. Nagel, pp. 17–46. Orlando, FL: Academic Press.

———. 1992. *The Dynamics of Ethnic Competition and Conflict.* Stanford, CA: Stanford University Press.

Ortego, Philip D. 1973. "The Chicano Renaissance." In *Introduction to Chicano Studies,* edited by L. I. Duran and H. R. Bernard, pp. 568–84. New York: Macmillan.

Osako, Masako. 1984. "Japanese-Americans: Melting into the All-American Pot?" In *Ethnic Chicago,* edited by Melvin Holli and Peter Jones, pp. 69–76. Grand Rapids, MI: William B. Eerdmans.

Osborne, Stephen. 1989. *Indian-Hating in American Literature, 1682–1857.* Unpublished doctoral dissertation, University of Michigan, Ann Arbor.

Pace, David. 2001. "Indian Casinos." *IRE Journal* 24:8–10.

Padilla, Felix. 1987. *Puerto Rican Chicago.* Notre Dame, IN: University of Notre Dame Press.

Padilla, Raymond, and Alfredo Beravides (eds.). 1992. *Critical Perspectives on Bilingual Education Research.* Tempe, AZ: Bilingual Press/Editorial Bilingue.

Page, Bryan. 1980. "The Children of Exile: Relationships between the Acculturation Process and Drug Use among Cuban Youth." *Youth and Society* 11:431–47.

Paisano, Edna. 1992. "Selected Social and Economic Characteristics for the American Indian, Eskimo, and Aleut Population for Selected Areas: 1990." Presented at the Meeting for the Census Advisory Committees on the American Indian and Alaska Native, Asian and Pacific Islander, Black and Hispanic Population for the 1990 Census, November 5–6, Phoenix, Arizona.

Palm, Risa. 1985. "Ethnic Segmentation of Real Estate Agent Practice in the Urban Housing Market." *Annals of the Association of American Geographers* 75:58–68.

Paredes, Raymond. 1977. "The Mexican Image in American Travel Literature, 1831–1869." *New Mexico Historical Review* 52:5–29.

Park, Robert E. 1916. "The City: Suggestions for the Investigation of Human Behavior in an Urban Environment." *American Journal of Sociology* 20:577–612.

———. 1950. *Race and Culture.* Glencoe, IL: Free Press.

Park, Robert E., and Ernest W. Burgess. 1924. *Introduction to the Science of Sociology.* Chicago: University of Chicago Press.

Parker, Linda. 1989. *Native American Estate: The Struggle Over Indian and Hawaiian Lands.* Honolulu: University of Hawaii Press.

Passel, Jeffrey. 1976. "Provisional Evaluation of the 1970 Census Count of American Indians." *Demography* 13:397–409.

———. 1993. "Discussion: Racial Identity/Classification and Its Effect on the Undercount." In *Proceedings of the Bureau of the Census 1993 Research Conference on Undercounted Ethnic Populations,* pp. 345–53. Washington, DC: U.S. Bureau of the Census.

Passel, Jeffrey, and Patricia Berman. 1986. "Quality of 1980 Census Data for American Indians." *Social Biology* 33:163–82.

Pear, Robert. 1998. "Black and Hispanic Poverty Falls, Reducing Overall Rate for Nation." *New York Times* (Sept. 25): A1.

Pedraza-Bailey, Silvia, and Teresa Sullivan. 1979. "Bilingual Education in the Reception of Political Immigrants: The Case of Cubans in Miami, Florida." In *Bilingual Education and Public Policy in the United States,* edited by Raymond Padilla, pp. 376–94. Ypsilanti: Eastern Michigan University Department of Foreign Languages and Bilingual Studies.

Peng, Samuel. 1990. "Attainment Status of Asian Americans in Higher Education." In *Contemporary Perspectives on Asian and Pacific American Education,* edited by Russell Endo, Virgie Chattergy, Sally Chou, and Nobuya Tsuchida, pp. 56–77. South El Monte, CA: Pacific Asia Press.

Penrose, Eldon. 1973. *California Nativism: Organized Opposition to the Japanese, 1890–1913.* San Francisco: R & E Research Associates.

Perez, Lisandro. 1980. "Cubans." In *Harvard Encyclopedia of American Ethnic Groups,* edited by Stephan Thernstrom, pp. 256–61. Cambridge, MA: Belknap Press.

———. 1986. "Immigrant Economic Adjustment and Family Organization: The Cuban Success Story Re-Examined." *International Migration Review* 20:4–20.

Perez, Sonia, and Deirdre Martinez. 1993. *State of Hispanic America 1993: Toward a Latino Anti-Poverty Agenda.* Washington, DC: National Council of La Raza.

Pessar, Patricia. 1995. *A Visa for a Dream: Dominicans in the United States.* Boston: Allyn and Bacon.

Peterson, William. 1971. *Japanese Americans: Oppression and Success.* New York: Random House.

Pinkney, Alphonso. 1969. *Black Americans.* Englewood Cliffs, NJ: Prentice-Hall.

———. 1984. *The Myth of Black Progress.* New York: Cambridge University Press.

Pitt, Leonard. 1966. *The Decline of the Californios.* Berkeley: University of California Press.

Platt, Anthony. 1997. "End Game: The Rise and Fall of Affirmative Action in Higher Education." *Social Justice* 24(2):103–18.

Pohlmann, Marcus D. 1990. *Black Politics in Conservative America.* New York: Longmans.

Portes, Alejandro. 1990. "From South of the Border: Hispanic Minorities in the United States." In *Immigration Reconsidered: History, Sociology, and Politics,* edited by V. Yans-McLaughlin, pp. 160–84. New York: Oxford University Press.

Portes, Alejandro, and Dag MacLeod. 1996. "What Shall I Call Myself? Hispanic Identity Formation in the Second Generation." *Ethnic and Racial Studies* 19:523–47.

Portes, Alejandro, and Ruben Rumbaut. 1990. *Immigrant America: A Portrait.* Berkeley: University of California Press.

President's Commission on Mental Health. 1978. *Report of the Special Populations Subpanel on the Mental Health of Asian/Pacific Americans,* vol. 3. Washington, DC: U.S. Government Printing Office.

Price, John. 1978. *Native Studies: American and Canadian Indians.* New York: McGraw-Hill/Ryerson Limited.

Proctor, Bernadette, and Joseph Dalaker. 2002. *Poverty in the United States: 2001.* Washington, DC: U.S. Bureau of the Census.

Rable, George C. 1984. *But There Was No Peace: The Role of Violence in the Politics of Reconstruction.* Athens: University of Georgia Press.

Reed, Ishmael. 1993. *Airing Dirty Laundry.* Reading, MA: Addison-Wesley.

Reisler, Mark. 1996. "Always the Laborer, Never the Citizen: Anglo Perceptions of the Mexican Immigrant during the 1920s." In *Between Two Worlds: Mexican Immigrants in the United States,* edited by David G. Gutierrez, pp. 23–43. Wilmington, DE: Scholarly Resources.

Ricketts, Erol R., and Isabel Sawhill. 1988. "Defining and Measuring the Underclass." *Journal of Policy Analysis and Management* 7:316–25.

Robbins, Rebecca. 1992. "Self-Determination and Subordination: The Past, Present, and Future of American Indian Governance." In *The State of Native America: Genocide, Colonization, and Resistance,* edited by M. Annette Jaimes, pp. 87–121. Boston: South End Press.

Robinson, Cecil. 1963. *With the Ears of Strangers: The Mexican in American Literature.* Tucson: University of Arizona Press.

Rodriguez, Havidan. 1992. "Population, Economic Mobility and Income Inequality: A Portrait of Latinos in the United States, 1970–1991." *Latino Studies Journal* 3:55–86.

Rodriquez, Nestor. 1987. "Undocumented Central Americans in Houston: Diverse Populations." *International Migration Review* 21:4–26.

Roediger, David R. 1991. *The Wages of Whiteness: Race and the Making of the American Working Class.* New York: Verso.

Rogg, Eleanor. 1974. *The Assimilation of Cuban Exiles: The Role of Community and Class.* New York: Academic Press.

Rolph, Elizabeth. 1992. *Immigration Policies: Legacy from the 1980s and Issues for the 1990s.* Santa Monica, CA: The RAND Corporation.

Romo, Ricardo. 1989. "The Urbanization of Southwestern Chicanos in the Early Twentieth Century." In *Race and Culture in America,* edited by Carl Jackson and Emory Tolbert, pp. 235–49. Edina, MN: Burgess International Group.

Ross, Thomas. 1990. "Innocence and Affirmative Action." *Vanderbilt Law Review* 43:297–336.

Rowan, Carl T. 1993. *Dream Makers, Dream Breakers: The World of Justice Thurgood Marshall.* New York: Little, Brown.

Rubel, Arthur. 1966. *Across the Tracks.* Austin: University of Texas Press.

Rumbelow, Helen. 2002. "Dreaming of Homes on the Reservation." *Washington Post* (Oct. 13): A3.

Russell, James. 1994. *After the Fifth Sun: Class and Race in North America.* Englewood Cliffs, NJ: Prentice-Hall.

Russell, Katheryn. 2001. "Racial Profiling: A Status Report of the Legal, Legislative, and Empirical Literature." *Rutgers Race & The Law Review* 3:61–81.

Russell Sage Foundation. 1999. *The Multi-City Study of Urban Inequality.* New York: Russell Sage Foundation.

Safire, William. 2002. "Non-Indians Benefit Most from Casinos." *Seattle Post-Intelligencer* (Dec. 15): G2.

Sanchez, George. 1951. *Concerning Segregation of Spanish-Speaking Children in the Public Schools.* Inter-American Education Occasional Paper No. 9. Austin: University of Texas Press.

San Miguel, Guadalupe, Jr. 1987. *"Let All of Them Take Heed": Mexican Americans and the Campaign for Educational Equality in Texas, 1910–1981.* Austin: University of Texas Press.

Santiago, Anne M., and Margaret G. Wilder. 1991. "Residential Segregation and Links to Minority Poverty: The Case of Latinos in the United States." *Social Problems* 38:492–515.

Schaefer, Richard T. 1990. *Racial and Ethnic Groups,* 4th edition. Glenview, IL: Scott Foresman/Little, Brown.

Schafer, Daniel. 1993. "A Class of People Neither Freemen nor Slaves: From Spanish to American Race Relations in Florida, 1821–1861." *Journal of Social History* 26:587–609.

Schiavo, Giovanni. 1934. *The Italian in America Before the Civil War.* New York: Vigo Press.

Schick, Frank, and Renee Schick. 1991. *Statistical Handbook on U.S. Hispanics.* New York: Oryx Press.

Schmidley, A. Dianne. 2001. *Foreign-Born Population in the United States: 2000.* Washington, DC: U.S. Bureau of the Census.

Schneider, Mark, and Thomas Phelan. 1990. "Blacks and Jobs: Never the Twain Shall Meet?" *Urban Affairs Quarterly* 26:299–313.

Schoeni, Robert, Kevin McCarthy, and Georges Vernez. 1996. *The Mixed Economic Progress of Immigrants.* Santa Monica, CA: RAND Corporation.

Schrieke, B. 1936. *Alien Americans: A Study of Race Relations.* New York: Viking.

Schuman, H., C. Steeth, L. Bobo, and M. Krysan. 1997. *Racial Attitudes in America: Trends and Interpretations.* Cambridge, MA: Harvard University Press.

Select Committee on Aging. 1992. "Farmworkers' High Mortality: Government Neglect?" Washington, DC: U.S. Government Printing Office.

Selzer, Michael. 1972. *"Kike"—Anti-Semitism in America.* New York: Meridian Press.

Senate Committee on Housing and Urban Affairs. 2002. "Capital Investment in Native American Land." Washington, DC: U.S. Government Printing Office.

Shively, J. 1992. "Cowboys and Indians: Perceptions of Western Films among American Indians and Anglos." *American Sociological Review* 57:725–34.

Shorris, Earl. 1992. *Latinos: A Biography of the People.* New York: Avon Books.

Shrier, Arnold. 1958. *Ireland and the American Emigration, 1850–1900.* Minneapolis: University of Minnesota Press.

Simmons, Ozzie G. 1973. "The Mutual Images and Expectations of Anglo-Americans and Mexican Americans." In *Introduction to Chicano Studies,* edited by Livie Duran and H. Russell Bernard, pp. 112–20. New York: Macmillan.

Singleton, Royce, and Jonathan H. Turner. 1975. "Racism: White Oppression of Blacks in America." In *Understanding Social Problems,* edited by D. Zimmerman and L. Weider, pp. 130–60. New York: Praeger.

Sissons, Peter. 1979. *The Hispanic Experience of Criminal Justice.* New York: Hispanic Research Center at Fordham University.

Sklare, Marshall. 1971. *American Jews.* New York: Random House.

Smith, Geoffrey. 1992. "There's No Whites Only Sign But . . . " *Business Week* (Oct. 26): 78.

Smits, David. 1991. "Squaw Men, Half Breeds, and Amalgamators: Late 19th Century Anglo-American Attitudes toward Indian-White Race-Mixing." *American Indian Culture and Research Journal* 15:29–61.

Snipp, C. Matthew. 1986. "The Changing Political and Economic Status of the American Indians: From Captive Nations to Internal Colonies." *American Journal of Economics and Sociology* 45:145–57.

———. 1989. *American Indians: The First of This Land.* New York: Russell Sage Foundation.

Sodowsky, Gorgi, Edward Lai, and Barbara Plake. 1991. "Moderating Effects of Sociocultural Variables on Acculturation Attitudes of Hispanics and Asian Americans." *Journal of Counseling & Development* 70:194–204.

Spinden, Herbert. 1928. "The Population of Ancient America." *Geographical Review* 18:640–60.

Stampp, Kenneth M. 1956. *The Peculiar Institution: Slavery in the Ante-Bellum South.* New York: Vintage Books.

Staples, Robert. 1975. "White Racism, Black Crime, and American Justice: An Application of the Colonial Model to Explain Crime and Race." *Phylon* 36:14–22.

Starobin, Robert S. 1970. *Industrial Slavery in the Old South.* London: Oxford University Press.

Stedman, Raymond. 1982. *Shadows of the Indian: Stereotypes in American Culture.* Norman: University of Oklahoma Press.

Steele, Shelby. 1990. *The Content of Our Character.* New York: St. Martin's Press.

Stephan, Walter, and Cookie Stephan. 1989. "Antecedents of Intergroup Anxiety in Asian-Americans and Hispanic-Americans." *Journal of Intercultural Relations* 13:203–19.

Stewart, Omer. 1987. *Peyote Religion: A History.* Norman, OK: University of Oklahoma Press.

Stoddard, Ellwyn R. 1973. *Mexican Americans.* New York: Random House.

Sue, Stanley, Nolan Zane, and Derald Sue. 1985. "Where Are the Asian American Leaders and Top Executives?" *PLAAMARC Research Review* 4:13–15.

Suzuki, Bob. 1989. "Asians." In *Shaping Higher Education's Future: Demographic Realities and Opportunities, 1990–2000,* edited by Arthur Levine and Associates, pp. 87–115. San Francisco: Jossey-Bass.

Swinton, David. 1989. "The Economic Status of Black Americans." In *The State of Black America,* pp. 9–39. New York: National Urban League.

Takagi, Dana. 1990. "From Discrimination to Affirmative Action: Facts in the Asian American Admissions Controversy." *Social Problems* 37:578–92.

Takaki, Ronald (ed.). 1987. *From Different Shores: Perspectives on Race and Ethnicity in America.* New York: Oxford University Press.

———. 1989. *Strangers from a Different Shore: A History of Asian Americans.* Boston: Little, Brown.

———. 1993. *A Different Mirror: A History of Multicultural America.* Boston: Little, Brown.

———. 1996. "The Myth of the 'Model Minority.'" In *Taking Sides: Clashing Views on Controversial Issues in Race and Ethnicity,"* 2d edition, edited by Richard Monk, pp. 41–47. Guilford, CT: Dushkin.

Tamayo, William, Robin Toma, and Stewart Koh. 1991. *The Voting Rights of Asian Pacific Americans.* Los Angeles: University of California at Los Angeles Asian American Studies Center.

Tang, Joyce. 1991. *Asian American Engineers: Earnings, Occupational Status, and Promotions.* Paper presented at the Annual Meeting of the American Sociological Association, Cincinnati, OH.

Taylor, Marylee. 1998. "How White Attitudes Vary with Racial Composition of Local Populations: Numbers Count." *American Sociological Review* 63:512–35.

Taylor, Ronald. 1973. *Sweatshops in the Sun—Child Labor on the Farm.* San Francisco: Earthwork.

Therrien, Melissa, and Roberto Ramirez. 2001. *The Hispanic Population in the United States: Population Characteristics.* Washington, DC: U.S. Census Bureau.

Thomas, Gail. 1995. "Notes on Asian American Employment." In *Race and Ethnicity in America: Meeting the Challenge in the 21st Century,* edited by Gail Thomas, pp. 265–68. Washington, DC: Taylor & Francis.

Thomas, R. Roosevelt, Jr. 1990. "From Affirming Action to Affirming Diversity." *Harvard Business Review* 68:107–17.

Thompson, Laura, and Alice Joseph. 1944. *The Hopi Way.* Ann Arbor: University of Michigan Press.

Thornton, Michael, and Robert Taylor. 1988. "Intergroup Attitudes: Black American Perceptions of Asian Americans." *Ethnic and Racial Studies* 11:474–88.

Thrupkaew, Noy. 2002. "The Myth of the Model Minority." *The American Prospect* 13:38–42.

Tinker, George, and Loring Bush. 1991. "Native American Unemployment: Statistical Games and Coverups." In *Racism and the Underclass: State Policy and Discrimination Against Minorities,* edited by George W. Shepherd, Jr., and David Penna, pp. 119–44. New York: Greenwood Press.

Titiev, Misha. 1944. "Old Oraibi." Papers of the Peabody Museum of American Archaeology and Ethnology, vol. 22, no. 1. Cambridge, MA: Harvard University Press.

Tolnay, Stewart E., and E. M. Beck. 1992. "Racial Violence and Black Migration in the American South, 1910–1930." *American Sociological Review* 57:103–16.

Tomasi, Silvano, and Madeline Engel (eds.). 1970. *The Italian Experience in the United States.* New York: Center for Migration Studies.

Torres, Maria de los Angeles. 1988. "From Exiles to Minorities: The Politics of Cuban Americans." In *Latinos and the Political System,* edited by F. Chris Garcia, pp. 81–98. Notre Dame, IN: University of Notre Dame Press.

Trennert, Robert. 1982. "Educating Indian Girls at Nonreservation Boarding Schools, 1878–1920." *Western Historical Quarterly* 13:271–90.

Treviño, Fernando, M. Moyer, R. Valdez, and Christine Stroup-Benham. 1991. "Health Insurance Coverage and Utilization of Health Services by Mexican Americans, Mainland Puerto Ricans, and Cuban Americans." *Journal of the American Medical Association* 265:233–37.

Trueba, Henry. 1986. *Success or Failure? Learning and the Language Minority Student.* New York: Newbury House.

———. 1989. *Raising Silent Voices: Educating the Linguistic Minorities for the 21st Century.* New York: Newbury House.

———. 1993. "Race and Ethnicity: The Role of Universities in Healing Multicultural America." *Educational Theory* 43:41–54.

Tsosie, Rebecca. 1999. "Privileging Claims to the Past: Ancient Human Remains and Contemporary Cultural Values." *Arizona State Law Journal* 31:583–677.

Tsuchida, Nobuya. 1990. "The Evacuation and Internment of Japanese Americans during World War II: An Invaluable Lesson on the American Judicial System." In *Contemporary Perspectives on Asian and Pacific American Education,* edited by Russell Endo, Virgie Chattergy, Sally Chou, and Nobuya Tsuchida, pp. 160–91. South El Monte, CA: Pacific Asia Press.

Turner, Jonathan H. 1992. "Inequality and Poverty." In *Social Problems in America,* edited by G. Ritzer and C. Calhoun, pp. 73–138. New York: McGraw-Hill.

Turner, Jonathan H., and Edna Bonacich. 1980. "Toward a Composite Theory of Middleman Minorities." *Ethnicity* 7:144–58.

Turner, Jonathan H., and Alexandra Maryanski. 1993. "The Biology of Human Organization." *Human Ecology* 3:1–36.

Turner, Jonathan H., and Pedro Payne. 2002. "Power, Politics, and African Americans." In *Sociological Views on Political Participation in the 21st Century,* edited by Betty A. Dobratz, Timothy Buzzell, and Lisa K. Waldner, pp. 139–69. New York: JAI Press/Elsevier.

Turner, Jonathan H., and Royce Singleton. 1978. "A Theory of Ethnic Oppression." *Social Forces* 56:1001–8.

Turner, Jonathan H., Royce Singleton, and David Musick. 1984. *Oppression: A Sociohistory of Black-White Relations in America.* Chicago: Nelson-Hall.

U.S. Bureau of the Census. 1963. *U.S. Census of Population: 1960 (PC2–1B).* Washington, DC: U.S. Government Printing Office.

———. 1972. *The Excluded Student (Report III): Educational Practices Affecting Mexican Americans in the Southwest.* Washington, DC: U.S. Government Printing Office.

———. 1973a. *U.S. Census of Population: 1970 (PC2–1D).* Washington, DC: U.S. Government Printing Office.

———. 1973b. *1970 Census of Housing and Population (Subject Report PC2–1F).* Washington, DC: U.S. Government Printing Office.

———. 1975a. *Historical Statistics of the United States: Colonial Times to 1970.* Washington, DC: U.S. Government Printing Office.

———. 1975b. *The Navajo Nation: An American Colony.* Washington, DC: U.S. Government Printing Office.

———. 1976. *Puerto Ricans in the Continental United States: An Uncertain Future.* Washington, DC: U.S. Government Printing Office.

———. 1979a. *The Social and Economic Status of the Black Population in the United States: An Historical Overview, 1790–1978 (P-23-No. 80).* Washington, DC: U.S. Government Printing Office.

———. 1979b. *Civil Rights Issues and Asian and Pacific Americans: Myths and Realities.* Washington, DC: U.S. Government Printing Office.

———. 1980. *Success of Asian Americans: Fact or Fiction?* Washington, DC: U.S. Government Printing Office.

———. 1981. *Persons of Spanish Origin in the United States: March 1980 (P-20-No. 361).* Washington, DC: U.S. Government Printing Office.

———. 1983a. *U.S. Census of Population: 1970 (PC80–1).* Washington, DC: U.S. Government Printing Office.

———. 1983b. *1980 Census of Population (PC80–51–10).* Washington, DC: U.S. Government Printing Office.

———. 1983c. *Asian and Pacific Islander Population by State: 1980 (PC80-51-12).* Washington, DC: U.S. Government Printing Office.

———. 1983d. *America's Black Population: 1970 to 1982, A Statistical View (PIO/POP-83-1).* Washington, DC: U.S. Government Printing Office.

———. 1983e. *Ancestry of the Population by State: 1980.* Washington, DC: U.S. Government Printing Office.

———. 1985. *1980 Census of Population (Subject Report PC80-2-10).* Washington, DC: U.S. Government Printing Office.

———. 1986. *Recent Activities Against Citizens and Residents of Asian Descent.* Washington, DC: U.S. Government Printing Office.

———. 1988. *The Economic Status of Americans of Asian Descent: An Exploratory Investigation.* Washington, DC: U.S. Government Printing Office.

———. 1989a. *Money, Income and Poverty Status in the United States: 1987 (P-60-No. 161).* Washington, DC: U.S. Government Printing Office.

———. 1989b. *Civil Rights Issues in Maine.* Washington, DC: U.S. Government Printing Office.

———. 1991a. *Current Population Reports, The Hispanic Population of the U.S. Southwest Borderland (P-23-No. 172).* Washington, DC: U.S. Government Printing Office.

———. 1991b. *Current Population Reports, The Hispanic Population in the United States: March 1990 (P-20-No. 449).* Washington, DC: U.S. Government Printing Office.

———. 1991c. *The Black Population in the United States: March 1990 and 1989 (P-20-No. 448).* Washington, DC: U.S. Government Printing Office.

———. 1991d. *Studies in American Fertility (P-23-No. 176).* Washington, DC: U.S. Government Printing Office.

———. 1992a. *The Asian and Pacific Islander Population in the United States: March 1991 and 1990 (P-20-459).* Washington, DC: U.S. Government Printing Office.

———. 1992b. *Population Trends in the 1980's (P-23-No. 175).* Washington, DC: U.S. Government Printing Office.

———. 1992c. *Civil Rights Issues Facing Asian Americans in the 1990s.* Washington, DC: U.S. Government Printing Office.

———. 1993a. *1990 Census of Housing—Detailed Housing Characteristics: American Indian and Alaska Native Areas (1990 Ch-2-1A).* Washington, DC: U.S. Government Printing Office.

———. 1993b. *Statistical Abstract of the United States: 1993.* Washington, DC: U.S. Government Printing Office.

———. 1993c. *Ancestry of the Population in the United States: 1990.* Washington, DC: U.S. Government Printing Office.

———. 1994a. *The Hispanic Population in the United States: March 1993* (Series P20-475). Washington, DC: U.S. Government Printing Office.

———. 1994b. *Characteristics of American Indians by Tribe and Language: 1990.* Washington, DC: U.S. Government Printing Office.

———. 1995. *Statistical Abstract of the United States: 1995*. Washington, DC: U.S. Government Printing Office.

———. 1999a. *Poverty in the United States: 1998*. Washington, DC: U.S. Government Printing Office.

———. 1999b. *The Black Population in the United States: March 1998*. Washington, DC: U.S. Government Printing Office.

———. 1999c. *Asian and Pacific Islander Population in the United States: March 1998*. Washington, DC: U.S. Government Printing Office.

———. 2001a. *Current Population Survey Racial Statistics Branch, Population Division* (Internet release, February 2001).

———. 2001b. *Profile of the Foreign-Born Population in the United States: 2000*. Washington, DC: U.S. Bureau of the Census.

———. 2002a. *The Asian Population: 2000*. Washington, DC: U.S. Bureau of the Census.

———. 2002b. *Money Income in the United States: 2001*. Washington, DC: U.S. Bureau of the Census.

———. 2002c. *Racial and Ethnic Residential Segregation in the United States: 1980-2000*. Washington, DC: U.S. Bureau of the Census.

U.S. Commission on Civil Rights. 1970. *Mexican Americans and the Administration of Justice in the Southwest*. Washington, DC: U.S. Government Printing Office.

———. 1972. *The Excluded Student: Educational Practices Affecting Mexican Americans in the Southwest*. Washington, DC: U.S. Government Printing Office.

———. 1976. *Puerto Ricans in the Continental United States: An Uncertain Future*. Washington, DC: U.S. Government Printing Office.

———. 1979. *Civil Rights Issues and Asian and Pacific Americans: Myths and Realities*. Washington, DC: U.S. Government Printing Office.

———. 1980. *Success of Asian Americans: Fact or Fiction?* Washington, DC: U.S. Government Printing Office.

———. 1986. *Recent Activities against Citizens and Residents of Asian Descent*. Washington, DC: U.S. Government Printing Office.

———. 1988. *The Economic Status of Americans of Asian Descent: An Exploratory Investigation*. Washington, DC: U.S. Government Printing Office.

———. 1989. *Civil Rights Issues in Maine*. Washington, DC: U.S. Government Printing Office.

———. 1992. *Civil Rights Issues Facing Asian Americans in the 1990s*. Washington, DC: U.S. Government Printing Office.

———. 1996. *Briefing on Efforts to End Discrimination in Mortgage Lending: Executive Summary*. Washington, DC: U.S. Commission on Civil Rights.

U.S. Department of Commerce. 1989. *Poverty in the United States, 1987*. Series P-60, No. 163. Washington, DC: U.S. Government Printing Office.

U.S. Department of Health, Education and Welfare. 1976. *A Statistical Portrait of the American Indian*. Washington, DC: U.S. Government Printing Office.

U.S. Department of Health and Human Services. 1993. *Health United States 1992 and Healthy People 2000 Review*. Pub. No. 93-1232. Washington, DC: U.S. Department of Health and Human Services.

U.S. Department of Housing and Urban Development. 1991. *Housing Discrimination Study*. Washington, DC: U.S. Department of Housing and Urban Development.

U.S. Department of Justice. 1980. *National Hispanic Conference on Law Enforcement and Criminal Justice*. Washington, DC: U.S. Department of Justice Law Enforcement Assistance Administration.

———. 1991a. *1990 Statistical Yearbook of the Immigration and Naturalization Service.* Washington, DC: U.S. Government Printing Office.

———. 1991b. *Teenage Victims: A National Crime Survey Report.* Washington, DC: U.S. Government Printing Office.

———. 1991c. *School Crime: A National Crime Victimization Survey Report.* Washington, DC: U.S. Government Printing Office.

———. 1995. *Bureau of Justice Statistics Sourcebook of Criminal Justice Statistics—1994.* Washington, DC: U.S. Government Printing Office.

———. 1999a. *Legal Immigration, Fiscal Year 1998.* Washington, DC: U.S. Government Printing Office.

———. 1999b. *Refugees, Fiscal Year 1997.* Washington, DC: U.S. Government Printing Office.

———. 1999c. *Asylees, Fiscal Year 1997.* Washington, DC: U.S. Government Printing Office.

———. 2002. *Criminal Victimization 2001.* Washington, DC: U.S. Government Printing Office.

U.S. Department of Labor. 1989. *Monthly Review* 112. Washington, DC: U.S. Government Printing Office.

———. 1991. *Preliminary Report on Discrimination in the Workplace and the Existence of the "Glass Ceiling."* Washington, DC: U.S. Government Printing Office.

U.S. General Accounting Office. 1989. *Equal Employment Opportunity: Women and Minority Aerospace Managers and Professionals.* Washington, DC: U.S. Government Printing Office.

———. 2002. *Native American Housing. GAO Report GAO-02-654.* Washington, DC: U.S. General Accounting Office.

Valdez, R. Burciaga, Julie DaVanzo, Georges Vernez, and Mitchell Wade. 1993. "Immigration: Getting the Facts." RAND Issue, Paper #1. Santa Monica, CA: The RAND Corporation.

Van Ausdale, Debra, and Joe R. Feagin. 2001. *The First R: How Children Learn Race and Racism.* Boulder, CO: Rowman and Littlefield.

van den Berghe, Pierre. 1978. *Race and Racism: A Comparative Perspective,* 2d edition. New York: Wiley.

———. 1981. *The Ethnic Phenomenon.* New York: Elsevier.

Vargas, Sylvia. 1998. "Deconstructing Homo[geneous] Americanus: The White Ethnic Immigrant Narrative and Its Exclusionary Effect." *Tulane Law Review* 72:1493–1596.

Verdun, Vincene. 1993. "If the Shoe Fits, Wear It: An Analysis of Reparations to African Americans." *Tulane Law Review* 67:597–668.

Vernez, Georges. 1990. *Immigration and International Relations: Proceedings of a Conference on the International Effects of the 1986 Immigration Reform and Control Act (IRCA).* Santa Monica, CA: RAND Corporation and the Urban Institute.

———. 1993. *Needed: A Federal Role in Helping Communities Cope with Immigration.* RP-177. Santa Monica, CA: Program for Research on Immigration Policy.

Vernez, Georges, and Allan Abrahamse. 1996. *How Immigrants Fare in U.S. Education.* Santa Monica, CA: RAND Corporation.

Vernez, Georges, and Kevin McCarthy. 1990. *Meeting the Economy's Labor Needs Through Immigration: Rationales and Challenges.* Santa Monica, CA: RAND Corporation.

———. 1996. *The Costs of Immigration to Taxpayers: Analytical and Policy Issues.* Santa Monica, CA: RAND Corporation.

Villareal, Roberto. 1988. "The Politics of Mexican-American Empowerment." In *Latino Empowerment: Progress, Problems, and Prospects,* edited by Roberto Villareal, Norma Hernandez, and Howard Neighbor, pp. 1–9. New York: Greenwood Press.

Vitucci, Jeff. 1999. "The State of Hispanic Health." *Hispanic Business* 21:40–2.

Wagenheim, Kal (ed.). 1973. *Puerto Ricans: A Documentary History.* Garden City, NY: Doubleday, Anchor.

Wallace, Steven P. 1989. "The New Urban Latinos: Central Americans in a Mexican Immigrant Environment." *Urban Affairs Quarterly* 25:239–64.

———. 1990. "Race versus Class in the Health Care of African-American Elderly." *Social Problems* 37:517–34.

Wang, L. Ling-chi. 1988. "Meritocracy and Diversity in Higher Education: Discrimination against Asian Americans in the Post-Bakke Era." *The Urban Review* 20:183–209.

Warner, W. Lloyd. 1941. "Introduction." In *Deep South,* edited by Allison Davis, Burleigh Gardner, and Mary Gardner, pp. 1–6. Chicago: University of Chicago Press.

Warner, W. Lloyd, and Leo Srole. 1945. *The Social Systems of American Ethnic Groups.* New Haven, CT: Yale University Press.

Weber, Max. 1905–1906 [1930]. *The Protestant Ethic and the Spirit of Capitalism,* translated by T. Parsons. New York: Scribner and Sons.

Weinberg, Meyer. 1977. *A Chance to Learn: The History of Race and Education in the United States.* New York: Cambridge University Press.

Welch, Susan. 1990. "The Impact of At-Large Elections on the Representation of Blacks and Hispanics." *Journal of Politics* 52:1050–76.

Welch, Susan, J. Gruhl, and C. Spohn. 1984. "Dismissal, Conviction, and Incarceration of Hispanic Defendants: A Comparison with Anglos and Blacks." *Social Science Quarterly* 65:257–64.

Wellner, Alison. 2002. "Beyond City Limits: Asian Americans Are More Likely Than Ever to Call the Suburbs, or Even Small Towns, Home." *American Demographics* 22:2–5.

Whetstone, Muriel. 1993. "The Story behind the Explosive Statistics: Why Blacks Are Losing Ground in the Workforce." *Ebony* (Dec.): 102–4.

White, John. 1985. *Black Leadership in America: From Booker T. Washington to Jesse Jackson.* New York: Longmans.

Whitmore, John, Marcella Trautmann, and Nathan Caplan. 1989. "The Socio-Cultural Basis for the Economic and Educational Success of Southeast Asian Refugees (1978–1982 Arrivals)." In *Refugees as Immigrants: Cambodians, Laotians, and Vietnamese in America,* edited by David W. Haines, pp. 121–37. Totowa, NJ: Rowman & Littlefield.

Wildavsky, Ben. 1990. "Tilting at Billboards: Butts (et al.) vs. Poutts." *New Republic* (Aug. 20): 19–20.

Williams, David, and Chiquita Collins. 2001. "Racial Residential Segregation: A Fundamental Cause of Racial Disparities in Health." *Public Health Reports* 11:404–17.

Williams, Robert. 1990. *The American Indian in Western Legal Thought: The Discourses of Conquest.* New York: Oxford University Press.

Williamson, Joel. 1984. *The Crucible of Race: Black/White Relations in the American South Since Emancipation.* New York: Oxford University Press.

Wilson, Kenneth, and Alejandro Portes. 1980. "Immigrant Enclaves: An Analysis of the Labor Market Experience of Cubans in Miami." *American Journal of Sociology* 86:295–319.

Wilson, William J. 1987. *The Truly Disadvantaged.* Chicago: University of Chicago Press.

Wirth, Louis. 1945. "The Problem of Minority Groups." In *The Science of Man in the World Crisis,* edited by R. Linton, pp. 347–72. New York: Columbia University Press.

Wong, Bernard. 1976. "Social Stratification, Adaptive Strategies and the Chinese Community of New York." *Urban Life* 5:33–52.

Wong, Eugene. 1978. *On Visual Media Racism: Asians in the American Motion Pictures.* New York: Arno.

Wong, Paul, Chienping Lai, Richard Nagasawa, and Tieming Lin. 1998. "Asian Americans as a Model Minority: Self-Perceptions and Perceptions by Other Racial Groups." *Sociological Perspectives* 41:95–119.

Wood, Andrew. 2001. "Anticipating the Colonias: Popular Housing in El Paso and Ciudad Juarez, 1890–1923." *Journal of the Southwest* 43:493–505.

Woodward, C. Vann. 1966. *The Strange Career of Jim Crow,* 2d edition. New York: Oxford University Press.

Wound, Barbara Bad. 2000. "American Indian Youth Outnumber Others in Justice System." *The Aboriginal Youth Network* (August). Available at: www.ayn.ca/news.

Wright, Bobby, and William Tierney. 1991. "American Indians in Higher Education: A History of Cultural Conflict." *Change* 23:11–18.

Yen, Earl. 1988. "Flames Leave Massachusetts Cambodian Families Homeless." *Asian Week* (Dec. 2).

Yu, Jin. 1980. *The Korean Merchants in the Black Community.* Elkins Park, PA: Philip Jaisohn Foundation.

Zambrana, Ruth, and Claudia Dorrington. 1998. "Economic and Social Vulnerability of Latino Children and Families by Subgroup: Implications for Child Welfare." *Child Welfare* 77:5–28.

Zo, Kil. 1978. *Chinese Emigration into the United States, 1850–1880.* New York: Arno.

Zweigenhaft, Richard L., and G. William Domhoff. 1982. *Jews in the Protestant Establishment.* New York: Praeger.

Photo Credits

Index